C000049272

Rock climbing in Snowdonia

Rock climbing in Snowdonia

Paul Williams

Constable London

First published in Great Britain 1990
by Constable & Company Limited
3 The Lanchesters
162 Fulham Palace Road
London W6 9ER
Copyright © 1990 Paul Williams
Reprinted 1992, 1994, 1996
Set in Baskerville 9pt by
Rowland Phototypesetting Limited
Bury St Edmunds, Suffolk
Printed in Great Britain by
BAS Printers Limited
Over Wallop, Hampshire

British Library CIP data
Williams, Paul, *1946 Mar. 24–*
Rock climbing in Snowdonia
1. Gwynedd. Snowdonia. Rock climbing – Manuals
I. Title
796.5′223′0942925

ISBN 0 09 468410 3

TO MY SON, CHRISTOPHER

Contents

Contents

Contents   ix

Rhoscolyn   451

Illustrations

Maps and diagrams (by Phil Gibson)

Crag photo-diagrams

Photographs

Acknowledgements

This guidebook is, to a certain extent, a by-product of nearly twenty years of pleasure that I have had climbing in Snowdonia. The 'selected 500' are just some of the many fine routes that I have enjoyed in the company of rope mates almost too numerous to mention, especially John Allen, Ron Fawcett, Andy Grondowski, Dougie Hall, Trevor Hodgson, the late Phil 'Big Jim' Jewell, Dave Lawson, Jim Moran, Dave Roberts and John Redhead.

The photographers have played an extremely important part in the production of this book and my thanks go to Steve Ashton, John Beatty, Andy Brazier, Dave Croaker, Leo Dickinson, Chris Lyon, Chris Griffiths, Malcolm Griffiths, Les Holliwell, Crag Jones, Tony Riley, Edgar Siddall, John Sumner, Bill Wayman, John Woodhouse; and also to Iwan Jones, Tom Jones and Wendy Grondowski, who used my camera to good effect. Phil Gibson drew the maps and diagrams.

Other people who accompanied me out on the odd occasion, checked route descriptions and grades, posed for photographs and generally offered much helpful advice and criticism were Dave Bailey, Martin Barnicott, Bob Bradley, Dave Bradshaw, Simon Brown, Stuart Cathcart, Martin Crook, Dave 'Smiler' Cuthbertson, Phil Davidson, Steve Durkin, Marian Evans, Rowland Edwards, Mel Griffiths, Fred Hall, Steve Haston, Richard Head, Joe Healey, Adam Heynes, Steve Howe, Alan Hughes, Jesse James, Chris Jewell, Iwan Jones, Tom Jones, Steve Lewis, Pat Littlejohn, Stan Lowe, Leigh McGinley, Anthoine Le Menestrel, Heather Mills, Jerry Moffatt, Jon de Montjoye, Dave Nottidge, Mike Owen, Jim Perrin, Andy Pollitt, Mick Pointon, Paul Pritchard, Dave Pyecroft, Nigel Riddington, Lynn Rogers, Andy Sharp, Tony Shaw, Chris Shorter, Paul Simkiss, John Sumner, Phil Thomas, Dave Towse, Crispin Waddy, Hugh Walton and Richard Williams.

Thanks must also go to Andy Newton and Tony Shaw for some useful criticism and proof-reading. And last but not least, thanks to Geoff Milburn at the eleventh hour. I apologize to anyone whose name I may have inadvertently omitted.

P.W.
1990

Introduction

Snowdonia contains some of the finest and most accessible cliffs in Britain and its place in climbing history will need little introduction. This guidebook describes, in around 500 routes, the essence of quality rock climbing to be found in the Snowdonia region. The selection of routes is aimed at climbers of all abilities, so the novice or newcomer to the area will find it just as useful as the seasoned specialist.

The guidebook covers all the well-known (and many not-so-well-known) and worthwhile climbing grounds within (and some just outside) the Snowdonia National Park. It is divided into seven sections: North Wales Limestone – including recent developments on the short but fierce Pen Trwyn outcrop and some, not so recent, on Little Orme; Carneddau and Ogwen – an extremely popular mountain area where many climbers have 'cut their teeth', especially on the polished holds of the Idwal Slabs or the Milestone Buttress; Llanberis Area – the almost hallowed walls of Dinas Cromlech, the dark sweeping lines of the majestic Clogwyn Du'r Arddu, and that stomping ground of 'The Ancients', Lliwedd, are a world away from the climbing-wall-orientated-crag-rat-bolt-protected-designer-climbs of the Dinorwic Slate Quarries; Snowdon South – Tremadog, a gem of a crag with its sound dolerite, good protection, and sunny aspect (not to mention its close proximity to the café) should be on the agenda of any self-respecting modern climber. But what of the secret cliffs tucked away down on the mysterious Lleyn Peninsula? And what about the unknown mountain crags, such as Llechog, and Craig Cwm Ddu; Snowdon East – starting from that most amenable of mountain areas, The Moelwyns, with their rough pocketed rock, fair weather and classic easy climbs, we work north, past the ramparts of Carreg Alltrem and beyond the riverside crag of Craig Rhiw Goch, to the beautiful Crafnant Valley, where Clogwyn yr Eryr and some spectacular rock await; Central Wales – largely unknown and unfrequented, a forgotten world where the cliffs are supposedly buried beneath a mantle of grass and heather. Climb the soaring aretes of Gist

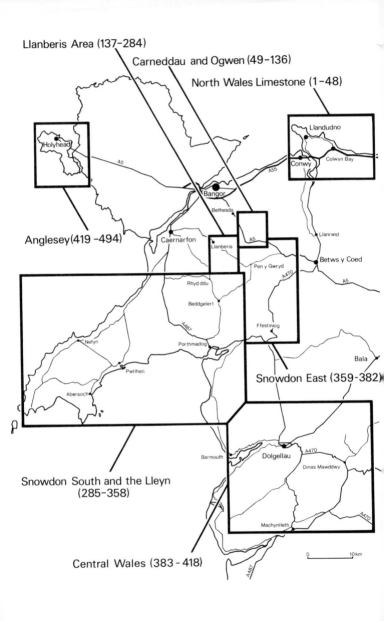

Llanberis Area (137-284)

Carneddau and Ogwen (49-136)

North Wales Limestone (1-48)

Anglesey (419-494)

Snowdon East (359-382)

Snowdon South and the Lleyn
(285-358)

Central Wales (383-418)

Holyhead

Llandudno

Conwy   Colwyn Bay

Bangor

Bethesda

Caernarfon

Llanberis

Llanrwst

Betws y Coed

Pen y Gwryd

Rhyd ddu

Beddgelert

Ffestiniog

Nefyn

Porthmadog

Pwllheli

Bala

Abersoch

Barmouth

Dolgellau   A470

Dinas Mawddwy

Machynlleth

0   10 km

Ddu, follow the jugs up the overhanging Diamond Wall of Bird Rock, or tackle some of the pleasant slabby South Buttress routes in scenic Cwm Cywarch where the massive crag stretching across its upper reaches shyly conceals some 'Shrike-like' walls from the casual visitor . . . and you will return, time and again; Anglesey – Britain's premier sea cliff, Craig Gogarth, offers a wide variety of routes ranging from the fiercely overhanging horrors of the Main Cliff to the delightful off-vertical jug-pulling so characteristic of Castell Helen; not far away, Rhoscolyn is a small cliff, but with a big feel about it!

The coverage of each area has been to a certain extent governed by its popularity, so an area like Llanberis, or Gogarth, is more extensively covered than, say, the Moelwyns or Central Wales, which despite having a number of fine routes have never been particularly trendy.

The format consists of detailed route descriptions, incorporating standard adjectival, technical and E grades, as well as a star system. In many cases the descriptions are slightly longer than those found in the definitive guidebooks and it is hoped that these, in conjunction with the many excellent crag photo-diagrams, will make the climbs easy to locate and follow without prior knowledge of the area. Special attention has been paid to the easier and medium grade routes (from Diff to VS) and descent details are usually included after their descriptions.

The task of selecting a limited number of routes from a total of well over 4000 throughout the area was particularly daunting. The idea was to provide a coverage which would encompass as many aspects of Welsh rock climbing as possible without putting too strong a bias on either hard or easy routes, or on any one area. However, if a fair representation of current climbing standards is to be made, it is inevitable that any selected guide will contain a considerable number of harder routes. Nonetheless, a whole host of classic routes in the easier grades are included and it is hoped that these will continue to give much pleasure and enjoyment. Thus the guide contains both The Wrinkle and The Wrinkled Retainer, and climbers have the option of three Ordinary Routes – on the Idwal Slabs, on Craig yr Ogof in Cwm Silyn, or on Gogarth Main Cliff – depending on the degree of commitment sought.

Grading

The standard adjectival/numerical system has been used throughout:

Mod	Moderate	
Diff	Difficult	
V Diff	Very Difficult	
HV Diff	Hard Very Difficult	
S	Severe	
HS	Hard Severe	4a, 4b
VS	Very Severe	4b, 4c
HVS	Hard Very Severe	5a, 5b
E1	Extremely Severe	5b, 5c
E2	Extremely Severe	5b, 5c
E3	Extremely Severe	5c, 6a
E4	Extremely Severe	5c, 6a, 6b
E5	Extremely Severe	6a, 6b
E6	Extremely Severe	6a, 6b

There is also one artificial route included for the 'whack-and-dangle' brigade: the difficult Big Overhang, A3.

It should be noted that the numerical, or technical, pitch grades are shown to correspond with their normal adjectival rating (i.e. VS, 4c, or HVS, 5a) and that some overlapping will occur depending on certain factors. Thus the grade VS, 5a would indicate that whilst the hardest moves on the route are not commonly found on VSs, the climbing is both short and well-protected enough to warrant a VS grade. Conversely, E1, 5a means that although the route is not as hard technically as a standard E1, it is either serious or sustained enough for an E1 grade. The higher up the scale of difficulty one climbs, the more subjective the grade becomes; on the hardest routes, such criteria as height, personal fitness and motivation can all play an important role in how hard one finds the moves. At the lower end of the scale, it has been decided to omit pitch grades for routes below 4a. The technical grade was introduced into the mountain areas purely for use with the harder routes and the adjectival grade alone suffices for routes in the Diff–S bracket.

Apart from the grades, other abbreviations used are: L, left; R, right; PR, peg runner; BR, bolt runner; TR, thread runner; BB, bolt belay; PB, peg belay; TB, thread belay; FFA, first free ascent; AL, alternate leads; VL, varied leads.

Bolts, pegs and threads are subject to wear and corrosion through prolonged exposure to the elements, and should be treated circumspectly!

Although the selected climbs represent the best that each crag has to offer, in response to general demand a star system has been included: no stars, Good; *, Very good; **, Excellent; ***, Utterly amazing . . . outstanding routes which are classics amongst classics!

Access

The inclusion of a route in this guide does not mean that there is an automatic right to ascend it. Some crags lie on private land, and permission to climb should be sought. *This is most notably the case at* CRAIG Y FORWEN.

Definitive guidebooks

The space-consuming nature of a selected climbs guidebook means that much interesting information has to be omitted. The definitive guides to the areas covered in this book are produced by the Climbers Club and regular visitors to North Wales will find them invaluable. The present set numbers nine volumes which are regularly updated and revised.

Maps

Ordnance Survey maps are by far the easiest and quickest way of locating crags and should be carried if going into the mountains, especially if there is a chance of bad weather closing in. The following 1:50,000 Landranger maps cover all the areas: Anglesey, 114; Caernarfon and Bangor, 115; Lleyn Peninsula, 123; Dolgellau and Surrounding Area, 124. On a larger scale, the 1:25,000 Outdoor Leisure series contains much more information; Snowdon, 17 and Cadair Idris, 23 should prove invaluable to those who really wish to 'get their teeth' into the area.

Photo-diagrams

The somewhat challenging task of providing a series of crag photographs suitable for use as photo-diagrams was fulfilled in the main by Malcolm Griffiths of Snowdon Camera, with the author plugging most of the remaining gaps. Although it was neither possible nor practical to cover every crag mentioned in the book, the end result is a superb and unique collection of photographs which drastically eases the task of route location. Most routes are indicated, though the occasional one may have been omitted due either to the topography of the cliff or to the congested nature of the routes. In such latter cases, careful scrutiny of the descriptions should quickly untangle the mass of lines.

Accident and rescue procedure

In the event of any accident which will require a rescue and/or medical attention, dial 999 and ask for the police. Give concise information about the location and suspected injuries of the casualty and the police will summon the local rescue team or take other necessary action.

North Wales Limestone

Delightfully situated close to the holiday towns of Llandudno
and Colwyn Bay, North Wales limestone lies happily in the
rain-shadow of the Snowdonia massif: it receives more
sunshine, enjoys better weather and dries more quickly than
either Tremadog or Gogarth. Until the mid-seventies, few
climbers realized the area's potential and the limestone cliffs
were dismissed as vegetated backwaters, the preserve of the
eccentric in pursuit of the esoteric . . . but all that has changed!
A new route boom in 1983, along with its attendant publicity in
the mountain media, thrust Welsh limestone into the spotlight,
establishing it as one of Britain's premier climbing areas.

There are three main areas. First, near the village of
Llanddulas lies Craig y Forwen, a steep outcrop around
100ft/30m in height which provides a fine selection of open
climbs with natural protection on sound rock. Next comes the
Great Orme which forms the end of the Llandudno peninsula,
and is littered with outcropping rocks and buttresses, most
notably the spectacular Castell y Gwynt and the extensive cliffs
of Pen Trwyn, perhaps the ultimate roadside playground with
sharp holds, good friction and the occasional bolt ladder to go
at. On both these cliffs, any route can be reached within five
minutes; this is in marked contrast to the Great Zawn, lying at
the seaward end of the Little Orme (the massive headland
towering over the east end of Llandudno beach), where the
approach takes twenty minutes, the routes are committing and
there is an incredible feeling of isolation.

Local amenities

The area is generally visited on a daily basis as it lies only
forty-five minutes by car from Llanberis and a little over an
hour from Manchester. It is also well served by public
transport: British Rail has stations at both Llandudno Junction
and Llanddulas and the L1 Cymru Coastliner bus shuttles
back and forth between Chester and Caernarfon at regular
intervals with stops at Llandudno and Llanddulas.

The nearest campsite is opposite the Technical College at

Llandrillo yn Rhos (old Llandudno–Colwyn Bay Road).
Please note that under no circumstances should climbers camp
at Craig y Forwen unless given permission by the farmer who
owns the caravan site beneath the cliff (which in view of the
current (1988) access problem seems extremely unlikely).
Bivouacking under the roadside caves at the start of Pen Trwyn
is frowned upon by the local council.

Llandudno sports a host of pubs and cafés, plus the odd
nightclub or two. The trendiest places to drink are Tiffanys and
the Cottage Loaf (the latter being a good place to spot the
Charlton Chestwig Medallion Men). Nearby, at the Upper
Mostyn Street roundabout, is the Princes – the best café to
breakfast at – while Parisella's Ice Cream Parlour, less than
five minutes' walk from Pen Trwyn, takes over for midday and
afternoon refreshments. Lyon Sports on Mostyn Street sells
climbing equipment, and is the repository for new route
information.

Most of the cliffs are subject to certain access conditions and
limitations which should at all times be respected; these are
outlined in the preamble to each crag.

Craig y Forwen (907767)
This delightful crag is situated approximately one mile up an
open valley which runs inland from the main coast road at the
small village of Llanddulas. On approach from Colwyn Bay,
turn off the A55 dual carriageway into the village itself. At the
far end make a sharp turn R at the old school and follow the
narrow lane, keeping R at the junction to the Plas Newydd
Farm and Caravan Site. The cliff lies above this in the trees and
is reached across private land which stretches up to the foot of
it. Before attempting to climb here, permission should be
obtained from the farmer who owns this strip of land, across
which there is NO RIGHT OF WAY. At the time of writing, owing
to several heated clashes with climbers who have been abusive
(not to mention the litter), the farmer may refuse permission.

The BMC and local Manpower Services Commission are

negotiating an access agreement which involves the building of stiles, new fences and the clearing of a car-park. Further details will probably be issued from the BMC in the climbing press. Meanwhile, if permission is granted, special care should be taken not to cross the fence at the top of the crag and to obey all signs and notices.

Cars should be parked up the road beyond the caravan site entrance by a small gap in the trees. Go through this and scramble up the slope to the L-hand end of the main crag – a path runs R-wards along the foot of it. The gully just L is the normal descent route – Staircase Gully (Mod) – and 30ft/9m R of this a sentry box, overhang and crack give the line of Knightsbridge (VS). The shallow groove R again is Pterodactyl (HVS), whilst The Flue (VS) follows a wide crack up the R-hand side of the wall.

1 Softly Softly   S   80ft/24m *

D. Williams, C. Goodey, 1967

The huge corner R of The Flue has a large perched block in it at 30ft/9m and gives a fine route.

1. Climb directly up the corner and go over the block to a roof. Move R under this then climb back L to finish up a steep little corner. To the R are two steep chimney cracks, The Y Chimneys (HVD), an excellent introduction to the easier grade climbs here. 25 yd/23m R, through some bushes, lies the Great Wall buttress. The R-hand side of the front face has a huge roof 30ft/9m up, while around its R arete, the side wall gently overhangs for its entire height: this is The Great Wall itself.

2 Fido's Redemption   HVS   100ft/30m *

N. Sherry, D. Williams, 1965/A. Ingham, K. Farrimond, 1983

A quality route with a surprising top pitch up the L arete of the buttress. Start below the arete.

1. 50ft/15m. 5a. Climb up to the R for a few feet then continue directly up the wall passing a TR and PR to belay at the prominent yew tree.

2. 50ft/15m. 4c. Go up L behind the tree to gain the arete after

a few feet. Continue up for a few more feet then move R to finish straight up.

3 Great Whaler/High Plains Drifter
E3   230ft/69m **
P. Livesey, R. Fawcett (AL), 1976/A. Pollitt, C. Lyon, 1981

A superb tour around the entire Great Wall Buttress. Start 10ft/3m R of the L arete of the buttress at a steep black corner (Jugular Start to Fido's).

1. 60ft/18m. 5b. Climb the corner for 15ft/5m to an obvious R-ward traverse line leading across then around the arete into Mojo. Follow this up to the roof and a wooden wedge runner. Move R and pull up to the next roof, PR. A delicate traverse R gains a PB on the arete.

2. 90ft/27m. 5c. Step down and move R, PR. Continue traversing into Great Wall, PR. Move up to a TR then do the traverse of Great Wall into the centre of the face. Climb up to the next TR then move out R and traverse R again until steep climbing up over the bulge gains a tree belay. An escape can be made up the easy (4b) groove behind the trees exiting L at the top.

3. 80ft/24m. 6a. Step L and climb the black groove to the break. Traverse airily L across Great Wall with increasing difficulty to a mean finish up a crack near the arete.

4 Freedom   E2   100ft/30m *
R. Edwards, L. Holliwell, 1974

An entertaining route with two contrasting pitches. Start in the centre of the wall at the foot of a corner/groove leading up to the L-hand side of the large roof.

1. 50ft/15m. 5c. Climb the wall just R of the corner to an overlap. Step into the corner and go up to the roof. Traverse L to the arete, PR. Go round the lip of the roof via a good R-handhold into a crack in the wall above. Move R to a small ledge and PBS.

Craig y Forwen

2. 50ft/15m. 5c. Step up R into a thin slabby crack which leads awkwardly up to a large overlap. Traverse L to a ledge then finish direct, or move R and go straight up. Harder.

5 **Mojo**   E1   100ft/30m ***

F. Corner, B. Thompson (aid), 1959/FFA: R. Edwards, N. Metcalfe, 1975

A sensational but surprisingly easy roof.

1. 50ft/15m. 5b. Go up to the large roof as for Freedom. Move R for 10ft/3m then climb to the next roof, PR. Traverse L along the roof (easy after the first move) to a PR on the lip. Pull round to the Freedom belay.
2. 50ft/15m. 4a. Traverse L and move up into groove which is taken easily past a tree to finish. It is better to traverse easily L to the yew tree belay of Fido's Redemption, and finish up this.

The arete R of Mojo is Quickstep, E4 6a. This also delineates the left edge of The Great Wall.

6 **Great Wall**   E4   90ft/27m ***

C. Goodey, P. N. Dilly (aid), 1967/FFA: P. Livesey, 1975

An excellent route with sustained climbing on perfect rock. As good a single pitch as any in the area. Start below some prominent pockets in the middle of the wall.

1. 5c. Climb diagonally L to a PR at 15ft/5m. Traverse back R to a TR in a black hole. Move up with difficulty to a long slot (good runners and a poor rest). Swing L and climb a little white pillar. Trend R-wards to a small flake crack then move across L to a broken flake. Finish direct past a BR.

7 **Twisting Chimney**   VS   100ft/30m

F. Corner, K. Forder, 1960

The obvious chimney R of Great Wall gives an interesting pitch.

1. 50ft/15m. 4a. Scramble up into the cave at the base of the chimney. Bridge up for 30ft/9m to belay at the back.

2. 50ft/15m. 4c. Back-and-foot the outside of the chimney which eases just after it narrows. Go straight up past a jammed block to finish.

20yd/18m R around the next corner, the crag steepens and increases in height giving two classic climbs.

8 **Scalar**   VS   120ft/36m ***
D. Patrick, C. Bartlett, 1963
A fine and varied route which crosses the large wall before finishing up the crack at its R edge. Start at the L of the buttress in the corner under the overhang.
1. 60ft/18m. 4c. Go up to the overhang and make a rising traverse R into the obvious corner/crack. Ascend this to a good ledge and belay.
2. 60ft/18m. 4c. Continue up the corner and over the roof to gain a wide crack. Finish up the steep corner.

9 **Ivy Sepulchre**   VS   110ft/33m *
C. Goodey, D. Thomas (bach), 1959
A few feet R of Scalar, the large crack running the full height of the crag gives a strenuous workout. Start at the foot of the crack.
1. 60ft/18m. 4c. Climb the crack swinging out L to avoid the overhang. Continue up the crack to a ledge and belay on the R.
2. 50ft/15m. 4c. Move back L into the crack and follow it to the top of the crag.

To the R of Ivy Sepulchre is a large wall with a somewhat vegetated slanting groove on its R side. Just beyond this is the obvious Sinister Chimney (S) in the back of a bay. Ash Groove (VS) takes the crack/groove just to its L.

10 **Space Mountain**   E5   90ft/27m **
G. Gibson, P. Gibson, 1982
A very fine testpiece, steep and fingery with only sufficient protection. It takes a line of shallow scoops up the white wall L

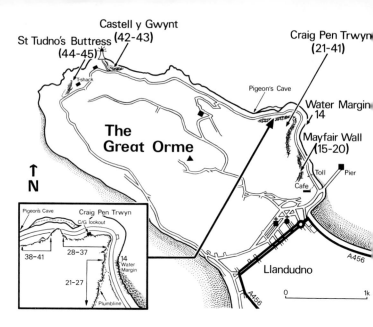

of Ash Groove. Start just L of Ash Groove.

1. 6a. From the tree stump, step L and climb up into the first scoop. Balance up R-wards to good holds in the break, PR, then make fingery moves up and L into a second scoop. Go up R-wards past a TR to jugs, then move back L to enter a slim groove. Climb this to more jugs below the final bulge. Step L and surmount the bulge finishing direct past another TR.

The next three routes all lie at the bottom R-hand end of the crag and are reached by continuing along the path and crossing the fence that abuts it. On the L is a large red and black coloured buttress with a deep chimney on its R-hand side. Next comes a large black slabby wall.

11 **Route 66** VS 140ft/42m *
D. Patrick, C. Bartlett, 1963
An excellent route at this standard which is very popular. Start

40ft/12m R of the deep chimney in a corner at the foot of the large black slab.
1. 90ft/27m. 4c. Climb the L-hand corner of the slab for 20ft/6m. Make a delicate R-ward traverse to its far side. Ascend the arete to a steep wall which is taken to a good ledge.
2. 50ft/15m. 4b. Follow the corner to the top of the crag.

12 **Sangfroid**   HVS   160ft/49m **
R. Edwards, L. Holliwell, 1973
A sensational route crossing the huge wall R of Route 66. The best of its grade on the crag. Start 30ft/9m R of Route 66 below a prominent flake high on the wall which can be reached via a crack system.
1. 30ft/9m. 4a. Go easily up the crack to ledges. Belay.
2. 130ft/40m. 5a. Follow the cracks up on to ledges which get progressively smaller, aiming for the overhanging flakes. Follow these L until it is possible to traverse L across the wall to gain the arete. Go round this and finish up the corner – an exhilarating pitch!

13 **Sangfroid Direct Finish**   E2   120ft/37m ***
A. Pollitt, J. Moffatt, 1981
A tremendous pitch at the top end of the grade.
2a. 5c. Follow Sangfroid to the traverse L. Step R and climb a flake crack with an awkward move to gain a small ledge. Take the rib and wall just to the L with a long reach for another ledge. Traverse L to finish as for the normal route – an adrenalin-surging experience!

Great Orme
The Great Orme is the limestone peninsula which lies at the west end of the Llandudno promenade. It is encircled by a one-way toll road – the Marine Drive – which provides quick and easy access to all the crags and outcrops described. Please note that under no circumstances should drivers turn around or attempt to reverse vehicles back through the toll gate.

CRAIG PEN TRWYN   (781836)

This, the most popular and extensive crag in the area, lies just above the Marine Drive and starts 100yd/93m along from the toll gate where a double sloping cave system sports many dynamic and gymnastic problems. In fact, the crag is well known for its short, fierce and fingery routes. Just a little further along is the main Mayfair Wall, the finest of the Pen Trwyn crags, with the small compact buttress of Hanging Rock at its far end. Diagonally up to the R above a long grassy slope is an undercut crag capped by roofs with a prominent arched overhang curving over from its R side. Beyond this, the crag becomes smaller, and continues as a long series of walls around 60ft/18m high, stretching around the headland, past the coastguard look-out and an old disused pill-box, to terminate at a descent gully which sports some telegraph poles. On the R is Monster Buttress with its huge central overhang, leaning out over the road. Next comes a narrow white pillar before the aptly named Yellow Wall, with Black Wall immediately to its R. Down below, at sea level lies Pigeon Cave which gives immaculate bouldering and is reached down the path starting opposite Monster Buttress, and then bearing round to the L.

The rock of Pen Trwyn is generally sound, especially on these selected routes, but if any rocks are dislodged, and land on the Marine Drive, they should be removed as soon as possible!

The number of climbers at the crag has increased dramatically since the 1983 new route boom. The borough council has become deeply concerned at the many reports of falling rocks barely missing tourists walking, cycling or driving round the Orme during the busy summer months. The council believes that in the event of an accident caused by climbers, or climbing, it and the owners could be held liable, thus having to pay substantial compensation for any damage or injury so caused.

A local access agreement has been negotiated between the BMC and the borough council to the effect that no climbing is allowed on Pen Trwyn (save in the roadside caves) from 9 a.m. to 5 p.m. during July, August and the first week in September, plus Easter and all other bank holidays. This agreement should be strictly adhered to, as disregard for it could jeopardize future climbing here – possibly resulting in a permanent ban!

The Lower Tier of Pen Trwyn, a long bulging wall at sea-level, easily visible from the Mayfair Wall area, has no such restriction – access is dependent on the state of the tide only. Hop over the wall opposite the first roadside cave and descend a steep grassy gully to land on a boulder beach. Stumble L-wards along this to reach . . .

14 **The Water Margin**   HVS   550ft/170m ***
N. Clacher, K. Simpson, 1982

A thrilling sea-level girdle taking the obvious horizontal break around the headland. Very straightforward providing care is taken with the tides. Start well R of the prominent cave; a curving line of weakness leads up to the break. The first section is by far the steepest and most awkward (5a), and sometimes accommodates a belligerent seagull during the nesting season. Traverse the break more easily now. It dips slightly as it rounds the headland before continuing on sharp spiky jugs below the high-tide level, to reach a narrow zawn. Belay as necessary. Either climb the easy arete on the L to finish over grass, or climb the R wall of the zawn to rejoin and follow the break around into a similar zawn to finish – harder, 5b!

15 **Axle Attack**   E5   70ft/21m ***
M. Griffiths, L. McGinley (both led), 1981

An outstanding pitch taking the obvious bolt ladder which rises from a small black bottomless corner at the foot of the highest part of the Mayfair Wall, a few yards beyond the roadside caves. Superbly sustained at the lower limit of its grade. Start from two embedded boulders below the corner.

1. 6b. Climb the corner with difficulty and move out R-wards on to the wall. Go directly up to a semi-rest below a shallow groove. Enter the groove and ascend via a digit-wrecking move, crux, to a flake jug at its top. Continue to a PR then trend diagonally L-wards to a ledge and BB. Abseil off.

A few yards R of Axle Attack, from the lowest point of the crag, a bolt ladder climbs up over a bulge and into a cave; the substance of Mayfair E4, 6b. Next to it lies the short R-facing Carrigan's Groove E5, 6b.

16 The Disillusioned Screw Machine
E6   120ft/36m***
J. M. Redhead, A. Pollitt (1 pt), 1982/FFA: A. Pollitt, P. Williams, 1983
A sensational route of great character which weaves a tortuous line into and out of the first and highest of two large scoops, prominent features in the next part of the wall. The classic of its grade at Pen Trwyn. Start from a point 20ft/6m R of Mayfair below a L-facing flake leading up to the L-end of the large lower terrace.
1. 50ft/15m. 6a. Ascend to a large hole and good spike. Continue past a BR with difficulty then pull L-wards over the bulge to get established on a steep slab. Climb up, keeping L of the flake to gain the end of the terrace – Masterclass, E7 6c takes the awesome headwall above. Step R to a stance and BB.
2. 70ft/21m. 6b. Traverse R to twin BRs. Grope blindly up to the R for a small hold above the bulge, the key to entry into the large scoop above – powerful! Exit L from this, past a BR to reach a huge pocket. Continue boldly to a resting place in the middle of the headwall. Climb direct to the horizontal break. Step L and finish straight up passing a PR just below the top. PBS on the higher terrace which runs down R-wards to join the road just beyond Hanging Rock.

On the R side of the Mayfair Wall, a large L-facing flake at the foot of the crag gives easy access to the lower terrace, launching point for the next three routes.

Great Orme – Mayfair Wall

17 **The Bearded Clam** E5 110ft/33m **

A. Pollitt, P. Williams, 1983

The R-facing groove above and L of the lower large scoop is full of surprises! Start at the L-facing flake.

1. 40ft/12m. 4a. Climb the flake then move across to an obvious belay just L of the scoop.

2. 70ft/21m. 6b. Surmount the initial bulge to reach horizontal slots then follow a ladder of in-situ gear up L-wards to a poor rest at the overhang – Oyster, E6 6c breaks L here! Dramatic moves R past a BR lead up into a bottomless groove. Climb this to a PR at its top. Step out R on to the arete and go up to a break. Move R a few feet then follow a second groove to a BB. Abseil off.

18 **Rapture** E4 110ft/33m *

J. Moffatt, E. Jones, 1983

The large groove just R of the second large scoop gives a fine outing.

1. 40ft/12m. 4a. As for The Bearded Clam.

2. 70ft/21m. 6b. Move up R-wards into the scoop – Needle in the Groove, E6 6b takes the bulge above by desperate moves! Step R to a PR. Make fierce moves out and up the short wall past a BR to gain the groove above on the R. PR. The groove is straightforward to an awkward step R at its top. PR. Finish straight up the flake above to a BB. Abseil off.

19 **Anchovy Madonna** E2 110ft/33m *

A. Pollitt, P. Williams, 1983

The major groove line just R of Rapture is by far the most amenable on this section of crag and is justifiably popular.

1. 40ft/12m. 4a. Climb the L-facing flake to the terrace. Belay; or continue . . .

2. 70ft/21m. 5c. Move R and go up to a bulge sporting three TRS. Surmount the bulge at this point to enter a groove on the L. Continue to the next bulge then step R on to a small ledge. Climb back up L on deep pockets to the foot of a short rib which is taken to a stance and BB. Abseil off.

20 Connor's Folly   E1   70ft/21m
J. Connor and party (1 pt), 1972/FFA: A. Pollitt, N. Clacher, 1982
This is the prominent R-facing disjointed groove, a short way
up the grass bank, just before the crag drops down to terminate
on the roadside at Hanging Rock. A steady pitch and a good
introduction to Pen Trwyn.
1. 5b. Awkwardly enter the groove – the slim groove in its L
arete is The Wall of Blutes, E3 6a. Follow it trending slightly R
and continue up to the terrace. PBS on the L (in and L of a small
chimney).

Moving along beyond Hanging Rock, the huge arched
overhang is clearly visible above a long grass slope. To its L is a
long groove/corner:

21 Jungle Jive   E2   150ft/45m **
P. Williams, T. Taylor, 1985
Varied and exposed; one of the better 'easier' routes on the
crag. The groove rises from the L end of a long overhang which
blocks entry to this part of the cliff. Start several yards to the R
where a flaky crack provides a suitable entry point.
1. 100ft/30m. 5c. Pull over the bulge and move up to the
obvious hole. TR. Step down and make a descending L-ward
traverse to enter the groove/corner just above the lip of the
overhang. Ascend the interesting corner to a hanging nut and
BB a few feet below the terrace.
2. 50ft/15m. 5b. Climb carefully up to the terrace and a BR.
Step R and ascend the airy groove system past a hidden PR to
finish. Scramble up grass for 30ft/9m to a peg and large nut
belay in a short wall. Escape a few feet to the R, then traverse
L-wards over the top of the hill to descend in front of the sloping
cave system.

Parallel leaning corners R of the arched overhang mark the
start of the smallest part of Pen Trwyn. A short distance to the
R is the wide crack of Uriah's Neck, VS 4c with two shallow
corners starting 25ft/8m up the rock face just beyond.

22 **Gold Digger** E1 60ft/18m*
P. Williams, A. Pollitt, D. Lyon, 1983

An entertaining pitch with a memorable finish. Start beneath the first corner at a L-facing flake.
1. 5c. Climb the flake and trend slightly R up the wall to reach the corner. Technical moves up this gain a small overhung ledge. PR. Move L to a '5.9 mantel' to land on top. Traverse R along the edge of the crag for about 160yd/148m to the abseil chains at the top of Plumbline.

About 20ft/6m R of the second shallow corner – Golden Goose, E3 6a – is a grey slabby wall:

23 **It** E1 60ft/18m*
M. Roberts, A. Francis, 1982

A popular and pleasant trip up the centre of the wall.
1. 5b. Climb twin cracks then step R and continue straight up. The finish gives an anxious moment or two if at all damp! The obvious line coming in from the R to join It 20ft/6m from the top is Precious Metal, E1 5b.

150 yd/139m R-wards, at the centre of this long low section of cliff, past a plethora of hard routes on rock of varying quality, is a well-trodden patch of mud and grass from which rises a superb goove; this lies a few yards L of the prominent corner, Zag, HVS 5a.

24 **Plumbline** E3 65ft/20m***
R. Edwards, 1973

A fabulous pitch which receives almost as much traffic as the M1!
1. 5c. Pull up into the groove; there is a steepening at half-height where it changes into a crack and proves stubborn. Fight up stepping L at the top to a precarious exit. BB. Abseil off.

Great Orme – Craig Pen Trwyn

60yd/55m R of Plumbline the base of the crag becomes severely undercut with a ramp at the far end of this overhanging area. In the centre the flake/groove of Solid Gold, with its small sloping ledge at 20ft/6m, is fairly obvious.

25 **Klondike**   E4   60ft/18m *

W. Wayman, F. Crook, 1983

Just L of Solid Gold, the open groove with a prominent undercut at 30ft/9m gives a cracking pitch.

1. 6a. Pull L-wards over the bulge into a niche. Climb steeply L-wards up to the undercut. Friend. Move up and slightly R to finish up the open groove above.

26 **Solid Gold**   E3   60ft/18m ***

W. Wayman, F. Crook, 1983

A well-named route which is toughly graded!

1. 6a. Steep and strenuous reachy moves up the wall lead to a narrow sloping ledge – an occasional bivouac spot! Move R and layback up to stand on it, fiendish! Continue up the still steep flake/groove to the top.

R of Solid Gold are two L-trending grooves: the L one is Captain Fingers, E5 6b; the R-hand and larger groove is:

27 **Firefly**   E3   60ft/18m **

M. Crook, D. Towse, 1983

Another fine and popular pitch. Start from the foot of the ramp at the R end of the overhangs.

1. 6a. Move up and pull over the roof past a BR to stand on a short slab. Move L on side-pulls and surmount the bulge into the upper groove. Flit up this to finish.

As the Marine Drive turns the headland, a broad white wall looms above. Beneath its L side which is diagonally undercut is a crumbly gargoyle-like pinnacle.

28 **The Arc of Eternity**   E4   80ft/24m **

P. Williams, A. Grondowski, 1983

A superb voyage along the lip of the overhangs on the L side of the wall. Start below a shallow weakness in the centre of the wall.

1. 6b. Climb easily up for 20ft/6m then traverse L into an open recess. Swing out L and continue airily but steeply with a desperate move past a BR to enter a shallow groove. Hard moves gain a second BR. Finish L-wards at a small ledge.

29 **Excursion**   E2   70ft/21m **

I. Alderson, M. Roberts, 1981

A classic trip. Start in the centre of the wall as for The Arc.

1. 5b. Ascend trending L-wards to a prominent vertical slot. Move L on to a small ramp to reach jugs at its end. Finish steeply, straight up past an old PR.

30 **Clear White Light**   E3   70ft/21m ***

K. Howett, D. Towse, S. Jenkins, 1982

Superb open climbing up the highest part of the face. Start 10ft/3m R of Excursion at a short flake crack above a block.

1. 6a. Climb direct to two black streaks then pull up and move L to an obvious slot. Runners. Make hard moves directly up over the bulge, crux, to reach good holes and wires. Traverse R to a TR on the arete. Climb up then step L to a flake crack which leads to an awkward finish – a bold pitch.

Continue along the road to the coastguard look-out.

31 **Bruno His Wall**   HVS   60ft/18m

G. Roberts, H. Williams, 1979–80

An entertaining climb starting 20ft/6m R of the look-out.

1. 5a. Climb the short steep wall to finish via the prominent L-facing flake crack. Descend way over to the R down the gully containing some telegraph poles.

The next three climbs lie in the immediate vicinity of a derelict pill-box a little further along the road.

32 **Big Licks**   E3   80ft/24m *
T. Freeman, G. Roberts, 1982

A fearsome flake precedes an enjoyable juggy groove. Start at a leaning flake-crack just L of the pill-box.

1. 6a. Struggle up the initial crack to get established on the wall above. Move first R then back L to enter and climb the open groove. Exit R at the top on to a ledge on Beachcomber. PR. Finish over the bulge.

33 **Pil**   E1   80ft/24m
M. Roberts, I. Alderson, 1981

Start from on top of the old pill-box.

1. 5b. Step off the pill-box and climb a crack for 10ft/3m. Step R and ascend direct into Beachcomber. Continue to the ledge on the L. PR. Finish direct.

34 **Beachcomber**   HVS   80ft/24m
R. Edwards, 1973

Start a few feet R of the pill-box below a huge overhanging crack.

1. 5b. Thrutch up the steep initial crack. Continue along the huge flake to a ledge on the L. PR. Descend below the roof on the L to finish on the path, or finish direct past the PR.

35 **Mr Olympia**   E5   65ft/20m **
R. Fawcett, P. Williams, W. Wayman, 1983

A powerful pitch to 'prime the pump'. It takes the centre of the leaning wall R of Beachcomber. Start a few feet R of Beachcomber below a short crack with a TR at its top.

1. 6b. Boulder problem moves gain the crack and TR. Move up L to PR. Go straight up to a sloping jug and small wire slot – sustained. Traverse 5ft/1.5m R to undercuts below an overhang. Surmount this strenuously to finish with relief up the juggy groove and bulge above. BB.

The next line of weakness R of Mr Olympia is The Chain Gang, E5 6b, beyond which a side wall comes out towards the road. An open groove just before the arete gives two pleasant routes:

36 **Kanly**   E2   65ft/20m
D. Towse, 1981
A bold little climb.
1. 5b. Climb the groove then move out L on to the ramp. Move up and R-wards to a small roof. Surmount this to an easy finish up the final groove.

37 **Bauxed**   E1   65ft/20m *
G. Roberts, T. Cunningham, 1979–80
The better of the pair.
1. 5b. Climb the groove then pull out R on to the wall. Continue up on good holds and finish up L-wards with a tricky move near the top.

A short distance further along the Marine Drive, Monster Buttress with its massive roofs and R-ward trending ramp – Gorgo, E5 6a – is easily identifiable.

38 **The Continuing Adventures of Charlton Chestwig**   E4   80ft/24m **
A. Pollitt, P. Williams, 1983
A fine pitch at the top end of the grade. Strenuous and delicate. Start at the R side of the buttress below the huge roof, where a ferocious crack – Charlton Chestwig (The World's Finest Climber), E5 6b – rises up from the R arete.
1. 6a. Attack the crack from the R and battle strenuously up to a bulge. Traverse thankfully out L, PR, to the arete and climb it past a BR to finish. PB. Walk off L.

Just a bit further on is Yellow Wall with a short ramp at its foot, a little R of centre.

39 **The Pirates of Pen Trwyn** E4   50ft/15m **

A. Pollitt, P. Williams, R. Fawcett, G. Fawcett, 1983

A fingery pitch – the best on the wall. Start below the ramp.

1. 6a. Climb up on to the short ramp then ascend past a BR to a TR just above a good hold. Move R-wards past this to finish direct. BB. Abseil off.

40 **String of Pearls** E3   50ft/15m *

D. Towse, M. Raine, 1983

Another classic pitch. Start just R of Pirates.

1. 6a. Climb a narrow ramp/groove to a slab and TR. Pull up and L past a TR to a slim R-leaning groove. TR. Follow this boldly to the ledge. BB.

41 **Pale Shelter** E1   50ft/15m *

D. Lyon, N. Clacher, 1983

Pleasant climbing at a reasonable standard. Start 10ft/30m R of String.

1. 5b. Climb up first R then L to reach an obvious groove in the R side of the wall. Continue up on positive holds to a L-ward exit on to the ledge at the top. BB. Abseil off.

CASTELL Y GWYNT   (757845)

This very impressive crag lies directly below the lighthouse and gives sensational climbing on sound rock. From the car-park and tea shack just beyond the lighthouse, approach by walking back to cross the wall just R of the lighthouse entrance. Go down and traverse round to the L below the lighthouse wall to reach a narrow gully. Descend steeply to the bottom. Traverse R along a footpath. The crag appears dramatically with its massive capping roof under which Appian Way traverses. Below lie walls on the wrong side of vertical for most climbers. Over on the L is a stunning black and white overhanging prow which is Psychic Threshold, E5 6b whilst in the middle, the old aid route Central Pillar, E7 6c starting from the large stalagmite and climbing direct to finish over the capping roof, represents 'State of the Art' rock athleticism in the late eighties.

However, on a crag bedecked with around a dozen routes at E5 or above, two middle-grade Extremes are outstanding:

42 **New Dimensions**   E3   140ft/43m ***

R. Edwards, T. Jepson (3 pts), 1975/FFA: R. Edwards, 1976

A spectacular, classic and high-quality route. Its crux pitch takes the prominent black groove high up, just R of the centre of the cliff. Start from a small cave at the foot of the buttress. Huge TBS.

1. 65ft/20m. 5c. Climb out of the cave via an awkward crack and continue up to the top of a short slab on the R below a roof. PR. Go up the arete above which forms a bulging groove to a PR. Swing R around the arete to reach a steep groove and climb it precariously. Exit L at the top to a poor stance and BB. TRS in the roof above.

2. 45ft/14m. 6a. Move L to the foot of a steep black groove. Climb this over a couple of bulges passing a BR and PR *en route* to the roof. Traverse R on good holds past a PR on the arete and continue to a small groove around the corner. Good belays.

3. 20ft/9m. 5a. Move up and L into a steep corner and so to a PR on the arete. Move L on to the steep wall to finish carefully over some loose rock.

43 **The Appian Way/Watling Street Finish**
E2   250ft/76m ***

R. Edwards, G. Perry, 1977/R. Edwards, F. Smith, 1977

An exciting girdle which follows the fault line below the capping roof from R to L. Protection is good and the positions even better. Start 50ft/15m L of the gully, just R of a cave and a large boulder.

1. 60ft/18m. 5a. Enter the groove from the R and climb it to a steepening. Move out L on to the wall then ascend diagonally to a ledge. Belay round a corner on the R, or continue . . .

2. 45ft/14m. 5b. Climb the wall to a groove and large flake on the L. Descend slightly to the arete, move on to a steep slab. Follow the fault line L-wards under the roof dropping down to the New Dimensions belay.

3. 65ft/20m. 5b. Move L to the prow and cross the top of the
New Dimensions groove continuing to a TR after another
20ft/6m. Traverse strenuously to a small ledge and belays.
4. 80ft/24m. 5c. Watling Street Finish. Continue L to the
overhanging prow and swing round to a poor rest. The traverse
continues with increasing difficulty until the angle of the rock
eases. Finish up a grassy groove on the L.

ST TUDNO'S BUTTRESS   (756844)
A pleasant open crag giving enjoyable climbing, situated
directly below the tea shack car-park, which is on the R-hand
side of the road a little farther on from the lighthouse. From the
far end of the car-park, continue on to descend a wide grassy
gully with a scree slope in it. Descend it; the crag is on the R,
comprising a short upper tier above a slabby main buttress.
Follow the path down to the latter.

44 **Oceanside**   E2   440ft/134m **

R. Edwards, F. Harvey (5 pts), 1972/FFA: R. Edwards
A delightful girdle which follows a strong natural line from R to
L across the main buttress. Start at the R-hand side of the
buttress below a chimney and climb up to the end of the fault
line.
1. 125ft/38m. 5b. Descend slightly moving L to a PR. Hand
traverse L across a shallow groove, PR, and continue round the
bulge to another PR. Continue L past yet another PR until a step
up is made at a downward-pointing flake. Go L and descend to
a scoop (and PBS).
2. 80ft/24m. 5c. Move up L-wards to the roof and continue
traversing to a crack. Move L round the bulge past two PRS then
stand on the fault line and move L into a groove. Drop down to
the break again and traverse L past a PR to a PB.
3. 60ft/18m. 5b. Move L to a TR and descend to a ledge. Rejoin
the break and follow it across a shallow groove, PR. Descend L
to PBS – poor rock.

Great Orme – Castell y Gwynt

4. 150ft/46m. 5a. Move up L-wards to an overlap which forms a long shallow groove. Follow this via a wide crack near the top to land on a loose ledge after 100ft/30m. Climb the crack, or the shallow groove 10ft/3m to the R; and so reach the arete on the L. Climb direct to a cave. Bolt/stake belay.

5. 25ft/8m. 5a. Bridge up and over the roof, finishing up a short gully.

45 **Gritstone Gorilla**   E3   65ft/20m ***
P. Williams, R. Edwards, 1977

An excellent route crossing the largest roof on the upper tier to finish just below the car-park netting. Very strenuous for all, save those possessed of some of the characteristics of an anthropoid! Start at some large blocks underneath the wide overhang.

1. 5c. Climb the R-hand corner of the cutaway for 10ft/3m. Undercut L and ascend to the large roof, PR. Launch out across this to good holds on the lip. Layback up a flake to a PR. Traverse steeply L for 10ft/3m then pull up into a chimney groove. Finish up this – a little gem!

Little Orme

Sitting at the east end of the Llandudno promenade, the headland of Little Orme attracts only a fraction of the attention, climbing-wise, that its larger brother – Great Orme – receives. When viewed across Llandudno Bay from the Great Orme its topography is clearly revealed. One vast complex face, comprising isolated buttresses, smooth faces and steep-sided zawns, juts out into the sea; many of its features are invisible from the beach.

Colonies of seabirds known as auks, i.e. guillemots, puffins and razorbills, plus several other protected species nest here each year, so in certain areas, including the L-hand side of the

Great Orme – St Tudno's Buttress

Great Zawn, there is a climbing ban in operation from 1 March to 15 August – the routes selected are unaffected by this.

GREAT ZAWN   (816827)

This, the most remote climbing spot on Little Orme, lying at the seaward tip of the face below an old look-out post, guarantees adventure, mainly on good-quality rock – with some vegetation mixed in to 'enhance the experience'. There is an incredible feeling of isolation here; situations are dramatic; routes are long, demanding and atmospheric. It is a place for COMPETENT PARTIES ONLY and should be avoided when wet!

The approach takes 15–20 minutes along a footpath which quits the Llandudno-Rhos-on-Sea road near the crest of the hill, just below the R end of a small fierce outcrop – the Manor Crag. (There is lay-by parking down the side road which turns off some 300yd/279m farther on, where the main road becomes a dual carriageway as it drops down into Rhos-on-Sea.) After 100yd/93m the path forks. Take the lower hedgerow branch which gently leads to a kissing gate. Continue up to the L of a row of hawthorn trees before crossing through and heading for a grassy col. Cross this then turn R and continue for 100yd/93m to a rise. The old look-out post is now visible, perched on top of a grass knoll about 200yd/186m away. Just before one reaches the look-out, a slippery path runs L-wards down the hillside below it, before cutting back to reach a large sloping field – The Meadow, which lies at the top of Great Zawn. A weird-looking cave above and on the L is an obvious and accommodating spot in which to dump gear. It is also the substance of . . .

46 **The Hole of Creation**   E3   60ft/18m **

P. Williams, J. Taylor, 1983

A gynaecologically intriguing experience! The most bizarre rock formation on The Ormes yields a good 'party' route!

1. 6a. Bridge up the back of the cave (easier on the L) around a weird bulge to enter an orifice. Move out precariously, huge TR, then grope up for a good jam and thus gain a sensuous

arm-lock in a small hole above the bulge. Make a hard move up and then L to finish direct up the slender rock wall. Belay well back in a rocky outcrop over on the L. (The Magic Flute E6, 6b climbs the bolted stalagtite on the R wall of the cave.)

Down below and to the R (looking out) is a non-tidal rock bay known as The Amphitheatre. L of this, a vast undercut slab capped by a long overlap rises steeply from the sea providing the main challenge of the zawn. Sadly, the mild climate and hours of sunshine conspire to ensure that its upper reaches rapidly grass over, despite periodic cleaning by local climbers. In grassy conditions, it may be prudent to leave an extra rope dangling down the summit lawn from the final belay to assist escape should the battle through it prove too great a demand on the leader's resolve . . . The final belay is a bolt and thread in the small wall, a few yards after the approach path cuts back L.

From The Meadow traverse back R, facing out, to the abseil point – a large bolt beside thread and nut placements – sited at the R-hand end of the long overlap. Abseil 140ft/43m down the pocketed wall of Mur yr Ogof, E3 6a to land in The Amphitheatre. Escape is now only possible (a) up the selected route (b) up the abseil rope (c) across 300ft/93m of greasy slabs on the R at VS, 4c, followed by some 'hairy' grass scrambling – the alternative approach in reverse (d) by boat (e) by helicopter.

47 **Old Sam** E3 250ft/75m ***
C. Lyon, D. Lyon, 1981
A tremendous route up the centre of the slab. Start from a small ledge down on the L of The Amphitheatre.
1. 50ft/15m. 5b. Step off the ledge and ascend L-wards to two excellent holds. Descend slightly and traverse delicately L to belay in a small recess. Good nut slot on the L.
2. 100ft/30m. 5c. Climb directly up for 20ft/6m then make difficult moves R to the base of a thin crack, crux. Go up this past a TR until level with the top peg on Quietus (to the R).

Ascend a second crack slightly L-wards then climb up to a
small ledge and PB; junction with Quietus.

3. 100ft/30m. 5b. Go straight up to the overlap and surmount
this R-wards on to a rib. Climb this and continue over steep
grass to finish on the approach path. BB and TB on the L. If this
pitch is completely overgrown, and if a hanging rope is to hand
. . . prussik!

48 **Quietus**   E2   320ft/98m **

R. Edwards, K. Toms, 1971

A superb route taking a slim hidden L-facing groove above the
initial traverse on Old Sam, with which it shares a common
start.

1. 150ft/46m. 5c. From the L end of the ledge, ascend L-wards
under a long open L-facing groove. Climb up R to a PR at its
foot. Climb the interesting groove to a PR at the top. Continue
straight up to another PR. After a further 10ft/3m, traverse
15ft/5m L and climb direct to the small ledge and PB on Old
Sam.

2. 50ft/15m. 4c. Climb directly up to a belay beneath the
overlap (in common with Old Sam which continues . . .).

3. 120/37m. 5a. Ascend L-wards to the roof and pull round it to
gain the slab above. Follow the secondary overlap L-wards into
a small gully to belay in a crack on the R. If the top pitch looks
uninviting, an escape may be made up Old Sam . . . by rope?

Little Orme – Great Zawn

Carneddau and Ogwen

Running north-west from Capel Curig towards Bangor, the main A5 road cuts through a beautiful wilderness of mountain scenery – the Ogwen Valley. To the north the large rounded rolling expanse of the Carneddau hills stretches right up to the A55 coast road, whilst to the south the Ogwen area throws up the stark peaks of Tryfan and the Glyder massif.

Ogwen is the more popular of these two areas. It is the home of many of North Wales's finest traditional climbs, some of them dating back to the earliest scramblings on the Idwal slabs around the turn of the century. The cliffs here range from the Milestone Buttress, Bochlwyd Buttress, the Gribin Facet and the slabs and walls at the head of Cwm Idwal – all low-lying, a short distance from the road – to the high mountain crags of Glyder Fawr, Glyder Fach and the East Face of Tryfan.

With a uniquely high quota of medium and easy grade routes, the Ogwen area is a particularly fine place for the novice, as well as providing all the delights and tradition to suit the temperament of the middle-grade climber.

North of the A5, the selected routes lie mainly on large remote mountain crags, in dramatic settings: Llech Ddu, Ysgolion Duon, Craig Lloer and Craig yr Ysfa all have lengthy approaches and require a few days of good weather to come into condition. In marked contrast, Braich Ty Du and Carreg Mianog are readily accessible outcrops taking little or no drainage.

Local Amenities

Cheap accommodation in Ogwen is both plentiful and traditional. The main drawback, however, is the lack of a regular bus service through the valley – buses from Bangor travel as far as Bethesda, and there is a summer service from Llanrwst to Capel Curig. Those without transport will need a base close to the cliffs. Gwern y Gof Isaf, better known as Willy's Barn, provides camping and a barn (685601), whilst

Gwern y Gof Uchaf (673604) is for camping only. For the mobile climber with a vehicle, alternative campsites can be found at Capel Curig: Dol-gan (745574) and Garth Farm (701571).

The pubs in Capel Curig – Cobden's, Tyn y Coed and Bryn Tyrch – are all very popular and serve as good meeting places. All provide bar meals. The Douglas Arms in Bethesda is also popular. Take-away food is available at Capel Curig Post Office, Idwal car-park, and – in summer – from tea vans in the lay-by below the Milestone Buttress. There are cafés in Capel Curig and Bethesda. Food can also be bought from the Capel Curig Post Office which is open on Sundays. Climbing and camping equipment may be purchased at the branches of Joe Brown's and Ellis Brigham's at Capel Curig, and at Arvon's in Bethesda.

Carneddau Area

LLECH DDU (666636)

This sombre north-facing crag, tucked away on the ridge which runs north-west from Carnedd Dafydd into Cwm Llafar, is slow to dry even in fine weather. At first glance the cliff seems grossly vegetated, but this is a façade, for the routes described are some of the finest in the Carneddau, well worth the walk in from Gerlan (633655) which is the easiest access point for both Llech Ddu and Ysgolion Duon – the Black Ladders.

It is best to park in the village where there is limited space near the water works (638658), from which a poorly defined path leads across marshy ground to a good track running parallel to the Afon Llafar. This leads into the cwm to a point directly below a steep escarpment which rises to the foot of the crag (approach time about forty-five minutes).

Above a large grassy area in the centre of the cliff about 200ft/61m up, a large groove runs up to a huge square roof; this is The Great Corner. About 100ft/30m R of this is The Groove, a massive feature looking as though it was gouged out by the

mighty blow from a giant chisel. Just L of the top of The Groove
is a huge semi-detached flake, invisible from below – The
Pinnacle. R of this, and next to it, is an even larger flake – The
Pillar. Both are separated from the main cliff by a narrow gash
– The Pillar Chimney. The Pillar Traverse (Diff) comes across
here from the R side of the crag following The Pillar Chimney
behind both of these flakes. Descent: from the top of the cliff, go
diagonally R, beyond its west flank, to where a path zigzags
(with a little scrambling) down to the bottom.

49 Central Route/Scarface Finish Direct

VS   440ft/133m **

G. Dwyer, R. Morsley, 1946/L. E. and L. R. Holliwell, 1967

The original line of weakness up the centre of the cliff. Start just
R of the centre of the cliff below a V-chimney, and above two
large boulders lying just below the path.

1. 110ft/34m. 4c. Climb the V-chimney until the wall
overhangs and a rib leads diagonally R. This is followed to a
bulge where an awkward step up L leads to a stance at the foot
of a groove.

2. 100ft/30m. 4b. Go up the slab and corner crack to a recess
below the steep wall. Step on to the R wall which eases to
become a slab. Climb this to a belay.

3. 80ft/24m. 4b. Ascend a diagonal crack on the R until a
shallow groove is reached. Follow this to a grassy stance at the
top of The Groove or, for The Great Corner, climb the flake on
the L to a large terrace.

4. 60ft/18m. 4b. Climb the wall on the R to a grassy bay and
belay in the chimney beyond.

5. 90ft/27m. 4a. Go up a slab on the L which leads back R to a
small gully. This in turn leads to the top.

50 The Great Corner   E2   230ft/70m **

J. H. Clements, D. Potts (AL) (1 pt), 1965/FFA: Unknown

An excellent route taking the huge corner high up on the
central part of the cliff. Good protection and airy situations
make this a classic! It is best approached by ascending Central

Llech Ddu

Route and traversing L to belay at the foot of the corner.
1. 130ft/40m. 5b. Climb the corner passing a PR on the R wall into a niche. Stance and belay a few feet higher under the roof, just R of a large detached flake.
2. 100ft/30m. 5b. Traverse L across the wall on good holds to the arete. Step down 5ft/1.5m and L into the R-hand of two grooves. Climb this with difficulty where it overhangs, crux.

'Spaced out' on The Great Arete

Continue to a small roof. Surmount this and finish up the groove.

51 **The Groove** E1 450ft/135m ***
J. V. Antoine, I. F. Campbell (some aid), 1961/FFA: Unknown
A magnificent route taking the most obvious feature of the cliff. Once loose and vegetated, it has now cleaned up to provide an exciting and airy expedition. Difficulties are continuous rather

than excessive. Start 30yd/27m R of Central Route at the base
of a narrow groove leading up to a feeble-looking Y-shaped
tree.

1. 80ft/24m. 5a. Climb the groove, PR, to the tree.
2. 60ft/18m. 5a. Go up the deceptively steep corner behind the
tree to a bulge which is turned on the R wall. Step back L to PBS
but a poor stance.
3. 70ft/21m. 5a. Traverse delicately L into The Groove itself.
Climb this, PR, for 30ft/9m to an uncomfortable stance and PBS.
4. 100ft/30m. 5a. Follow the groove direct to a grass ledge –
superb!
5. 50ft/15m. 4b. Take the wall on the R to a grassy bay and
belays in the chimney beyond.
6. 90ft/27m. 4a. Finish as for Central Route, or escape down
the Pillar Traverse to the R.

52 **The Great Arete**   E4   440ft/133m***
*E. Drummond, B. Campbell-Kelly (some aid)/FFA: P. Livesey,
S. Foster, 1975*
The most sensational climb in the Carneddau! The R arete of
The Groove is, to quote the first ascensionists, 'A route of utter
exposure and difficulty in a position of great cheek'.

1. 80ft/24m. 5a. As for The Groove.
2. 60ft/18m. 5a. Climb the corner to belay – as for The Groove
(cleaner and better than the original second pitch).
3. 120ft/37m. 6a. Move L to the bottom of the groove in the
arete, PR, to a poor resting place below a small deep hole. A
very precarious and sustained series of moves leads to the first
overhang, and a poor rest, PR. Reach up and pull over the
overhang using a crack on the R to enter a groove on the R of
another overhang, PR. Climb the narrowing groove until level
with a PR then swing R on good holds where the angle eases.
Ascend diagonally R for 25ft/8m to belay on the slab.
4. 90ft/27m. 4c. Follow the L arete in a superb position to the
top of The Pinnacle with poor protection and some dubious
rock.
5. 90ft/27m. 4a. Finish as for Central Route or The Groove.

53 **Elliw**   E1   290ft/89m **

A. A. Bell, J. H. Clements (AL), 1965

A fine climb on superb rough rock. It lies on the west flank of
the crag in an area split by chimneys and grooves of various
sizes, above the obvious grassy dyke – Pillar Traverse. The
most noticeable feature here is Y Chimney – the large groove
starting 75ft/23m along the traverse and, if taken direct, VS.
Our route tackles the open light-coloured groove in the next
recess, 50ft/15m to the L.

1. 140ft/43m. 5b. Climb up into the groove via the crack and
go directly up to an overhanging wall. Follow the groove past a
poor PR, crux, diagonally L then continue straight up to an
overhang. Poor stance and PBS 10ft/3m to the L.

2. 150ft/46m. 4c. Traverse R and follow a slim groove, stepping
R at an overlap. Scrambling remains to the top.

YSGOLION DUON (THE BLACK LADDERS)   (668632)

This impressive cliff, nearly three-quarters of a mile wide and
800ft/250m high, lies at the head of Cwm Llafar. It is
approached as for Llech Ddu, beyond which another twenty
minutes of scrambling over an unpleasant boulder field leads to
the foot of the crag. There are few continuous lines here as the
steep black walls and dripping overhangs give way to broad
undulating terraces running horizontally at many levels –
Ysgoleinciau (the rungs of the ladder). Two prominent gullies
run the full length of the face, the one on the L being Central
Gully (Diff), whilst the other is:

54 **Western Gully**   S   1060ft/325m ***

P. H. Cooke, T. Brushfield, H. Owen, 1901

One of the finest gully climbs in Wales. Hard and serious for its
grade, in less than ideal conditions. Though it is rarely climbed
in summer, queues form at the foot of it in winter when it
becomes a first-rate Grade IV ice route. Start directly below
the gully where the stream has cut a groove through the lower
rocks to the scree.

1. 250ft/77m. Go up the unpleasant water-worn grooves for

80ft/24m to grass and slime in the gully bed; the same point can be reached via easier rocks and a little chimney to the L. Scramble up the gully in two pitches to belay.

2. 75ft/23m. Turn the chockstone on the R and continue up into the gully.

3. 55ft/17m. Tackle a nice clean pitch to a smooth section.

4. 60ft/18m. Bridge up into the chimney, face L and go up to reach a large stance.

5. 25ft/8m. Continue easily to a mossy cave.

6. 40ft/12m. Exist R past jammed blocks to belay at the foot of a groove.

7. 70ft/21m. Climb the awkward groove to grass and vegetation above. Stance on the L.

8. 35ft/11m. Traverse L until it is possible to climb the R-hand side of a huge jammed boulder to a large cave.

9. 80ft/24m. Take the slab on the R, crux, to reach scree. Scramble up into a little amphitheatre to belay on the L.

10. 70ft/21m. A chimney on the L gives the best exit. Go up past a boulder bridge whence 300ft/93m of scrambling leads to the summit.

CRAIG BRAICH TY DDU   (649609)

This little-frequented crag comprises an area of broken buttresses and grass/scree-filled gullies, about 300ft/93m above the A5 on the lower slopes of Pen yr Ole Wen. It is the most accessible cliff in the Carneddau and makes a pleasant change for those who tire of the crowds in Cwm Idwal.

The buttresses are actually the ends of faint spurs which drop down from high on the mountain and are numbered from R to L as one looks at the cliff. The climbs described lie on Buttresses Five, Seven and Eight, and are approached along a faint path which starts from the Alfred Embleton stile by the Ogwen Falls and traverses up to meet a drystone wall running up from the road to the toe of Buttress Three. Above and R are two smaller buttresses, One and Two, and on the L, high up the grass/scree gully with a drystone wall across it, sits Buttress Four.

Pinnacle Ridge Route

Down on the L is a line of prominent pinnacles forming a castellated ridge; a tongue of rock shoots down from the base of a spur almost to the A5 – this is Buttress Five.

55 **Pinnacle Ridge Route**   V Diff   330ft/101m *

K. U. Ingold, Miss P. J. Fearon, J. M. Ball, 1950

Start from the bottom of the buttress. Scramble up to the foot of an obvious clean-cut ridge leading up to the pinnacles: 'PR' is scratched on the rock.

1. 130ft/40m. Climb the slabby rib to a large block at 60ft/18m. Make a high step up R into a groove and continue up another groove to belay on a heather terrace.

2. 50ft/15m. Scramble easily up the ridge to a spike belay.

3. 75ft/23m. Traverse R and climb the ridge easily to a stance on its R side.

4. 75ft/23m. Climb up steeply to the crest and go over, or round, the pinnacles to the top.

Just above Buttress Five sits an extensive crag which is broken and vegetated with a water course on its R – this is Buttress Six. Above and to the L lies Buttress Seven with two large diamond-shaped overhangs at half-height above a clean-cut corner, the line of:

56 **Decameron Rib**   VS   190ft/57m **

S. M. Lane, F. A. Boydell, 1955

One of the best routes on the crag. Start at the foot of the short chimney 15ft/5m R of the foot of the corner.

1. 90ft/27m. 4a. Go up the chimney for 15ft/5m, traverse L into the corner which is taken to the roof. Step L to belay.

2. 70ft/21m. 4b. Climb into the bottomless chimney and ascend past a dubious block to continue up the crack. Move R to another crack which is followed for 15ft/5m until a large flake is passed on the L. Go up a slab to belay.

3. 30ft/9m. 4a. Trend up L-wards to the top of the final pinnacle and step across to easy ground. Scramble up for 200ft/60m then traverse L into the gully.

Buttress Eight faces Buttress Seven and starts 100ft/30m higher up, on the L of the easy wide gully leading up from the foot of

Decameron Rib. At the lowest point of the buttress is a huge detached flake with a curved chimney on its R.

57 Route 2 S   110ft/33m **
C. H. S. R. Palmer, G. W. Furlong, 1927
Start 40ft/12m R of the curved chimney at the bottom of some large jammed blocks.
1. 50ft/15m. Climb the jammed blocks then pull into a niche which is quitted with difficulty on the R using a horizontal spike. Stance and belay 10ft/3m higher.
2. 60ft/18m. Take the steep wall direct – on jugs . . . a classic pitch!

58 Cuckoo Groove HVS   150ft/45m *
J. R. Lees, T. R. Wilkinson, 1960
A good climb taking the large groove 30ft/9m R of Route 2. Start at a 10ft/3m bollard.
1. 50ft/15m. 4c. Enter the groove with difficulty, crux. Follow it to a poor stance and belay on the L.
2. 50ft/15m. 4b. Step back down; move out on to the R arete and climb it with difficulty to a stance.
3. 50ft/15m. 4c. Go up into the overhanging corner and escape R to easier ground.

CRAIG LLOER   (663619)
This lonely cliff sits hidden away on the north-east side of Pen yr Ole Wen above Ffynnon Lloer. It is usually reached in around forty minutes along the path which runs from the east end of Llyn Ogwen, past Tal-y-llyn Farm, before zigzagging up the hillside on the west bank of the stream issuing from Cwm Lloer.

   The cliff consists of two buttresses separated by a wide scree-filled amphitheatre, and our route lies on the R-hand (west) one which is seen in profile on approach from the *llyn*.

Craig Braich Ty Ddu

59 **Kirkus's Route**   HS   280ft/84m *

C. F. Kirkus (solo), 1928

The best route on the crag with continually interesting moves on sound rock. Start 25ft/8m L of the toe of the buttress and immediately R of a wide grassy bay, at a cairn below an easy sloping chimney.

1. 90ft/27m. Climb the chimney then step out R to enter a groove. Go up for a few feet then traverse L to the edge of a slab. This leads delicately to a heathery stance.
2. 50ft/15m. An awkward little rib gains the foot of an obvious crack. Struggle up this, crux, to good holds and a TB.
3. 90ft/27m. From a heather shelf, TR diagonally R to a rib and follow this up the edge of the buttress until forced back L into a square-cut groove above the stance. Bridge up and climb a slab to a large spike belay directly above.
4. 50ft/15m. Scramble up easy slabs to finish. To descend, scramble higher to a short steep section leading down into the amphitheatre on the L.

CARREG MIANOG   (686618)

This steep outcrop lies low on the south-east flank of Carnedd Dafydd, about half a mile north of the farm at Glan Llugwy. It is easily seen, and best approached (in thirty minutes), from the A5 along the well-surfaced gated road (as for Craig yr Ysfa). At the top of the initial steep section, follow the leat (canal) L-wards to a bridge, just before the Afon Llugwy. Strike directly up now, crossing a boulder field that lies below the crag. Please note that on no account should an approach be made along the private road to Glan Llugwy.

The cliff has two main facets: high up on the L, the West Buttress has a prominent arete at its centre; then comes a grassy central area, before the more broken East Buttress down to the R, seamed by a couple of horizontal breaks with an arete at its lower R end. Descend up and over to the L of the cliff.

Carreg Mianog

60 **The Cracked Arete** VS 110ft/34m *

A. D. Ferguson, R. A. Williams, 1945

The central arete of the West Buttress is well protected and on good rock. Start just L of the arete above a small cave.

1. 75ft/23m. 4b. Climb directly up the edge to a ledge then step back L and follow an easy crack to another ledge. Take the thin curving crack above, crux, to a large ledge.

2. 35ft/11m. The wide corner crack gives an easy finish.

30ft/9m to the L, Zip Wall (S) gives a fine pitch.

61 **Biceps Wall** VS 100ft/30m

D. H. Haworth, G. A. Horridge, 1948

A good strenuous pitch just L of the arete on the East Buttress, though not quite in the class of its neighbour. Start a few feet L of the arete, below a cannon of rock.

1. 70ft/21m. 5a. Climb awkwardly up to join the arete at 15ft/5m and continue to the grass ledge. From the large block at the back, pull round the roof and take the short slab to another ledge and the 'cannon'.

2. 30ft/9m. 4c. Finish straight up the tricky wall above the 'cannon' . . . Starting up a groove just R of the arete is Funny Bone (VS) which climbs the wall via two interesting mantelshelves – usually dirty.

CRAIG YR YSFA   (694637)

This large rambling crag faces north-east and sits high up on the flanks of Carnedd Llewelyn. It consists of two great buttresses split by a huge gully, the Amphitheatre, which has a magnificent wall on its R-hand side; a prominent scree shoot runs out of its mouth down towards the valley. The R-hand buttress is vegetated and split by a large diagonal gully – Great Gully. Three gullies divide the L-hand buttress. From L to R these are: Pinnacle, Bending and Avalanche Gullies.

The cliff is reached in around seventy-five minutes via the well-surfaced, gated road which starts from the A5 at 687603. Parking is limited here and care should be taken not to block the gateway. Follow the road north up the hillside and where it bears L, carry straight on along a path over a rise, skirting the R side of the Ffynnon Llugwy reservoir. The path now rises steeply up to a col at 695633, from which point the top of the cliff can be seen on the R shoulder of Carnedd Llewelyn.

For routes on the Amphitheatre Wall, it is best to follow the ridge to the top of the cliff and scramble carefully down keeping towards the L-hand side (looking out) of The Amphitheatre.

For Amphitheatre Buttress, Great Gully and the longer climbs, a path leads from the col down and round to the foot of the crag.

62 **Amphitheatre Buttress**   V Diff   960ft/293m ***
G. D. and A. P. Abraham, D. Leighton, J. W. Puttrell, 1905

A very popular and classic mountaineering route. Start at the foot of the buttress which forms the L-hand side of The Amphitheatre, just above the path.

1. 100ft/30m. Easily up to a good stance.
2. 120ft/37m. Continue via slabs and a tricky groove.
3. 180ft/55m. Two pitches of easy climbing gain a large ledge below a steep wall.
4. 70ft/21m. The crux: climb the very polished corner on the R to a large detached block. Continue up, finishing on rounded holds.
5. 200ft/61m. Vegetated scrambling.
6. 110ft/34m. Follow the ridge horizontally, traversing a gap, two gendarmes and a sharp edge to reach the main mass of the mountain.
7. 180ft/55m. Climb the ridge on the R to the top.

Amphitheatre Wall

On the R-hand side of the Amphitheatre is a great sweep of clean steep rock split at two-thirds height by a shelf: the Bilberry Ledge. The climbing on this wall is comparable in quality to that found on the East Buttress of Cloggy, perhaps finer as an aesthetic experience – the setting is better, the wall gets the sun until mid-afternoon, and the crowds seldom come.

Below the Bilberry Ledge, high up on the extreme L, is The

Craig yr Ysfa

Crack (HVS). Lower down, the next line of weakness is a short chimney with an obvious V-groove offset above and ʀ – Plumbagin (HVS). Further ʀ and lower still is a long ledge about 20ft/6m up; above its ʀ end a huge, ʀ-leaning, open V-groove gives the second pitch of Mur y Niwl. The bulging wall ʀ again is taken by Amadeus, E4 6a and Agrippa (HVS).

63 **Aura**   E2   200ft/61m **

R. Carrington, A. Rouse, B. Hall, 1975

A superb climb up the wall between Plumbagin and Mur y
Niwl. Start about 40ft/12m R of Plumbagin's V-chimney, lower
down the gully where an obvious line of holds leads
horizontally R.

1. 150ft/46m. 5b. Climb directly to a PR below a small roof at
30ft/9m. Move R to stand on a block on a narrow ledge. Step
back L to climb the obvious thin crack slanting up to the R, past
a PR, to the top of the wall.

2. 50ft/15m. Easily up to the terrace.

64 **Mur y Niwl**   VS   250ft/75m ***

A. J. J. Moulam, J. B. Churchill, 1952

One of the great Welsh mountain classics – not to be missed!
Start in the gully bed, R of a small damp chimney and below
the L-hand end of a long grass ledge at 15ft/5m.

1. 40ft/12m. 4c. Go up the wall to the ledge which is traversed
to its R end. Or, start 15ft/5m further L in a recess and traverse
R along an obvious flake to the ledge and PB. Much harder
when wet.

2. 100ft/30m. 4c. Climb the wall to a small niche, move R and
go up on good holds to the base of the large V-groove – possible
belay. Hand traverse R along the upper of two ledges, step
down and move delicately R into a diagonal crackline which
leads to a 'perch' stance. Nut and poor PBS.

3. 60ft/18m. 4c. Step down, then move R on sharp handholds
beneath the overhang to a ledge. Move up and on to another
ledge, PR. Climb the arete on the L to a grassy stance and block
belay.

4. 40ft/12m. 4b. Ascend a groove to land on a glacis. Move L to
below a short cracked wall.

5. 10ft/3m. 4c. Finish up the short tricky wall to belay
80ft/24m further back at the base of the upper wall.

65 **Girdle of the Lower Amphitheatre Wall**

E1   500ft/150m ***

R. James, J. Wilkinson, 1966

Another superb mountain classic! One of the most enjoyable
girdles around. After the first two pitches, the climbing is
around the VS/HVS standard. Start at the foot of the crack on
the L of the wall.

1. 65ft/20m. 5b. Climb the crack for 30ft/9m until it is possible
to step R to reach a good spike. Descend the steep diagonal
crack, crux, to reach the top of an overhang. Step across this
and pull on to a stance.

2. 100ft/30m. 5b. Descend R and make a bold step to gain a
horizontal crack which is traversed until it is possible to move
into a niche. Move R into another niche, then semi hand
traverse 30ft/9m R to near an arete. PR and ancient nut. Abseil
30ft/9m and swing into a stance on the second pitch of Mur y
Niwl. PBS.

3. 70ft/21m. 4c. Descend, traverse R then go up the diagonal
crack to the 'perch' – as for Mur y Niwl.

4. 70ft/21m. 5a. Descend a groove (below the traverse R on
Mur y Niwl) and go down over a small overhang until a short
traverse leads to a jug on the arete. Using a sling on the jug (5c
free) descend to the start of a hand traverse which leads to a
stance.

5. 70ft/21m. 4c. Step down and round the corner, then go up
over two sloping ledges, continuing on large holds to a stance.

6. 120ft/37m. 4c. Move R on to a steep wall. Pull up into a
groove and go to the top. Carry on for 80ft/24m to the Bilberry
Terrace and belays.

Pinnacle Wall

The next couple of routes are on Pinnacle Wall, the upper wall
on the R of the Amphitheatre above the Bilberry Terrace.

Craig yr Ysfa – Amphitheatre Right Wall

66 **Pinnacle Wall** S 230ft/69m**

C. F. Kirkus (solo), 1931

A fine wandering climb which is very exposed. It is the ideal continuation to Mur y Niwl. Start at the R-hand end of Bilberry Terrace, below the quartz ledge at a stepped corner leading up R-wards.

1. 40ft/12m. The stepped corner to a good stance.
2. 90ft/27m. Go up 10ft/3m to the quartz traverse. Follow this L-wards with ease, until an awkward step at the end leads to a small stance. PBS.
3. 100ft/30m. Climb the corner above for 30ft/9m. Good holds in a rough-edged diagonal crack lead to the pinnacle. Step L, finishing up a slab.

67 **The Grimmet** VS 160ft/49m *

A. D. M. Cox, R. L. Beaumont, 1938

Steep and well-protected. Start at the L-hand end of Bilberry Terrace, in the R-hand corner of a smaller terrace.

1. 110ft/34m. 4c. Climb the steep corner crack to a cave. Move out L on good holds. Continue up the corner until forced L into a narrow groove: awkward. Go straight up and bridge round the final overhang to reach grass and a stance up R.
2. 50ft/15m. 4b. Traverse back L to reach excellent holds on a steep rough wall. Take this to more ledges. Two mantelshelves above lead to the top.

68 **Great Gully** V Diff 730ft/223m *

J. M. A. Thomson, R. I. Simey, W. G. Clay, 1900

The huge gully splitting the North Buttress, not to be confused with Vanishing Gully, gives an excellent route of its type, with bags of character and atmosphere. It is reached by walking round the foot of the buttress on the R of the Amphitheatre past an indistinct gully – Vanishing Gully – and ascending scree for 200ft/61m to a cavernous gully entrance . . . scramble up for 150ft/46m.

Mur y Niwl, just below 'the perch'

1. 90ft/27m. Turn the chockstone on the L then scramble up for 80ft/24m.

2. 120ft/37m. Go over the chockstone on the L then scramble a further 100ft/30m to The Door Jamb (taken direct in deep snow conditions).

3. 60ft/18m. Move up a short groove on the R, past a ledge on the L to a larger one. Move back L into the gully bed.

4. 35ft/11m. Continue up the steep, wet gully bed, or take the deep chimney on the R.

5. 45ft/14m. The chimney proves awkward to a R-stepping exit at the top – this pitch can be avoided on the R wall by a traverse and grass.

6. 110ft/34m. Take the R-hand groove then scramble up scree for 80ft/24m.

7. 200ft/61m. Go up the chimney R of the rib, or go up over mossy chockstones on the L. Scramble up for 60ft/18m then go out over a large jammed block to another one.

8. 20ft/6m. Ascend an awkward undercut chimney on the R, or the R wall stepping into the top of the chimney. The L-hand chimney may also be climbed.

9. 50ft/15m. The Great Cave Pitch. Go up the L wall of the cave with difficulty, crux. Traverse L to reach the outer chockstone. Scramble to the top . . . The last two pitches can be avoided by chimneys which leave the gully part way up pitch 8. The L one is strenuous, and the R one leads to easy ground in a few feet. A superb winter route.

Ogwen Area

MILESTONE BUTTRESS   (663602)

This popular crag lies just west of the foot of Tryfan's North Ridge, directly above the Tenth Milestone from Bangor on the A5. Easily seen from here, it can be reached from any one of the lay-bys in around ten minutes via a series of well-defined paths running up to its foot; the shortest but steepest one goes up just L of the stone wall, before continuing round to the East Face of

Tryfan, and is one of the usual approaches for climbing on that part of the mountain also.

The cliff is split in half by a line of vegetated broken rocks leading up to the base of the massive Central Block. The front face has a shallow groove running its full height which gives the Ogwen Valley its hardest climb – The Wrinkled Retainer. To the R is an area of easy-angled slabs and ribs, whilst on the L are steeper grooves and corners. Routes are described from R to L.

69 **Pulpit Route** and **Ivy Chimney**   Diff   290ft/87m
G. Barlow, Miss E. M. Barlow, 1911

At the R edge of the crag is a wet gully (Little Gully) which provides the usual descent. Our climb follows the rib to its L by a series of slabs and then takes the prominent chimney. Start at the foot of the rib beside the descent gully.

1. 90ft/27m. Climb the juggy slabs trending L then continue straight up a narrow slab with a step at the top to a TB at a large block – The Pulpit.

2. 80ft/24m. Climb the steep slab on the L of The Pulpit to reach an easier slab. Continue up through the little trench in the wall to ledges.

3. 40ft/12m. Scramble up and walk across to a chimney with some large wedged blocks at its top.

4. 50ft/15m. The entry is steep! Continue up the chimney to an exposed exit through a hole on the R to a ledge and TBs.

5. 30ft/9m. Take the slab on the R, stepping L to finish.

L of Pulpit Route, a prominent rib gives the line of Rowan Route (Mod) whilst a few yards lower down on the L is:

70 **Direct Route**   V Diff   250ft/75m ***
G. Barlow, H. Priestly-Smith, 1910

A popular climb up the R-hand side of the Central Ridge – a large blunt rib forming the L-hand boundary of the slabs. Very polished! Start on a terrace at the foot of a diagonal crack which runs up a slab in the R side of the Central Ridge.

1. 100ft/30m. Climb the diagonal crack to a niche. Move L and
go up slabs to good flake belays.
2. 100ft/30m. Step up, and move L up a corner and short
leg-jamming crack into a niche (optional belay). Carry on up a
steep crack to the Bivalve – a large flake. Hand traverse L under
this and go up round the corner to belay. Low thread on the R
. . . Scramble up to a large ledge a few yards higher to reach:
3. 30ft/9m. The Corner Chimney. The smooth chimney in the
back L-hand corner is climbed with difficulty, facing R until it is
possible to finish up its L edge.
4. 20ft/6m. Finish up the short slab.

71 **Superdirect**   HVS   280ft/84m **

G. Barlow, H. Priestly-Smith, 1910/Pitch 4 – J. M. Edwards, 1941
An enjoyable route taking the crest of the Central Ridge prior
to an exciting finale on the Central Block. Start at the foot of
the ridge below a thin slanting crack.
1. 100ft/30m. 4c. Layback up the crack, round into the easier
crack which leads to an inverted scoop and continue up the
blunt rib to a ledge.
2. 100ft/30m. 4c. From the L-hand end of the ledge, turn the
overhang and climb steeply up the arete to another ledge
(possible belay). Take the obvious line up the edge to belay on
the Bivalve.
3. 20ft/6m. 4a. Easily up the rib overlooking the gully.
4. 60ft/18m. 5a. Traverse airily out L along the front of the
Central Block to a good ledge from which a steep crack leads to
the top.

72 **The Wrinkled Retainer**   E5   100ft/30m ***

*M. Boysen, J. Yates – with a tree, as Desecration Crack E3, 6a,
1979/FFA: J. Redhead, C. Shorter – without!, 1980*
An infamous route, the rediscovery of which led to the demise
of the only oak tree on Tryfan. The felling of the tree (which is
to be strongly condemned) has, from a climber's point of view,

Milestone Buttress

left a line of purity, beauty, and no little difficulty. No aid is required on the first 25ft/8m although expertise in the art of levitation could prove useful. Start at the foot of the Central Block by the remains of the oak.

1. 6c. From the stump of the tree, finger-shredding moves up the boulder problem lower wall lead to a welcome resting ledge. Climb the deceptively awkward crack in the shallow groove above to join and finish up Superdirect – a tremendous pitch.

73 Wall Climb/Soap Gut/Chimney Route

HS   210ft/64m **

W. R. Reade, 1927/C. W. F. Noyce, 1936/E. W. Steeple, 1913

A fine hybrid giving interesting climbing from the toe to the top of the crag. Start 30ft/9m R of the drystone wall at the foot of a wall.

1. 65ft/20m. Go up the wall on polished holds until a sharp-edged crack is reached after 40ft/12m. Either step round to the R and ascend, or climb the crack (VS). Move diagonally up L, then go down and across on a ledge leading to the foot of a large corner – Soap Gut.

2. 95ft/29m. 4b. Ascend easily for 40ft/12m to a ledge. Continue for 20ft/6m until a mantelshelf enables a ledge on the L to be gained. Step on to the R wall to reach the Narrows. Awkward moves up this corner, crux, lead to good ledges. Move across the rib on the R and traverse down to reach the corner of Chimney Route.

3. 50ft/15m. Climb the smooth crack in the R of the corner with a hard move at 20ft/6m. After this the pitch eases to a tricky finish.

EAST FACE OF TRYFAN   (665594)

Tryfan's major climbing area rises from the Heather Terrace, a prominent well-trodden rake crossing the face from R to L. The face comes into view, weather permitting, some two miles beyond Capel Curig as one drives towards Bangor. It generally

Soap Gut, approaching the Narrows

takes around one hour to reach the crag up the scree path
(starting from the Tenth Milestone and L of the stone wall)
which leads up to a shoulder on the North Ridge. Here the path
splits, the upper branch following the crest of the North Ridge,
the lower branch contouring round to the start of the Heather
Terrace. Alternatively, an approach can be made along a path
starting from Gwern Gof Uchaf (673604), passing the slabs of
Little Tryfan to a stony couloir which leads to the start of
Heather Terrace. Park as for the Milestone Buttress or at
Gwern Gof Uchaf.

   The climbing on the East Face centres on the three large
buttresses whose tops denote the three summits of the
mountain. These buttresses are separated by two prominent
gullies: North Gully on the R and South Gully on the L. The
R-hand buttress, North Buttress, is climbed by Grooved Arete,
whilst to the L, across North Gully, Central Buttress is taken by
the absorbing First Pinnacle Rib. Finally, L again beyond
South Gully(from which Munich Climb rises) lies South
Buttress which provides the pleasant but well-worn Gashed
Crag route.

74 **Grooved Arete**   HV Diff   810ft/244m ***
E. W. Steeple and party, 1911

One of the finest routes of its standard anywhere in Wales. An
early start is recommended at weekends to avoid queuing! Start
from the Heather Terrace on the R side of the North Buttress at
the foot of a groove in a little rib – 'GA' scratched on the rock.
1. 100ft/30m. Go up the groove, then awkwardly L to the foot
of a slab. Climb this and scramble up to a stance by a large
spike.
2. 90ft/27m. From the belay, step on to a rib on the L. Take
this for 40ft/12m until a step L gains a delicate groove leading
to a good stance.
3. 100ft/30m. Go over a little overhang on the R, then go L and
scramble up rock to a grassy path. Walk 100ft/30m R to the

Tryfan – East Face

edge of the gully where an elegant rib rises to meet the main
mass of Terrace Wall.

4. 90ft/27m. Climb the rib, first on the R then on the L, to a
block stance.

5. 120ft/37m. Ascend round a bulge to enter the main groove
and climb it to a step L into a smaller groove. Follow this, and a
rib on the L to a grassy ledge – The Haven – below the Knight's
Move Slab. Belay on the L.

6. 50ft/15m. Climb the crack on the L side of the slab, then
move delicately across on the lattice of cracks which make up
the chess-board, crux, to a small sloping stance on the R edge.

7. 60ft/18m. Climb the groove, or the R arete.

8. 100ft/30m. Continue steeply on good holds, finishing up the
rough black wall . . . Descend by walking down L into North
Gully; go up this to the col between the main and North peaks,
then straight ahead down the West Face.

75 North Buttress by the Terrace Wall Variant
V Diff   645ft/196m *
O. G. Jones, G. D. Abraham, J. W. Puttrell, 1899
This climb takes the L-hand side of the North Buttress then
weaves its way up Terrace Wall – a steep area of rock starting
about 450ft/140m above Heather Terrace. Start below a deep
groove just R of North Gully.

1. 70ft/21m. Go up the corner with difficulty to a good stance.

2. 60ft/18m. Move R, then follow a steep scoop in the middle of
the main rib to a belay.

3. 60ft/18m. Climb the edge on the L or the groove further R.

4. 250ft/77m. Scramble up to the foot of Terrace Wall.
Towards the L end of the wall, North Buttress Ordinary route
goes diagonally L to a terrace, up a 20ft/6m slab then easily
back R behind some large flakes, continuing R until a little
groove leads to Belle Vue Terrace. In the middle of the ledge at
the foot of the wall is a pointing finger stone. Start between this
and the North Buttress groove, below a hollow in the face on
the L.

5. 75ft/23m. Go up the groove to a bulge in the wall. Turn this

on the R to the First Ledge. Continue direct for 15ft/5m to the Second Ledge.

6. 80ft/24m. Walk R to reach the L wall of an obvious groove – Long Chimney. Traverse the groove and go up the rib on the R to Bollard Slab. Climb the slab and move back L into the groove which leads to the traverse and Belle Vue Terrace.

7. 50ft/15m. Straight up on easy rock to the top . . . descend as for Grooved Arete.

76 **Belle Vue Bastion** VS 160ft/48m ***
I. Waller, C. H. S. R. Palmer, 1927

The best route on Terrace Wall with fine situations. Start at the R end of the ledge running along the foot of the wall.

1. 90ft/27m. 4c. Easy climbing up large blocks for 30ft/9m leads to a possible stance on the edge. Continue by following grooves up the edge of the slab until a small exposed ledge is reached at about 65ft/20m. Make a hard move up L to a niche, crux, and go straight up, or move round the corner (after the crux) and climb to the Grove of Bollards.

2. 70ft/21m. 4b. Traverse R on to the lip of the exposed overhang, then move R round the corner and back up L to easier climbing which leads directly to the terrace. Descend as for Grooved Arete.

77 **First Pinnacle Rib** V Diff 635ft/195m **
E. W. Steeple, G. Barlow, A. H. Doughty, 1914

A fine varied route, the best on Central Buttress. There are three broad ribs between South Gully and a large grassy bay to the R. This route takes the middle one. Start 30ft/9m R of South Gully – '1 PR' is scratched on the rock.

1. 120ft/37m. Go easily up blocks to the overhang. Move R and climb the R-hand groove to a step back L on to slabs which lead to a ledge. Go up steep slabs to a belay where the ridge narrows.

2. 260ft/80m. Enjoyable climbing up the ridge in two or three pitches to reach the huge pinnacle.

3. 45ft/14m. The Yellow Slab – crux. From the ledge behind

the pinnacle, go up the edge of the slab on polished holds until a move R at 10ft/3m to a groove is possible. Take this more easily to a stance. This pitch can be avoided by a wall and bulge on the R (just S).

4. 150ft/46m. Go up L on curving suspect flakes until the climbing eases at about 70ft/21m. Scramble up a scree terrace to below the final wall. Walk round to the R and ascend easily to Adam and Eve – two large monoliths denoting the summit. Or better:

5. 60ft/18m. Thomson's Chimney. From the terrace, climb the chimney to a ledge at 20ft/6m, move R to another chimney and continue up this to the top. Descend down the West Face.

78 **Munich Climb** VS 275ft/83m **

H. Teufel, H. Sedlmayer, J. R. Jenkins, 1936/FFA: J. M. Edwards, 1936

A good steep route, fairly well protected, which requires competent rope work and a steady leader: the home of an infamous piton! Start half-way up South Gully on the L wall, opposite and just below the level of the pinnacle of First Pinnacle Rib; beneath a triangular grass ledge with a block sitting on it. Gain this from the gully.

1. 30ft/9m. 4a. Climb any of the three slabby grooves on the R to a grassy stance.

2. 35ft/11m. 4c. Go up the rectangle of slab on the L for 20ft/6m, then move R and up using a good handhold on the R edge of the slab to a stance among some perched blocks.

3. 60ft/18m. 4c. From the blocks, move up to the nose on the L to gain a traverse line which leads to a steep flake crack – Teufel's Crack. Climb this past one awkward move to a grassy rake and belay.

4. 50ft/15m. Easily up the rake passing behind a large block to a wide terrace.

5. 100ft/30m. 4b. Ascend the groove behind the block, awkward at 35ft/11m and 55ft/17m, to gain a rocky ledge at 70ft/21m. Climb the steep wall trending R to finish. Descent: go over to the main peak then down the West Face.

First Pinnacle Rib, the Yellow Slab

79 **South Buttress by the Gashed Crag**

V Diff   525ft/160m *

H. B. Buckle, G. Barlow, 1902

A classic route with a masochistic crux! Start 20 yd/18m L of South Gully at a groove directly below The Gash – a huge roof some 200ft/61m up the buttress.

1. 100ft/30m. Follow the groove, exiting R on jammed blocks at the top.
2. 80ft/24m. Go straight up to The Gash, then step R to belay below a chimney.
3. 60ft/18m. Thrutch up to the top of the chimney and continue scrambling for a few feet until a wall leads up to the crest of the ridge.
4. 120ft/37m. Follow the broad back of the ridge.
5. 120ft/37m. The ridge narrows and becomes more broken until two grooves lead to the foot of the final wall.
6. 45ft/14m. The narrow chimney which splits the wall is awkward and exposed, easing towards the top near the South Summit. Descend as for Munich Climb.

BOCHLWYD BUTTRESS   (656597)

This small cliff of compact rock gives enjoyable climbing, mainly in the easier grades. It lies on the east bank of the stream which flows down from Llyn Bochlwyd. Approach along the Miners' Path from Ogwen Cottage until near the crag, whence a short traverse brings one to its foot in about twenty minutes. There is parking space around Ogwen and Idwal Cottages. The buttress is split down its centre by twin chimneys which give our first route:

80 **Chimney Climb**   V Diff   105ft/32m

F. Aldous, A. C. Adams, O. Thorneycroft, 1909

The original route of the crag. Start at the R-hand chimney.

1. 30ft/9m. Climb the chimney until it is possible to swing on to the face on the L. Go up on good holds to a stance and belay; or go up the L-hand crack(S); or go up the L-hand chimney (VS).

2. 35ft/11m. Move L into the chimney which is climbed past the overhang to a stance in the chimney above.
3. 40ft/12m. Continue up the chimney until a move L leads to easier climbing and the top.

The wall on the R of Chimney Climb provides two pleasant 'Severe' routes: Two Pitch Climb, a line 20ft/6m R, and Five Pitch Climb, which lies 20ft/6m R again.

81 **Arete and Slab** Diff 105ft/32m
C. H. S. R. Palmer, D. G. MacDonald, 1927
An enjoyable route taking the R arete of the buttress before moving L to climb its final slab. Start at the foot of a crack in the arete.
1. 45ft/14m. Climb the steep crack on good holds, then scramble up to belay in the corner.
2. 20ft/6m. Traverse L for 15ft/5m, then go up to a sloping ledge.
3. 40ft/12m. Awkwardly mantelshelf on to the slab on the L which leads to the top.

82 **Marble Slab Start** HS 60ft/18m *
C. F. Kirkus, C. Brennand, 1935
Start 20ft L of Arete and Slab, just L of a bollard.
1. Climb to the top of the bollard. Go up to a little bulge on good holds. Pull over this and continue delicately up and R to better holds and the second stance of Arete and Slab climb.

83 **Wall Climb** HS 150ft/46m *
F. E. Hicks, C. J. A. Cooper, W. E. Woosnam-Jones, 1929
Exposed and interesting; the easiest line up the wall L of Chimney Climb. Start just L of the L-hand twin chimney by two sloping gangways.
1. 85ft/26m. Move up on to a ledge then follow the upper gangway L-wards. Descend from the top and step L. Continue by moving up R, past an awkward mantelshelf. Go straight up to a grass ledge on the L.

2. 65ft/20m. Climb the groove near the R-hand end of the ledge for 10ft/3m before moving R on to the steep exposed wall. Finish airily up this – an excellent pitch.

84 **Bochlwyd Eliminate**   HVS   110ft/33m **

R. James, R. Barber, 1962

A good pitch up the smooth wall between Wall Climb and Chimney Route. Start at the foot of the buttress by a quartz slab.

1. 5a. Easy climbing up the slab leads to a step R on to the rib. Ascend this to the Wall Climb traverse then continue up the small open groove. A rounded hand traverse gains a ledge on the R. Climb up to a block above then step down and R to follow holds which lead back up and L, easing towards the top.

GLYDER FACH – MAIN CLIFF   (656587)

This north-facing cliff sits high on the side of Glyder Fach above Llyn Bochlwyd. The rock here is exceptionally clean and rough, providing good friction and large holds which allow climbing in even fairly bad weather.

Follow the Miners' Path to Llyn Bochlwyd which is skirted on the L. Continue steeply up scree paths to the foot of the crag: approach time, about sixty minutes. Park as for Bochlwyd Buttress.

The cliff is divided into three parts: the Central Mass – a triangular area of rock containing the smooth Alphabet Slab on its L side – is defined on the L by the broken Main Gully (the descent route) and on the R by East Gully (a classic HS climb). To the L of Main Gully lies the very steep and columnar East Buttress, whilst to the R of East Gully lies the smaller and more broken West Buttress.

85 **Gamma** S 155ft/47m *

C. F. Kirkus, G. G. Macphee, 1936

A delicate line up the centre of the Alphabet Slab. A diagonal chimney/crack line is the prime feature of this slab – Beta

Bochlwyd Buttress

Glyder Fach – Main Cliff

(Diff) and Alpha (VS) climb the slabs on the L, whilst Delta (V Diff) lies R of Gamma. Start below the chimney/crack on a subsidiary terrace.

1. 45ft/14m. Climb up and R to a shallow groove. Follow this and continue until a horizontal traverse L leads to a stance and belay on the edge of Beta.

2. 80ft/24m. Move 10ft/3m L into a narrow crack which leads to easier ground. Continue easily, straight up to a poor stance below the final wall.

3. 30ft/9m. Go up the wall on small holds to a tricky finish from a V-scroop. Belay well back.

The previous climb finishes on the terrace just below the bottom of Main Gully. To the L is East Buttress, and two landmarks to note are The Capstan, a large bollard, slightly higher and 40yd/37m L, and The Luncheon Stone, a block 50yd/46m horizontally L. The following routes are described from R to L.

86 Chasm Route V Diff   265ft/80m **

J. M. A. Thomson, H. O. Jones, L. Noon, 1910

The deep narrow fissure just L of Main Gully gives an interesting climb! Start directly below the Chasm at a rocky rib, 10yd/9m R of The Capstan.

1. 50ft/15m. Go up the rib to spike belays.

2. 50ft/15m. Climb the cracked wall until forced easly R into the gully bed. Continue for 20ft/6m to a belay.

3. 40ft/12m. Climb the gully bed to some jammed boulders. Take the R wall and exit between the boulders into the gully.

4. 60ft/18m. Climb an easy crack, then ascend the steep L wall moving diagonally L to a flake. Go behind this then follow a crack back R into the gully.

5. 45ft/14m. The Vertical Vice – a masochist's delight! Climb a crack in the L corner, then go up into a chimney cave out of which one can step into the Vice. Ascend strenuously facing either way, or avoid it on the R.

6. 20ft/6m. A tricky crack on the R leads to the top.

Chasm Route: in the clutches of the Vertical Vice

The next two climbs are best approached up Chasm Route.

87 **Lot's Wife** VS   110ft/33m **

C. F. Kirkus, A. M. Robinson, 1931

A fine climb taking the face of the pillar between the Direct
Route and Chasm Route. Start at the foot of the Chasm proper,
or slightly lower.

1. 40ft/12m. 4c. Traverse L below the main groove (Lot's
Groove) to gain a little corner with pocketed walls; or better,
reach this point from below via a little overhang. Go delicately
up and swing L on to the rib, then step up and stride into a
crack on the L. Follow this to a stance.
2. 50ft/15m. 4b. Jamb and bridge up to better holds at
25ft/8m. Take the R-hand crack, then slabs which lead to a
large recess.
3. 20ft/6m. A slanting crack on the R leads to a large ledge, the
Verandah. Finish as for The Direct Route.

88 **Lot's Groove** HVS   110ft/33m ***

C. F. Kirkus, F. E. Hicks, 1929

A superb pitch at the lower end of its grade; both delicate and
strenuous with good protection. Start as for Lot's Wife.

1. 90ft/27m. 5a. Move L into the groove which is jammed with
increasing difficulty to a move up R on to the wall overlooking
the Chasm at 40ft/12m. Go up for a few feet, then step back
into the groove and bridge up to the overhang. Pass this
awkwardly using a crack out on the L wall for the feet, until it is
possible to bridge again. A couple more moves gain better
holds and a good stance.
2. 20ft/6m. Climb the crack on the R to the Verandah. Finish
as for Lot's Wife.

89 **The Direct Route** HS   300ft/91m ***

K. M. Ward, H. B. Gibson, 1907

An excellent traditional expedition which, when combined with
the Rectangular Excursion (avoiding Gibson's Chimney, VS)
and the Winter Finish (as described here), has only one short

difficult section – the Hand Traverse. Start at The Capstan on
the L of a rib.

1. 85ft/26m. Climb up and cross the rib. Go up a little then
recross it heading for the Arrowhead Belay at the foot of the
chimney/crack. Go up the chimney/crack on good holds until a
move R on to the face is possible. Continue up and R into a
bulging corner which leads to a grass stance and security
behind a huge bollard.

2. 20ft/6m. Easily up to a sheltered bay.

3. 50ft/15m. Climb the often greasy scoop heading for a ledge
on the L at 20ft/6m – Gibson's Chimney goes straight up here.
The Rectangular Excursion: traverse down to the L and move
round the rib on to a jammed block in a gully. Belay over to
the L.

4. 40ft/12m. Move back R to reach the large flat ledge, then go
up another 10ft/3m to the Hand Traverse. TR. This is best
climbed as a semi-hand traverse with the L foot wedged in the
crack (it may also be foot traversed) to a stance at the top of
Gibson's Chimney.

5. 35ft/11m. Ascend the crack and chimney passing a large
grass ledge on the R – the Verandah – to a stance 10ft/3m
higher.

6. 70ft/21m. The Winter Finish. Move L along a broad flake
then go up the corner crack to the top. Descend by scrambling
up and across R-wards to Main or East Gully.

From the Verandah, there are four alternative finishes. From L
to R these are: Left Hand Crack (VS) and Right Hand Crack
(HVS) which go up either side of the Final Flake; Hodgkin's
Variation (S) which gives superb crack climbing starting from
the R-hand corner of the ledge; and last but not least, around
the corner are Coffin Chimney and the Final Crack (HS) which
give the normal finish.

Lot's Groove: the tricky finish

90 Slab Climb by the Spiral Variant

V Diff   235ft/71m *

K. M. Ward, H. B. Gibson, 1907

An enjoyable route taking a line up the buttress L of the Direct Route. Start at The Capstan.

1. 50ft/15m. Climb the rib just L of The Capstan, then trend L towards a chimney with twin pinnacles near its top.

2. 30ft/9m. Move L and make a long step into the chimney which is climbed to an exit L.

3. 30ft/9m. Gain a ledge 10ft/3m higher, then go up the R-hand crack (hard to start) and so to a stance. The direct way (V Diff) reaches this point by a diagonal slab, hard near the top, starting from 30ft/9m up Pitch 1.

4. 40ft/12m. Traverse R for 10ft/3m and climb mossy slabs to the Arch and a junction with the Direct Route at the start of its Hand Traverse.

5. 45ft/14m. Climb the L-hand corner past large flakes, then go across the wall on the L on huge holds to an airy stance on the rib.

6. 40ft/12m. Climb to the top of the clean rib and belay.

Descend by scrambling up R-wards until it is possible to drop down into Main Gully.

91 Oblique Buttress   S   200ft/59m *

C. F. Holland, I. F. Richards, 1918

A fine climb taking the L-hand side of the East Buttress. Start from the foot of the lowest rocks, 40yd/37m L of The Luncheon Stone, where a rib runs up to a prominent crack.

1. 70ft/21m. Climb a slab, then the R edge of the rib to a grass ledge below the crack.

2. 40ft/12m. Climb the difficult crack and move R to a pinnacle. Step R to belay.

3. 85ft/26m. From the top of the pinnacle step on to the face and climb it easily to a ledge at 30ft/9m. Traverse 10ft/3m L across a shallow corner to a rib. This is taken to an awkward mantelshelf on the R, crux, and so to the top. Descend as for Slab Climb.

92 **Hawk's Nest Buttress**   S   185ft/56m **

G. D. and A. P. Abraham, A. Thomson, 1905

This delightful route lies on the West Buttress and climbs a
narrow pillar of rock, the L edge of which forms a prominent
knife-edged arete, 50 yd/46m R of East Gully. Best approached
by a traverse R from the top of the Alphabet Slab. Start below
the arete, on the terrace.

1. 55ft/17m. Scramble up to a grass ledge and continue up easy
slabs to a flake stance.

2. 50ft/15m. Climb the rib on the R to a small ledge and
continue to a niche. Lean out to reach a mantelshelf ledge on
the R. Standing on this is very awkward, crux, and leads in a
couple of moves to a belay.

3. 80ft/24m. Easily up trending R to a chimney in the R-hand
corner. This is taken to an easy slab leading up to the Shark
Pinnacle. Descend well over to the R, or reverse Needle's Eye
Climb, a relatively enclosed V Diff which squeezes up the
R-side of the buttress.

93 **Hawk's Nest Arete**   VS   120ft/36m ***

P. W. W. Nock, H. Harrison, 1940

An excellent route giving some of the best climbing on the crag.
Start at the L-hand side of the terrace, 20ft/6m L of Hawk's
Nest Buttress.

1. 90ft/27m. 4c. Climb the edge of the buttress to a large block
at 40ft/12m. Climb the arete with difficulty to gain a small
ledge. Toe traverse R to a chimney/crack which leads to a flake.
Swing back L, then go straight up the wall to a stance.

2. 30ft/9m. Follow the crack to the top. Descend as for Hawk's
Nest Buttress.

THE GRIBIN FACET (CLOGWYN Y TARW)   (649596)

This is the long, broken cliff overlooking the Ogwen Cottage –
Cwm Idwal path. It is very popular with middle-grade
climbers and is reached from the Ogwen Cottage car-park in
about fifteen minutes.

   The Gribin is split into four sections. From L to R these are

the Far East Buttress, a rambling area of short walls and large
ledges. Next comes East Buttress, comprising a steep face
whose main line is taken by Synapse, E2 4c, 5c, with the
prominent triple overlapping nose of the Insidious Slit, E5 6a
immediately R again, and whose R flank is formed by a large
easy-angled slab. At the foot of the slab sits a huge flat boulder,
useful as a base camp. Beyond this the cliff becomes more
broken, offering an easy descent. To the R lies the Central Area
bounded on its L by a slim tower, taken by Playtime. Further
over, past a vegetated wall, is a clean rock buttress consisting of
huge blocks through which Monolith Crack weaves its way.
The cliff now starts to lose height, and the next feature is the
steep, tree-filled Wooded Gully which offers another descent.
After this the crag becomes smaller until it fizzles out where the
fence runs up from the Idwal Gate.

94 Yob Route   VS   135ft/47m *

K. R. C. Britton, G. N. Crawshaw, 1957

A good way up the East Buttress via a L facing, square-cut
corner which starts 30ft/9m up, a few feet R of the triple
overlapping nose. Start about 100ft/30m L of the flat boulder by
a deep crack which becomes a chimney higher up, and at the
foot of a ramp leading up L towards the corner.

1. 4c. Go easily up the ramp to a groove. Go up again to reach
a jug. Swing on to the wall and climb the square-cut corner
which leads to a small ledge. Continue straight up the crack
and swing R on to the wall. Move back into the continuation of
the crack and make a stride R to another small ledge. Climb
past a small tree to gain two steep cracks leading up the wall on
the R to join Slab Climb; or: Original Finish (4b). From the
small ledge, traverse the slab on the R to reach Slab Climb by a
groove.

Yob Route

95 **Llyn**   HS   100ft/30m **

C. H. S. R. Palmer, J. M. Edwards, 1931

A classic of its grade taking the deep crack and chimney just R
of Yob Route. Steep with adequate protection. Start as for Yob
Route.

1. 4b. Traverse diagonally R to gain the foot of the crack. This
is steep at first and then eases to below a second steep section.
Layback and jam up to gain the rib on the R (runner at its top),
then step back L into the crack/chimney which leads more
easily to join Slab Climb.

The large easy-angled slab to the R has four Mod-V Diff routes
on it, the best being:

96 **Slab Climb**   Diff   165ft/50m *

J. Laycock, S. W. Herford, 1912

A good exposed climb. Start at the foot of the R-hand side of the
slab.

1. 50ft/15m. Climb up a few feet then make a long horizontal
traverse L (easy but unprotected) to belay in a sandy corner.
Or, reach this point from below via a steep little corner (Slab
Intermediate Route – V Diff).
2. 30ft/9m. Go up the cracked slab on the L to a crevasse
stance.
3. 45ft/14m. Continue up the slab using diagonal cracks to a
good flake, runner. From the top of this reach the slab above
and a stance a few feet higher.
4. 40ft/12m. Climb L around an exposed corner and go straight
up over blocks, or more easily R, to finish.

97 **Rocking Chair**   VS   100ft/30m *

R. L. Roberts, E. Birch, 1958

Start at the prominent V-groove in the R-wall, just above the
start of Slab Climb.

Gribin Facet

1. 4c. Climb the groove to a ledge on the R at 30ft/9m. Move back into the chimney/groove which becomes smooth and polished. A few thin moves lead to a jug at the end of the major difficulties. Continue up more easily to finish up a slab.

98 **Playtime** VS 100ft/30m
R. James, C. T. Jones, 1959

The crack in the face of the tower on the L of the Central Area lies at the top end of its grade. Start below its L-hand side, 30ft/9m up the gully at a large tree.

1. 40ft/12m. 4b. Move R round a rib and climb a steep greasy groove to a smaller tree.
2. 60ft/18m. 5a. Traverse R on to the front of the tower. Climb delicately along some flakes until a hard move enables the crack to be reached. Climb this direct past a flat-topped spike – quite energetic and a connoisseur's delight. Alternatively, from the flat-topped spike, move R to a ledge and bridge up a square groove to finish – 4c.

99 **Monolith Crack** S 150ft/45m ***
G. D. and A. P. Abraham, 1905

An amusing expedition which is usually enjoyed in retrospect! At the foot of the buttress consisting of huge fallen blocks, one of these blocks has tilted over forming a cave on its R side. Start at the mouth of this cave.

1. 30ft/9m. Wriggle through a hole under the block to a stance below a chimney.
2. 30ft/9m. Climb the chimney or its twin further L. Both Hard!
3. 50ft/15m. Either squeeze into the chimney facing R and climb up through a hole behind the chockstone to the surface (traditional), or step R from the pedestal to climb a crack around the corner to the same place.
4. 40ft/12m. An easy slab and chimney lead to the top.

100 Zig-Zag   S   140ft/42m*

S. W. Herford and party, 1912

The best route of its grade on the crag. Start about 15yd/14m R
of Monolith Crack on a large boulder which blocks the path.
1. 70ft/21m. Climb the corner, then move L at the overhang to
a crack which leads to a sloping ledge. From its R-hand end,
climb an open V-chimney facing R, crux, to reach a quartz slab.
Belay a little higher.
2. 40ft/12m. Continue up the slab to belay below twin cracks.
3. 30ft/9m. Either climb the R-hand crack (S), or the L-hand
crack – much harder.

To the R of Zig-Zag beyond Wooded Gully – the descent for
this area – the cliff becomes more broken and diminishes in
height. A tall thin flake stands proud from the rock face giving:

101 Flake Crack   VS   90ft/28m

O. Thorneycroft, 1909

A novel climb up the chimney behind the wobbly flake! Start
on a rock ledge directly below it.
1. 45ft/14m. 4c. Gain the slab on the R and climb to a holly tree
further R. Move back L and reach the crack on the R of the flake
with difficulty. Go up this to a stance behind the flake.
2. 45ft/14m. 4b. Bridge up to the tip of the flake, runner, and
step across on to the wall. A few delicate moves lead to easier
climbing and the top.

CWM CNEIFION (THE NAMELESS CWM)   (647585)
This remote cwm, tucked away high on the flanks of Glyder
Fawr between the Gribin and Senior Ridges, contains four fine
routes: the first, leading up to the cwm, is Sub-Cneifion Rib, a
steep rib of clean rock which drops down the hillside half-way
between the Gribin Facet and the Idwal Slabs. The hillside
above is a maze of jumbled rock which eventually attains some
semblance of order at its R end, at the entrance to the cwm
itself, to form our next choice, the exhilarating Cneifion Arete
which leads up to the Gribin Ridge. Finally, at the head of the

cwm, the steep sombre crag of Clogwyn Du is the setting for that superb duo – Manx Wall and Hebenwi.

The normal approach is via Sub-Cneifion Rib (or the gully on its L): just above, a well-defined path runs across up into the lower cwm.

102 **Sub-Cneifion Rib** V Diff 340ft/103m (648593)
J. M. Edwards, 1931

The clean compact rib of rock about 400ft/123m above Llyn Idwal, below the entrance to the cwm, can be reached in around thirty minutes. Start 50ft/15m up to the L of the toe of the rib, between a pointed block and the rib itself.

1. 35ft/11m. Step on to the rib and climb it to a crack, then step L and continue on good holds to a stance on the L.
2. 40ft/12m. Step R and climb a groove to a bulge which is turned on the L. Step back R and take an open groove to easier climbing and a stance.
3. 40ft/12m. Scramble up L-wards to the foot of the next rib.
4. 80ft/24m. Go up the crest of the rib with a few interesting moves until a smooth slab leads to a belay. From the belay, scramble down and around the rib on the R to a stance on some flat blocks 20ft/6m below the final nose of steep rock.
5. 105ft/32m. Mantelshelf on to the nose and traverse delicately R round the corner to a cracked slab. Go up this to the crest of the rib, then follow a crack to reach easier climbing up more cracks to a stance.
6. 40ft/12m. Climb the final crack to the top.

103 **Cneifion Arete** Mod 400ft/123m (648587) ***
G. Barlow, Miss E. Clark, 1905

An enjoyable, exposed climb with large holds and an 'Alpine feel' about it. A path leads R from the top of Sub Cneifion Rib along the hillside and as it reaches the mouth of the cwm, a prominent slabby ridge can be seen on the L starting 200ft/61m up the screes. Start just R of the foot of the ridge.

1. 75ft/23m. Climb steeply up on good holds for 35ft/11m. Move R for 15ft/5m then climb easily up the crest.

2. 25ft/8m. Move back L to reach a little chimney and follow it to easier ground. Continue by around 300ft/92m of scrambling over huge flakes and pinnacles, taking belays as required. The difficulties diminish as the height increases towards the Gribin Ridge.

CLOGWYN DU   (646583)

Lying close to the summit of Glyder Fawr and towering over Cwm Cneifion, this is one of the highest and most inaccessible climbing grounds in Wales, with a tedious approach (by local standards) of over an hour. Unfortunately, the cliff receives little sun and takes several days of fine weather to come into condition. Even then, there is some seepage, and the rock tends to be rather dirty when compared to that of the lower Idwal crags. Nonetheless, the aspect is excellent with sensational views down the Ogwen Valley and out across Anglesey.

The R-hand side of the cliff is defined by the obvious Clogwyn Du Gully – a classic Grade IV ice route which seems to come into condition every winter. The L wall of the gully is formed by a narrow buttress which tapers into a pillar, bounded on its L by the chimney/rake of Pillar Chimney (Diff). Next comes the impressive main face, undercut at its base with the prominent chimney/crack of Travesty (VS 1 pt) running up its L edge. L again, that deep, slimy, eponymous fissure – The Crack (E1, 5b 2 pts) – is the last coherent feature before the crag peters out into the hillside.

104 **Manx Wall**   HS   180ft/56m ***

A. J. Lowe and party, 1942

An exposed and thrilling route which breaks out L from Pillar Chimney to cross the upper section of the main face. Start 150ft/46m up the chimney/rake at the foot of the main pillar.

1. 45ft/14m. Take the obvious line of weakness out L to a stance and good belay.

2. 35ft/11m. Enter a groove on the R and climb it on small sharp holds to a ledge. Stance and belay on the L.

Clogwyn Du – Cwm Cneifion

3. 35ft/11m. Climb the tricky corner behind the belay, then move L to a narrow grass ledge. TB.

4. 65ft/20m. 4b. Climb the delicate slab to the top of the crack. Traverse L under the overhangs. Turn these on the L using good holds on the wall above. Finish up a steep crack on the L. An atmospheric pitch!

105 **Hebenwi** E2 250ft/75m *
M. Boysen, D. Alcock (AL), 1969

A powerful and impressive route which swaggers up the centre
of the main face. Start at the end of the large grassy ledge that
runs across from the L below the steep central wall, by a
shallow grassy gully.

1. 30ft/9m. 4b. Climb steep grassy rock trending R to a ledge
below bulges.
2. 90ft/27m. 5b. Move R under the bulges and climb straight
up a very steep wall past a PR, crux. Continue up and R to a
small ledge. Good nut belays on the R.
3. 40ft/12m. 5a. Climb up L on a diagonal line to a large ledge.
4. 90ft/27m. 5a. Ascend the arete to the overhang. Pass it on
the L up an overhanging wall to reach easier ground. Or, from
the stance, traverse R to the foot of a slab, pull round a corner to
gain a wall which is climbed on large holds to the top.

IDWAL SLABS AND WALLS (645591)

This most popular of Ogwen climbing areas lies at the far end
of Llyn Idwal. It offers routes of all grades including some of
the hardest and most poorly protected pitches in Wales. It is
easily reached along the Cwm Idwal path in about twenty
minutes from Ogwen Cottage car-park.

The crag consists of a large sheet of easy-angled overlapping
slabs which rise to the foot of a steep wall, Holly Tree Wall.
This in turn is topped by the smaller Continuation Wall. The
R-hand side of the main slab abuts a steep escarpment of slabs
and walls – the West Wall. To the L, the edge of the slab drops
steeply forming a cliff between 100ft/30m and 200ft/60m high
running up parallel to the hillside. This is the East Wall and it
continues further up in the same line, becoming steeper, to give
the Suicide Wall area, easily recognized from its streaky
appearance. On this superb section of cliff, some magnificent
routes forge a path up seemingly blank sections of the face
using small holds and pockets, invisible from below. The bold
may proceed confidently; the rock is immaculate but the
protection is spaced!

The East Wall

This wall has three main facets. The lowest one falls from the initial pitches of Tennis Shoe, which runs up the L edge of the main slab to finish at an obvious tower topped by a perched boulder. Below this tower the wall kinks at right angles before rising up the hillside once again to the Suicide Wall Area.

106 Heather Wall   VS   170ft/51m*

F. E. Hicks, A. B. Hargreaves, E. A. Stewardson, 1929

One of the most enjoyable routes on the wall with an exposed crux. The lowest facet is bounded on the R by the first pitch of Tennis Shoe, and on the L by the corner of Rake End Chimney (S) which is reached from the R by a diagonal ramp. Start at the foot of the ramp on a grass terrace which bisects the easy slabs of the descent route, 200ft/61m up from the base of the cliff.

1. 100ft/30m. 4b. Move up R on a little gangway and continue on pockets to a small ledge. From the R climb up to a cone of slab and ascend to a small stance just L of its apex.

2. 70ft/21m. 4c. Traverse L to a groove, then move up L again to reach the rib, just below a bulge. Climb the bulge direct, crux, or diagonally from a good foothold on the L (easier). Step up L into another groove and continue more easily to a good stance. Descend by scrambling across Tennis Shoe on to the main slab to reverse down Ordinary Route, or escape up to the L as for Ash Tree Wall.

107 Ash Tree Wall   VS   175ft/52m*

F. E. Hicks, J. A. Smalley, 1929

Steep and exposed with good holds, this climb takes the second facet of the wall, below the tower and perched boulder (at the top of Tennis Shoe). Start about 100ft/30m above the Heather Wall start, at the top of a broken slab just L of centre of the wall facing the foot of the crag.

1. 100ft/30m. 4b. Climb the wall on good holds to below a

Idwal East Wall

bulge at 50ft/15m. Turn this on the R to easier-angled rock. Move up slightly L to a ledge with spike belays at its L end.

2. 45ft/14m. Step down and around to the L then go up on good holds past a couple of ledges to a stance below and L of the final tower.

3. 30ft/9m. 4c. Move R on to the face of the tower and climb it until a hard move up and round leads on to a polished slab and the last few moves of Tennis Shoe.

Descent: the easy way off scrambles up to the L for 300ft/93m over a couple of rock steps until a well-defined path leads to the edge of the gully. After 50ft/15m of climbing descent, the gully bed leads down to the foot of the top end of the East Wall (Suicide Wall Area). From here, either carefully descend the steep scrambling path which runs down below the East Wall to the foot of the slabs, or follow a diagonal path towards Idwal Gate until a grassy traverse leads easily back L to the same place.

108 **East Wall Girdle** VS 500ft/150m ***
J. M. Edwards, C. H. S. R. Palmer, 1931

The best climb on the wall, taking a pleasantly sustained line at half-height across its first two facets. Start as for Tennis Shoe, just L of the main slab at the foot of a narrow subsidiary slab and R of a short slab around the corner (Hargreaves Slab, V Diff).

1. 90ft/27m. 4a. Climb up and move round to follow a narrow slab near its L edge. Move R to a ledge and belay.

2. 30ft/9m. Continue direct up the quartzy slab to a spike belay.

3. 110ft/33m. 4a. Follow the next slab until it steepens. Make a long step L to join the conical slab of Heather Wall. Go up to the apex of the slab. Step L to belay (as for Heather Wall).

4. 40ft/12m. 4c. Traverse L as for Heather Wall, across a groove and over to the rib. Move down L to reach a grassy

East Wall Girdle, pitch 4

ledge, then traverse L to reach a stance at the top of the ramp of
Rake End Chimney.

5. 70ft/21m. 4b. Step up on to the small slab on the L, then
move across round a couple of bulges to gain the slab section of
Ash Tree Wall. Follow this to the ledge with belays at its L end.

6. 90ft/27m. Traverse low and round to the L without difficulty
to reach a long grassy ledge. Continue along this to a stance
below the final slabby wall on the L.

7. 70ft/21m. 4b. Climb the middle of the wall on the L to a
flake. Step L and climb to a small ledge. Step L again into an
awkward exposed groove which is followed delicately to the
top. Belay well back. Descend as for Ash Tree Wall.

109 Suicide Groove E1 110ft/33m *

J. B. Lawton, D. H. Haworth, 1948

This is the easiest route on Suicide Wall and takes the large
L-slanting groove low down at the extreme R end of the streaked
wall. Difficulties are short and sharp. Start at the foot of the
groove.

1. 80ft/24m. 4b. Climb the slab on the L of the groove to a
small stance. Belay 15ft/5m below the overhang.

2. 30ft/9m. 5b. Go up the scoop to the overhang (PR on the R
wall) which is overcome by a few thin moves to reach a good
hold in the corner. Layback directly up the groove to finish.

The centre of the slab to the L is taken by Suspended Sentence
E2, 5c which surmounts an overhang before moving R to join
Suicide Groove for its final moves.

110 Suicide Wall Route 2 E2 150ft/46m **

P. Crew, B. Ingle, 1963

This takes a curving line below the blankest section of wall and
gives a fine pitch on reasonable holds with a delicate and poorly
protected crux. Start about 150ft/46m up the hillside from the

Capital Punishment: the final rib

foot of Suicide Groove below a crescent-shaped scoop a few feet up the wall and above a step in the path.

1. 5b. Climb the short wall into the L-hand end of the scoop. Descend a little, then follow the blunt rib on the R to a line of flakes. Climb the flakes strenuously to an old PR. Move up R round a rib to a shallow groove which is climbed on small pockets to a little ledge, crux. Go up a slabby groove on the R for 30ft/9m. Continue up the arete R again, to finish by grassy ledges.

111 Capital Punishment E4 160ft/48m ***

M. Boysen, D. Alcock (1 pt), 1971/FFA: M. and R. Berzins, C. Hamper, 1976

A brilliant route, one of the finest in the area. Difficulties are sustained and the paucity of protection makes them well felt. From the scoop of Route 2 a slab, shallow groove and ramp offer a tenuous line diagonally L-wards up the face. Start as for Suicide Wall Route 2 below the crescent-shaped scoop.

1. 20ft/6m. 5a. As for Route 2 to belay on the PR at the top of the scoop.

2. 80ft/24m. 5c. Move up to the steep triangular slab and climb it to the foot of a shallow groove (small wires round to the L – if you can find them). Climb the groove using pockets on the R wall to reach a 'Thank God' hold and TR. Continue steeply on positive holds to a ledge. Poor belays.

3. 60ft/18m. 5b. From the L end of the ledge, climb the steep ramp passing a good runner to join Route 1 for its last couple of moves. Belay well back. Pitches 2 and 3 may be run together.

112 Suicide Wall Route 1 E2 100ft/30m ***

C. Preston, R. Morsley, J. Hines, 1945

An amazing first ascent: the hardest route in the country at the time it was climbed. A classic pitch which remains a grave undertaking! Start below and L of a conspicuous grass ledge situated 25ft/8m up on the L side of the wall.

1. 5c. The start is very polished. Step up R, then continue passing a tiny spike in a pocket by some difficult moves, crux.

Continue more easily to reach the L end of the grass ledge.
(Wall of the Dead, E4 6b reaches this point direct via the thin
crack below and continues direct to finish.) A PR normally
protrudes from the wall 10ft/3m above – lasso this with a long
sling to provide a runner. From the R end of the ledge, make a
few fingery moves up a rib and scoop to reach good holds on the
L at the start of a traverse line. Follow this R-wards on
reasonable holds to an awkward move on hidden pockets
leading to the final break. This leads easily back L to the top.
(Death Row, E3 5c is a serious pitch up a groove just R of the
ledge of Route 1 which finishes up the parent route.)

The Main Slab

This large sweep of easy-angled slab gives several outstanding
routes – all in the easier grades – and is an ideal setting for
newcomers to be introduced to the sport.

113 Tennis Shoe   S   465ft/141m ***

N. E. Odell, 1919

This classic route follows the L edge of the main slab enjoying
fine situations. Start just L of the main slab at the foot of a
narrow subsidiary slab.

1. 95ft/29m. Climb up and round to follow a narrow slab near
its L edge. Move R on to a ledge and belay, or go straight up the
edge of the main slab to the same point – VS.
2. 50ft/15m. Reach the main slab on the R via a scoop and
delicately continue up the edge to a large ledge.
3. 60ft/18m. Step back on to the slab which is taken on positive
holds to reach a large flake. Belay on this, or in the gully on
the L.
4. 110ft/33m. Ascend the gully moving on to its L-hand rib as
soon as possible. Continue up keeping L to a rounded ledge.
Nut belay low on the R.
5. 100ft/30m. Move easily up the slab to the L to reach a grass
terrace and awkward belays. Walk to the L end of the terrace by
the rock tower capped by the perched boulder.
6. 50ft/15m. Move out on to the front face of the tower and

climb it on polished holds. A tricky move into a scoop leads to a delicate move on to the final slab and a finish over the perched boulder.

Descent: as for Climb 107, Ash Tree Wall, scrambling up to the L of Holly Tree Wall before a climbing descent to the top end of Suicide Wall.

114 **The Ordinary Route** Diff   460ft/140m *

Sir T. K. Rose, C. C. B. Moss, 1897

The easiest way up the slabs. The route follows a deep polished crack 20ft/6m in from the L-hand edge. Start below this.

1. 150ft/46m. Go easily up the crack passing a couple of large spike runners to a good stance in a niche.

2. 150ft/46m. Climb the rib on the R for 20ft/6m then traverse L to reach another groove. Step L and climb the edge for a few feet, then go back into the groove and continue to a polished scoop. Exit R from the top of the scoop on to a slab with incut holds. Continue up easier rocks to a good spike belay.

3. 80ft/24m. Follow the polished crack above the belay until the slab steepens. Step across R on good holds, then go straight up the crack above to land on a good stance.

4. 80ft/24m. Easily up L then back R to the terrace with a huge perched boulder; or climb direct to the boulder (V Diff).

Descent: as for Climb 107, Ash Tree Wall; scramble up to the L of the steep walls above until a path leads to the edge of a gully and 50ft/15m of climbing descent.

About 30ft/9m R of Ordinary Route, polished twin cracks leading to a shallow scoop at 20ft/6m denote the start of Charity (V Diff) whilst, to the R again, a well-defined rib rises to meet the upper wall – Central Rib (S). Just R of the foot of Central Rib lies:

Idwal Slabs and Walls

115 **Hope**   V Difff   450ft/137m ***

Mrs E. H. Daniell and party, 1915

Probably the best route on the slabs: a delightful excursion, well maintained as its standard. Start about 25yd/23m R of Ordinary Route, just R of Central Rib below a flat ledge at 30ft/9m.

1. 140ft/43m. Climb the quartz slab, or the groove on the L to gain the flat ledge. Climb the slab behind, trending R then back L to reach a crackline leading up to a patch of quartz. Go up the quartz to a ledge on the L edge and continue via a small groove to belay on a large ledge below the Twin Cracks.

2. 100ft/30m. The Twin Cracks are polished and difficult to start, but an enormous hold appears just when it is needed. From this hold, step up R then move delicately L to a thin crack. Climb this to good holds and pockets and a ledge by the overhang. Continue up and round to a small ledge at the bottom of the groove/corner. Good nut belays.

3. 150ft/46m. Climb the slab just L of the groove to a tricky bulge which is passed on the L, then back R: the final rib of Faith (V Diff), which starts 40yd/37m R of Hope on the next sheet of slab, comes in from the R here. Either belay up and to the R in the steeper quartz area for Faith, or climb diagonally L up a slab to reach a crack and stance (care needed with belays here).

4. 60ft/18m. From the Faith stance, move up and round to the L to gain the large terrace with the perched boulder sitting on it. Or, from the crack stance, finish direct over quartzy rock.

Descent: as for The Ordinary Route.

Holly Tree Wall

Above the terrace with the perched boulder on it (not to be confused with the boulder at the finish of Tennis Shoe) is the steep Holly Tree Wall. Behind and L of the boulder is a smooth section. Below this, starting 20ft/6m above the terrace, is a polished scoop. From its top end, a gangway runs diagonally up to join a deep chimney/crack on the R of the blank area.

This is the line of:

116 **Original Route** VS 130ft/39m **
I. A. Richards, C. F. Holland, Miss D. E. Pilley, 1918
Start at the foot of the wall, by a boulder which leans against it, 15ft/5m below the polished scoop.
1. 90ft/27m. 5a. Climb up to the scoop which is eventually entered with difficulty, and so to a niche under an overhang. Or, 10ft/3m R of the top of a quartzy pinnacle, a mantelshelf R then another back L lead more easily to the niche. Step R and follow the gangway to a ledge below the chimney/crack. Step down L a little to a narrow ledge. From its end, a delicate move up R and a mantelshelf lead to better holds and a stance above the chimney/crack. Alternatively, take the chimney/crack direct.
2. 40ft/12m. 4b. There are three options: continue directly up the corner; the wall just to the L stepping back R after 25ft/8m; or a series of short walls at the L side of the bay, stepping R to finish. Descend by traversing L to join the normal descent before the final rock step and path leading to the gully.

Holly Tree Wall is split into two segments by the deep Javelin Gully (HS) on its R side.

117 **Lazarus** S 140ft/42m **
No first ascent was recorded but the crux was climbed by I. A. Richards and Miss D. E. Pilley during their Other Kingdom ascent in 1922.
The easiest way up Holly Tree Wall breaks out L from Javelin Gully. Start at the foot of this.
1. 50ft/15m. Go up the gully over two rock steps (both climbed from R to L) to a large ledge and belay.
2. 90ft/27m. Move L round a block, then traverse delicately L trending up towards a shallow corner, past a runner on the L. A polished little wall is surmounted via a couple of thin moves up and R to gain better holds, crux, and a slabby groove. Climb this trending R at the top to easier ground and a large terrace. Descend as for Original Route.

118 **Javelin Buttress** VS 120ft/37m **

F. Graham, C. E. Jerram, 1925

A fine open climb on perfect rock up the long groove splitting
the front face of the buttress R of Javelin Gully. Start from the
R-hand side of the main terrace, R of the foot of Javelin Gully.
1. 4c. Follow the ledge R-wards and go up into the groove.
Climb this on good holds until a slab leads out L. Ascend for a
few feet then move R to a natural TR. Traverse R and go up via a
couple of mantelshelves on narrow ledges to an easing of the
angle and the large terrace below the Continuation Wall.
Descend up and across L-wards as for Original Route.

119 **Javelin Blade** E1 120ft/37m *

J. L. Longland, C. Williams, 1930

A remarkable route for its period, delicate and poorly
protected, it takes the edge of the buttress L of the parent route.
Start as for Javelin Buttress.
1. 5b. Follow Javelin Buttress to the natural TR. Descend to the
pock-marked slab and climb it to the L edge of the buttress.
Bridge up the groove above, or step into it from the L (small
wires). A bold move on to the rib on the R leads to jugs and
easier rock. Continue to the terrace. Descend as for Original
Route.

Continuation Wall

Above Holly Tree Wall, the next tier is shorter but offers a
couple of interesting routes as a prelude to further climbing on
Glyder Fawr.

120 **The Arete** VDiff 80ft/24m *

F. E.Hicks, C. M. B. Warren, A. L. Spence, 1929

Start at the L side of the main facet below a L-facing corner with
a slab to its L.
1. Climb the corner for a few feet then traverse L across the
slab to the arete. Take this directly to the top – a superb pitch.
A direct start can be made L of the corner.

121 **Groove Above**   S   80ft/24m *
T. S. Knowles, H. Poole, 1926
Start R of the centre of the facet below a short wall leading up to
a deep V-groove.
1. 4b. Enter the groove, problematic on first acquaintance, and
go up to a steepening. Exit R on to the rib which is followed to
finish. (10yd/9m to the R, Diagonal Route (VS) climbs twin
cracks into a scoop, before moving L to finish up Groove
Above.)

West Wall
At the R side of the main slab, a series of broken walls and slabs
run up to merge wtih Holly Tree Wall.

122 **Demetreus**   E3   80ft/24m ***
D. Beetlestone, G. Gibson, 1979
An elegant and demanding pitch on perfect rock. The highest
facet of the West Wall is smooth and rectangular with a faint
seam/crack running up its centre. Start from a grassy bay at the
foot of the wall reached by a R-ward traverse from the upper
reaches of Hope.
1. 6a. Move up and L to reach the faint seam/crack; this is
technical, sustained and stubborn. Struggle precariously up to
where it peters out. Quick thinking, strong fingers and nifty
footwork now come into play if success is to be achieved . . . a
classic!

Idwal Buttress
Low down, way over on the R-hand side of the slabs, above the
dark seepage line of Idwal Staircase, is a prominent
pock-marked undercut wall:

123 **Homicide Wall**   E2   125ft/38m ***
D. G. Peers, J. Whittle, (1 pt) 1971
This uniquely pocketed wall gives a climb of great character
which rises up from the R to tackle its bold and intimidating
central face. Protection is spaced, and one week of good

weather should be allowed to enable the pockets to dry out.
Start at the toe of the buttress.

1. 80ft/24m. 4c. Follow the pockets steeply up to a quartz
ramp. Continue delicately, around a blunt rib to a good stance
above the lip of the overhangs.

2. 45ft/14m. 5c. Move L past an old PR. Climb steeply up on
massive pockets to an impasse. Make a difficult move L to a
horizontal spike in a pocket, crux, then continue strenuously up
past a PR to better holds. Finish boldly on large widely spaced
holds – a memorable pitch!

GLYDER FAWR (THE UPPER CLIFF)   (644586)

This large broken cliff sits 2250ft/700m above sea level on the
north face of Glyder Fawr, above and R of the Idwal Slabs. It is
usually reached via a route on the Slabs, Holly Tree Wall and
the Continuation Wall, followed by a section of interesting
scrambling until a quartzy traverse leads R to its foot. A more
direct but laborious approach can be made by toiling up the
screes well R of the Slabs to reach the cliff in around an hour
from Ogwen Cottage car-park.

   The most striking features of the cliff are the two deep
L-facing corners running its full height which define either side
of the East Buttress; East Gully (V Diff) and Central Gully
(S–VS) are grassy sluices separated by the large slabby ridge of
East Arete (Diff). The prominent arete R again gives an
excellent mountaineering route, Central Arete (Diff), whilst
way over on the L, a smaller but obvious area of compact grey
rock, the Grey Group, has several quality climbs.

124 **Grey Slab**   VS   270ft/82m ***

J. M. Edwards, F. Reade, 1932

The most obvious feature of the Grey Group is the pronounced
rib taken by Grey Arete. To the L, separated from it by a scarp
wall, is a smooth slab providing a superb pitch of a delicate and

Glyder Fawr – the Upper Cliff

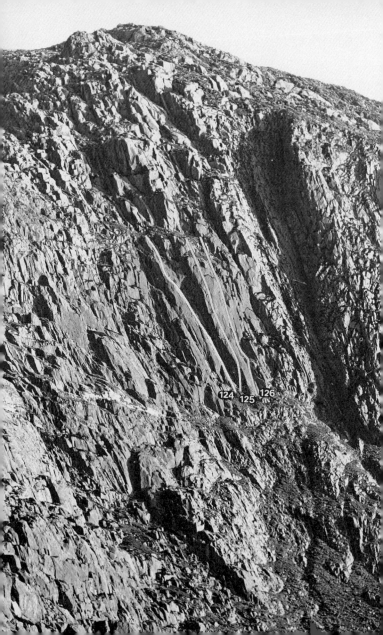

sustained nature – a classic – which just merits its grade. Start
at the foot of the corner formed by the slab and scarp wall.

1. 120ft/37m. 4a. Climb the corner passing a ledge and
continue up to gain some pock-marks on the L. These lead to
another ledge. From its L end, an awkward move up a little
corner leads to a poor stance with good belays below an
overhang.

2. 150ft/45m. 4b. Surmount the bulge and move up a few feet.
Traverse delicately L to a faint rib which is followed to a good
foothold at its top. Follow a line of pockets up R then back L
under the overlap to reach the slab edge. Climb the shallow
groove to reach another line of pockets on the R. Take these to a
stance and poor belay – a serious pitch which is often wet in
places.

Scramble up to the summit or traverse L to upper Cwm
Cneifion.

125 **Grey Arete**   HVS   270ft/82m **

R. James, P. Benson, 1959

An excellent route with varied climbing in a fine position up the
crest of the rib R of Grey Slab. Start at the foot of the damp
corner (as for Grey Slab) on a grass ledge just L of the arete
which is blunted by a scoop at its base.

1. 120ft/37m. 4c. Step into the scoop and follow it by
semi-laybacking for 15ft/5m until it is possible to move R on to
the slab. Go up this near the L edge to a horizontal grass ledge.
Belay on the R.

2. 40ft/12m. 4c. Climb the middle of the pock-marked wall to
reach a stance on the L.

3. 80ft/24m. 5a. Layback the steep crack above until a hard
move leads to a small ledge. Continue up the crack until it leans
back R, then step awkwardly into it and follow it to a grass
ledge. Belay well to the R.

4. 30ft/9m. Easily up the wall above the crack.

126 **Procrastination Cracks** VS 120ft/37m **

J. M. Edwards, A. M. D'Aeth, 1932

A good pitch taking the twin cracks R of the steep part of Grey
Arete. Start from the top of Pitch 1 of Grey Arete (which
provides the best approach) at the R-hand end of the horizontal
ledge, 20ft/6m below the foot of the cracks.

1. 5a. Climb up to the L-hand crack and traverse R at 20ft/6m
to gain the wide R-hand crack. Follow it until it narrows: move
boldly on to the wall on the L, and after some difficult moves,
regain the L-hand crack from a small ledge. Climb directly up
the scoop to the impending wall above. Swing L on to a rib,
then follow a thin crack to finish – a very good pitch.

127 **Central Arete Direct** V Diff 650ft/200m **

G. and H. B. Buckle, 1909/Mrs E. H. Daniell, G. Barlow, 1909

A fine mountaineering expedition up the crest of the ridge R of
Central Gully. Smooth and steep at first, the ridge eases higher
up to give some interesting scrambling over a castellated
section. Immediately R of Central Gully is a slim grassy rake –
High Pasture (V. Veg). Start at the foot of slabs below the large
buttress R of this.

1. 150ft/46m. Climb the foothill slabs to a good grass ledge.
2. 110ft/33m. Climb directly up the exposed arete on small
holds. Belay in a groove on the R.
3. 50ft/15m. Traverse back L and continue up the arete.
4. 340ft/106m. Follow the edge, up, along, and over a line of
assorted sawteeth – spikes, pinnacles and gendarmes – which is
eventually blunted by the hillside.

CLOGWYN Y GEIFR (639589)

This huge crumbling cliff lies at the head of Cwm Idwal and
can be reached from Ogwen Cottage in about forty-five
minutes. At the centre of the crag and cutting it in half is a
massive dark cleft, the Devil's Kitchen. From the foot of this,
two synclinal terraces lead diagonally up L (South Syncline)
and R (North Syncline), subdividing the cliff further and
providing easy ways of ascent or descent.

Below and L of the South Syncline is the South Cliff which is loose, broken and wet; the area of cliff just L of the Kitchen contains much moss and vegetation and is decidedly unpleasant; the area of rock R of the Kitchen is steeper and cleaner, and is split by two gullies. To the R, and below the North Syncline, lies a smooth and impressive face – the North Cliff.

At close quarters, the climbing is found to be of a better quality than the appearance of the cliff would suggest, especially on its R side. However, the rock tends to be friable in places, sometimes snapping under heavy usage, thus the routes have a serious feel about them. There is also great botanical interest in this cliff, as it is the home to several species of rare flora; climbers are asked to refrain from needless trundling and unnecessary gardening operations.

In a good winter, Clogwyn y Geifr sports a dramatic array of frozen seepage lines and gullies; icy curtains, pillars and mushroom-shaped hoods exert a magnetic pull on all serious winter climbers. This is probably the premier ice-climbing venue south of the border – some would say on either side of the border! Pride of place goes to the spectacular Devil's Appendix, Grade V, the 300ft/93m frozen waterfall between Devil's Staircase and Hanging Garden Gully; when in condition, it cannot be missed as it dominates the cwm.

128 **The Devil's Kitchen (Twll Du)**   V Diff   80ft/24m ***
W. R. Reade, W. P. McCulloch, 1898

A great traditional classic steeped in atmosphere which follows cracks up the L wall, just before the waterfall, deep in the bowels of the Kitchen. Start by scrambling up the bed of the stream to reach a boulder blocking the gully floor. It is known as the Waterfall Pitch and gives a short problem: easiest on the R; wettest underneath; hardest and driest on the L. Continue easily up the gully floor passing a huge pinnacle which leans

Clogwyn y Geifr

against the R wall, until a capstone overhangs the gully,
causing the waterfall.

1. About 20ft/6m before the waterfall, cracks slant up the L
wall to the level of the capstone. Gain the cracks and climb
them on large holds until an awkward move leads to a traverse
line. Follow this to the top of the capstone and the end of all
difficulties.

129 **Advocate's Wall**   VS   220ft/66m *

C. Preston, R. G. Morsley, D. McKellar, 1945

A serious but atmospheric expedition which will appeal to
traditionalists and others of that ilk who enjoy dark, dank
places. Start just before the Waterfall Pitch, under the large
overhangs on the R wall.

1. 60ft/18m. 4a. Climb the corner and continue across the
black slab to reach a ledge at its top. TB.

2. 70ft/21m. 4b. Go up the corner on the L for 10ft/3m. Make a
difficult traverse L around the corner on to the front face, crux.
Climb steeply up into a chimney on the L.

3. 90ft/27m. 4a. Climb the chimney, then exposed rock on the
L to finish.

130 **Devil's Staircase**   S   285ft/86m *

O. G. Jones, G. D. Abraham, 1899

The first major gully R of the Kitchen gives a tremendous route;
start directly below it.

1. 85ft/26m. Easily up to a smooth shallow chimney which
proves difficult for 20ft/6m. Continue on good holds past a
large ledge on the R to a better one.

2. 110ft/33m. Climb up the L side on looser rock to reach the
foot of the cave. Climb up for 40ft/12m, then exit L round the
capstone and continue up the gully bed to a stance.

3. 90ft/27m. The L-hand crack above provides a hard wet
struggle and is rarely ascended. The normal finish climbs up a
wall to reach the R-hand crack (The Drainpipe) into which one
can disappear. Wriggle up inside it past a chockstone to emerge
gasping into the open. From here, scramble up to the top of the
cliff.

131 **Devil's Bastion**   E2   280ft/85m **
T. Herley, D. Blythe (AL), 1965

A bold and interesting route up the buttress R of Devil's
Staircase. Start from the top of the large pedestal R of the
Staircase (gained from the R) below a small hanging groove.
1. 90ft/27m. 5c. Climb the grey slab into the groove. Surmount
the bulge with difficulty, PR. Go up the slab trending L then
back R to a large loose flake. Move L along a line of holds to
reach a sloping ledge where a good hold enables a long swing L
to made on to easy ground, and so to the horizontal break.
Spike belay on the R.
2. 40ft/12m. 4b. Climb up to the R of the spike to a grassy
ledge. Flake and nut belays in a small cave on the L.
3. 150ft/46m. 5a. Climb directly to a niche and go over a bulge
on the L, PR. Continue L along the obvious traverse line to reach
the arete. This gives a sensational finish . . . an airy pitch not
over-endowed with protection!

Further R, past an evil-looking corner that is normally dark,
wet and slippery (the summer line of Devil's Appendix, VS), is
another large gully line, Hanging Garden Gully (V Diff), first
climbed by O. G. Jones and the Abraham brothers in 1899 – a
must for the aspiring botanist as it contains possibly the largest
quantity and variety of flora of any Welsh rock climb. It is even
possible to get to grips with the rock in places! The north (R)
side of the cliff has in fact two synclinal terraces running down
from the R. Between them is The Band, a steep area of rock
split by a wet curving gash, the Devil's Cellar (HV Diff). Just L
of this, a steep arete, slabby at the top, gives:

132 **Devil's Delight**   E1   195ft/59m *
R. Edwards, E. G. Penman (AL), 1966

A serious little pitch with the main difficulties occurring in the
first 25ft/8m. Scramble up to start at a prominent orange rock
scar.
1. 85ft/26m. 5b. Make difficult moves up to reach better holds
at about 20ft/6m – strenuous, with some suspect rock.

Continue up trending L for 30ft/9m to reach the foot of a steep R-ward rising ramp. Follow this for 10ft/3m then move up to a Friend and nut belays just L of the large shattered flake.

2. 110ft/33m. 4b. Go up behind the belay, then move R under an overhang and continue until just past a rockfall scar. Trend up and L to pull on to an amazing slab and continue, keeping to the L, to the top.

133 **Devil's Nordwand** HVS 380ft/115m **

R. James, J. V. Anthoine, 1959

An excellent route on sound rock running up the centre of the North Cliff. Start in the centre of the crag directly below an obvious 10ft/3m square niche 60ft/18m up the face.

1. 60ft/18m. 4b. Climb the front of a flat pedestal until forced into a grassy crack on the L. Go up this easily to the top.

2. 100ft/30m. 5a. Climb a thin crack for 10ft/3m then traverse L into the niche. Exit from this via its top L-hand corner. Step L, runner, then diagonally R to a small grass ledge. From its R end, climb a crack then traverse a thin slab to a stance and nut belays.

3. 100ft/30m. 5a. Reverse the last few moves of the previous pitch and continue the tricky traverse L to a ledge below an open chimney. Take this direct to a large sloping ledge on the R – poor belays.

4. 120ft/37m. 4c. Climb easily up the wall on the L for 40ft/12m, then go up steeply on good holds for another 15ft/5m. Traverse L to a spike, then go diagonally across to the arete. Finish up this.

THE RED SLAB (626631)

This superb sheet of impeccable red rock lies at the entrance to Cwm Graianog, the large hollow nestling in the eastern slopes of Carnedd y Filiast. High up on the R side of the cwm, the long, low-angle slabby area running up towards the summit of the mountain with its 1000ft/300m routes, up to VS in

Devil's Nordwand

standard, provides a haven for the climber in search of a quiet day out.

Park on the old Ogwen Road near the Naval Hut – Tai Newyddion (630635). A path climbs steeply up the hillside behind it, following a stone wall. Cresting the rise, the slab stands out on the R. Scramble across to its base. Approach time about twenty minutes.

134 Central Route   S   280ft/86m **

F. Graham, 1924

The slab is smooth and compact with few runner placements, but the angle is low and the friction fabulous! Start below its centre.

1. 140ft/43m. Climb the slight weakness with just sufficient holds to belays that are difficult to find, and awkward to arrange!

2. 140ft/43m. Finish more or less directly up the open slab to belay just below the top – a 50m rope reaches the top.

CRAIG CWRWGL (THE PILLAR, AND SLABS OF ELIDIR)   (615616)
This lonely crag perches high on the flanks of Marchlyn Mawr above the dam and reservoir for the CEGB's Dinorwic Pump Storage Scheme. It is conveniently reached up the well-surfaced road from a parking area and padlocked gate on the mountainside below the cwm (596633). It takes about forty-five minutes to reach the dam and another ten across scree to the foot of the crag, which has two main facets: the Pillar of Elidir is an obvious feature separated from the mountainside by East Gully and The Rift (Diff) on its L, and by West Gully behind. Up and to the R, above a long scree slope, the Elidir Slabs give open climbing on excellent rock.

Craig Cwrwgl – the Pillar and Slabs of Elidir

135 **Corrugated Cracks** HS 150ft/45m *

A. W. Evans, P. Smith, 1937

A strenuous and varied route – the best on the Pillar! Scramble round the toe of the Pillar to belay on a quartz and grass terrace on its east side. Above lies a steep face with the twin crack systems of Siesta Cracks (HVS) and Mexico Cracks (HVS) on the L. Next comes our selected route, with a slabby rib below a smooth rock wall – The Arete (Diff) – to its R, and the largest gash in the front face, North Chasm (S) just beyond.

1. 70ft/21m. From the terrace, climb a grassy corner to the foot of the prominent crack.
2. 40ft/12m. 4b. The narrow chimney proves strenuous and unhelpful at the start. Pull over a chockstone into a wider section and thrutch violently up to the next chockstone, and a ledge. A strength-sapping and ungradable pitch!
3. 40ft/12m. 4a. Continue up the wider chimney above, facing R, until a crack on the R leads to a terrace. Descend by slithering down the Rift, behind the Pillar, then abseiling or climbing down West Gully.

136 **Janos** VS 265ft/80m **

A. J. J. Moulam, C. T. Jones (AL), 1967

A surprisingly good route up the centre of the Elidir Slabs. The rock is compact but protection is spaced; the climbing is straightforward. Start by a quartz vein just L of the lowest slabs.

1. 100ft/30m. 4b. Go straight up to the end of the large overhang and gain the top of a block on the R. Move L to get established above the roof. Climb up to an overlap, turn it on the R and continue direct, stepping R to a stance.
2. 60ft/18m. 4b. Traverse L across a steep groove, with a stride to gain its L rib. Climb this to a ledge and poor belays.
3. 105ft/32m. 4b. Ascend directly up the slab above, keeping L of the long groove. The holds keep coming until the climbing gradually eases off to broken ground above – an excellent pitch. Scramble up diagonally R-wards to descend the shoulder of the mountain down to the dam.

Llanberis Area

The Llanberis Pass, or The Pass as it is known locally, runs between the massifs of Snowdon and the Glyders forming a steep craggy valley along the bottom of which the A4086 connects Pen y Pas Youth Hostel to the village of Llanberis. Facing Llanberis from across the twin lakes, Llyn Padarn and Llyn Peris, the vast Dinorwic quarry workings on the lower slopes of Elidir Fawr stand out starkly, a monument to the times when slate was king! To the south is Snowdon and beneath its summit lie two huge but contrasting cliffs – Lliwedd to the south-east, and Clogwyn Du'r Arddu (or Cloggy) to the north-west.

Of these four climbing venues, the south-facing Dinorwic Quarries with their quick-drying, radical slate routes, a mere stone's throw from Pete's Eats café, are by far the most popular during the winter months. Catching what sun is available year round, and with severe variations in local weather patterns, the quarries are often in condition when there is bad weather in the mountains, a couple of miles away!

Next comes the Llanberis Pass, comprising several low-lying crags on each side of its valley slopes as well as high crags on its southern side. The low-lying cliffs are all easily accessible from the road and those on the north side – Craig Ddu, Clogwyn y Grochan, Drws y Gwynt, Carreg Wastad and Dinas Cromlech – tend to be steeper and cleaner than their counterparts opposite. On the south side, the main crag is Dinas Mot, fronted by a distinctive slabby pyramid of rock – The Nose; whilst higher up are the large cliffs of Craig y Rhaeadr and Cyrn Las which seldom see the sun, and take several days to come into condition during a dry spell. Higher still, in Upper Cwm Glas, Clogwyn y Person and Clogwyn y Ddysgl with their rough clean rock are a sheer delight to climb on in late afternoon summer sunshine.

As well as offering a wealth of rock, a severe winter produces many good snow and ice routes, the most notable being the frozen waterfalls that drop down over Craig y Rhaeadr – Central Icefall Direct VI and Cascade V.

In marked contrast is Lliwedd, a huge rambling cliff, 1000ft/300m high and half a mile wide, whose long routes capture the best traditions of mountaineering. Never a popular cliff, Lliwedd provides peace, solitude and all the charms of a forgotten era.

Clogwyn Du'r Arddu, on the other hand, provides a balance between The Pass and Lliwedd. It is a massive cliff whose stunning appearance and great atmosphere add much flavour to the high percentage of quality routes that criss-cross its buttresses. With its celebrity status in British climbing history, Cloggy never fails to draw climbers on to its steep walls and slabs.

Local Amenities

The most convenient and popular accommodation is unofficial camping or bivouacking in the Llanberis Pass itself. There are numerous sites, particularly below Clogwyn y Grochan and Dinas Cromlech – discretion is needed and great care must be taken to avoid leaving litter, causing water pollution and damaging walls. Alternatively there is Humphreys Barn and campsite at Nant Peris (605585), a site on the south side of The Pass (619569) and numerous others between Llanberis and Caernarvon. Unofficial high camping amongst the boulders overlooking Llyn Du'r Arddu is not unknown if there is a dry spell during the summer months.

There is a regular bus service between Caernarvon and Nant Peris and, in the summer only, from Nant Peris through The Pass to either Capel Curig or Beddgelert.

The most attractive pubs from a climber's point of view are the Pen y Gwryd which lies just over the top of The Pass at the junction with the Beddgelert–Capel Curig road; The Vaynol, in Nant Peris, where there is also a combined post office and shop; the Padarn Lake and Victoria Hotels in Llanberis. Llanberis has a wide variety of shops and cafés. Most notable amongst the latter is Pete's Eats, a popular climbers' meeting place and watering hole on the High Street, with a New Routes book to brighten up those rainy days. Just along the road from

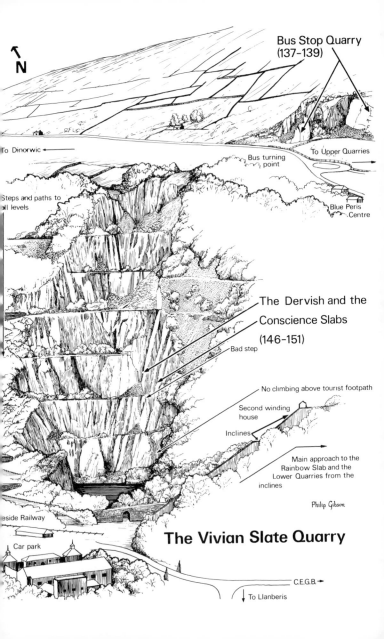

Bus Stop Quarry
(137-139)

To Dinorwic ←

Bus turning
point

To Upper Quarries →

Steps and paths to
all levels

Blue Peris
Centre

The Dervish and the

Conscience Slabs

(146-151)

Bad step

No climbing above tourist footpath

Second winding
house

Inclines

Main approach to the
Rainbow Slab and the
Lower Quarries from the
inclines

Philip Gibson

eside Railway

Car park

The Vivian Slate Quarry

C.E.G.B. →

↓ To Llanberis

there, climbing gear is available from two shops: Joe Brown's or The Rock Shop. For those who feel like a short trip to Caernarvon, The 14th Peak is a large climbing retail outlet which also has a very good café on its premises.

Llanberis Slate

At first sight, when viewed from across the lake in Llanberis, the Dinorwic Slate Quarries look like a random hotch-poch of holes, tips and inclines. But on closer inspection, it can be seen that the workings have a carefully structured layout. Fortunately, for ease of description, if nothing else, a wide fenced slate track – the Nant Peris footpath – runs from the bus terminus at Dinorwic (591611) and contours along the side of Elidir Fawr, providing an arbitrary demarcation line between the Upper and Lower Quarries, before it zigzags down to the valley floor to meet the A4086 at 600587, just before Nant Peris.

Buried in the mountainside, deep under the slopes of Elidir Fawr, lies the Dinorwic Pump Storage Scheme run by the CEGB, who have their main site offices on the lakeside at the centre of the Lower Quarries. *The quarries are on private land owned by the* CEGB who seem to tolerate climbers, providing that they do not indulge in anti-social behaviour. *There is no official access for climbers.* Please do not leave litter or damage walls or fences when crossing them, and refrain from trundling, even though the temptation may be great. Remember, future unofficial access may depend on your behaviour!

On the L-hand side of the Lower Quarries, Vivian Quarry is managed by the Country Park Organization which allows access providing that no climbing takes place above the tourist path in the quarry bottom.

Initially, climbing on slate is a strange experience. The low friction and friability of the rock conspire to give a feeling of insecurity which is rather unnerving for the uninitiated. The selected routes are all recognized as slate classics of their grade and thus should be virtually free from loose rock. However, climbers should still be wary; seemingly solid slate holds have an alarming tendency to 'disappear' rather suddenly!

Bolts are used to protect some of the selected routes, but so little is known of their holding power or durability in slate that their reliability cannot be guaranteed 100 per cent.

Beware trailing ropes along the ground both above and below your route; sharp edges on slate cut like a scalpel and rubble is easily dislodged from the top of quarried faces owing to the rock's poor surface friction – there have been many cases of chopped ropes, and a couple of incidents where climbers have been badly injured by falling debris.

Although slate dries quickly, if rain is imminent, retreat – quickly! The rock becomes as slippery as ice within *seconds* of the 'heavens opening'.

The inclusion of this slate section in the guide in no way implies that climbers have a right to climb in the Dinorwic Quarries.

THE UPPER DINORWIC QUARRIES

These are the workings which lie above, and within easy reach of the Dinorwic–Nant Peris footpath. They are described from L to R as one encounters them whilst walking from Dinorwic.

Bus Stop Quarry   (592612)

This is the amphitheatre encircling the grassy field on the L, immediately before the Dinorwic bus terminus, where the road ends in a turning circle. The quarry may be reached on foot from Llanberis via the Zig-Zags, a stepped path rising up the hillside on the opposite side of the causeway separating Llyn Padarn and Llyn Peris. Alternatively, one can drive to the head of Llyn Padarn at the Bangor turning (from the Llanberis – Caernarfon road). After 100yd/93m turn R, then L over the old bridge with wonderful views up the lake to The Pass and Snowdon. Turn R along the side of the lake and follow a steep winding road for two miles up through Fachwen to an awkward (steep) T-junction by the old school. Turn R again. The end of the road is less than a couple of minutes' drive away. From Bangor, turn off for Deiniolen; the bus terminus lies two miles beyond the village centre.

Bus Stop Quarry – the Rippled Slab

The crag has two main facets: the Rippled Slab with its brushed lines is immediately obvious. On the L, and set at R-angles to it, are the Dinorwic Needles – a thin knife-edged ridge running down towards the road.

137 **Fool's Gold**   E1   80ft/24m **

P. George, A. George, 1985

A superb crack with good protection. Just as one reaches the Needles, there is a prominent L-facing V-groove capped by a roof; start below this.

1. 5c. Climb the groove for 15ft/3m Step R and make a fierce pull up for good holds, crux. Follow the crack past a couple of awkward sections to the top.

138 **Scarlet Runner**   E4   90ft/27m **

W. Wayman, P. Williams, 1985

A sustained pitch up the L-hand side of the Rippled Slab. The line is delineated by four BRs, the top two close together. Start below these.

1. 6a. Climb up trending slightly R with a committing move to clip the first BR. Continue to a break. Hand traverse L, then stand up to clip the second BR. Move L to a tiny ledge then climb diagonally R passing the third BR on the R by a very hard move – and so past the fourth BR just above to finish direct. Belay on a tree 30ft/9m back.

The central line of the slab receives seepage from trees and vegetation above – Virgin on the Ridiculous, E4 6a. Next comes:

139 **Massambula**   E2   100ft/30m *

P. Williams, W. Wayman, 1985

A fine route which finishes just R of the clump of trees crowning the top of Virgin. The upper section is 4c/5a, but 'run out'. Start below a short wall and flat rib.

1. 5b. Climb the wall to a ledge at 12ft/4m. Continue to a good nut in the crest of the rib. Follow the L-ward traverse line above to a BR. Move slightly L, then go up and R to pass the second BR and gain a good ledge. Ascend diagonally L up tiny ledges then climb direct to the apex of the slab, exiting R-wards via a heathery pull. Belay to a tree 40ft/12m back. The brushed area R of Massambula is Gnat Attack, E1 5c.

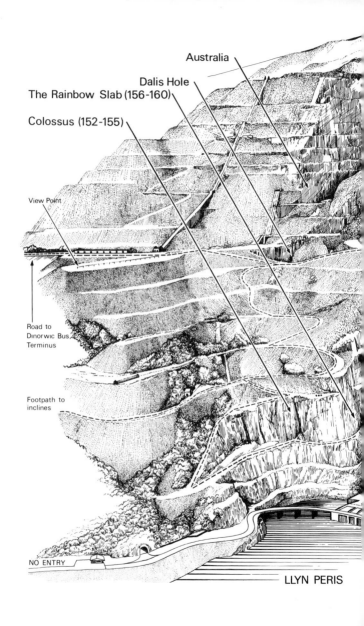

Australia

Dalis Hole

The Rainbow Slab (156-160)

Colossus (152-155)

View Point

Road to
Dinorwic Bus
Terminus

Footpath to
inclines

NO ENTRY

LLYN PERIS

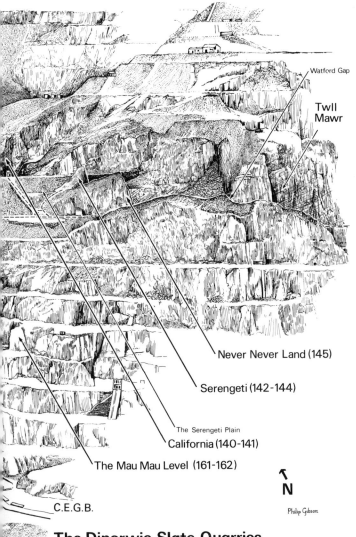

Watford Gap

Twll
Mawr

Never Never Land (145)

Serengeti (142-144)

The Serengeti Plain

California (140-141)

The Mau Mau Level (161-162)

C.E.G.B.

N

Philip Gibson

The Dinorwic Slate Quarries.

Go through the gate and follow the track (Nant Peris footpath) for about a quarter of a mile past a huge derelict cutting shed – Watford Gap, a prominent cleft in the quarried walls, lies a few hundred yards in front, and is an obvious landmark. Next comes a small slate building where the track turns sharply L through a kissing gate – turn R to reach the 'Viewpoint'. Directly in front, a long incline rises up the mountainside, just beyond the point where the track turns back R, dropping steeply down into a dip. On the L, on the other side of a gate, lies Dali's Hole – a sunken quarry with dead trees rising ghostly-white from its floor: a surreal landscape which floods almost completely during prolonged rainy spells. Directly above Dali's Hole is a vast open man-made cwm with a scree slope falling down from its top L corner – Australia.

California

Go through the gate as for Dali's Hole. Bear R and walk, then scramble up a scree slope to reach the obvious tunnel mouth, just below a terrace. At the other end of this is a circular hole hemmed in on three sides from which one gets a dramatic first view of California Wall, a magnificent sweep of rock fully 200ft/61m in height, and flanked on its L by a narrow pillar which bears the scars of a rockfall on its L side. The L arete of the rock face through which the tunnel continues is a fine feature and gives:

140 **Californian Arete**   E1   140ft/43m ***
C. J. Phillips, solo, 1984

A tremendous pitch for its grade which takes the superb wavy arete, marked with horizontal quartz striations, jutting out into the quarry floor around and to the L of the tunnel exit. The climbing is unique; protection is imaginary, but the belay at the top is sound! There is a hidden blast shelter in a hole through the base of the arete.

California

1.4c. Start on the R for 20ft/6m then cross the arete which is taken steeply on its L side for a few feet. At about 50ft/15m, pull back R round the crest to reach a good hold. Continue more easily in an airy position, without runners, to finish up a short groove. The rope can be looped round the top of the arete to belay, plus wires as a back up . . . Escape by walking across to gain a heather ledge on the L. Follow this L-wards, staying roped up for a 'bad step', then continue round a blunt rib (where the path narrows) and go through a hidden tunnel, emerging on to a slate plateau. Scramble down easy scree to regain the Nant Peris footpath.

141 **Central Sadness** E5 220ft/67m ***

J. Silvester, C. Dale, 1986

A powerful climb accepting the challenge thrown down by California Wall at its highest point. One of the finest slate routes around with two contrasting pitches: the first serious, and the second 'wild' but well protected! Start below the centre of the face, a few feet R of a slim R-facing groove that drops down from the top end of a ledge system about 50ft/18m up.

1. 100ft/30m. 6a. A hard start, crux, up a finger-crack leads to a small recess. Continue up on sloping holds, undercuts and layaways for 30ft/9m. Tape runner. A protectionless wall gives some anxious moments before the security of a long narrow ledge with a two bolt belay is reached; an heroic lead!

2. 120ft/37m. 6a. Step L into a crack. After 5ft/1.5m, trend slightly R along the obvious line for about 20ft/6m to reach a crack running down from the top of the face. The crack is steep, the friction poor, but the protection is good; so climb it via some superb technical moves. Make a reachy move R-wards over a bulge about 30ft/9m from the top, to finish easily up a dog-legged hand crack; a pitch for the safety-conscious married man with a large rack of wires! Scramble up the hillside to reach steps running down L-wards along the edge of Australia to a col. Continue down to Dali's Hole.

Serengeti Area

From the dip in the track by Dali's Hole, continue for about 200yd/186m in the direction of Nant Peris; the track rises at first, then levels out passing a circular slate air vent. Go through a gate just beyond, then walk back past the vent and scramble up one level. Bear R between a heather-topped island and a large hut with a slate slab for a door, on to the Serengeti Plain, a large slate clearing with steep walls on the R which diminish in height towards their R end. On the L, facing them, is the smooth Seamstress Slab, split by two slanting cracks – the slab forms merely one side of the aforementioned heather-topped island and the descent path runs down to its L end.

142 **Seamstress**   HVS   70ft/21m *

S. Haston, solo, 1983

1. 5a. The original route up the slab gives a neat little pitch. Start below the L-hand crack, and climb it. The standard is well maintained throughout.

The wall direct L of Seamstress gives Slug Club Special, E4 6a.

143 **Seams the Same**   E2   70ft/21m

S. Haston, solo, 1983

1. 5b. Despite its name, the R-hand crack proves to be a stiffer proposition than its neighbour, giving fine sustained climbing, and a very long reach a few feet up. Protection is only moderate!

R of Seams the Same, a blank area of slab gives two desperate routes – My Halo, E7 6b and the excruciating Windows of Perception, E6 7a – before a slim groove 15ft/5m L of the arete gives another trip into the realms of fantasy for 99.9 per cent of climbers – The Medium, E7 6c. However, there is hope for the aspiring hard man just L of the arete:

144 **Heading the Shot**   E4   75ft/23m **

S. Haston, N. Walton, 1984

An exceptionally fine pitch, both technically hard and
sustained. The line is indicated by three bolts and a peg, the
first one being difficult to clip!

1. 6b. Climb the slab just R of the bolts on a series of tiny holds.
Powerful cranking and deft footwork enable one to reach the
third bolt. Move L and finish direct, stretching L to clip the final
peg *en route* – fingery!

Never Never Land Area

Go through the gate a few yards after the air vent, as for the
Serengeti, but instead of turning L, go straight ahead past a
ruined building. Bear round L-wards to the foot of an
impressive slab, split by a stepped groove in its lower section,
the line of:

145 **Never Never Land**   E5   145ft/44m **

M. Crook, N. Walton, A. Newton, 1984

An excellent, committing route with some friable rock. The
crux is protected by an iron spike which protrudes somewhat,
adding to the dangers of an already difficult ascent! A third
rope may be needed to reach the safest belay – about 60ft/18m
back.

1. 6a. Start below the stepped groove. Climb awkwardly up to
the roofs. Move L and go up to the protruding spike, runner!
Hard moves past this, crux, then a sustained section on a flaky
edge gain a rest, and a runner. Make a tricky shuffle up a rib to
the overlap, and better holds. Move up and L, then follow a line
of holds to the L arete. Finish direct on large sloping holds and
ledges – no protection. Cosmic. Walk down R-wards to the
Serengeti.

Further along the track, immediately on the other side of
Watford Gap, is Twll Mawr, The Big Hole, with its shattered

Serengeti Area – Seamstress Slab

back wall and an enormous smooth face on its L climbed by several desperate routes, the most celebrated of which is The Quarryman, E8 6c, 6b, 7a, 7a – worth the walk to look at if climbing nearby.

THE LOWER DINORWIC QUARRIES

Both Vivian Quarry and the Rainbow Slab Area are approached from the large visitors' car-park by the Padarn Country Park and Lakeside Railway. Take the road which turns off opposite the Snowdon Mountain Railway and cuts across between Llyn Padarn and Llyn Peris: the car-park is signposted at the first turning on the L. Vehicles should not be parked on the slate verges by the approach roads.

Vivian Quarry

The narrow multi-tiered quarry rising up the hillside just beyond the Lakeside Railway is part of the Padarn Country Park, a designated conservation area of outstanding botanical interest; the management, who seem sympathetic to climbing, ask that climbers stick to the paths and avoid trampling on regenerating vegetation.

A slate archway connects the car-park to the quarry bottom where there is a still, dark lake beyond a wooded area of birch, sycamore, willow, oak and ash. A prow juts out from the far shore sporting many hard routes and the ungradable jump from its tip – Nicki's Leap, wet suit recommended! Above, on the R-hand side of the second tier up, is an impressive slab with an overlap cutting across it at two-thirds height. One reaches the slab via a path and steps running up the hillside to the L of the quarry, before crossing a stile and contouring round past a 'bad step' to a scree slope below it.

The Dervish Slab Area

A steep wall on the L runs across to meet the slab. All the routes on it are hard, perhaps the best known being The Manic Strain, E7 6c – a line of five bolts up the smooth face, L of the hanging bomb-bay flake chimney – and Gin Palace, E5 6b – a

frantic, frictionless fight, fraught with frustration! To the R of
the Dervish Slab, and reached via a 'bad step' around its R
arete, lies the smaller, Conscience Slab.

146 **Comes the Dervish**   E3   130ft/40m ***
S. Haston unseconded, 1982

The central crackline of the slab gives the most celebrated of all
slate routes. An immaculate piece of climbing on small positive
holds, with good protection after the first 20ft/6m. Usually well
chalked up. Start below the slotted hairline crack.

1. 5c. Climb up with a hard move to gain the slot at 20ft/6m,
crux! Follow the crack with the occasional long reach for a good
finger-lock or face hold past a precarious move R, on to better
holds, and a good rest at the overlap. Pull over this and
continue up the easier slab above, passing a small wire, to
finish. A solid gold pitch. TBS and BBS. Abseil off.

147 **Flashdance**   E5   150ft/46m **
A. Pollitt, T. Freeman, 1983

A sizzling pitch requiring a certain 'cool'. The route takes a
rising line of shallow scoops to join Comes The Dervish at a
good hold about 10ft/3m below the overlap. Start just R of the
centre of the slab.

1. 6a. Climb up R-wards along twin diagonal cracks, then
break out L along the line of scoops. Follow these by a series of
fingery and insecure moves, without much protection, easing
slightly to a junction with Comes The Dervish. Breeze up this
to finish!

148 **Last Tango in Paris**   E2   150ft/46m
M. Roberts, C. Edwards, 1985

A worthwhile route up the R side of the slab, but a little loose
above the overlap. Start just R of the centre of the slab as for
Flashdance.

1. 5c. Follow the twin diagonal cracks to the arete and
continue up to a small ledge. Break out diagonally L and ascend
via a crack to the overlap. Climb over this and finish carefully
up the top slab, over some suspect rock.

149 **The Sweetest Taboo**   E4   80ft/24m *
M. Raine, J. Dawes, 1986

A very fine pitch up the centre of the Conscience Slab; bold at
the outset. Start below the highest part of the slab, 10ft/3m L of
the rising break which delineates its R edge.

1. 6a. Trend slightly L for 15ft/5m to an ankle-snapping move,
then continue fairly direct to good holds. Move R with a long
reach, then climb up past a good wire placement to a BR. A
couple of desperate moves just above lead to a pleasant few
finishing moves and a BB. Abseil off.

150 **Never as Good as the First Time**   E3   75ft/23m
M. Raine, C. Dale, 1986

The easiest way up the slab; start at the foot of the rising break
at its R edge.

1. 5c. Climb up to a BR. Traverse L for 6ft/2m (a long span)
then ascend direct to the large flake on The Sweetest Taboo.
Continue to the BR, then step R and follow the crack to a BB.
Abseil off.

151 **Is it a Crime?**   E3   75ft/23m *
M. Raine, C. Dale, 1986

1. 5c. Follow Never as Good to its first BR. Make a difficult
move diagonally R and continue up to another BR (a long clip)
below a small overlap. Finish up the thin crackline to a BB.
Abseil off.

The Rainbow Area

This lies just above the CEGB main site and is the most
sensitive area: park as for Vivian Quarry at the Lakeside
Railway car-park. Follow two successive inclines (the lower one
starts just R of the Vivian entrance arch) to the second winding
house. Follow the track for another 50 yd/46m to the foot of a
third incline. Cross the fence and go along the wide terrace

Vivian Quarry – Dervish and Conscience Slabs

contouring around the hillside. After about 300 yd/280m, the
track turns L, then passes some ruined buildings to reach a
culvert where it turns R. Cross the fence and follow a scree path
down for about 50 yd/46m to a vegetated area with some
decaying tree stumps: the top of Colossus Wall. From here the
path continues for another 80yd/73m or so, bearing round to
the L and the top of Rainbow Slab; opposite and on the L are
the Rainbow Levels.

Colossus Wall
From on top of Colossus Wall turn R (looking out) and follow a
path down across some pipes, descending alongside the culvert,
to the terrace below, which contours back round below
Colossus Wall, to the Rainbow Slab around the corner.

152 Bella Lugosi is Dead   E1   80ft/24m *
M. Crook, N. Walton, 1984
On the L of Colossus Wall, an 80ft/24m slab is split by a
prominent thin crack near its L edge. Quite a serious little
pitch.
1. 5b. Climb the crack which has positive holds, but some
suspect rock. Go up past a PR to some difficult finishing moves
in a wide crack – the prudent climber will carry a Friend 2½ for
this!

Colossus Wall is fully 150ft/46m high, with quality routes
taking the natural weaknesses in the face. Just around to the L,
a unique leaning groove system gives the precarious Jack of
Shadows, E4 6a, 6a. The L arete of the wall gives Big Wall
Party, E5 6b, 6b, which finishes up the smooth, steep crack
splitting the front face. Next, fairly low down on the L side, are
two long V-slots one above the other; in the centre, two superb
vertical shallow L-facing corners rear up nearly 100ft/30m
before curving over to merge with the wall. On the R, the
prominent L-slanting line of weakness with a circular niche at

Colossus Wall

75ft/23m, and a 15ft/5m groove just above it, is the line of Colossus.

153 **Major Headstress**   E5   150ft/46m ★★
P. Williams, C. Gilchrist, 1986

An excellent pitch, both bold and exposed! Start just R of the arete at a prominent crack which leads up to the first V-slot.
1. 6a. Climb the crack up into the niche at 25ft/8m. Pull out into the steep V-groove. BR. Take the L arete of this with a long reach at the top for the second BR. Climb steeply up the wall passing another BR on layaways. Traverse R to good holds and a BR. Take the difficult groove above passing yet another BR and mantel on to a ledge. Step R and cruise the headwall past BR number 6. An airy mantel at the top gives a fitting finale.

154 **Ride the Wild Surf**   E4   150ft/46m ★★★
P. Williams, O. Jones, 1986

A fabulous route; the best on the wall. It takes a very direct line up the L-hand corner/groove and sports the famous/infamous Chipadeedoodah hold – one of the more obvious chipped holds on slate. Start near the centre of the wall below a hanging flake/groove.
1. 6a. Go up to clip a BR on the L, then move across to clip another one on the R. Traverse back, feet on Chipadeedoodah, and layback the flake to a small ledge. Continue directly up the corner with the occasional long reach, passing a BR or five to the small roof. Grit your teeth and go for the next BR, 20ft/6m above (junction with Major Headstress). Float up the enigmatic groove and sail up the top wall on a tidal wave of elation!

Great Balls of Fire, E4 6a climbs the other corner/groove into the circular niche on Colossus before breaking out diagonally R-wards via a short overhanging groove, and ledge system, to finish with an exposed mantelshelf!

Cruising up Ride the Wild Surf

155 **Colossus** E3   150ft/46m ***

P. Williams, A. Holmes, 1986

A classic of its grade, well bolted, well positioned and very popular. It takes the major line of weakness starting on the R side of the wall. Unfortunately, the crux crack normally seeps, and when wet can be very hard indeed – the BR at its foot normally sports a couple of slings, the sure sign of an epic retreat! Start by a boulder at the base of the wall.

1. 5c. Make a hard move up for a ledge. Follow the line curving over R-wards to a ledge. Two BRs. Step L and pull up awkwardly for better holds, then move R past a sapling stump to a good hold. Climb a crack to the top of a pinnacle. Go straight up to enter a slanting V-groove, or reach the same point via the circular niche on the L. The V-groove is hard to start; exit L into a crack at the top of it. Struggle up the crack past a couple of BRs. From a hold just above the second one, make a couple of difficult moves L to an easy but sensational mantelshelf on to a good ledge. (It is possible to move L slightly higher – easier, but not as good as the original way.) Gain a higher ledge on the R, and continue steeply to an awkward finishing move. A third rope may be necessary to arrange belays some way back.

Rainbow Slab

This, the most elegant of the slate slabs, an immaculate, smooth, grey sweep of rock, rises up for 140ft/43m and is over 200ft/61m across. A curving line of rippled rock arches up from L to R, the dominant feature which gives the slab its name. All the routes on the slab are E1 or harder; in fact, most are E5 or harder! For the connoisseur of 'rockover and mantelshelf', of 'fingertip cranking' and 'cosmic cruising', Rainbow Slab is Nirvana!

An abseil bolt is in situ at the apex of the slab (this is usually backed up with a wire and Friend) from which one can easily reach the foot of the climbs. For those who prefer to walk, an approach can be made down alongside the culvert by Colossus Wall.

156 **Red and Yellow and Pink and Green, Orange and Purple and Blue**   E1   130ft/40m *

M. Lynden, solo, 1983

A soft touch technically, but serious. The easiest way up the slab. There are arbitrary runners at 80ft/24m – these will save you from the mortuary, but not from the Casualty Department at Ysbyty Gwynedd! Start just in from the L arete.

1. 5a. Trend up to the R along a line of holds with an awkward move to gain a good ledge. Move up then trend back L on positive holds to a broken area and poor runners. From the L end of the ledge make a hard move up for an obvious hold, then finish up the slab above – a good pitch which can be split.

157 **Pull My Daisy**   E2   125ft/38m ***

M. Lynden, J. Silvester, 1984

The prominent crack splitting the L side of the slab has a metal bar protruding from it at about 60ft/18m and is very popular.

1. 5c. Climb up to a runner at 20ft/6m, then continue up to the metal spike. Continue boldly up on small hidden holds to an easing in the angle, trending up L-wards to finish – a superb pitch! Belay well back.

158 **The Rainbow of Recalcitrance**   E6   200ft/60m ***

J. Silvester, M. Lynden, 1984

A magnificent route which tiptoes tenuously and elegantly along the arching ripple – The Rainbow – in its entirety! Once the initial crack is left behind the protection is really spaced! There have been several massive pendulums by both leaders and seconds during various ascents – about 100ft/30m seems to be the record, so far! Start below a thin crack just L of The Rainbow.

1. 100ft/30m. 6b. Climb the difficult crack for 40ft/12m (as for Naked Before the Beast, E6 6c which finishes direct) then step R on to The Rainbow. A friction move up on frictionless rock, crux, enables one to pad up the ripple to stepped ledges and good wires above. Step back down and continue balancing along the ramp to a BR which is difficult to clip (a poignant

moment to recall the slab-climber's maxim – 'Smear or Disappear'). Continue ʀ-wards again, relieved, to a belay on small ledges (on Cystitis by Proxy).

2. 6a – hard! Move ʀ, then ascend the obvious line, with no protection, to a ᴘʀ on a small ledge at 40ft/12m. Finish on the ʀ up the lower of two black grooves.

159 **Poetry Pink** E4   140ft/43m ***
J. Redhead, D. Towse (both led), 1984

A superb pitch; the easiest of the harder routes on the slab. There is bolt protection at 25ft/8m and 50ft/16m, with a tricky step up to reach the latter. A sprinter/doctor for a belayer should relieve some of the mental stress! Start a few feet ʀ of The Rainbow.

1. 6b. Climb the slab to two ʙʀs. Move up with difficulty and continue via an awkward step up, or mantelshelf, to reach another ʙʀ. Hard moves to pass this gain The Rainbow. Teeter ʀ along it for a few feet to the stepped ledges and good wires. Enter the groove above with difficulty and climb it to the top. If the pitch is split at a bolt stance on the prow to the ʟ of the final groove, a third rope to belay with will not be necessary.

160 **Cystitis By Proxy** E5   150ft/46m **
D. Towse, J. Redhead (AL), 1984

The original route of the slab gives bold climbing up the line of the abseil. Its fierce and fingery crux is protected by two ʙʀs. Although the climb may be split (as on the first ascent) it is usually done in a single run-out.

1. 6b. From the foot of the abseil climb up into shattered cracks. Continue up a hairline crack (poor micro-wires) to a hard step ʟ. Climb boldly up to small ledges and move up ʀ to a flake. ʙʀ above and a possible belay. Climb up just ʀ of the ʙʀ to a second ʙʀ. Pass this and step ʟ on to a flat hold with great difficulty, a tendon-ripping crux. Move up ʟ, then follow a line of holds diagonally up ʀ, to the top. Belay at the abseil point.

Rainbow Slab

The Mau Mau Level (Level 2)
This is the second quarried tier up from the base of Rainbow
Slab. It is also the largest of the Rainbow Levels. Approach by
following the original track past the culvert (the turn-off point
for The Rainbow and Colossus Areas) and up a rise for a short
distance to where the track bends L. Cross the fence and
contour round the back of the bay along Level 3 to stand on top
of a narrow greenstone prow which presents a smooth face to
the mountainside as it juts out on to Level 2. Two of our
selected routes climb this prow and are reached by abseil from
slate blocks on its top – care should be taken to avoid the rope
running over sharp edges.

161 The Mau Mau E4 70ft/21m***
P. Williams, unseconded, 1986
No longer the man-eater it once was, the compelling,
bow-shaped finger-crack in the smooth wall on the R-side of the
prow (facing out) is still quite a 'pumper'. Start below the
centre of the wall.
1. 6a. Climb the crack on layaways to reach a ledge on the R (a
wide flake crack leads up to the R end of this ledge – 5b). The
fun now begins. Step back L and fight up the continuation crack
which is superbly protected by wires – the trick is to avoid
resting on them. Finish using holds on the L wall – a quality
pitch.

162 German Schoolgirl E2 70ft/21m***
M. Crook, N. Walton, 1984
A very good pitch up the superbly clean-cut corner in the back
on the next bay, diagonally across the top of the narrow pillar
on the opposite side to The Mau Mau. Start below the corner.
1. 5c. The corner is hard near the bottom, crux. Continue by
sustained bridging, jamming and laybacking to the top. Well
protected by lots of small wires.

The Mau Mau

Llanberis Pass (North Side)

CRAIG DDU   (618574)

This is the first cliff on the L, lying just above the road about a mile beyond Nant Peris as one drives towards Pen y Pass. It is easily recognized by its jet black, smooth, main face which perpetually seeps until there is a prolonged dry spell. Despite this seepage, the cliff offers some excellent climbing, seemingly slabby routes turning out to be much steeper than expected when one gets to grips with them.

The main L-hand section of the cliff is divided from the slab-topped R-hand section by a wet vegetated gully – Garlic Groove (S), and is bounded at its L-end by an obvious chimney with a tree above it – Short Tree Chimney (Diff). To the R of this, a prominent watercourse running down the face of the cliff marks the start of:

163 **Crown of Thorns** S   135ft/41m*
P. R. J. Harding, C. W. F. Noyce (AL), 1949

A pleasant outing, best tackled when dry! At the R edge of the watercourse, start from a boulder which protrudes 3ft/1m from the ground.

1. 65ft/20m. Climb to a grassy ledge at 25ft/8m. Move R into a groove which leads to the top of a pedestal.
2. 40ft/12m. Go up the wall on good holds to a sloping ledge. Climb a grassy groove on the R until it is possible to enter a large scoop. Belay in the corner.
3. 35ft/11m. Climb the flaky wall to the R. Move up and across the groove on the L to reach the top via a difficult move; or climb directly up the corner above the wall and struggle through the 'thorny crown' on to the grass. Belay well back. Descend by traversing L-wards to join a path which descends steeply then cuts back along the foot of the crag.

Craig Ddu

164 **Zig-Zag**   VS   220ft/66m **

D. Belshaw, J. Brown, 1952

A good open climb, somewhat lacking in protection. Small
wires are useful. Start under a prominent overhang 20ft/6m up
and about 50ft/15m R of the Crown of Thorns starting boulder.
1. 130ft/39m. 4b. Climb up L to a grassy ledge at 30ft/9m. Go
diagonally R to another grassy ledge then move L into a groove
which is taken up R-wards to a large sloping ledge. Move L into
another groove and climb it to a stance.
2. 90ft/27m. 4b. Climb the obvious line diagonally R for
20ft/6m. Finish up the black groove. Descend as for Crown of
Thorns.

165 **Canol**   E1   230/69m *

J. Brown, D. Belshaw, 1952

A steep climb with a short technical crux. Start 20ft/6m R of
Zig-Zag and 40ft/12in L of the slanting crack on the L side of a
large pinnacle. A holly tree sits above.
1. 80ft/24m. 4c. Climb steeply up to the holly tree. Cross a field
and climb diagonally L-wards to a sloping shelf which leads L to
a blocky belay.
2. 80ft/24m. 5b. Move 15ft/5m L to an indefinite crack in the
steep wall. Layback up this to a good hold and a ramp. Move R
along this to a PR below the overhang. Go up the overhanging
wall, moving L then R to reach a long ledge, crux; follow this
past a tree to a large block.
3. 70ft/21m. 4b. Climb the groove behind the tree to a
shattered overhang which is turned on the L to finish. Descend
as for Crown of Thorns.

To the L of Garlic Groove, at the point where the approach
path meets the cliff, is a large pinnacle which marks the start of
Black Wall (E1) and Scrog (E1), two routes which take
complex lines up the wall above it. To the R is a prominent low
angle rib:

166 **Rib and Slab**   V Diff   250ft/76m *

V. J. Wiggin, D. R. Meldrum, 1948

A popular beginners' climb. Start at the foot of the rib of rock just R of Garlic Groove.

1. 100ft/30m. Climb the rib which steepens near the top to the broad terrace.

2. 150ft/46m. The slab above is a delight. Climb via a line just L of centre to finish. Care is needed with the final belay.

Descent: traverse L round a grassy couloir, then go up a rock step on its L side; go across keeping well above the crag until a steep slippery grass slope leads down to join the path on the L of the crag.

167 **Rift Wall (Anthropology)**   VS   200ft/60m **

J. M. Edwards, K. N. Davies, F. J. Monkhouse, 1949

An interesting route up the slabs and overhanging corner-crack which are just L of a huge flat-topped pedestal. Start 25ft/8m R of the stone wall which runs up to meet the crag.

1. 70ft/21m. 4b. Climb easy rocks diagonally L to a ledge. A rising traverse back R across steep rock leads to the lower slab. Climb this to belay below the overhanging corner-crack.

2. 90ft/27m. 5a. The crack provides a tough struggle, crux. Go up the easy slab to the top of the pedestal.

3. 40ft/12m. 4a. Go up L to the foot of a steep corner. Swing airily on to the L arete on large flakes. Finish easily. Descent: Scramble up and over L-wards as for Rib and Slab; or carefully reverse its top slab to a good abseil tree at the top of the rib.

168 **Orpheus**   E2   180ft/54m *

C. J. Phillips, R. J. C. Kirkwood, J. Arthy, 1967

A bold steep but juggy route up the front face of the large pedestal. Start 20ft/6m R of Rift Wall by two quartz bands.

1. 80ft/24m. 5b. Ascend diagonally up a shallow groove to a good flake runner. Traverse R for 20ft/6m to a small ledge on the arete. Climb strenuously up on good holds and pockets with little protection to a poor rest in a niche. Move up L to surmount the overhang at its weakest point to reach a sloping ledge and belay.

2. 50ft/15m. 4c. Climb diagonally R up a little wall and continue to a small bay (on Pedestal Route – V Diff). From the R end of the bay move R, round a bulge and climb the arete to the top of the pedestal.

3. 50ft/15m. 4c. Move R to climb a crack and a small overhang into a groove. Finish up this. Descend as for Rift Wall.

169 **Yellow Groove** VS 140ft/42m **

J. Brown, D. D. Whillans, 1955

A superb little route up steep rock on the L side of the yellow wall, well up and to the R of Orpheus. Start on the R-hand side of a rock pyramid, below the steep wall.

1. 50ft/15m. Scramble easily up L-wards to the large block at the apex of the rock pyramid.

2. 90ft/27m. 4b. Climb the groove above the block to an overhang. Move R to a ledge below a clean-cut groove. Climb this on good holds then step L to a delicate finish up the wall, crux. Descend as for Rift Wall.

170 **Yellow Wall** E2 160ft/48m **

D. Yates, D. Potts (AL), 1962

A fine sustained climb of interest and character. Start just R of Yellow Groove at the foot of a steep wall.

1. 90ft/27m. 5b. Climb the steep wall to a resting place at 20ft/6m. Trend up L-wards to the base of a shallow groove. Climb this and continue to a large foothold below the overhang. Turn this on the R and go up to a ledge and belay.

2. 70ft/21m. 5b. Traverse L past a perched boulder, under a roof to a sloping ledge. A strenuous pull over the roof leads to awkward and precarious climbing up the groove above. Face L to finish. Descend as for Rift Wall.

171 **Petite Fleur** HS 110ft/33m

C. E. Davies, G. D. Verity, 1961

Pleasant but short. Start R of Yellow Wall below a huge boss of rock and an overhanging chimney.

1. 4b. Climb the steep crack and wall to a ledge below the

chimney (Fever – HVS – goes L up the hanging groove here).
Move up into the chimney and follow it R-wards into the
continuation groove, crux. Finish easily to a grassy ledge and
belay. Descent: Scramble up for about 150ft/46m then traverse
L keeping well above the top of the crag to the steep grassy
slope and footpath on its L-hand side.

CLOGWYN Y GROCHAN   (621572)
This is the next cliff on the L after Craig Ddu. It is very
popular, lying only a couple of hundred yards' walk from the
lay-bys situated directly below it. In summer these are
occasionally full, so the large car-park east of Nant Peris
(606583) may have to be used instead.

   Two repulsive gullies split the cliff into three large buttresses.
On the L is Goat's Buttress which offers three classic routes on
clean steep rock. To the R, past Goat's Gully (VS), is the
central section of cliff, gently overhanging at its base and
offering climbs of a fierce and sustained nature – the
V-chimney at the lowest point of this buttress is an obvious
feature: Brant Direct (HVS). Higher up, the buttress
deteriorates somewhat and there is little to commend it. R again
lies Central Gully (HS) and beyond this the last buttress,
broken and with much loose rock – definitely not
recommended!

172 **Phantom Rib**   VS   245ft/74m **

G. W. S. Pigott, Miss M. Kennedy-Frazer, W. H. Stock, 1949
An entertaining climb with its crux reserved for a delicate and
exposed rib just to the L of the corner of Nea. Start at the L side
of Goat's Buttress where a small gully runs up R-wards to a
large grassy ledge on Nea.
1. 40ft/12m. 4b. Reach parallel cracks in the L wall of the gully
and climb these past trees to a ledge.
2. 40ft/12m. 4c. Go up the small groove behind the stance,
then traverse steeply to a hidden ledge on the rib. Climb the rib
delicately on small holds, crux, until better holds lead up R to a
stance in a wooded gully.

3. 60ft/18m. 4b. Climb diagonally R up a series of little grooves near the R arete. At the highest of these make a blind move R, around the arete into another groove. Ascend this on finger-jams to blocks at its top.

4. 45ft/14m. 4a. Traverse R, go up the corner and follow a ledge back L. Climb 10ft/3m to a good stance directly above the previous one.

5. 60ft/18m. Go easily up R to an oak tree, then diagonally R to a corner. Finish up this to gain the Nea ledge. Descend as for Nea.

173 **Nea**   VS   245ft/75m **

Mme N. E. Morin, J. M. Edwards, 1941

The central curving corner of Goat's Buttress gives a very popular climb which only just warrants its Very Severe status. Start 30ft/9m up in a large grassy bay below a corner, reached by scrambling up an easy gully from the L.

1. 65ft/20m. 4b. Climb the corner until it divides. Follow its L branch for 15ft/5m to a steepening. Step delicately R around the rib to gain a crack, crux, which soon leads to a cramped stance and belay.

2. 75ft/23m. Follow the slabby corner crack until a little chimney leads to a large ledge and excellent belays.

3. 65ft/20m. 4b. Swing out on to a ledge on the steep L wall and move up to a short corner. Make an exposed step L to reach the start of a shallow bottomless groove. Climb this on improving holds to a large ledge.

4. 40ft/12m. Climb more easily up the wall behind then scramble well back to belay. Descent: *this is quite difficult and requires care.* To reach the Nea ledge (the start of the descent path) from the finish of higher routes, an awkward little chimney, marked by a finger stone at its top, is reversed. Scramble L-wards down and round along the loose path to descend a sometimes wet and greasy gully on the L side of the cliff; the face to the L of the gully (looking out) may also be

Clogwyn y Grochan

descended over several rock steps although most climbers use a combination of the two to reach the bottom.

174 **Spectre** HVS 300ft/91m **

P. R. J. Harding, E. H. Phillips, 1947

A well-protected route of interest and character with a problematic crack which climbs up to the R of Nea. Start at the lowest point of Goat's Buttress.

1. 65ft/20m. 4c. Climb the thin crack to a ledge on the R. Continue up to the R on easier rock to belay below a steep groove.
2. 70ft/21m. 5a. Climb the difficult groove to a ledge below a butterfly-shaped overhang. Move up and delicately around the arete on the L on to a steep slab. Cross this either high or low then climb a groove to a stance.
3. 30ft/12m. Climb easily across R-wards to the foot of a steep wide crack.
4. 30ft/12m. 5a. The crack is best started by layback. Quit it on perfect jams and so gain the stance at the end of Nea Pitch 2.
5. 65ft/20m. 4b. Swing out on to the L wall and climb a shallow groove. Step L and ascend the bottomless groove to a good stance (Nea Pitch 3).
6. 40ft/12m. Finish up the wall behind the stance (Nea Pitch 4). Descend as for Nea.

175 **S.S. Special** E2 150ft/46m **

D. Roberts, P. Williams, B. Dunne, 1977

A superb eliminate taking a direct line up the Sickle Wall. Start below twin cracks L of the Sickle flake.

1. 5c. Climb either crack to a ledge at 30ft/9m. Step R and ascend awkwardly to reach the 'letter-box' on the Sickle traverse. Continue straight up to join Sickle below the roof (moving L and climbing the Sickle groove is considerably easier, E1 5b). Step L and pull boldly over then follow a R-curving flake until a few delicate moves lead to easy slabs and

Nea, just after the hard moves round the rib on pitch 1

a belay in a short corner. Either finish diagonally L across the slabs as for Sickle Pitch 3, or climb up L to the prominent tree and abseil 150ft/46m to the ground below.

176 **Sickle**   HVS   190ft/57m *
J. Brown, D. Cowan, 1953

A steep and satisfying route crossing the white wall R of Goat's Gully. Start at the foot of the massive flake just L of the V-chimney of Brant Direct.

1. 70ft/21m. 5a. Ascend the crack on the R side of the flake to a ledge at its tip. Step L on to the wall and climb a thin crack to a ledge. Continue to a niche then traverse R past some blocks and go up to a sloping stance.

2. 60ft/18m. 5a. Step down and cross the steep wall on the L (hands in the horizontal slot) with difficulty to a groove which leads to a resting place under the roof. Move delicately out L to pass the roof then go up slabs to a stance in a small corner on the R.

3. 60ft/18m. 4c. The slabs on the L are crossed diagonally to reach a short steep crack in the L wall of Goat's Gully. Climb it to the perched block stance of Nea. Finish up this, or climb up L to the prominent tree and abseil off – as for S.S. Special.

177 **Brant Direct**   HVS   75ft/23m ***
P. R. J. Harding and party, 1949

A popular and well-protected exercise in bridging and jamming. Start at the foot of the obvious V-chimney/groove splitting the toe of the buttress, immediately R of the large flake.

1. 5a. Climb the chimney/groove via several awkward moves to a long narrow ledge and belay on the R. Abseil from the holly tree just R again.

178 **Cockblock**   E5   75ft/23m ***
J. Redhead, C. Shorter, K. Robertson, 1980

A fierce and fingery problem. Start below the R arete of Brant Direct.

1. 6b. Boulder up to a rest at 10ft/3m. Continue with difficulty

past a small pillar to a good nut (often fallen on!). Make a long
reach up and R, then pull up fiercely, all very tiring, to an
easing at 50ft/15m. Belay thankfully on the long ledge above.

179 **First Amendment**   E1   150ft/45m *
D. Roberts, P. Williams (AL), 1978
An enjoyable route with an airy top pitch. Start 6ft/2m L of the
rock step, below a thin crack which leads up to a L-facing
corner (Slape Direct, E1 5c takes a crack just L again which
finishes up a R-facing corner).
1. 70ft/21m. 5c. A difficult start gains good holds. Layaway up
to the jug at the end of the Brant traverse, crux, and continue
steeply up the L-facing corner to a holly tree belay.
2. 80ft/24m. 5b. Behind the holly tree is a large flake. Step off
this and climb the smooth wall, unprotected, then the stepped
hanging groove to the top, well-protected. Descent: make a
rising R-ward traverse, then step delicately round an arete to
abseil off the tree at the top of Hangover.

180 **Brant**   VS   360ft/109m ***
J. M. Edwards, J. E. Q. Barford, 1940
A popular and traditional Welsh classic. Start on top of the
rock step below a sentry box a few feet up.
1. 70ft/21m. 4c. Climb up to the sentry box and make a
delicate L-ward traverse to a good hold. Continue L more
easily, then go up to holly trees. Climb the short corner and
move round the flake on the L to a long ledge.
2. 50ft/15m. 4c. Traverse L then step down and round into a
short problematic V-chimney. Squirm up this to a large ledge
on the R.
3. 140ft/43m. 4a. A rising L-ward traverse up the wall leads to
a slab. Climb the overlap and slabs above heading for a
prominent corner. Ascend this for 50ft/15m, then step R and
amble up over easy slabs to belay on a yew tree.
4. 100ft/30m. 4a. Climb directly up the nose of the buttress
behind the belay to the top of the cliff. Descend over to the L, as
for Nea.

181 **Surplomb** E2   130ft/39m *

J. Brown, D. D. Whillans (1 pt-AL), 1953

A steep and strenuous route with a bold first pitch. Start as for Brant, below the sentry box.

1. 80ft/24m. 6a. Climb up into the sentry box. Make a difficult and long move R to reach a finger-hold, crux – this can be reached direct: harder! Continue up on widely spaced holds, soon easing to the traverse ledge of Slape (a VS which comes in from the R). Thrutch up the short overhanging chimney to a good belay ledge.

2. 50ft/15m. 5b. Bridge up the chimney until a swing out on to the L arete can be made. Continue up a shattered crack to a stance. Descent: traverse R stepping round the arete to abseil off as for First Amendment.

182 **Stroll On** E3   130ft/40m ***

R. Fawcett, P. Livesey, 1976

A splendid eliminate line with one extremely hard move. Start below an obvious groove 10yd/9m R of the Brant/Surplomb sentry box.

1. 6a. Climb the groove for a few feet then step R to a ledge. Go up to the tip of a pinnacle and follow the steep crack above to the overhang. Surmount this with a long reach for a good hold, crux, and continue up stepping R, then back L to finish up a small corner. Move R round the arete to abseil off as for First Amendment.

183 **Hangover** E1   150ft/45m **

J. Brown and party, 1951

An exposed and enjoyable classic. Start as for Stroll On.

1. 70ft/21m. 5a. Climb the groove for a few feet then step R to a ledge at the foot of a rounded groove. Climb this then step L and go up a crack to a small ledge. Care is needed with belays here.

2. 80ft/24m. 5b. Move round the arete and climb the wall just

The difficult Quasar

to its R to reach a ledge, crux. Traverse back L into the main
groove, directly above the stance and ascend it with difficulty to
a ledge and belay. Abseil off the holly tree at the top of the
groove – carefully!

184 **Quasar**   E3   120ft/37m **
J. Moran, A. Evans, E. Marshall, 1977
Another excellent eliminate in the Stroll On mould. Start
25ft/8m R of Hangover below a narrow groove which snakes up
to an overlap at 30ft/9m.
1. 6a. Climb the groove strenuously to the overlap and pull out
R to a large flake and good resting ledge. Follow the thin crack
above the flake, and using a hidden slot, reach a ledge on the L.
Climb the wall (as for Hangover) to another ledge. Take the
steep shallow groove (as for Kaisergebirge Wall) to belay on a
ledge on the L. Descend as for Hangover.

185 **Kaisergebirge Wall**   HVS   100ft/30m **
P. R. J. Harding, J. I. Disley, A. J. J. Moulam (7 pts), 1948
A much fallen-off and exposed route which takes an exciting
traverse across steep rock. Start 30ft/9m L of Central Gully at
the foot of the prominent diagonal line.
1. 5b. Follow the rising traverse L-wards to an awkward step
up and continue to the foot of a steep shallow groove. Enter this
with difficulty and continue for 15ft/5m to an easing, crux.
Continue up the groove, still awkward, to a ledge on the L.
Descend as for Hangover.

186 **Wind**   HVS   90ft/27m **
M. Crook, J. Moran, 1977
A popular little test-piece. Start as for Kaisergebirge Wall.
1. 5b. Go steeply up the crack to a tricky move at 50ft/15m,
crux. Continue more easily up a groove to finish on a large
ledge – Lords. Abseil off.

DRWS Y GWYNT   (621574)
This steep outcrop sits on the hillside above and just L of

Clogwyn y Grochan. Its dominant feature is a large, clean R-angled corner (reminiscent of Cenotaph). The finger-crack in the centre of its R wall is Too Hard for Jim Perrin E1, 5c with the wider crack at the arete taken by Cracked Wall (V Diff). The L arete is Demi Sec Dame, E3 6a.

187 **Little Sepulchre**   VS   80ft/24m *
J. I. Disley, P. R. J. Harding, A. J. J. Moulam, 1948
The central corner gives a superb pitch.
  1. 4b. Scramble up to some tall spikes, then move into the corner. Continue up the delightful corner crack – easier than it looks!

CARREG WASTAD   (625571)
This crag sits on the hillside a few hundred yards up the valley from Clogwyn y Grochan, opposite the Climbers Club Hut – Ynys Ettws, and is reached from the road in about ten minutes. On the L side, the ribbed slabby area is taken by Wrinkle, and in the centre, the large open corner running the full height of the cliff – Erosion Groove – is an obvious feature. Just R, the steep face with the long slanting overhang of Shadow Wall crossing it at two-thirds height also dominates this central area. R again, a line of yew trees marks the path of Dead Entrance (V Diff) after which the cliff becomes more broken, terminating in a reddish tower of friable rock. There are easy descent gullies at either side of the cliff.

188 **The Wrinkle**   V Diff   235ft/71m ***
M. P. Ward, J. E. Q. Barford, B. Pierre, 1947
One of the most popular routes of its grade in The Pass. The rock is very polished in places. Start at the L side of the cliff, L of an overhang, low down, and below a bulge at 60ft/18m (taken by Skylon, HS).
  1. 80ft/24m. Climb the steep wall, first R, then L to the Skylon overhang. Traverse R, exposed, to a ledge and nut belays in a corner.
  2. 65ft/20m. Climb the corner then make a strenuous move to

gain a ledge on the R. Climb a groove slanting back L and go up
a wrinkled slab to a good ledge.

3. 90ft/27m. Take the short crack on the R to the top of a small
pedestal. Climb the slabby grooves to a ledge. Finish up the
broken corner on the R to the top of the crag. The protection is
spaced! Belay well back.

189 **Lion** VS 285ft/86m **

P. R. J. Harding, A. J. J. Moulam, 1949

An entertaining route with a technically interesting second
pitch. Start well R of The Wrinkle, below a prominent groove,
just R of a large overhang at 60ft/18m – Brute 33, E2 5b 5c.

1. 60ft/18m. 4a. Take the easiest way up the wall to cracked
blocks. Go over these to a good belay ledge. (Unicorn, HVS
takes the groove above.)

2. 80ft/24m. 4c. Move R on to a step black slab and cross it
diagonally to the chockstone of Overhanging Chimney.
Surmount this awkwardly and cross the R wall to a stance. A
delightful pitch.

3. 65ft/20m. Climb the slab on the R. Go across a short
chimney and on to Crackstone Rib. Continue up a short wall to
a ledge and belays (as for Crackstone Rib).

4. 80ft/24m. 4a. Climb an easy groove on the R to a sloping
ledge (as for Crackstone Rib). Traverse R a few feet, then go up
to a tree on the L. Climb the huge flake. From its top, go up the
wall trending slightly L to the top.

190 **Elidor** E1 200ft/61m *

J. Harwood, R. High, 1964

A steep and exposed route tackling the blank-looking groove
above the Lion traverse. Start as for Lion.

1. 60ft/18m. 4a. As for Lion.

2. 140ft/43m. 5b. Step R on to a slab and go straight up
heading for the blank little groove (runners at its foot). Bridge
up this and move out L. Continue up to a R-ward traverse

Carreg Wastad

leading to a small ledge on the obvious arete. Ascend this in an airy position, then scramble to the top.

191 **Overlapping Wall**   E1   250ft/75m **

M. G. Hughes, unseconded, 1948

An open route of interest and character. The crux is much harder than the rest of the climb. Start below Overhanging Chimney, just L of a large overhang.

1. 90ft/27m. 4c. Climb up for 20ft/6m until a traverse R on good holds gains a small ledge. Ascend L then R to a quartzy ledge. From its L end, a shallow groove leads to a stance below the large chockstone of Overhanging Chimney.

2. 70ft/21m. 5b. Climb the groove until its L rib can be gained. Move L to climb the bulging overlap at its weakest point, crux. From a good nut, traverse L a little, then go up and follow a groove back R to a ledge. Move R to belay in the corner: an exciting pitch.

3. 90ft/27m. 4c. Make a rising R-ward traverse up on to the rib. Follow this in a superb position to finish at the top of Crackstone Rib.

192 **Crackstone Rib**   S   175ft/53m ***

J. M. Edwards, J. B. Joyce, 1935

A classic route which has become justifiably popular. Pitch 2 is very photogenic! Start below the central corner of Erosion Groove and slightly to its L.

1. 30ft/9m. Climb a short crack to a ledge. Belay on the L.

2. 80ft/24m. A well-worn traverse L leads towards the arete passing a depression, runners. Step boldly round on to the arete and climb it delicately up to a ledge. A short wall leads to a better ledge.

3. 65ft/20m. Climb the easy groove on the R to a corner, runner. Continue to a traverse line on the L wall. Follow it to a thin crack which quickly leads to the top.

193 **Ribstone Crack**   VS   160ft/48m *
J. I. Disley, A. J. J. Moulam (AL), 1951
A well-protected climb at the upper end of its grade. Start as for
Crackstone Rib.
1. 110ft/33m. 4c. Climb the short crack to a ledge, as for
Crackstone Rib. Step R and follow the continuation crack to a
small resting spot at 80ft/24m. Go up awkwardly to an open
groove and so to a sloping stance and belay on Crackstone Rib
– a sustained pitch.
2. 50ft/15m. 4a. Traverse back R and go up to a tree and flake
crack. Follow this to the top of the flake and finish up the wall.

194 **Erosion Groove/Direct Finish**
HVS/E2   180ft/55m **
D. D.Whillans and party (1 pt), 1953/D. D. Whillans, J. Brown, 1955
A disappointing route which follows the central corner;
however, the Direct Finish is a stunning little pitch! Start just R
of the foot of the corner below some holly trees.
1. 50ft/15m. Scramble up past the first holly and step L into a
crack which leads to a stance and belay on a huge flake.
2. 65ft/20m. 5a. Move across into the main corner which is
hard to start. Continue passing a small roof at 45ft/14m on the
L, crux, to an overhanging groove. Go up this awkwardly to a
stance. A pitch with its share of friable rock . . . one may now
finish quite easily up the corner, but better:
3. 65ft/20m. 5c. The Direct Finish. Step R and make a difficult
entry into the groove by thin bridging – good protection.
Follow the groove more easily to a final steepening, TR. A short
strenuous section leads to the top.

195 **Shadow Wall**   VS   150ft/45m ***
J. M. Edwards, J. B. Joyce, 1935
A good climb with an exciting crux traverse under the large
slanting overhang that more than compensates for a scrappy
start! Start just R of Erosion Groove where a corner slants up to
the L end of the overhang.

1. 90ft/27m. 4a. Climb the groove to a holly tree and continue up to a stance and belay below the huge roof.
2. 40ft/12m. 4c. Traverse under the roof using a system of three ledges. Each ledge is more difficult to gain than its precursor. From the final ledge, step round the corner, crux, and climb a groove to a tree belay.
3. 20ft/6m. Go easily up behind the tree to finish.

196 Yellow Crack HVS 160ft/48m *

H. I. Banner, C. T. Jones, 1958

A strenuous and satisfying climb – a gritstoner's delight. Start as for Shadow Wall.

1. 40ft/12m. Climb the groove on the R to a large holly tree.
2. 100ft/30m. 5b. Step R to the foot of a steep corner crack and climb it fairly easily for 20ft/6m. The crack soon bulges, leans L and becomes a 'real pig'. Jam up awkwardly to a wide ledge. Make a long step R into a groove (on Zangorilla) and take this for a few moves until a swing up L leads to a narrow ledge and the crux of Shadow Wall. Swing R round the rib and climb a groove to the Shadow Wall tree belay. Trilon (VS) reaches this point directly up a prominent rib.
3. 20ft/6m. Finish straight up behind the tree.

197 Zangorilla E3 160ft/48m **

A. Sharp, C. Dale, 1977

An impressive climb with a technical first pitch and a spectacular top pitch through the Shadow Wall roof. Start 10ft/3m R of Shadow Wall by a large flake.

1. 110ft/33m. 5c. Gain the steep groove above and climb it strenuously, with a difficult R-ward exit on to a ledge below the bulge on Trilon. Move back L to reach a steep leaning groove about 8ft/2m R of Yellow Crack. The groove proves very hard to start, but soon relents a little. Continue up and move round L to belay on the final ledge of Shadow Wall.
2. 50ft/15m. 5c. Undercut boldly out L across the large roof on the obvious line. Climb the wall above, passing a rattling block (if it's still there) to reach the top.

198 **Old Holborn** HVS 240ft/77m *

P. Crew, B. Ingle, D. Potts (1 pt), 1963

An uninspired start leads to an open and exhilarating finish. Start at a small rib with a groove either side, 40yd/37m R of Shadow Wall, below a steep tower which starts 70ft/21m up the crag, just to the R of a line of yew trees.

1. 90ft/28m. 4c. Climb the R-hand groove until a swing L gains the crest of the rib. Continue to a possible holly stance. Traverse R with difficulty to a slanting rake and climb to another holly tree stance – this is as for Bole Way (VS) which finishes up to the R of the Old Holborn tower.

2. 30ft/9m. 4a. Follow the steep L-slanting groove to the large ledge and tree belay at the foot of the tower.

3. 60ft/20m. 5b. Move L and climb a steep groove to the large overhang, PR. From a good handhold under the roof, make a bold swing out L to a hidden ledge. Move back R and follow the arete to small ledges. Poor belays.

4. 60ft/18m. 4c. Climb the wall behind the stance trending R to finish. A pitch requiring steadiness on the part of the leader.

DINAS CROMLECH   (629569)

This magnificent cliff stands like a sentinel 600ft/180m above Pont y Cromlech, guarding the upper reaches of The Pass. It is reached from the lay-by near the bridge in around twenty minutes – the easiest line is on the R.

The cliff is dominated by the massive open-book corner at its centre, the apex of which forms Cenotaph Corner. To the L of this, the next corner is Sabre Cut, rising from a large sloping rocky ledge about 80ft/24m up – The Forest. Further L, beyond the cracks of Dives, and Holly Buttress, lie three smaller corners: Pharaoh's Wall, Pharaoh's Passage and Parchment Passage, before the overhanging groove/niche of The Thing, and then more broken rock. To the R of Cenotaph Corner, beyond the impressive crack in its R wall, Cemetery Gates, the next large corner is Ivy Sepulchre. Way over on the R side of the cliff, past a heathery field, The Heath, the castellated Flying Buttress rises up in steps to join the main mass before

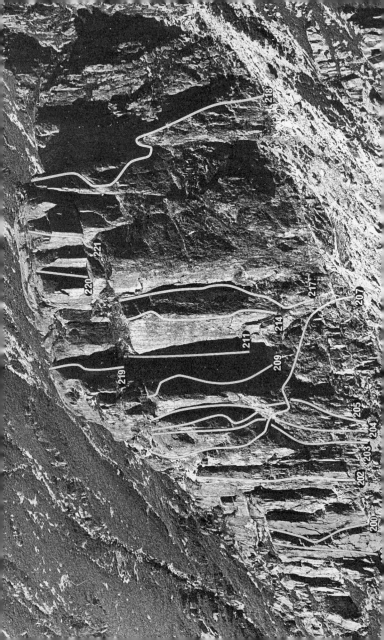

Castle Gully (Diff), a shattered buttress and the descent gully.
Above Cenotaph Corner, a series of grassy ledges and trees,
The Valley, traverse the cliff, above which lies a shorter section
containing several fierce cracks.

Descents: for routes finishing L of Sabre Cut, scramble up
and around over the top of the cliff to find the steep but easy
descent gully which curves round and down the R-hand side.
There is also a path which runs down to the L of the cliff, but
this is hard to locate and not recommended.

For climbs finishing on The Valley, it is easiest (and usual)
to abseil down just R of Cenotaph Corner. For those who hate
abseiling, the easy diagonal flake, Tributary Crack (Diff),
which splits the short wall above and L of Cenotaph, leads to an
easy ledge just below the top. Scramble over R-wards to the
descent gully.

199 **The Thing**   E2   125ft/39m **

J. Brown, D. D. Whillans, 1956

An exciting and well-protected route up the intimidating black
wall L of Parchment Passage. Start below an overhanging crack
that slants up R-wards to a groove/niche.
1. 80ft/24m. 5c. Climb the thin crack with difficulty and after a
couple of thin bridging moves, pull strenuously into a niche.
Jam up to the overlap and, using a flake, layback L on to a good
foothold, continue up past a sapling, trending R, then move
round the arete to belay on Parchment Passage.
2. 45ft/14m. 4c. Move back L and rejoin the crack which leads
amenably up to the top.

200 **Parchment Passage**   V Diff   140ft/43m

J. M. Edwards, O. S. Bell, 1933

A pleasant climb up the L-most corner of the cliff. The upper
section is very polished. Start at the foot of the corner.
1. 55ft/17m. Scramble up to a tree and belay.
2. 85ft/26m. Climb up to the L where an exposed high step on

Dinas Cromlech

polished holds gains a ramp leading back into the corner and an ancient holly. Possible belay. Move up to reach the L-hand of two short cracks. Follow this, then step R to avoid difficulties and finish direct. Scramble up over the top of the crag to descend down the gully on its R.

201 **Cobweb Crack**   VS   110ft/33m *
J. Brown, M. T. Sorrell, 1951

A sustained climb up the wall just R of Parchment Passage. Start a few feet L of that route at the foot of a short crack.

1. 40ft/12m. 4a. Take the crack on good holds then traverse L to a stance.
2. 70ft/21m. 4c. Above is a pocketed T-shaped crack, undercut at the start. Climb steeply up for 20ft/6m to better jams. Continue, fairly strenuous, until a couple of moves lead L into Parchment Passage. Finish up this.

The corner R of Cobweb Crack is taken by the disappointing Pharaoh's Passage (VS), whilst the corner R again gives the pleasant Pharaoh's Wall (VS). Next comes a steep, slanting pocketed crack, Pitch 1 of:

202 **Noah's Warning**   VS   220ft/67m ***
J. Brown, M. T. Sorrell, 1951

A fine sustained route, high in its grade. Start below the pocketed crack.

1. 130ft/40m. 4c. Ascend the crack past a large pothole and several bulges to an overhang. Turn this on the L to a ledge and belay.
2. 90ft/27m. 5a. Climb the chimney/crack behind the stance to reach an overhanging flake. Step R round this. Go straight up then back L to a thin crack. This leads to a difficult, rounded, and memorable finish on the L!

Cobweb Crack

203 **Dives/Better Things** HS 210ft/63m **

J. M. Edwards, T. E. Davies, 1933/T. D. Bourdillon, J. W. T. Tomlinson, M. J. Bell, 1949

A classic climb finishing up the slim corner L of Sabre Cut. R of Noah's Warning is the prominent wide corner/crack of Holly Buttress (VS). Just R of this is a steep corner/crack which leads to the L end of a black diagonal overhang; start below this.

1. 80ft/24m. 4a. Climb the crack on good holds then traverse diagonally R under the black overhang, through a wet section to belay as for Spiral Stairs on a large sloping ledge, The Forest.

2. 40ft/12m. Climb the crack on the L (as for Spiral Stairs) and belay above it, below the steep shallow V-corner.

3. 90ft/27m. 4a. The V-corner is taken direct, the first 30ft/9m providing the crux. The rest is airy but relatively easy!

204 **Sabre Cut** VS 180ft/55m ***

E. Pentir Williams, R. G. Williams, 1935

This excellent route has a fine finish up the first prominent corner L of Cenotaph. Start at a vertical corner 10ft/3m R of Dives.

1. 105ft/32m. 4c. Climb the corner until it divides. Step R and ascend the wall to The Forest. Go easily up to a fine belay at its top R-hand corner, below the arete.

2. 75ft/23m. 4b. Traverse L and climb the enjoyable corner crack to the top; the spaced protection adds to the buzz!

205 **Curfew** E1 220ft/67m *

J. Moran, G. Milburn, 1977 (Pitch 1 – Sabre Cut Direct Start by D. T. Roscoe and party, 1957)

A popular eliminate which just merits its grade. Start 15ft/5m R of Sabre Cut, below a rib R of a black overhang.

1. 100ft/30m. 5a. Climb the rib to a ramp which leads R-wards. From the end of this, step R into a steep corner leading to Spiral Stairs and thus reach a stance on The Forest.

2. 120ft/37m. 5b. Ascend the steep wall R of the tree on Spiral Stairs. Take the L arete past a ledge to a break running R.

Follow this until the wall above bulges. Make a couple of bold moves up to the R, crux, then continue up the exposed arete on good but slightly friable holds to finish.

206 **Foil**   E3   80ft/24m ***
P. Livesey, unseconded, 1976

A superb, sustained and well-protected crackline splitting the face R of Sabre Cut. Start from The Forest.

1. 6a. Follow the crack which increases in difficulty to some thin moves at 50ft/15m. Continue strenuously to a semi-rest at a large pocket. Undercut this and progress via finger jams and layaways to a precarious exit. Traverse L to belay at the top of Sabre Cut.

Now come the flanking walls of Cenotaph Corner, two huge sheets of rhyolite, pitted with pockets, dotted with small sharp holds, and split by the occasional crack. The climbs here are some of the best single pitches around . . . anywhere! However, though the next route starts below these sheer walls, it immediately scuttles off L in search of easier-angled rock.

207 **Spiral Stairs**   V Diff   280ft/84m **
J. M. Edwards, S. B. Darbishire, 1931

A polished and exposed route: by far the easiest way up this part of the cliff. Not recommended for complete novices as the traverse on Pitch 2 is quite serious to second. Start on the scree directly below the R arete of Cenotaph Corner.

1. 100ft/30m. Scramble easily up the rock steps and follow the path round to below the L wall of Cenotaph Corner. Good nut belays if you can find them.
2. 70ft/21m. Climb the short polished crack to an obvious L-ward traverse line. Follow this descending slightly for 50ft/15m until a rib leads up to a stance on The Forest.
3. 70ft/21m. Move up and traverse L to a crack. Climb this to a ledge on the L and continue up L on good holds until an easy slab leads to good belays but a poor stance.
4. 40ft/12m. Climb the crack/groove to finish up easy slabs.

Scramble to the top of the cliff and descend via the gully on the
R-hand side.

208 **Memory Lane**   E3   145ft/44m **

P. Livesey, J. Lawrence, G. Price, 1976

A fine, open and thrilling route, both serious and sustained.
Start below the L arete of Cenotaph Corner at the Spiral Stairs
belay. A crack leads up to The Forest.

1. 5c. Climb the polished crack and its steeper continuation to
The Forest. Step round on to the L wall of Cenotaph Corner.
Go directly up on pockets and finger-holds to the ledge of
Epitaph (which joins our route from Foil, a few feet to the L).
Continue steeply past a flake runner up the poorly protected
arete in an exhilarating position to finish . . . a runner in Left
Wall on the lower section is usual, although the route has been
done without it!

209 **Left Wall**   E2   140ft/43m ***

*R. Moseley, J. Smith, J. Sutherland (some aid), 1956/FFA: A. Garlick,
1970*

A fabulous pitch with good protection. The crack presents no
real difficulty (although leaders psyche out) until it forks L at
the top where it is sustained for 20ft/6m. The most fallen-off
route in The Pass. Start from the large sloping ledge below
Cenotaph Corner, about half-way up.

1. 5c. Climb diagonally L to stand on a broken ledge below the
crack proper. The crack is hard to start but soon eases.
Continue on good holds, steep, to an awkward few moves
where it bends to the R. A good resting spot below a flake soon
arrives. The crack forks just above. The L-hand branch is quite
strenuous and gives some anxious moments before a series of
'Thank God' holds lead L to the arete. Scramble up to finish.

Dinas Cromlech – the central walls

210 **Resurrection**   E4   145ft/44m ***

R. Edwards, N. Metcalfe (4 pts), 1975/FFA: P. Livesey, J. Lawrence, 1975

A magnificent wall climb. Sustained and fingery with a desperate (on first acquaintance) crux right at the top. Start just L of Cenotaph Corner.

1. 6a. Climb up trending L for 15ft/5m. Continue direct on pockets passing a faded TR to reach The Girdle Ledge. Move R to a flat rib of rock. Go up the L side of this, passing two PRs by a very hard move to reach better holds, then move across to join Left Wall, just below where the crack forks. Gain the R-hand branch with difficulty and follow the very sustained crack for 30ft/9m to a good spike and runner. The crack now closes. Either trend R-wards via a finger-wrenching sequence to reach a flat hold then finish direct (the most popular), or, from the spike, make a long reach L to sharp finger-holds and finish up the little groove just L again.

211 **Cenotaph Corner**   E1   120ft/37m ***

J. Brown, D. Belshaw (2 pts), 1952

Probably the most famous British rock climb. This perfect line in the middle of two almost featureless walls provides an immaculate pitch. Start below it.

1. 5c. Climb the corner to a difficult move at 25ft/8m. Continue more easily and use a crack on the L wall to reach a widening of the corner crack. Jam, bridge and wedge up past a chockstone (the Pudding Stone) to gain a shallow niche. Bridge up delicately past a couple of PRs (and good wires) and pull into the crack above with difficulty. A couple of quick moves gain good finishing holds. Belay on a tree to the R.

212 **Lord of the Flies**   E6   130ft/40m ***

R. Fawcett, C. Gibb, 1979

A simply stunning route of impeccable quality. A classic pitch

On the cruxes of Resurrection (right) and Left Wall

just R of Cenotaph Corner. Start about 12ft/4m R of Cenotaph below some thin vertical cracks.

1. 6a. Climb the cracks until they peter out, then go straight up on good pockets to a finger-ledge. Traverse boldly R on this and move up to a broken pocket. Make some very thin moves up L crux, to another pocket. Step R and climb direct to reach better holds leading up to The Girdle ledge. Take the wall behind a good runner to a finger ledge. Bold moves lead to the base of a shallow groove and improving holds. Finish up the groove past a bomb-proof runner . . . there is one very hard move!

213 **Right Wall**   E5   150ft/46m ***

P. Livesey, unseconded, 1974

This excellent route, the original way up the wall, was a quantum leap forward in climbing concepts at the time it was put up. Its fearsome reputation has long since been dispelled and the route is now sought after by every aspiring 'tiger'. It should not, however, be underestimated! Start at the R-hand end of the grassy ledge below a short wall and shallow corner leading up to a L-slanting crack.

1. 6a. Move up on to a ledge. Step L out of the shallow corner and take the diagonal crack to a runner at its top. Step back R and climb direct to a finger ledge. This leads up and R to a good resting place. Step up on to a large square foothold and climb diagonally L to reach a large shattered pocket. From the top of this, step L and go up on small pockets to The Girdle ledge. Traverse R until directly below a shallow pocket, The Porthole, 20ft/6m above. Climb the wall just to the R, then step into it and thus reach a series of good holds leading R past a prominent spike. At the end of these, finish direct up a thin crack . . . a fantastic pitch!

214 **Cemetery Gates**   E1   170ft/51m ***

J. Brown, D. D. Whillans (AL), 1951

Yet another of the great Cromlech Classics! An exciting and open route which is quite serious for a couple of steep moves at 40ft/12m but is otherwise well protected. It takes the obvious

crack up the edge of the right wall of Cenotaph Corner. On the
R-hand side of the ledge at the foot of the Corner is a large flake.
Descend this to a tree belay below the R arete.

1. 110ft/33m. 5b. Go up to the R of the arete, then move L to
the foot of the crack. Enter it with difficulty and continue
steeply, but easily, past a couple of fingery moves at 60ft/18m
on to a ledge. Take the crack above, with some difficult moves
to reach The Girdle ledge. Belay.

2. 60ft/18m. 4c. From the R-hand end of the ledge, climb a
wide crack for 15ft/5m. Step round the arete and climb steeply
up on a series of large incut holds to finish. An airy pitch.

215 The Cromlech Girdle E2 240ft/72m ***

D. D. Whillans, J. Brown (3 pts), 1956

A splendid route of interest and character. Only the best part of
the full route, the pitches crossing the L and R walls of
Cenotaph Corner, are described here. Start from The Forest, at
a belay on the edge of the L wall of Cenotaph Corner.

1. 100ft/30m. 5b. Step round the corner on to the wall. Climb
up a few feet then move R to join the crack of Left Wall. Follow
this to a good flake and nut. Climb back down for 10ft/3m and
make several fingery moves across to reach the horizontal
break. Traverse this more easily into Cenotaph Corner. Climb
up to where the crack widens and belay. Care should be taken
to protect the second on this pitch!

2. 80ft/24m. 5b. Ascend the wide crack to put a runner on the
Pudding Stone – a strong party may not find this necessary.
Descend to the start of a narrow ledge which runs across the R
wall. Follow this using pockets on the wall above until a
difficult move leads to the wide ledge which extends R-wards to
the Cemetery Gates belay.

3. 60ft/18m. 4c. Finish up the wide crack on the R for 15ft/5m,
then step round the arete and go up on 'Thank God' holds – as
for The Gates.

216 **Ivory Madonna**   E5   260ft/80m ***

R. Fawcett, P. Williams, 1980

A superb R to L girdle of the main Cromlech walls. Start at the
foot of Cemetery Gates.

1. 140ft/43m. 6b. Ascend Cemetery Gates to the first good
resting ledge at 60ft/18m. Follow a narrow ledge L-wards to
Lord, from which a desperately sustained 20ft/6m of
doigt-dinging technicality sometimes gives access to Cenotaph
Corner. Go up for 15ft/5m to belay.

2. 120ft/37m. 6a. A hard move L (hands level with the start of
The Girdle ledge crossing the R wall, and just below an overlap
on the L wall) gains two good pockets. Continue L to a flake
runner, step down and go across to meet Left Wall below its
crux. Move boldly out L along a rising line of widely spaced
pockets to join Memory Lane at a perched block 15ft/5m from
the top. Finish up the arete.

217 **Ivy Sepulchre**   E1   210ft/63m **

P. R. J. Harding, E. H. Phillips (2 pts), 1947

An interesting climb up the great corner R of Cemetery Gates
with one short difficult section moving out of a niche. Start
directly below this corner on a grassy ledge.

1. 80ft/24m. Climb vegetated rock and go up L to reach a crack
leading to trees. Traverse R along a path then scramble up over
two rock steps to the foot of the corner proper. Or, reach this
point by a traverse from the start of Cemetery Gates.

2. 110ft/33m. 5b. Climb steeply up the corner to a good hold
on the L. Continue more easily and jam up into the large niche
below an overhang. The next section is difficult until
fingerholds on the R wall enable better holds on the L to be
gained. Follow the corner without further difficulty to belay by
an oak tree just below the top.

3. 20ft/6m. Step L and finish direct.

218 **Flying Buttress**   V Diff   305ft/92m ***

J. M. Edwards, solo, 1931

A classic of its grade, steep and exposed but with good holds.

Very, very polished. Start high up on the R side of the cliff
below a well-worn castellated ridge.

1. 60ft/18m. Climb the crest of the ridge on large holds.

2. 60ft/18m. Continue up to the pinnacles on top of the ridge.
Belay.

3. 20ft/6m. Climb down over pinnacles to belay on the L wall
of the gully – Castle Gully.

4. 50ft/15m. Climb the large rock steps on the L wall, then step
round the corner crossing a little groove (or reach this point
from below) to a traverse line. Take this easily L-wards to an
exposed stance by a large flake.

5. 65ft/20m. Climb the steep wall behind the flake to gain a
gangway. Take this R-wards past a ledge to belay below a
chimney.

6. 50ft/15m. Enter the chimney, crux, and continue more
easily to the top. Descend via the gully well to the R.

219 Misty Wall   E1   60ft/18m
L. McGinley and party, 1979

A smart but serious little pitch, useful as a finish to Cenotaph
Corner. Start by a flake at the foot of the wall above and L of the
top of Cenotaph Corner.

1. 5b. Climb up to reach a ledge just L of the sapling. Move R
and go steeply up the bulging wall on good holds to finish
awkwardly via a short crack in the centre.

220 Grond   E2   60ft/18m ***
D. D. Whillans and party, 1958

An immaculate jamming problem. Start below a clean-cut
overhanging corner/crack, above and just R of the finish of Ivy
Sepulchre.

1. 5b. The first 20ft/6m are best tackled by laybacking . . . and
now it's up to you. If you're strong, you will love it! Superbly
butch!

221 **The Monster**   E1   70ft/21m *
M. Boysen, E. Volas, 1972
A good exposed crack pitch: rather on the physical side! Start
below the corner R of Grond.
1. 5c. Move up and traverse R to gain the wide crack by a
tricky move. Follow the sustained crack which widens
uncomfortably near the top. Finish awkwardly L of a perched
block.

Llanberis Pass (South Side)

DINAS BACH   (632560)
This delightful little crag lies 200yd/186m to the R of the road
as one travels up from Pont y Cromlech to Pen y Pass. It is best
approached from the Cromlech lay-by in about twenty
minutes. Walk up the road for about 500yd/450m then strike
directly up the hillside towards it.

The cliff has two main facets separated by the obvious Ash
Tree Gully (Diff). The East Wing presents a clean smooth
slabby wall facing down towards Nant Peris; there is a huge
flake at its lower end. The West Wing is much more broken,
comprising short walls, ledges, slabs and overhangs. Descents
are either via abseil, Ash Tree Gully, or well over to the R.

222 **Flake Chimney**   Diff   100ft/30m *
H. R. C. Carr, M. W. Guinness, 1925
An interesting little route up the flake and continuation wall at
the lowest point of the East Wing; start at the R-hand side of the
flake.
1. 50ft/15m. Climb the chimney: a bit of a struggle.
2. 50ft/15m. Step across on to the wall and move R to a good
ledge. Finish up the steep crack on the R.

Flake Traverse

223 **Flake Traverse**   Diff   85ft/26m *
P. L. Roberts, R. D. Crofton, 1931

An exposed climb on huge holds. Start R of Flake Chimney, past the R side of the slabby wall, below a series of flakes running up the L wall at the mouth of Ash Tree Gully.

1. Climb up and L on well-scratched holds. Follow large flakes up and R (very polished) to a ledge just below the top. Step up and L to finish steeply. Good nut belays.

DINAS MOT   (627563)

Dinas Mot lies at the end of the N ridge of Crib Goch, about fifteen minutes' walk from the Pont y Cromlech car-park. The dominant feature of the cliff is a huge triangular area of slabby rock at its centre, The Nose, which is flanked on the L by a towering buttress bristling with overhangs, the Eastern Wing. To the R lies the Western Wing, split by two gullies and ending in the superb Plexus Buttress. Both Wings contain routes that take in some impressive territory and are generally steep with perhaps a small amount of lichen, in marked contrast to The Nose, which offers delicate climbing on clean sound rock.

   Descents: from the top of The Nose, descend down either of the gullies which separate it from the main ridge – Eastern Gully (Diff) on the L which has a nasty step near its foot (a 'stopper' when wet) or Western Gully (Mod), by far the easiest and most pleasant way down. For the Eastern Wing, descend the shallow gully and rocky hillside well to the L of the buttress (i.e. beyond Staircase Gully which defines its L edge), while for routes on the Western Wing, Jammed Boulder Gully (Mod) provides the normal descent route though this needs care; alternatively, it is easy enough to walk around to find the descent L of the Eastern Wing.

The Eastern Wing
The Eastern Wing is split at half-height by a series of grassy

Dinas Mot – the Eastern Wing

breaks. Above and to the L is a steep tower of rock with a line of undercut slabs which slant up R-wards, cutting through the overhangs, the line of:

224 **The Mole**   HVS   275ft/83m ***

J. Brown, E. D. G. Langmuir, 1961

An enjoyable route on sound rock. Start on the L side of the crag at a small grassy rake, just above the large grassy rake of Troglodyte Wall (VS).

1. 90ft/27m. 4a. Follow the rake to a steep slab. Climb this to a grassy ledge just R of a huge flake.
2. 110ft/33m. 5a. Surmount the huge flake and move L to a steep rib. Ascend this, crux, and move R to a diagonal slab. Go up the corner for a few feet then traverse R under the roof until a short groove leads to a ledge and belays.
3. 75ft/23m. 4c. Follow a groove on the L until a R-ward traverse leads to ledges. Finish with care up rock and grass. Descend well over to the L.

225 **Gollum**   HVS   300ft/90m **

B. C. Webb, A. Harris, V. Cowley (2 pts), 1964/FFA: J. Perrin, 1966

A wandering but continually interesting line with some sensational moves over an overhang on its third pitch which atone for a grassy ramble on the second! Start on a large grassy pedestal at the foot of the buttress.

1. 40ft/12m. 5a. Climb diagonally R and surmount a small bulge, PR, to reach a slab with a belay above and L.
2. 60ft/18m. 4b. Move R into the flake crack and climb this on good holds to a tree on the grassy rake of Troglodyte Wall. Walk 50ft/15m along the rake to reach the huge flake stance of The Mole.
3. 110ft/33m. 5b. Climb diagonally R up the slab for 30ft/9m to a weakness in the overhangs. Pull strenuously over, PR, to finish on large holds on the L. Continue up a delicate groove then move L and go up to the second stance of The Mole.

Gollum: turning the overhang on pitch 3

4. 90ft/27m. 4b. Traverse R across the slab to reach a steep arete and climb this to the top. Descend as for The Mole.

The Nose

This is by far the most popular area of Dinas Mot. All the climbs described required a certain amount of finesse on their slabby lower sections where good footwork enables the arms to be saved for the steep cracks and corners of the final headwall.

226 **The Cracks** HS 290ft/90m **

B. L. Bathhurst, H. C. H. Bathhurst (4 pts), 1930/FFA:
C. F. Kirkus, 1930

This enjoyable climb is a classic at its standard and takes a line up the L edge of The Nose. Pitch 6 has a 4c mantelshelf, which can be avoided! Start just L and up from the lowest point of the buttress.

1. 40ft/12m. Climb easily up R, then follow a shallow groove to a small stance on the R.
2. 60ft/18m. Step up and climb a narrow slab trending L to reach a short crack. Take this to a stance below an overhang.
3. 45ft/14m. Undercut delicately R under the overhang into a chimney which soon leads to a good stance.
4. 45ft/14m. Climb twin cracks in the slab on the L to gain a large ledge and pinnacle belay on the R.
5. 60ft/18m. Climb the pinnacle and step awkwardly R on to a ledge below a corner. Go up the steep crack in the L wall to a stance overlooking Eastern Gully.
6. 45ft/14m. 4c. Move up R to make a difficult mantelshelf on to a rounded ledge. Traverse L and ascend to the top of The Nose with ease. The crux can be avoided by climbing the arete above the stance or escaping into Eastern Gully.

227 **The Direct Route** VS 245ft/74m ***

C. F. Kirkus, J. B. Dodd, 1930

The obvious shallow groove up the centre of The Nose is a must

Dinas Mot – The Nose

for all competent VS leaders! Start at the lowest point of the buttress, L of the prominent rock scar.

1. 50ft/15m. 4a. Scramble up broken rocks past a pedestal then continue up for 30ft/12m before stepping round L on to The Cracks belay.

2. 90ft/27m. 4b. Climb diagonally R-wards over a blunt rib to the foot of a light-coloured groove. Step L up a ramp then step back into the groove which is followed pleasantly to reach a large stance in a bay.

3. 50ft/15m. 4c. The Hand Traverse. Move easily up R on large holds to the start of a steep diagonal crack. Hand traverse this until a few moves up gain a long flat ledge with huge flake belays.

4. 55ft/17m. 5b. The smooth corner on the L is a 'little poser' to start, crux – or use combined tactics! Shimmy up the flake above to finish with care via a short corner which is often damp.

228 **Superdirect**   E1   245ft/75m **

R. Evans, H. Pasquill, 1974

A high-calibre eliminate which sneaks up in between The Direct and Diagonal. Since part of the first pitch collapsed, the route is now reached from The Direct Route; start at the lowest point of the buttress, L of the rock scar, as for The Direct, and Diagonal.

1. 70ft/21m. 4b. Scramble up over twin pinnacles and continue to a spike, a few feet higher. Move down to the R and traverse across the obvious line just above the rock scar. Move up to a ledge about 20ft/6m below a small overhang. Belay.

2. 130ft/40m. 5b. Climb up past the overhang to a good runner slot and continue for another 8ft/2m whence a couple of delicate steps L gain a crack. Follow this and move R on to a precariously balanced flake. Step back into the crack which leads to the long ledge and flake belays of The Direct.

3. 45ft/14m. 5b. Climb the pointed flake and bridge up the

Climbers on The Direct Route (left) and Diagonal

short corner to the overhang. A strenuous layback soon gains good finishing holds.

229 **Diagonal**   HVS   260ft/78m ***
A. Birtwistle, G. F. Parkinson, 1938

This superb route meanders boldly out across the centre of The Nose, with only moderate protection. Pitch 3 is guaranteed to get the adrenalin flowing. Start at the lowest point of The Nose, as for Superdirect.

1. 80ft/24m. 5a. Go up to and over twin pinnacles. Continue up the groove to the L side of a huge flake. From the tip of this move up a few feet then make a difficult R-ward traverse to a stance under a small overhang – this is more in keeping with the following pitches. Or, climb the first pitch of Superdirect and belay on a ledge below – easier.

2. 40ft/12m. 5a. Above is a large overhang terminating on its R in a prominent V-chimney. The chimney can be reached in two ways: either climb up to the L side of the overhang, good nut slot, and make a hard traverse underneath it, or, more easily, follow a diagonal line to good holds below and R of the chimney, then pull up into it. Exit L at the top on to a good ledge.

3. 100ft/30m. 5a. Traverse delicately R into a shallow scoop. Climb this and move R to make the famous mantelshelf on to a small ledge. Use a good pocket up on the R to reach an easy crack which leads to a ledge. Possible belays. Continue along the crack and scramble up to a stance below the final steep corner crack.

4. 40ft/12m. 4c. The strenuous corner crack succumbs to a forceful attack!

230 **West Rib**   HVS   225ft/68m *
C. F. Kirkus, I. M. Waller, 1931

A fine route in the Diagonal mould though not quite as good. It takes the faint rib R of The Link – a prominent dark overhanging chimney/crack. Poor protection makes the exposure well felt. Start directly below The Link, at the foot of the buttress.

1. 60ft/18m. 4b. Climb straight up to a good nut. Traverse R and then go up to a stance by two flakes 15ft/5m L of the rib.
2. 105ft/32m. 5a. Traverse R past a flat-topped spike to the crest of the rib. Follow this with a difficult step up to reach a ledge at 30ft/9m. Continue delicately, trending L, then climb direct to belay at a large flake on Western Slabs.
3. 60ft/18m. 4c. Move L around the arete. Climb a thin crack with some creaking flakes to a mantelshelf exit on to the arete. Move delicately R to finish up Western Slabs; or climb the finger-crack from the top of the large flake – The Chain, E1 5b.

231 **Western Slabs** VS 200ft/60m **

J. M. Edwards, A. R. Edge, A. M. D'Aeth, 1931

This enjoyable route finds the easiest way up the R side of The Nose. Start just L of the stile.

1. 50ft/15m. 4b. From the top of a quartzy block pull up on to a ledge and climb to a groove slanting up to the R. From the top of this move round the arete to a ledge with small belays. This point can also be reached direct – 4c.
2. 90ft/27m. 4b. From the ledge above go up to the lower of two small overlaps. Pass this on the R to a small sharp spike. Sling. Move across R under the next overlap into a groove. Climb this to a ledge. Continue up into a shallow groove which leads R-wards to a ledge overlooking Western Gully.
3. 60ft/18m. 4b. Move L and climb an easy groove to another ledge with a huge flake (at the top of West Rib Pitch 2). Climb the groove on the R to a hard R-ward exit above a block to gain a ledge. Finish easily.

The Western Wing

The large buttress on the R of The Nose is split at half-height by a series of huge grassy ledges, The Great Terrace. Below this, and just R of Western Gully, is a large black slab which is often wet, the lower part of:

232 **Black Spring**   HVS   580ft/176m **

M. Boysen, A. Williams, 1965

An excellent route which is long and rambling. Some
route-finding nous is required although the line is fairly
obvious. Start 10yd/9m R of Western Gully.

1. 50ft/15m. Go up a wet wall to a grassy terrace below the
steep black slab.

2. 90ft/27m. 5a. Climb a prominent crack for 30ft/9m then
move L for 10ft/3m until pockets lead up the steepening slab to
a bulge. Go over this and ascend delicately L-wards to reach a
cave stance. PBS.

3. 110ft/33m. 5a. Pull over the roof just R of the stance then
move R on to a steep slab. Climb this trending L to reach an
obvious quartzy crack/groove. Climb this more easily to a
grassy break – The Great Terrace.

4. 90ft/27m. 4a. Climb straight up over broken rock past two
small trees to a steep wall below a large overhang. Flake belay.

5. 120ft/37m. 4c. Layback up the crack on the L to below the
roof. A long easy traverse R leads to a stance where the roof
peters out.

6. 120ft/37m. 4a. Go easily up open slabs to the top. Descent:
Descend Jammed Boulder Gully (Mod) which defines the R
edge of the buttress (hard if wet) or walk along the top of the
crag to descend well L of the Eastern Wing – easier but longer.

R of Jammed Boulder is the slim but scruffy Groper Buttress,
bounded on its R by the Black Cleft (S) – a dark greasy gully,
best taken in a heatwave, or in the depths of winter.

Plexus Buttress

Just R of the Black Cleft, the large slabby Plexus Buttress is
split at two-thirds height by a barrier of massive roofs with
another roof above. Three superb climbs find their way up the
more amenable R side of the buttress, the first of which is:

233 **Plexus**   HVS   450ft/137m **
B. Ingle, P. Crew (AL), (2 pts), 1962
The original route of the buttress gives delicate climbing on
perfect rock. Start at the R-hand side of the buttress below a
large ledge.
1. 70ft/21m. Climb a groove to gain the ledge. Traverse easily
L to belay at the foot of a shallow groove.
2. 150ft/46m. 5a. Go up to a bulge (PR) which is overcome
awkwardly to reach a slab on the R. Step up and L to a crack.
Follow this and the groove above on good holds. Where the
climbing steepens, move L to an arete and continue up slabs to
a stance under the massive roof.
3. 120ft/37m. 5b. Move R to a groove in the overhang. Enter
this with difficulty (PR) then step L into a corner. Climb this
then move R to a very thin slab which leads to a ledge by a
detached block. Go over the block to a L-leading scoop. Mantel
out R and continue diagonally L to a stance.
4. 110ft/33m. 4b. Follow grooves and slabs to the top. Descend
down Jammed Boulder Gully.

234 **Ten Degrees North**   E2   430ft/129m **
A. Sharp, J. J. Zangwill, 1974
A bold and open climb which sneaks up in between Plexus and
Nexus. Start as for Plexus.
1. 70ft/21m. As for Plexus to the foot of the shallow groove.
2. 50ft/15m. 5b. Climb a short wall on the R then move R to a
PR. Climb up to a groove, step L and gain a slab with difficulty,
junction with Plexus. Nut belay. A deceptively steep pitch!
3. 110ft/33m. 5c. Precariously climb the open corner on the R
(good hold at the top on the L) and exit R on to a slab. Take this
delicately to a small overhang and continue up R-wards to the
large roof. Traverse R to flake belays, as on Nexus.
4. 90ft/27m. 5b. Ascend the crack on the L-hand side of the
flake to join the Nexus traverse. Follow this L-wards to belay on
Plexus.
5. 10ft/33m. 4b. Continue up grooves and slabs, as for Plexus.

235 **Nexus**   E1   430ft/130m ***

M. Boysen, P. Nunn (1 pt), 1963

An exhilarating climb with a magnificent second pitch, never unduly difficult, but nicely sustained. Start at the R side of the buttress, as for Plexus.

1. 30ft/9m. As for Plexus to the large ledge.
2. 150ft/46m. 5b. Go up the slab on the R of the corner to the overhang. Hand traverse L to a TR on the arete. Step up to the overhang, runner, then layback boldly round it on to a narrow ramp running up to the R. Follow the sustained ramp in a fine position to a steepening where a hard move gains a sloping ledge on the R. Climb the short overhanging crack and continue up a shallow groove to a good stance and flake belays.
3. 40ft/12m. 4b. Climb the slab on the R then move L to a ledge and PB.
4. 100ft/30m. 5b. Traverse L along the obvious horizontal crack. Swing round the arete on a hidden side-pull to reach a slab on the upper part of Plexus Pitch 3.
5. 110ft/33m. 4b. Finish pleasantly up grooves and slabs as for Plexus.

CRAIG Y RHAEADR   (622562)

This large red and white rambling crag lies on the L side of lower Cwm Glas Mawr and can be reached along the path leading up to Cyrn Las in around thirty minutes.

A waterfall cascades down the centre of the cliff, dropping from black overhangs 200ft/61m up and drenching the rock in all but the driest of summers. At its foot lies an enormous block, The Pedestal, and well over to the L sits the Cwm Glas Pinnacle, a detached rock pillar.

Although there are several fine routes on its walls, this crag has never been a popular place to visit in the summer, so one can find peace and quiet here, away from the noisy roadside crags. In winter, however, things change. The waterfall freezes, forming two huge ice curtains, given that the winter is a sharp

Dinas Mot – Plexus Buttress

one, and the ice climber has to queue for his chosen route, be it
Central Icefall direct VI on the L, or Cascade V to the R.

236 **The Wall**   E1   350ft/107m *

J. Brown, A. C. Cain, C. T. Jones, 1959

A good steep route up the large white wall, midway between
the red walls and the Cwm Glas Pinnacle. Protection is
moderate but the rock is generally rough and compact. Start at
the base of the wall.

1. 140ft/43m. 5a. Follow the obvious traverse line steeply up
R-wards, then move back L on another traverse to the foot of a
smooth grooved wall. Climb this for 20ft/6m, crux, then trend
up R making for the L edge of some grassy ledges. Move
diagonally L to a small grassy ledge and PB, directly above the
crux.

2. 150ft/46m. 4c. Traverse L for 10ft/3m, then go up on good
holds to enter a V-chimney. Follow this to grass and rock.
Continue more easily to a good grass ledge.

3. 60ft/18m. 4c. Climb the corner behind the ledge to finish up
easier ground above.

CYRN LAS   (615559)

This imposing cliff rises for some 500ft/154m from the screes
and dominates upper Cwm Glas Mawr. It is reached in about
forty-five minutes by taking the path to the R of the stream
which runs down from Cwm Glas.

The crag is divided into three buttresses by the deep gash of
Great Gully (V Diff) on the L, and Schoolmaster's Gully (S),
the narrow vertical chimney on the R. The two outer buttresses
have little coherent rock, but the magnificent central area,
Great Buttress, gives outstanding routes which are on good
rock in positions as exposed as any in North Wales. On its L
side is a slabby area taken by Main Wall, before the
groove/corner line of Subsidiary Groove, E1 4a, 4b, 5a, 4c, 5b.
Next comes the front of the buttress proper, a bulging area
taken by Lubyanka, The Skull and Great Buttress with the
prominent L-ward slanting cracks of The Grooves, R again.

Cyrn Las

There are two descents: either traverse across to the path from Upper Cwm Glas which lies *well over* to the L of the crag, or, for routes other than Main Wall, it is possible to scramble up and over the top of the crag to descend scree and a gully well to the R – this is more tedious than the L descent, but easier than the approach!

237 **Main Wall** HS 465ft/140m ***
P. L. Roberts, J. K. Cooke, 1935

One of the great classic routes of its standard in Britain! Good holds, good rock, impressive scenery and some awkward moves above the void combine to give a memorable outing up the L side of the Great Buttress. A serious mountaineering route demanding a competent approach. Start on a ledge below the L-hand side of the buttress, down and to the L of a triangular overhang with a grass ledge above.

1. 70ft/21m. 4a. Go diagonally L up the well-worn slab to a vegetated ledge at 30ft/9m. Move up a short corner for 10ft/3m, then go across a slab to step round a rib on the R and ascend to a pulpit stance.

2. 80ft/24m. 4b. A gangway slants up R to the chimney of Subsidiary Groove (which continues direct). Climb this awkwardly and then take the chimney for a few moves before a L-ward traverse along a ledge leads to a stance in a corner on the edge of the buttress. PB.

3. 45ft/14m. 4a. Climb the arete above. Good holds now lead diagonally R to a large triangular ledge in the corner.

4. 90ft/27m. 4b. Step down a few feet, move L and climb to the tip of a flaky pinnacle. Step across and pull up L-wards on to the steep wall and up into a niche. Traverse L around the corner to a ledge below a steep arete. Climb this on small but positive holds, then step across a chimney to a small slab which provides a stance and belay. A fine pitch on which problems of communication between leader and second are not uncommon!

5. 80ft/24m. 4a. Go up to an overhang then move L across a broken chimney to the base of a fine slab overlooking Great Gully. Ascend the L side of this on superb holds to a good stance.

6. 100ft/30m. A groove on the L, then a slab, lead to scrambling and the top.

Main Wall, just above the flaky pinnacle

238 **Lubyanka**   E3   400ft/120m **

E. Cleasby, J. Eastham, R. Matheson (AL), 1976

A bold, technical and sustained quality route with a thrilling finale. Start as for Main Wall.

1. 70ft/21m. 4a. As for Main Wall to the pulpit stance.
2. 80ft/24m. 4b. Follow the gangway up R-wards to the chimney (as for Main Wall) and climb it until a pull out R leads to a stance behind a large flake.
3. 60ft/18m. 5c. Above the flake is an obvious groove which is difficult to start. Enter it from the L and continue up to a large stance and PBS – a sustained pitch.
4. 50ft/15m. 5b. Go up the corner behind the stance, move out R at the top and descend a slab to a nut and PBS.
5. 70ft/21m. 5b. Climb directly up the slab, over the overlap on good holds to reach the foot of a short corner. Up this with one very hard move, then exit boldly L up a short slab to a small ledge and good nut belays.
6. 70ft/21m. 5c. Hand traverse the quartz band above the overhang in a wild position for 10ft/3m until a small hold on the rib above allows one to stand on it. Climb the groove (good holds round to the L) until it bends R to form a roof. Layback boldly through this to reach good holds and an easy slab. Go up this to nut belays.

239 **The Great Buttress**   E2   460ft/139m *

B. Ingle, P. Crew (AL), (1 pt), 1963/FFA: R. and A. Barley, c. 1964

Another fine open route which takes a line up the very centre of the buttress. The climbing is both delicate and strenuous. Start as for Main Wall.

1. 90ft/27m. 4c. A steep slab then a short strenuous chimney lead to a grassy terrace below the chimney of Subsidiary Groove.
2. 100ft/30m. 4c. Ascend a steep flake to the L of the arete. Climb down slightly and move R round the arete to a wall. Gain the foot of the L-shaped Helter Skelter Chimney on the L. Climb this to a stance, level with the flake on Lubyanka.
3. 80ft/24m. 5b. Traverse R to the arete and make a hard move

up to a small ledge. Move 10ft/3m R into a dark smooth
lichenous corner. Climb this then move L for 10ft/3m along a
narrow quartzy ledge. Go steeply up then diagonally R on flake
holds leading up to a niche. Belay.
4. 40ft/12m. 5c. The brutal overhanging crack above
succumbs to a combination of jamming, bridging, laybacking
(all very strenuous) – and swearing! – to a stance on the L.
5. 150ft/46m. 5a. Trend R to climb a steep cracked wall.
Continue up a R-ward leaning groove and the final groove of
The Grooves.

240 **The Skull**   E4   420ft/127m **

M. Boysen, A. Williams, J. Jordan (5 pts), 1966/FFA: R. Evans,
H. Pasquill, c. 1974

A tremendously exposed route, continuously difficult and with
a spectacular top pitch up a groove splitting the bulging central
headwall. Start as for Great Buttress.
1. 90ft/27m. 4c. As for Great Buttress.
2. 100ft/30m. 4c. As for Great Buttress.
3. 50ft/15m. 5c. Step down L and climb awkwardly L using a
suspect flake to reach a thin crack. Climb this strenuously to a
stance.
4. 50ft/15m. 6a. Move R round the overhanging arete to get
established in a shallow groove. Climb this with great
difficulty, then ascend the slab to a PR, and junction with
Lubyanka.
5. 130ft/40m. 5c. Climb the slab behind the belay, trending up
R to the foot of the prominent leaning groove. Make a hard step
R and continue up the R wall of the groove to a small ledge. The
groove now becomes mean and only yields to wide bridging
(good nut protection). At an old PR, the climbing eases and an
easy slab and block belay at the top of the groove are soon
reached. A sensational pitch.

241 **The Grooves**   E1   370ft/113m ***

J. Brown, D. Cowan, E. Price (1 pt), 1953

A superb route of interest and character up the series of

prominent grooves on the R-hand side of the buttress. Although nowhere desperate, interest is well maintained. Good protection. Start just L of Schoolmaster's Gully, below a prominent L-slanting groove line with an overhang at its base.

1. 120ft/37m. 5b. Go up easily to the overhang. Pull round this (hard if greasy), step L and back R into the groove. Straightforward climbing eventually leads to a grassy bay on the L.

2. 20ft/6m. 4a. Climb a short wall on the L to a stance below the second groove.

3. 120ft/37m. 5b. Climb a rib on the R to a little groove. A hard move up this and awkward jamming lead to an overhang. Step L on small holds to the foot of the main groove. Climb this for 60ft/18m by a variety of jamming techniques to land gasping on a ledge. Continue more easily up a short corner and exit R to a large ledge.

4. 110ft/33m. 5a. Step up R on to a sloping ledge. Traverse easily L round a corner to the foot of an overhanging groove. Take this on large holds, PR, until a tricky move R gains an easier groove leading up to finish.

242 **The Overhanging Arete**   E2   120ft/37m ***

H. I. Banner, J. O'Neill (1 pt), 1958

An awesome pitch up the arete R of the last pitch of The Grooves. Start up the large corner 10yd/9m R of the stance at the top of Pitch 3.

4a. 5b. Climb the corner for 30ft/9m until a line of holds leads L to a huge jug on the arete. Pull steeply up to another huge jug. Continue up to the remains of an old PR, whence a delicate step up R gains good holds. Follow these to finish up the easy top part of The Grooves – spacewalking!

CLOGWYN Y DDYSGL   (616554)

From the summit of Crib y Ddysgl, a ridge runs down into Upper Cwm Glas dividing it into two smaller cwms. At the end of the ridge is an obvious nose of rock, Clogwyn y Person, separated from the main spur by Eastern Gully (Mod) on the L and Western Gully (Mod), the normal descent, on the R.

Just R again, the west flank of the ridge consists of a large cliff, Clogwyn y Ddysgl, which becomes higher and more broken towards its R side. Both cliffs can be reached by following the Cwm Glas path to Cyrn Las then continuing steeply up L-wards to gain the upper cwm in around one and a quarter hours.

243 **The Parson's Nose**   Diff   250ft/75m**

A. H. Stocker, 1884

This, the best route on the nose of Clogwyn y Person, is one of the earliest routes in the area and offers exposed climbing on accommodating holds. Start at the lowest point of the nose beneath some slabs.

1. 80ft/24m. Climb the easy slabs.
2. 70ft/21m. Continue more steeply, veering slightly R towards Western Gully. Stance at the foot of a shallow groove.
3. 50ft/15m. Traverse R along a thin crackline to a ledge overlooking the gully.
4. 50ft/15m. Scramble up the edge of The Nose to the top. Descend down Western Gully, or continue up Clogwyn y Person arete to the summit.

244 **The Gambit Climb**   V Diff   325ft/99m***

J. M. A. Thomson, H. O. Jones, K. J. P. Orton, 1910

A very varied route on sound rock: an absolute classic! Llanberis's answer to Grooved Arete! Start at the foot of a 10ft/3m flake crack, 55yd/53m R of Western Gully and 15ft/5m L of a pocketed wall.

1. 75ft/23m. Climb the short flake until a step L, then down, lead to a traverse across a slab into a deep corner crack. Go up this to a good ledge. Continue up a short awkward crack to a large stance.
2. 55ft/17m. Traverse R to a shallow chimney and climb it to a grassy ledge.
3. 45ft/14m. A difficult traverse R leads to a short chimney which is taken to a good ledge.

Clogwyn y Ddysgl

4. 70ft/21m. Ascend the chimney at the back of the ledge to the top of the pinnacle. Hand traverse into an easy corner crack which leads to a scree-covered ledge – an excellent pitch.
5. 80ft/24m. Move R up a sloping grassy ledge to a R-angled corner with a thin crack. Climb this strenuously to the top.

Descend Clogwyn y Person arete and continue down Western Gully to the foot of the crag.

245 **Fallen Block Crack**   VS   265ft/81m *
I. M. Waller, 1927

A fine traditional climb which is slightly easier in boots, and much harder if it is at all wet! Start 150yd/139m R of Western Gully along a wide rake, The Parson's Progress, at a huge fallen block with a prominent crack above it.

1. 30ft/9m. 4a. Struggle up the initial crack to a chockstone belay.
2. 85ft/26m. 4c. Surmount the overhang, crux, and follow the crack to a resting place after 30ft/9m. Continue up the crack, eventually easing to a large ledge.
3. 150ft/46m. Ascend a chimney on the L, from the top of which 120ft/37m of easy climbing leads to the top of the cliff. Descend as for Gambit Climb.

CRIB GOCH   (625553)

This crag rises from the screes of Upper Cwm Glas to terminate at the summit of the prominent pinnacles which lie at the far end of the Crib Goch ridge. The easiest(!) and best approach is from Pen y Pass, by traversing up the Crib Goch ridge in about one and a half hours.

The cliff has two main sections, the tall compact Crib Goch Buttress on the L, with Crazy Pinnacle Gully (Mod) separating it from Crazy Pinnacle Buttress (Diff), on the R.

246 **Reade's Route**   V Diff   220ft/66m *
W. R. Reade, G. L. Bartrum, 1908

This classic mountaineering route which enjoys spectacular views takes a line up the clean R-hand edge of Crib Goch Buttress. Best combined with a trip round the Snowdon Horseshoe. Descend from Bwlch Coch and traverse across scree to start immediately L of Crazy Pinnacle Gully. Broken ground leads to a belay and stance overlooking the gully, at the foot of steeper rock.

Crib Goch

1. 100ft/30m. Go easily up the rib past several ledges to a l arge stance.
2. 70ft/21m. Climb a short wall with difficulty to the foot of a large pinnacle. Climb to the top of the pinnacle and make the

celebrated stride across to a crack in the wall, crux. Follow this
to a stance at the top of another pinnacle.
3. 50ft/15m. Go straight up the rib via a shallow groove to the
top.

CRAIG ADERYN   (639543)
This neat crag is tucked away in Upper Cwm Dyli, below and
south of Llyn Teryn, and is reached in less than thirty minutes
from Pen y Pass via the Miners' Path and a grassy descent. A
pipeline runs down from Llyn Llydaw between the Teryn
Bluffs, two prominent hummocks, and Craig Aderyn is the
most southerly of these, lying just beyond it. The main interest
centres around a superb south-east-facing slab which is
quick-drying.

247 **Jacob's Ladder/Via Media**   S   160ft/49m ***
F. Graham, 1924/F. Graham, M. W. Guiness, 1925
The slab can be climbed on almost anywhere at up to VS in
standard, but this combination gives the best route. 50m of
rope are necessary to do the climb in a single pitch unless an
intermediate stance is taken at around 80ft/24m – or both
members of the party are prepared to climb together for a few
feet. Start 15ft/5m L of the R arete, taken in its entirety by The
Arete Climb (Diff).
1. Ascend direct to quartzy holds at 45ft/14m. Continue up
parallel to the arete. At 80ft/24m trend L and follow the L-ward
slanting crack to the apex of the slab. Belay. Instead of moving
L at 80ft/24m, one can continue direct to finish up The Arete
Climb at V Diff. Descent: from the top of the arete make a
slightly descending R-ward traverse for 40ft/12m to the top of a
low relief rib. Follow this carefully down and round to the L
(facing out) then back R below a short rock face, with a rowan
tree and a spiky stump, to a sloping slabby step then a short
grass gully leading to the base of the crag.

LLIWEDD   (623534)

This massive north-facing cliff, 1000ft/300m high and half a mile wide, towers over Llyn Llydaw forming part of the L-hand half of the Snowdon Horseshoe. It is easily approached from Pen y Pass car-park along the Miners' Path to the lake. From here a path runs up L round its south side to reach screes leading up to the foot of the face in about an hour.

Although the cliff is fairly easy-angled with many breaks and grass ledges, in some areas there is a paucity of incut holds, and on many climbs protection is widely spaced. Wet rock dramatically affects route grades here, more so than on other crags, with even easy pitches becoming a very serious proposition if one is caught in a downpour.

A certain steadiness and route-finding ability are required on the part of the leader for most climbs. Three gullies divide Lliwedd into four main buttresses. Central Gully (HVS) separates the West and East Buttresses, whilst to the L, East Gully is the dividing fault between the East and Far East Buttress. Over on the R, the West and Slanting Buttresses are separated by Slanting Gully

The best climbing is located on the lower half of the East Buttress, especially on its front face, near the bottom of which are two large grass ledges. These should be positively identified along with several other important features before one gets too near to the foot of the cliff. The higher L-hand ledge is the Heather Shelf which runs horizontally for 50ft/15m and starts 25yd/23m R of East Gully, whilst lower down to the R is Birch Tree Terrace, about 80ft/24m long, which can be identified by some prominent quartz veins slanting up from the L to meet it.

Two-thirds of the way up the face lies the Great Terrace, a huge ledge which slants up L from Shallow Gully (which splits the East Buttress from top to bottom) for over 200ft/61m to a mass of quartz blocks marking the start of Terminal Arete. One-third of the way up the buttress, immediately R of Shallow Gully, is a ledge slanting up R-wards – the Bowling Green.

248 **Horned Crag Route**   V Diff   800ft/250m ***
J. M. A. Thomson, O. Eckenstein, 1905

This classic mountaineering climb takes a well-worn line up the
L-hand side of the East Buttress to pass between two huge
L-leaning pillars, The Horns, from which easy ground leads to
the summit. Start from the L-hand end of the Heather Terrace,
best reached by a scramble from the L to its L end.

1. 60ft/18m. Descend a line of ledges and traverse round a faint
rib to gain a broader rib. Go up this to good ledges and a stance
below a steep corner.

2. 80ft/24m. Climb the corner for 20ft/6m and step L on to the
front of the main rib. Take this on its R edge to a heather
stance.

3. 90ft/27m. Continue up the R-hand side of a broader rib
above to land on a large heather ledge.

4. 100ft/30m. Ascend diagonally R-wards across a wall and
climb a shallow chimney. Continue R along a quartz band to a
good ledge.

5. 80ft/24m. Scramble up L of easy-angled rock to the foot of
the Horned Crag.

6. 30ft/9m. Go up a groove in the middle of the wall to a
stance.

7. 40ft/12m. Climb a steeper groove above for a few feet, then
step out R, crux, and follow the edge on good holds to a ledge
below The Horns.

8. 20ft/6m. Climb the polished slab between The Horns with
difficulty. There now remains 300ft/93m of climbing or
scrambling, gradually easing towards the summit. Descent: go
down the gully forming the L-hand boundary of the Far East
Buttress. Or if there is no gear to retrieve from the foot of the
climb, walk along the summit path down to Pen y Pass, as for
the Snowdon Horseshoe.

249 **Paradise/Terminal Arete**   V Diff/Mod   880ft/267m *
H. O. Jones, R. F. Backwell, 1909

A delicate, sustained and open climb up the centre of the wall

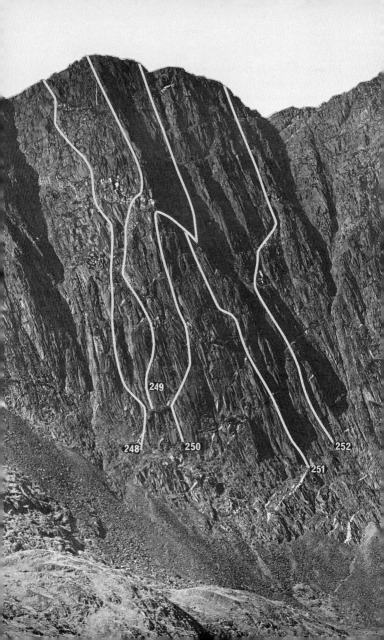

above the Heather Shelf. Start at the foot of a groove in the centre of the wall.

1. 90ft/27m. Climb the groove to where it divides at 50ft/15m and take the R-hand fork to a wall on the R which leads to a grass ledge.

2. 20ft/6m. Cross the ledge and go up quartzy rock to a better stance.

3. 80ft/24m. Move up L to climb a slabby groove with an awkward finish on to a slab. Continue to a good ledge.

4. 90ft/27m. Move L round the steep rib above to the foot of a long groove. Climb this, awkward to start, to easy ground.
From here it is possible to escape by traversing L and reversing Horned Crag Route to the foot of the buttress . . . or:

5. 200ft/61m. Follow a system of ribs up R to the quartz blocks at the top of the Great Terrace.

6. 400ft/122m. From the quartz block, follow a steep and well-trodden line up the arete on good holds for about 200ft/61m. Scrambling remains. Descend L along the Snowdon Horseshoe path as for Horned Crag Route.

250 **Avalanche/Red Wall/Longland's Continuation**   HV Diff   870ft/261m***

J. M. A. Thomson, E. S. Reynolds, 1907/J. L. Longland and party, 1929

One of the great expeditions of the area and the best route up the buttress. Start from the R end of the Heather Terrace – this point can be reached from below via a curving groove.

1. 100ft/30m. Make a long rising traverse to the R on good holds until a rib leads to a small stance below a grooved corner.

2. 40ft/12m. Climb easily up to a ledge at the top of a slab, below and L of a quartz-marked wall.

3. 50ft/15m. From the R end of the ledge move steeply up the quartzy wall until forced L into a steep crack which leads to a small ledge. Move R to belay on the front of the rib.

4. 70ft/21m. The rib leads up to easier ground.

5. 100ft/30m. Go easily up a grassy gully to belay below an impending wall.

Lliwedd

6. 100ft/30m. Scramble up R below the wall to the Great
Terrace. Belay about 80ft/24m R of the quartz blocks at the foot
of Terminal Arete, below a narrowing slab which is topped by a
bulge.

7. 80ft/24m. Follow a line of holds up R on steepening rock. A
difficult move up gains the crest of the rib which leads to good
ledges.

8. 100ft/30m. Climb the broad rib above and a short wall to
the Green Gallery. On the R is Shallow Gully: Longland's
Continuation starts 50ft/15m to the L at a quartz outcrop below
a rib.

9. 80ft/24m. Climb the rib to a niche. Step R from a perched
block to a slab. Climb this trending R and ascend steeper rock
to a grassy rake leading up L.

10. 40ft/12m. Go R and up a rib over blocks to a stance near
Shallow Gully.

11. 70ft/21m. Climb the broken rib above to a large ledge
below a steep slab.

12. 40ft/12m. Climb the slab, working up L to a ledge at
20ft/6m. Finish easily over rocks to the top. Descend as for
Horned Crag Route.

251 **The Sword/Route 2**   VS/V Diff   430ft/130m **
*J. M. Edwards, J. H. Buzzard, F. A. Champion, 1938/J. M. A.
Thomson, O. Eckenstein, 1904*

A good open climb between Birch Tree Terrace and Shallow
Gully. Route 2 starts up Shallow Gully then traverses L to a
quartz pillar (The Quartz Babe) 150ft/46m up the face, whilst
The Sword starts just L of Shallow Gully and climbs directly up
the crest of the buttress to reach the same spot. Shallow Gully
itself can be recognized by a 200ft/61m long quartz band which
slants up R to peter out at its foot. Start in a small corner below
an overlap, just L of the foot of Shallow Gully and 40yd/37m L
of Central Gully.

1. 140ft/43m. 4c. Go up the corner for 15ft/5m to the overlap
and move L with difficulty, crux, to a small ledge on the crest of
the rib. Climb straight up the rib which gradually eases, past

narrow ledges at 70ft/21m to reach The Quartz Babe (slightly loose near the top). Belay on good spikes 15ft/5m further on.

2. 70ft/21m. Continue easily to a stance with bollard belays below steeper slabs.

3. 40ft/12m. From the tip of the highest block, climb R up the slab to finish on the original 'Thank God' holds. Climb up to a ledge slightly higher on the L.

4. 40ft/12m. A steep shallow groove splits the wall above; go up this on good holds.

5. 80ft/24m. Follow the easier groove to a stance.

6. 60ft/18m. Easy rocks lead to the Great Terrace from which Red Wall/Longland's Continuation provides a suitable finish.

252 **Mallory's Slab/Great Chimney**   V Diff
900ft/282m **

G. H. L. Mallory, 1908/J. M. A. Thomson, H. O. Jones, 1907

These two routes offer a fine mountaineering day. A clean open slab leads up to the L end of the Bowling Green, which is traversed to its R-hand end below a large curving chimney/crack; this provides a contrasting finish.

To the R of Shallow Gully, a pair of grassy cracks 5ft/2m apart slant up L to join at 70ft/21m. To the R is a tall narrow slab with an overlap at 100ft/30m. The climb takes the L edge of this slab. Start at the foot of the R-hand grassy crack, about 50ft/15m L of Central Gully.

1. 90ft/27m. Climb a vague rib parallel to the grassy crack passing a small ledge at 60ft/18m and continue in the same line to a stance just L of the overhang on the slab.

2. 70ft/21m. Continue up the rib and finish R-wards over a tall unstable pillar to a stance.

3. 60ft/18m. Pass the overhang on its L and ascend diagonally R on to the L end of the Bowling Green. Traverse R along the Bowling Green to where it almost levels out, below an easy-angled groove, and before its quartzy middle section.

4. 100ft/30m. Climb the groove for 30ft/9m. Traverse R for 70ft/21m along a line of holds which become a ledge running parallel to the Bowling Green. This ends in a niche at the foot

of the chimney. If the groove can't be located, it is possible to join the traverse line by climbing a groove further R – much harder.

5. 100ft/30m. Climb the chimney strenuously using holds on the L wall.

6. 90ft/27m. Follow the chimney more easily into where it opens into a large bay.

7. 60ft/18m. Ascend the crack in the L-hand corner to large ledges. Approximately 300ft/93m of scrambling leads to the col between the East and West Peaks. Descend along the Snowdon Horseshoe path, over the East Peak.

253 **Slanting Buttress Ridge Route**
Diff   700ft/209m **

G. D. and A. P. Abraham, 1904

This excellent climb takes the main ridge of the large, poorly defined buttress to the R of Slanting Gully. Large holds and plentiful protection make this a good choice in all but the foulest of conditions. Two huge quartz zigzags run up the lower slabs of Slanting Buttress. Start at the foot of the ridge, 10ft/3m L of the spot where the R-hand quartz band meets the ground.

1. 100ft/30m. Climb a shallow depression to belay slightly R of the tip of the L-hand quartz band.

2. 110ft/33m. Continue easily in the same line.

3. 90ft/27m. Work up slightly L-wards, aiming towards the L-hand of two obvious corner/grooves. Belay in a recess below it.

4. 50ft/15m. Climb the slab on the L of the recess to a ledge and continue up the slab above to a stance overlooking a shallow gully.

5. 60ft/18m. Go steeply up to a well-worn groove just L of the ridge crest. Climb this to a ledge below the ridge.

6. 80ft/24m. Climb up then step R on to the narrow ridge. Follow this steeply at first, then easing to run horizontally into the foot of the steep wall above.

7. 65ft/20m. Ascend R-wards to a rib on the R-hand skyline. Move round this and go up to a ledge at the foot of a groove.

8. 40ft/12m. Climb the corner crack then a short groove on its
R to a large ledge.

9. 100ft/30m. Go easily up L to a break which leads back R to
the summit. Descent: follow the Snowdon Horseshoe path,
either L over the top of Lliwedd and so to Pen y Pass, or R and
along Bwlch y Saethau before climbing to Yr Wyddfa, the
summit of Snowdon.

Clogwyn Du'r Arddu   (599556)

This magnificent cliff, the Mecca for many climbers, lies high
on the north face of a ridge thrown down westwards from the
summit of Snowdon into Cwm Brwynog. North-facing and
catching only the early morning and late evening sun, its
majestic architecture is dark and sombre, sitting starkly above
the little lake of Llyn Du'r Arddu.

The crag is normally reached from Llanberis in about an
hour (by the fit) along the narrow road opposite the Royal
Victoria Hotel, over a cattle grid and up a steep hill to a
parking place a couple of hundred yards after the first gate –
just beyond the point where the Snowdon footpath branches off
to the L. Follow this footpath for about two miles past a green
tin refreshment shack, Halfway House, to a point where the
path forks: the L-hand branch climbs steeply up, leading
walkers wearily up to the summit; fortunately, the R-hand
branch contours easily round the cwm above Llyn Du'r Arddu
allowing climbers some respite before they reach the cliff
bottom. Or, from the first gate, follow the road for one mile
through another two gates to a *limited* parking spot at the farm
of Hafoty Newydd. Walk up the slope to the Snowdon railway
track which crosses the footpath half a mile further up the
mountain.

Cloggy is divided into eight main climbing areas, the most
impressive being the triangular-shaped East Buttress,
dominated by the clean sweep of an almost featureless sheet of
rough rhyolite, Great Wall. Perched on top of this sits The
Pinnacle, a massive tower which presents two faces to the

climber. Beneath, the scree-filled East Gully runs up to the L of the East Buttress, whilst L of this is the huge two-tiered Far East Buttress. The Eastern Terrace defines the R edge of the East Buttress and is a large stony rake which runs the full height of the cliff, slanting up from R to L. From its bottom end, at the start of the West Buttress, The Boulder rises for 200ft/61m, a compact slabby wall bounded on its R by a dark wet drainage line, The Black Cleft, E2 5b, 5c, 5c, 5a. Below The Boulder is the steep ribbed subsidiary buttress of Middle Rock, split by three main grooves. Immediately R of The Black Cleft lies the main mass of the West Buttress, a vast area of overlapping slabs and corners tilted to the L, its base guarded by overhangs. Running diagonally up R-wards underneath them is another large rake, the Western Terrace, with an area of steep smooth rock, The Steep Band, lying below. Finally, down and R of The Steep Band, is the broad diamond-shaped Far West Buttress.

Most of the routes on the cliff, especially on the West Buttress, are serious undertakings. On weekends and bank holidays it is advisable to wear a helmet as stonefall is a real hazard!

The easiest descent for all climbs is down the Eastern Terrace. The Western Terrace may also be descended, but since a rockfall in 1986 it has become quite tricky, and scree and boulders are inevitably dislodged to hurtle down towards the queues waiting for Great Slab.

The Far East Buttress

The best climbing on the buttress lies on its upper L-hand side where the huge central R-curving groove of Woubits splits the nose of the prominent rock tower known as the Mostest Buttress. Both routes described are reached by scrambling carefully down the Far Eastern Terrace, just L of the buttress.

254 Woubits E2 207ft/83m **
J. Brown, D. D. Whillans (AL), 1955
A route of interest and character. Start near the foot of the

Clogwyn Du'r Arddu – the Far East Buttress

terrace, just R of the band of overhangs, below short twin grooves leading up into a large broken R-facing corner below the prominent groove.

1. 120ft/37m 5b. Move R and pull steeply over the bulge into the R-hand groove. Climb this or its easier L-hand twin and continue up the broken corner above. Move R to a stance and PBS below an overhanging wall.

2. 150ft/46m. 5b. Climb the groove above to a small overhang at 40ft/12m. Pass this by moving L to a flake, standing on it, then reaching a higher ledge before returning to the groove; or, by moving back into the groove from the top of the flake and laybacking up to the same spot. Follow the now easier groove to the top of a slab then move L to squirm up a chimney in the corner. Finish via a slabby groove on the R to block belays.

255 **The Mostest** E2 320ft/97m **

J. Brown, unseconded, 1957

A very fine open route which wanders across the steep wall before climbing the bottomless corner R of Woubits. The climbing is fairly straightforward save for a couple of difficult moves at the top of the third pitch. Start to the R of Woubits where the gully fades out into steeper rock.

1. 120ft/37m. 4a. Move out R to climb a grassy groove leading to a small slab. Go up this via the cracks and continue up a short gully to a grassy rake. Move L to a chimney/groove and climb this to a large stance and PB.

2. 90ft/27m. 5a. Climb the crack on the L to the top of the pinnacle. Move R and make a bold swing round the bulge on to the wall on the R. Go up to a good spike runner, descend a little, then make some difficult moves along a rising traverse leading to a tiny stance in a bottomless corner.

3. 60ft/18m. 5c. Climb the corner on good holds to the overhang. Step up L to reach better holds and another groove with difficulty. Continue to a stance.

4. 50ft/15m. Finish easily up the broken slab.

The Pinnacle

The Pinnacle sits squarely on top of the East Buttress and has two faces set at R-angles to each other forming a prominent arete which towers over the approach path. Its front face gives some interesting and open climbing, but it doesn't really compare with the impressive side wall rising out of the upper part of East Gully, the home of several classic routes. A scrambling approach may be made up East Gully, but this is

Shrike, pitch 2: on the edge

loose and precarious in places. The first two routes are perhaps best reached by abseil from a handy pinnacle at the top of the Shrike Wall.

256 Shrike E1 190ft/58m ***

J. Brown, H. Smith, J. Smith (4 pts), 1959/FFA: J. Perrin, 1968

A sensational and exposed route which breaks out of the gloom of East Gully to climb a slightly overhanging wall on large holds. There is one hard move on the first pitch and a couple more to surmount the roof at the start of the second, apart from which the climb is 4c/5a. Start 50yd/46m R of the steeper top part of East Gully in a corner, below overhangs. A large pinnacle leans against the wall.

1. 65ft/20m. 5c. Climb the crack on the L side of the pinnacle for 10ft/3m. Traverse horizontally L for 15ft/5m, then go up a thin crack past (or with, 5a) a PR to reach better holds and so to a small stance and belay.

2. 125ft/38m. 5b. Climb the groove above the stance to a PR. Jam strenuously over the roof to good holds on the L where the crack widens. Traverse easily L to the arete, climb up a little and traverse back into the crack. Continue up past two spike runners to a small ledge. Move L to the arete. Climb this to a narrow ledge on the R and finish up the tricky 10ft/3m wall to jugs. An amazing pitch.

To the R of Shrike lies the corner of East Gully Groove (VS) – rather dirty and with some suspect rock. Just R again is:

257 The Axe E4 150ft/46m ***

P. R. Littlejohn, C. King, 1979

This tremendous mountain route, one of the best in North Wales, accepts the challenge of the obvious and formidable undercut arete R of Shrike. 50m ropes are needed to reach the very top, but a crevassed ledge 10ft/3m lower provides a good stance. Large nut belays. Start R of Shrike in a shattered bay beneath overhangs just R of the arete.

1. 6a. Climb the flake crack to the roof. Make a difficult pull round this, crux, and continue to a juggy L-ward traverse line. Follow this to large hollow flakes. Climb a thin flake and the

Clogwyn Du'r Arddu – The Pinnacle

wall above to gain the arete proper. Take the arete to a spike on the R. Make a move up then regain the arete at a small overhang. Continue directly up the arete in a brilliant position passing a crevassed ledge (possible stance) 10ft/3m from the top.

R of The Axe, the smooth grey curtain of rock known as The Final Judgement wall is breached by Margins of the Mind, E7 6c, a very thin face climb up its centre; 15ft/5m further R lies:

258 **Psycho Killer**   E6   150ft/46m **
R. Fawcett, P. Williams, J. Moran, 1980
This, the original way up the wall, gives a fierce and sustained pitch. Strong nerves, as well as strong fingers, are required; protection is spaced, the climbing is technical and the setting is atmospheric. Start below the overlap, about 25ft/8m L of the huge crack at the R side of the wall, Octo.
1. 6b. Pull round the overlap and climb a shallow groove to an ancient PR. Pass this with difficulty, crux, then trend awkwardly R to get precariously established in a very shallow corner. Follow this up L-wards passing some unstable rock to reach a small overlap. Traverse L to an obvious crack which soon leads up to better holds and the start of The Hand Traverse.

259 **Octo**   HVS   160ft/48m ***
J. Brown, M. T. Sorrell, D. Belshaw, 1952
The impressive corner/crack split by an overhang at half-height, which defines the R edge of the great smooth wall, is well protected and popular. Start up East Gully, then a serious scramble up steep grass and rock on the R lead to the foot of the climb, below twin cracks, or make a 'hairy' traverse round from Pinnacle Arete.
1. 50ft/15m. 4b. Climb either crack, the L-hand one is better, to a stance in the chimney.
2. 110ft/33m. 5b. Climb the R wall to the overhang and struggle round this with more strenuous moves to enter the

crack above. Continue up the sustained crack until it can be quitted on the R. Easier climbing leads to a grassy platform. Scramble up R-wards to escape.

260 **Pinnacle Arete/The Hand Traverse**

E2   270ft/82m ***

M. Boysen, C. J. Mortlock, 1962/H. I. Banner, C. T. Jones, 1960

This exciting combination takes the arete formed at the junction of the two main faces of The Pinnacle, then traverses sensationally across the Final Judgement wall L of Octo. Best reached via a route on the East Buttress. Start at the foot of an obvious groove capped by a roof on the face of The Pinnacle, and just R of the arete proper.

1. 130ft/40m. 5b. Climb the groove for 30ft/9m (Taurus, E3 5b, turns the roof on the L then finishes up the groove above) and traverse L on large holds to a ledge near the arete. Climb up past a PR to the arete. A difficult 10ft/3m of ascent up a thin crack leads to a L-ward traverse for 15ft/5m to the foot of the groove. Climb this to a good stance and belays.

2. 20ft/6m. Go up to a higher ledge which leads L to a stance at the top of Octo.

3. 100ft/30m. 5c. Move down and launch out boldly along the obvious incut traverse line to an old PR at 20ft/6m. Make a hard move up L and take the thin crack, then the corner above past a boulder arch to a stance.

4. 20ft/6m. Continue easily to the top.

The East Buttress

The East Buttress is seamed with cracks and grooves, all very steep and powerful, whereas the walls in between them give high-quality, open face work requiring good technique, strong fingers and a 'cool' head.

To the R of East Gully, the first breach in the buttress is taken by the L-facing Sunset Crack. Next comes a wide steep wall crossed by Llithrig and bounded on its R by a series of large blocky steps and corners trending up to the R, the substance of Pigott's Climb. Just R of this, the obvious crack of

Chimney Route (also east-facing, like most of the East Buttress cracks) comes before the vast central sweep of the Great Wall. At the L side of this, discontinuous grooves mark the line of Daurigol, E3 5b, 5c, whilst a thin crack slanting R-wards up the 'holdless' sheet of rock, a few yards R, traces out the tenuous path of the Great Wall itself. The far edge of this wall is defined by a huge crack running the full height of the buttress, November, with the parallel crack of Vember starting from a ledge at half-height. Now comes a huge flake of rock with Curving Crack buried in the depths behind it; Troach climbs its front face. R again, the straight Pedestal Crack comes before a shorter wall taken by Silhouette, with the eponymous feature of The Corner, just beyond it.

Descents: the Green Gallery is a large grassy terrace running along the top of the main buttress; The Pinnacle rises from this point. For routes lying L of November, scramble off R-wards from here, up over short walls to descend the Eastern Terrace; or continue via a route up The Pinnacle.

261 **Sunset Crack**   VS   180ft/54m *

A. D. M. Cox and party, 1937

A popular climb taking a steep east-facing chimney crack on the L of the buttress. Scramble up to the foot of the crack.
1. 110ft/33m. 4b. Go easily up to a grass ledge. Move across into the crack which provides interesting climbing to reach a belay below an overhang.
2. 70ft/21m. 5a. With a runner on a flake above the belay. Make a very awkward step up into the chimney on the lip of the overhang. Continue more easily up a corner to a rake, then finish up an easy chimney to reach the Green Gallery, running along the top of the East Buttress. A well-trodden path leads up R-wards to the Eastern Terrace.

Clogwyn Du'r Arddu – the East Buttress

262 **Llithrig**   HVS (1 pt)   245ft/74m ***

J. Brown, J. R. Allen (1 pt), 1952/FFA: C. J. Phillips, 1967

A superb and varied route with an exciting pendulum.
Breaking out of Sunset Crack it traverses the wall on the R then
finishes direct. Start at the foot of Sunset Crack.

1. 45ft/14m. 4a. Follow Sunset Crack to a stance and belay a
few feet up the crack proper.
2. 70ft/21m. 5a. Move across the wall into a steep groove.
Climb this to a small ledge on the arete. Traverse R below an
overhang to a small corner, crux. Move R and go up to reach
better holds leading diagonally R to a good spike. From this,
either pendulum across to a good ledge and belays –
traditional; or free climb the pendulum at E1 5c.
3. 70ft/21m. 4c. Traverse R and follow the obvious break to a
stance at the foot of a L-facing corner.
4. 40ft/12m. 4c. Climb the corner for 15ft/5m. Move L to a
crack which leads up to better holds on the L wall and thus, a
grassy ledge.
5. 20ft/6m. Take the wall behind to the Green Gallery.

263 **Pigott's Climb**   VS   270ft/81m ***

A. S. Pigott and party, 1927

This historic climb is the original way up the buttress. It takes
the next line of weakness, the huge blocky steps and corners
which define the R side of the Llithrig wall. The pitches are
steep, but the stances are large. Start by a mossy spring at the
foot of the cliff.

1. 70ft/21m. 4b. Climb L-wards up grassy ledges for 40ft/12m.
Take a tricky groove to a good ledge.
2. 40ft/12m. 5a. From the R end of the ledge, climb a rib then
traverse R to a 10ft/3m corner. Surmount this with difficulty to
a wide grass ledge, The Conservatory.
3. 70ft/21m. 4a. Straightforward climbing up the corner gains
a ledge on the R at 50ft/15m. Follow the chimney above to the
top of a massive rock pillar.
4. 90ft/27m. 5a. Continue strenuously up the corner cracks to
finish. Alternatively, at 60ft/18m, move R below a small

Llithrig: the crux traverse

cracked overhang and surmount it with difficulty, 5b; or
traverse round the corner on the R and climb the L hand of two
grooves.

264 **Chimney Route** VS 360ft/108m **

C. F. Kirkus, J. M. Edwards, 1931

A good route taking the deep crack R of Pigott's. This, the easiest way up the buttress, has a fine traditional air about it. Start at the foot of the chimney line in the centre of the buttress, just L of Great Wall.

1. 60ft/18m. 4a. Climb the chimney, or the R wall to a stance.
2. 110ft/33m. 4b. Follow the chimney on good holds to a niche at 50ft/15m. PR and a possible stance. (The thin crack in the L wall is taken by The Sweeper, E2 5c, 5a.) Airy bridging above the niche eventually leads to a slab on the R. Climb this to a belay at its top.
3. 80ft/24m. 4c. The overhang above, the Rickety Innards, as it is known, is very unstable, but can be climbed by the brave or the foolish. However, it is better to descend to the R and step into a groove which leads to a large flake. Traverse R and climb the steep wall in a very exposed position to the Green Gallery. It is now possible to escape up grass to the L, or:
4. 110ft/33m. 4b. Climb the prominent Continuation Chimney in the corner. Escape diagonally R to Eastern Terrace.

265 **Diglyph** HVS 260ft/70m *

J. Brown, M. T. Sorrell, 1951

A well-protected and strenuous climb with a short hard crux. Start just L of Great Wall at the foot of Chimney Route.

1. 60ft/18m. 4a. As for Chimney Route.
2. 90ft/27m. 5b. Move R for 10ft/3m to the foot of a crack. Climb this to a small ledge and continue over a bulge, PR, to belay on the ledge above.
3. 110ft/33m. 4c. Go up to the foot of the obvious groove and climb it to the large flake at 80ft/24m. Move R and ascend the steep exposed wall to the top, as for Chimney Route. Escape up L-wards to the Green Gallery.

266 **Great Wall** E4 230ft/70m ***

P. Crew, 1962/FFA: J. Allen, C. Addy, 1975

The thin slanting crackline running up the L side of the smooth

central wall gives a magnificent route, both bold and technical.
Start a few feet R of the foot of the crack.
1. 80ft/24m. 6a. Ascend diagonally L to the small overhang at
20ft/6m. Go over this and continue up the crack and groove by
some very thin bridging, PR. A long reach gains the
continuation of the crack above, soon leading to a small stance.
2. 150ft/46m. 5c. Climb the shallow depression for 40ft/12m to
good nuts in a short thin crack. Climb this to a small L-facing
corner. Move R on a sharp sidepull with a long reach across for
the obvious jug. Traverse R awkwardly for a couple of moves
then follow a weakness back up L to easier ground (possible
belay in a niche just below the ledge). Scramble up the earthy
gully to belay at the foot of Continuation Chimney in a corner
on the R. Care should be taken to avoid dislodging stones on to
the second.

267 **A Midsummer Night's Dream**   E6   250ft/75m ***
*E. Ward-Drummond, P. Bartlett (Pitch 1, some aid), 1973/First free
and complete ascent: P. Whillance, D. Armstrong, 1977/1978*
A powerful and uncompromising route with three hard pitches,
the first of which is often climbed as a route in its own right at
E5 6a – scary! The climb gains the Great Wall stance via a
curving weakness on the R, before breaking out L to climb the
ferocious little arete at the top of Chimney Route. Once the first
pitch is 'chalked up' the climb becomes considerably easier.
Start from a small grassy ledge at the foot of the wall, midway
between Great Wall and the crack of November.
1. 80ft/24m. 6a. Trend up L-wards to ledges and a PR. Make
sustained moves up to a wire loop. Move up, then bear slightly
L for 10ft/3m (PR hidden round a corner on the L) until a hard
semi-layback and long pull over a vague bulge enable one to
reach a line of holds running across to a point just above the
Great Wall stance. Step down to belay . . . a stunning pitch.
2. 70ft/21m. 6a. Take the Great Wall groove above for
40ft/12m, then move out L to an obvious mini-ledge on the face.
Go steeply up on minute holds until moves L gain a stance on
Daurigol around the corner . . . hard.

3. 100ft/30m. 6b. Easy climbing L-wards over grassy ledges leads to a good belay on the slab of Chimney Route, below the steep arete. Go up to the arete which overhangs alarmingly at close quarters; small wire protection in a horizontal crack around to the R. Boulder up the arete and grope blindly for the crucial hold, to get established on the easier-angled rock above. Continue, still quivering, to the top. An awesome piece of rockwork!

The next three routes start up the prominent Drainpipe Crack at the R edge of Great Wall:

268 **Jelly Roll**   E2   310ft/94m ***

R. Evans, C. Rodgers, 1971

A well-positioned climb with a sensational top pitch on good holds up the R-hand groove above Great Wall. One of the best routes of its standard on the cliff. Start as for November, at the foot of Drainpipe Crack.

1. 110ft/33m. 5a. Climb the crack for 90ft/27m then climb the ramp on the R to good belays.
2. 70ft/21m. 5a. Descend a few feet and follow a line of holds back L into the crack of November. Continue up until the crack closes. Move L to a hidden flake and climb it to a sloping grass terrace.
3. 130ft/40m. 5b. Climb the groove above on hidden holds, all very steep, turning the final overhang by a crack on its L. Continue up to good finishing holds in the short chimney above.

269 **November**   E3   380ft/116m **

J. Brown, J. Smith (8 pts), 1957/FFA: A. R. McHardy,
P. Braithwaite, 1970

A classic climb taking the arcing crackline at the R edge of Great Wall in its entirety. Start at the foot of Drainpipe Crack – often wet.

Great Wall, pitch 1

1. 110ft/33m. 5a. Climb the crack, reasonable protection after 25ft/8m. At 90ft/27m move R up the ramp to a good belay.

2. 150ft/46m. 5c. Reverse the ramp to the crack and continue up to a ledge on the L where it narrows. The crack becomes difficult and strenuous for a few feet before it widens into a shallow chimney. From a ledge above this, move up to a larger grass ledge.

3. 120ft/37m. 5a. Climb the awkward corner at the back of the ledge and follow the cracks above to the Eastern Terrace.

270 **Vember**   E1   310ft/94m ***
J. Brown, D. D. Whillans, 1951

Another classic climb, continually interesting and varied, which takes the shallow chimney R of, and parallel to, November. Start below the Drainpipe Crack, as for November.

1. 110ft/33m. 5a. As for November.

2. 120ft/37m. 5b. Climb steeply up the short cracked corner to a small ledge. Take the shallow chimney above, awkward, and continue more easily up an open chimney to a large grass ledge. Junction with November.

3. 80ft/24m. 4b. Ascend the R wall of the corner and continue up cracks to the Eastern Terrace.

271 **Curving Crack**   VS   210ft/64m **
C. F. Kirkus and party, 1932

A pleasant, traditional and atmospheric climb up the curving chimney/groove buried behind the massive flake R of Vember. Start below a thin crack which is formed by the R-hand side of a pedestal at the foot of the main chimney line. This is reached via an easy slab.

1. 35ft/11m. 4c. Climb the crack to the top of the pedestal.

2. 60ft/18m. Move L round the corner into a shallow chimney. Climb this strenuously over the bulge and go up to a stance on the L wall.

3. 115ft/35m. 4c. Move back into the crack and continue up until the angle eases. Move on to the arete and finish airily up it on good holds.

272 **Troach**   E2   210ft/65m ***
H. I. Banner, R. G. Wilson (1 pt), 1959/FFA: R. Evans, 1967
A steep and exhilarating route climbing the wall R of Curving
Crack. The hard section is quite short, and aside from this
holds are good. Protection is well spaced. Start as for Curving
Crack.
1. 35ft/11m. 4c. As for Curving Crack to the top of the
pedestal.
2. 120ft/37m. 5b. Move R past a shallow corner until a long
stretch up gains good holds on a quartz ledge. Step up and
slightly L into a shallow groove. Continue for 40ft/12m to an
old PR. Step R and climb to a dubious PR driven up into a small
overhang. Step R and make thin moves to reach a line of holds
leading up to a large flake belay.
3. 55ft/65m. 5a. Climb diagonally L to the arete. Finish up this.

273 **Pedestal Crack**   VS   190ft/60m **
C. F. Kirkus, G. G. Macphee, 1931
The prominent vertical crack R of Curving gives steep jamming
with good protection. Start by scrambling across the glacis
below Curving to the foot of the main crack at the L side of a
massive rock pedestal.
1. 60ft/18m. 4b. The crack direct is 5a; so move out R on to a
rib and climb it. Continue more easily to the top of the
pedestal.
2. 30ft/9m. 4c. The crack above leads stubbornly up to a small
stance in the corner.
3. 100ft/30m. 4b. Continue steeply up the crack to an easing
after 40ft/12m. Continue to a grassy bay at the top.

274 **Silhouette**   E2   170ft/52m ***
R. Edwards, N. Metcalfe, 1975
A superb, sustained and well-protected crack splits the wall R
of Pedestal Crack. Although described in two pitches, the route
may be done in a single run-out on 50m ropes, providing a
large rack is carried. Start in the centre of the wall, L of the

obvious ʟ-facing corner which defines its ʀ edge. Best reached
up the first pitch of Pedestal Crack.

1. 50ft/15m. 5c. Climb steeply up the thin crack to a short
groove. Nut and flake belay. Scorpio, E2 5b, comes in from the
ʟ and continues up Silhouette before moving ʀ to finish up a
blind flake crack.

2. 120ft/37m. 5c. Climb the groove. Move ʟ and ascend to a ᴘʀ
(Scorpio moves ʀ here). Follow the crack to a small overhang.
A long reach up now gains a good hold. Pull up and continue
up the easier crack above to finish.

275 **The Corner**   HVS   120ft/37m ***

J. Brown, J. R. Allen, D. Belshaw, 1952

A really great jamming pitch up the corner ʀ of Silhouette.
Good protection and nicely sustained. Start at the foot of the
corner, reached from directly below, or via the first pitch of
Pedestal Crack.

1. 5a. Climb the corner for 20ft/6m, move on to the ʟ wall. Go
up a little, then move back into the corner. Continue
strenuously up until a crack appears on the ʀ. Continue up on
'sinking jams' at about VS, to finish.

The West Buttress

This, the largest buttress on the cliff, is shaped like an inverted
triangle, leaning on the Eastern Terrace to the ʟ, and resting on
the Western Terrace which runs up under the overhangs
guarding its base to join the summit ridge. The rock on the
West Buttress has good friction, but is rather flaky in general.
However, in certain areas, for example the main pitches of
White Slab, it is beyond reproach, being firm, solid and
exceptionally rough.

   Apart from The Boulder and the obvious gutter of the Black
Cleft, other prominent features of The West are a slim,
hourglass-shaped slab in the midst of a maze of slabs and
overlaps, White Slab; the huge slab at the centre of the
buttress, Great Slab, with the indentation of Bow-Shaped Slab
in its ʟ side; and finally, up near the top of Western Terrace,

just to the L of a prominent rock scar, Bloody Slab, named after its reddish colour.

As the descent path weaves down the Eastern Terrace it passes beneath an impressive overhanging wall. Around the corner to the R is the steep, slabby, almost featureless front face of The Boulder. A path runs along the foot of the crag to climb a series of rock steps on the R side of the East Buttress. These lead up and across to the foot of both the Eastern Terrace and The Boulder.

276 **The Boulder**   E1   360ft/110m ***

J. Brown, unseconded, 1951

An exciting and exposed route which crosses the front face of The Boulder via the obvious traverse line to join the upper reaches of the Black Cleft. Start at the foot of the L-hand edge of the face (climbed direct by Left Edge E1, 4c, 5a, 5a).

1. 40ft/12m. 4c. Climb the arete and continue to a small stance and PB.
2. 130ft/40m. 5a. A gently rising traverse line slants up to the R. Hard moves to get established lead to easier climbing. At 30ft/9m gain a higher line and continue delicately across a smooth scoop to reach better holds. Follow these to a flake stance 5yd/5m away from the evil-looking corner on the R.
3. 45ft/14m. 5a. Climb the slab above to the overhang, move L to a ledge and surmount the overhang via a shattered crack. Belay immediately.
4. 145ft/44m. Scramble carefully up the grassy gully, then trend R-wards to the top.

277 **The Boldest/Direct Finish**   E3   300ft/92m ***

P. Crew, B. Ingle, 1963/C. J. Phillips, P. Minks, 1969

This magnificent route takes a sustained and direct line up the R side of The Boulder with a frightening lack of protection. Fortunately there are only a couple of hard moves. Chalk and 'sticky' boots have helped to dispel its once dreaded reputation . . . but the route still demands respect! Start just L of the obvious groove down on the R.

1. 150ft/46m. 5c. Traverse the grass ledge into the groove and ascend to a large flake. Move R to awkwardly gain the arete. Climb up to the overhang, spike runner. Traverse L past a good nut placement to a small ledge. Climb the wall above, slightly L to a faint depression. Step R and go up to a small flake, runner. Make a hard move up for an incut hold, crux, then follow a line of handholds diagonally L to reach The Boulder. Stance and a good belay flake a few feet higher.

2. 150ft/46m. 5c. Climb the steep slab above making for the obvious L-facing groove. Climb this, technical and delicate, soon easing to the top. Scramble 50ft/15m up the grass and loose rock to belay. Beware of knocking loose rocks on the second's head from this final section.

To the R of the Black Cleft, the maze of overlapping slabs rising from the Western Terrace, above overhangs, provides several long and exciting expeditions which should only be attempted by fully competent parties.

278 Longland's Climb   VS   340ft/103m ***

J. L. Longland and party, 1928

An enjoyable and classic outing which was the original breach in the West Buttress. It takes the first slender slab R of the Black Cleft. Start by following the path up and over Middle Rock to the foot of the Black Cleft, where a scramble up behind a large flake leads to the foot of the slab.

1. 90ft/27m. 4a. Climb the slab and corner to a stance where the chimney widens.

2. 40ft/12m. 4b. Continue up for a few feet then step L and climb the slab. Where it narrows, mantel on to the R wall and go up this more easily to a stance on the R.

3. 120ft/37m. 4a. Climb easily up the edge of the slab in a fine position to reach a large crevassed ledge on the R.

4. 90ft/27m. 4c. From the R-hand end of the ledge, climb the overhanging arete strenuously on good holds. Continue up a

Clogwyn Du'r Arddu – The Boulder and the West Buttress

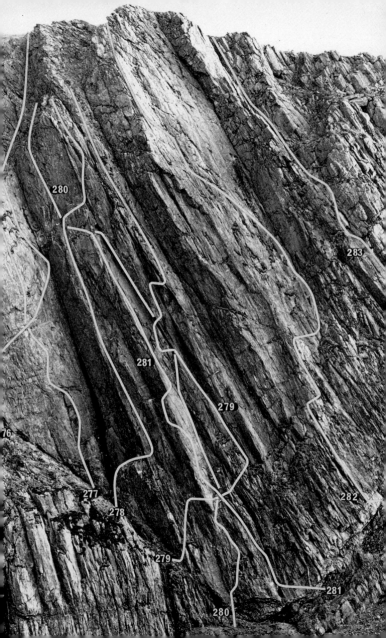

little, then move R to finish up a short chimney. Descend down
Eastern Terrace.

279 **Sheaf** VS 465ft/140m **

J. Campbell, A. D. M. Cox, 1945

An exposed and intricate route which weaves its way through
the bundle of ribs just R of White Slab. Excellent holds appear
when needed most. Scramble down below The Boulder to start
at the foot of Eastern Terrace, above a wet steepening at a
grassy crack.

1. 60ft/18m. 4c. Climb the crack and its continuation to a
small stance under the rib of White Slab. Or, make a
descending traverse from the start of Longland's to the same
spot.

2. 50ft/15m. 4c. Make a tricky move to gain the sloping ledge
on the R. Step round on to White Slab; move R for a few feet,
then descend with difficulty (Linnel's Leap) to a ledge at its
foot. Good flake belays higher on the R.

3. 85ft/26m. 3b. Descend a few feet, then move round the
corner on the R to the next slab which is rather broken. Climb
this via some grass to a ledge. Continue up to a large corner
stance above cracked blocks.

4. 70ft/21m. 4b. Move out L and climb the steep slab to a small
ledge on the arete. Move round the corner into a small broken
chimney. Traverse L on to White Slab and climb it to a PB.

5. 60ft/18m. 4c. Move R into a short groove. Climb this
awkwardly to good runners below the overhang. Boldly reach
up for good holds on the R arete. A spectacular swing out is
made to gain the groove on the R. Climb this to belay in a
corner in the groove above.

6. 60ft/18m. 4c. Make a long stride to a good hold on the
R-hand rib. Pull round this and go up for more good holds and
so gain the easier upper section of Narrow Slab, VS.

7. 80ft/24m. Grassy scrambling leads to a stance above the
Longland's overhang.

280 **West Buttress Eliminate** E3 515ft/157m ***

B. Ingle, P. Crew (AL), 1962

A tremendous route taking the corner-grooves up the R edge of White Slab. The climbing is sustained and absorbing, Walsh's Groove being a bit of a 'leg pumper'. From the point where the path divides below Great Wall, follow the lower branch below Middle Rock to reach the foot of the Western Terrace. The foot of White Slab is clearly visible (mist permitting) 100ft/30m above: start at the foot of the prominent red groove directly below it.

1. 125ft/38m. 5c. Climb steeply up the red groove for 20ft/6m then move R and climb boldly up on large widely spaced holds to grass ledges. Go up to a large block and optional stance. Take the steep slabby groove just to the L, then move slightly L, crux, and go up to a steepening. Move R then pull up on to a ledge with belays at the foot of White Slab.

2. 120ft/37m. 5b. Climb the groove above passing a hard move at 30ft/9m then follow the diagonal crack to belay at a flake on the R.

3. 150ft/46m. 5b. Walsh's Groove. Climb the short groove above, then back-and-foot the main groove using hand jams in the corner as required. Near the top move L to belay as for White Slab – a unique pitch.

4. 30ft/9m. Move L and climb up easily to the crevassed stance on Longland's.

5. 90ft/27m. 5a. Longland's Direct Finish. From the stance step L on to the continuation slab. Climb this, and the slightly suspect chimney above to the top. A well-positioned pitch.

281 **White Slab** E1 (1 pt) 570ft/176m ***

R. Moseley, J. Smith, 1956

The elegant hourglass-shaped slab R of Longland's is easily identifiable on approach to the crag, visibility permitting. A classic expedition of the highest calibre which gives sustained climbing at a reasonable standard. The route has a 'big feel' about it, especially if this is one's first visit to the cliff. About 100ft/30m R of the foot of Eastern Terrace, past the red groove

of West Buttress Eliminate, the overhangs are split by a smaller wet groove. Start just R of this at a small shattered pinnacle leaning against the overhangs.

1. 60ft/20m. 5b. From the top of the pinnacle, step down and traverse delicately L along the lip of the overhangs past a shallow groove to reach the wet groove. Climb it to a large flake belay. A serious pitch to second!

2. 80ft/24m. 4b. Climb the groove and crack behind the stance to belay just R of the foot of the main slab.

3. 120ft/37m. 5a. From the foot of the slab, climb up a little then move L to the arete. Follow this past a PR to a good spike at 60ft/18m. Move delicately R then continue up past a tiny flake until a step L round the arete leads into a groove. Ascend this for 20ft/6m to a small stance.

4. 65ft/20m. The Lasso Pitch. From the edge of the slab, lasso a small sharp spike in a groove on its far side. Swing across on the rope (or free climb across at E2, 5c) to reach it. Move L 10ft/3m and go up to a PB. A pitch easier for Rodeo Stars than Rock Stars!

5. 120ft/37m. 5a. Climb straight up the edge of the slab to a ledge at 60ft/18m. Continue up past a PR finishing direct to a stance and belay at the top of the slab.

6. 30ft/9m. Traverse easily L and go up to the crevassed stance of Longland's.

7. 90ft/27m. Climb the overhanging arete, then the chimney on the R, as for Longland's.

282 **Great Slab**   VS   600ft/184m **

C. F. Kirkus, G. G. Macphee, 1930

A very fine mountaineering expedition which climbs the largest feature on the buttress. The climbing is mainly 'Severe' in standard after the first pitch. However, in wet conditions, the Forty Foot Corner becomes the crux. Start about 50yd/46m up Western Terrace at an obvious break by a small pillar. Above is

White Slab: sustained climbing up the first big slab pitch

a small square slab capped by an overhang with a long groove just to its L.

1. 130ft/40m. 4c. Move up on to the slab then traverse delicately L to reach the long narrow groove. Climb this to a large ledge and cave stance.

2. 130ft/40m. 4a. Go round to climb the rib on the R for 40ft/12m. Traverse across R-wards to reach a shallow corner below a small overhang. Move R and continue up broken ground to belay at the foot of the Forty Foot Corner.

3. 60ft/18m. 4b. Climb the corner with a brief excursion on to the slab at 20ft/6m. From its top, move L to a stance and belay.

4. 150ft/46m. Continue more easily in a diagonal line across the slab to the L.

5. 130ft/40m. Climb to the edge of the slab in a superb position to the top.

283 **Slanting Slab**   E2 (2 pts)   450ft/138m *

D. D. Whillans, V. Betts (2 pts), 1955/FFA: I. Carr, 1983

An impressive and atmospheric route, somewhat lacking the continuity of White or Bloody with which it is so often compared. Nonetheless, the climb has a high adventure quotient! The initial overhang is usually aided with 2 or 3 PRs; free-climbed, it is much harder than the rest of the route, E3 6a. Start 60ft/18m L of and lower down from Bloody Slab where a pinnacle stands beneath the overhangs; there is a rock scar immediately above its lip, just to the L. At the time of writing, there are no in-situ PRs.

1. 120ft/37m. 5b. Use aid to surmount the overhang and gain the slab. Climb up and traverse L across a grassy patch, then continue along below a bulge to reach a grassy rake running up L-wards. Follow this to a stance and belay in a corner.

2. 40ft/12m. 4a. Climb to the end of the rake then step L round the corner to a crack in a large slab. Move up a little to good nut belays but a poor stance.

3. 140ft/43m. 5b. Climb the flake to a large overhang. Move L

Great Slab: the crux traverse on pitch 1

to climb a narrow quartz slab to another overhang. Step R and
pull round the overhang into the awkward groove above. Go up
this for one move then climb the R arete and continue to a good
stance on the R.

4. 150ft/46m. Go easily up the grassy gully to finish.

5. 130ft/40m. Climb the edge of the slab in a superb position to
the top.

284 **Bloody Slab**   E3   300ft/90m **

J. Streetly, unseconded, 1952

A superb route and a lonely lead with some sustained and
delicate climbing up the R-hand side of the red slab which sits
high up on the R near the top of the Western Terrace, just L of a
massive rock scar. Start up the Western Terrace from Slanting;
above a rock step and below a prominent boulder. Good thread
belay.

1. 100ft/30m. 5b. Climb up then traverse L and continue,
heading towards a runner in a slot at 40ft/12m. Climb up to the
bulge and turn it on the L. Step L and follow the flake crack to
the triangular overhang. Pass this on the L to a small sloping
stance and belay.

2. 90ft/27m. 5b. Traverse L and climb up to a tiny ledge.
Continue L, descending slightly to grass. Ascend the grassy
gully on the L.

3. 110ft/33m. Climb the rib on the L and continue up over
broken rock to finish.

Snowdon South and the Lleyn Peninsula

This section covers the large and diverse area to the south and
west of Snowdon. Many of the cliffs are low-lying, near the sea,
and out of the influence of the severe mountain weather
patterns; hence climbing is possible all year round.

The first three cliffs are in the Gwynant Valley, to the
south-east of Snowdon, just off the A498; Clogwyn y Bustach,
Clogwyn y Wenallt and Craig y Llyn lie in picturesque settings,
are of easy access and, although popular, are seldom crowded.

Running down the west side of Snowdon is the Cwellyn
Valley with its sombre lake, and another three crags; the
esoteric Craig Cwm Du and the impressively overhanging
Castell Cidwm lie almost back to back on Mynydd Mawr,
whilst further south, the little frequented but worthwhile
buttresses of Llechog sit tucked away in Cwm Clogwyn, on the
west flank of Snowdon. A mile or so south of Llyn Cwellyn, a
road runs due east from the village of Rhyd Ddu along the
dramatic Nantlle Valley, dominated by the buttresses and
pinnacles of Craig y Bera on its north side, and the Nantlle
Ridge, running parallel with the valley floor, to the south. At
the western end of the Nantlle Ridge, Craig yr Ogof in Cwm
Silyn has a mixture of classic easy slabs and exposed hanging
grooves which are well worth visiting. A couple of miles
south-east of Cwm Silyn, on the opposite side of the Nantlle
Ridge, is the 'lost valley' of Cwm Pennant and the isolated cliff
of Craig Cwm Trwsgl, reached from the A487, about four miles
before that road enters Tremadog village with its ever-popular
roadside cliffs. The term 'outcrop-style climbing' is most
appropriate for the clean, easily accessible and often sunny
Tremadog crags with their fabulous selection of routes at all
grades; Craig y Gesail, Craig y Castell, Craig Pant Ifan and
Craig Bwlch y Moch are more often than not in a dry condition
when rain clouds shroud the mountains. Nearby, to the east,
Carreg Hylldrem is a squat bulging cliff bristling with
overhangs, whose routes tend to stay dry in all but the foulest
weather.

Finally, slightly south and west of Tremadog, the mysterious

Lleyn Peninsula is an adventure playground with a wide variety of rock types and little-known cliffs hidden away in long-forgotten corners. Working clockwise: on the north-west coast, the huge cliffs of Yr Eifl and Carreg y Llam give long and rambling expeditions above the sea, yet with a mountaineering flavour. On the south-west tip of the Lleyn, opposite Bardsey Island, Pen y Cil provides some of North Wales's remotest routes. The next prominent headland due east, Trwyn Cilan, has the largest concentration of routes in the area, a cluster of zawns and crags which demand a competent approach – the rock here is occasionally suspect and the climbing situations are serious. This is in marked contrast to the holiday atmosphere of the Tyn Towyn Quarries next to Llanbedrog, and a stone's throw from a delightful sandy beach. There are also several nature reserves owned by the National Trust in the vicinity of, and including, Pen y Cil, which give superb coastal walking.

Local amenities

Eric's Café (Tremadog Café) below Craig Bwlch y Moch has both a barn and a campsite 'a couple of ropelengths' away from the foot of the nearest climbs. Other campsites can be found at the northern end of Llyn Gwynant (650525), at the forestry site a mile out of Beddgelert towards Rhyd Ddu (578490), and at Betws Garmon (535575). Unofficial camping, even at high level, is not recommended as the local farmers are unusually sensitive to casual intrusion. On the Lleyn Peninsula, there are several registered campsites near Abersoch, and one in the heart of Pwllheli (373347). Further north, there is also a site on the coast near the tiny village of Nefyn (313413).

There are pubs in all the main villages throughout the area, although the two in Tremadog village square are the most popular (closed on Sundays). Many cafés in the area are seasonal, but those in Porthmadog are open all year. Eric's Café at Tremadog is only open at weekends during the winter

The long traverse of Gallop Step

months. Supplies can be bought in all the main villages, and at Nant Gwynant. Cadwallader's Ice Cream Parlour in Criccieth, two minutes from the bouldering wall below the castle, is an excellent way to round off a training session – if one still has the strength left to clutch a cornet!

Two of the cliffs on the Lleyn Peninsula, namely Craig y Llam and Cilan, are subject to a 'bird ban' which lasts from 1 February to 1 August.

Gwynant Valley

CLOGWYN Y BUSTACH   (652535)

This large broken crag lies partially hidden on the wooded slopes of Gallt y Wenallt, about three-quarters of a mile upstream from the north end of Llyn Gwynant. It is reached in around twenty minutes from Cwm Dyli power station (654540) via a path which follows the valley floor before slanting diagonally up the hillside and over a col to the foot of the cliff. Cars should not be parked at the power station but may be left by the side of the old road.

The first buttress one comes to is North Buttress, with its huge curving band of overhangs.

285 **Gallop Step**   HVS   165ft/50m *
J. I. Disley, Denise Morin, 1956

An interesting climb which traverses the fault line under the great curving overhang from L to R. It is unique in that it starts and finishes on the ground! Scramble up L-wards to a block at the start of the fault line.

1. 65ft/20m. 5a. Climb up to the fault line and follow it R-wards to an arete at 50ft/15m. Move strenuously round this. A quick couple of delicate moves lead to a corner belay.

2. 100ft/30m. 4c. Move R along the line of weakness rising through a loose section to below the overhang. Follow the fault line descending R-wards (a bit vegetated) gradually easing to the foot of the crag.

286 **Lockwood's Chimney** Diff 220ft/66m *

A. Lockwood, 1909

A fine traditional climb up through the large vegetated buttress
to the L of North Buttress. Start: on the lower L-hand side of the
buttress and R of a steep loose black-streaked wall is an obvious
natural arch, Marble Arch. (This point may also be reached
from below by a 200ft/61m grassy scramble.)

1. 60ft/18m. Descend a few feet and follow ledges R-wards to
the foot of a short black crack topped by a birch tree.
2. 20ft/6m. Climb the crack to the foot of the chimney, or avoid
it 20ft/6m to the R.
3. 100ft/30m. Get into the crack behind the stance and go up
into the depths of the chimney. Climb over a chockstone and
scramble along the floor until it is possible to climb up round a
corner to a dramatic exit and fine stance.
4. 40ft/12m. Easy climbing to the top. Descend over on the L.

CLOGWYN Y WENALLT (647528)

This steep little crag is situated on the hillside just above the
campsite at the north-east end of Llyn Gwynant. It is reached
from the field at the end of the lake in about ten minutes.

The rock is generally sound and with incut holds which are
often surprisingly large. In the centre of the cliff, a stone wall
runs up to meet a large boulder, whilst on the L, a grassy
terrace cuts the cliff at one-third height fading out towards the
R. Descents are all down the well-trodden path to the L of the
crag.

287 **Ferdinand** E2 150ft/45m **

J. Brown, C. T. Jones, 1959

The main interest centres around a ferocious crack on the
second pitch. Several corners split the cliff face below the grassy
terrace, the L-hand of these being taken by Bovril (VS). Start
20ft/6m R of Bovril, below a shallow corner.

1. 60ft/18m. 5a. Climb the short wall into a niche. Move R on
good holds to a tree and continue across the grass ledge to
climb an easy slanting crack. Belay below a steep corner.

2. 90ft/27m. 5b. Ascend the corner for 15ft/5m until it is possible to step into the cruel crack on the R wall. Battle up this using almost every conceivable jamming technique to gratefully turn the top overhang by a much easier crack on the L to finish. Belay well back. (To step R a little lower and climb directly into the bottom of the crack is much harder, 5c.)

288 **Oxo**   VS   220ft/66m *

J. R. Lees, G. D. Roberts, W. A. Trench, 1953

Enjoyable climbing up the centre of the cliff. Start at the L-hand side of a bulging wall by a black recess 25ft/8m L of, and 10ft/3m higher than the Bovine start.

1. 100ft/30m. 4b. Traverse horizontally R to a black ledge and continue R below a detached flake to a short wall. Climb this to a gangway which is taken diagonally R-wards to a tree on the grass ledge to the R.

2. 30ft/9m. Take the easy slab on the L to belay by a tall tree at the foot of a crack.

3. 90ft/27m. 4c. Climb the steep crack and traverse R passing a small corner to finish direct on holds; or better, climb the difficult corner above the bulge, 5a, then step R to finish direct as for the usual way.

289 **Bovine**   HVS   210ft/63m ***

C. E. Davies, B. D. Wright, D. McKelvey, 1957

This fine route, the best on the crag, has a sensational top pitch up an impressive wall on huge holds. However, it is the first pitch which has slowed many leaders! The route becomes a superb VS if the Oxo start is used. Start at the toe of the buttress by a 4ft/1.5m flake, 8yd/8m L of the stone wall, and just L of a brown streak coming down from two corners, one above the other.

1. 90ft/27. 5b. Climb the bulging wall first R then back L to the detached flake on the Oxo traverse. Ascend the steep and precarious corner above, PR, crux, to a flat ledge. The R-facing

Clogwyn y Wenallt

corner above has a difficult start but quickly leads to a large grass ledge. Nut belays.

2. 30ft/9m. 4a. Climb down the slab on the R to belay below the steep wall.

3. 90ft/27m. 4c. Start up a short groove until a bold swing R on to the face gains good holds. Continue up in a fine open position to finish.

CRAIG Y LLYN   (619502)

This seemingly lichenous crag sits above the A498 just to the north of the head of Llyn Dinas. There is a car-park by the road from which fifteen minutes of steep scrambling up through a mossy wood leads to the foot of the lowest buttress. High on the L is a sheer smooth tower split by a crack with an overhang at half-height, Sybilla the Pun, E4 5c, 5c. Down and slightly to the L are two steep slabby diamond-shaped walls, each with its share of fine routes. However, the two selected climbs lie on the upper and larger of the walls, above a rocky step which splits the grassy hillside.

290 Wailing Wall   E4   160ft/49m **

P. Livesey, C. Crawshaw, 1978

A tremendous climb, both bold and delicate with a well-positioned and fingery crux. Start: climb the rocky step on its L-hand side then scramble 15ft/5m along the grassy gangway which runs up L-wards along the base of the upper diamond-shaped wall. Peg belay.

1. 6a. Step R on to the wall to a flake. Climb up on widely spaced but positive holds for 40ft/12m to the base of a groove. Traverse L to reach a ramp. Follow this for 40ft/12m to where it widens. Continue along another ramp leading up R-wards, until it joins a steep rib. Move up to clip a PR on the R, then descend and go up the exceptionally delicate and sustained rib which eases 20ft/6m above the runner. Move into a groove and step round L to a flake crack. Finish up this. Descend down an open gully 100yd/93m to the L.

Craig y Llyn

291 **Chance Encounter** E3 155ft/47m *

P. Livesey, P. Gomersall, B. Masson, 1978

An excellent companion to the previous route. Easier but still
poorly protected. Start as for Wailing Wall.

1. 5b. Step R on to the wall to a flake. Climb up on good widely
spaced holds to the foot of a groove, as for Wailing Wall. Climb

The crux rib of Wailing Wall on the second ascent

the groove and then move L to a flake crack leading up to a ledge. Go straight up the wall above on flakes to the base of a huge flake. Climb the face of this to finish.

CRAIG CWM DU (537551)

As one drives south-east along the A4085 from Waunfawr to Bettws Garmon, the R-hand skyline is dominated by the massive bulk of Mynydd Mawr (a.k.a. Elephant Mountain or Pachyderm Peak, derived from its profile when viewed from this stretch of road); Cwm Du is the huge hollow sunk into its north-west flank. Lining the back of this cwm, Craig Cwm Du is seen as a series of large broken buttresses, separated by gullies, which give over a dozen long mountaineering routes at up to VS in standard. Although relatively close to civilization, the crag feels very isolated, and it is rare to see another party on it.

An approach is usually made in around fifty minutes from a parking spot at Cerig-y-rhŷd (547564) on the Llyn Cwellyn side of Bettws Garmon. Cross the bridge by the waterfalls, which are signposted, and follow the track round L-wards to a barn. Head directly up the hillside through a gate and into a plantation. Follow the path up through the trees, atmospheric, to a stream which leads up L-wards to emerge in the bottom of the cwm; continue to a little knoll in its centre, a good spot from which to get one's bearings. Adam Rib takes the prominent slender R arete of Eden Buttress, the first of the main buttresses high up on the east side (L) of the cliff. It can now be reached by a soul-destroying slog up 400ft/122m of 'mobile' scree; or, more pleasantly, by trending up R-wards over heather to reach a narrow path which runs across the back of the cwm, just under the foot of the cliff.

292 **Adam Rib** HS 350ft/106 ** **

J. M. A. Thomson and party, 1911/Pitch 4: G. H. L. Mallory, R. Todhunter, 1912

The clean-cut R-hand edge of Eden Buttress gives a classic climb, continuously interesting, absorbing, and with airy situations. There is more than a hint of suspect rock in places, but this shouldn't cause any trouble for a steady leader. Start at the foot of the rib, just L of Eden Gully which defines the R edge of the buttress.

1. 100ft/30m. Straightforward climbing leads to a large grass ledge, above which the rib steepens and becomes smoother. Belay.

2. 90ft/27m. To the L of the main rib is a wide groove. Traverse up L-wards to climb the cracked L-wall of the groove until it is possible to step on to its L arete. Climb this easily past some grass until an obvious R-ward traverse is taken awkwardly back R to a grass ledge on the main rib. Thread belay round a corner to the R.

3. 90ft/27m. Take twin cracks just L of the rib to easier climbing and a small rock ledge. Step L and move up to belay on a fine rock saddle.

4. 70ft/21m. 4b. Above, the ridge narrows to a knife-edge and becomes quite steep and intimidating. Move up slightly on the R, then pull up over the bulge in a very exposed position. Continue steeply for a few feet until the angle eases off towards a good belay. Scramble up towards the main body of the mountain and descend down gentle slopes to the R of the cliff.

Towards the top of Adam Rib, a strangely contorted monolith on the L, just below the crest of the main ridge, becomes apparent; Crazy Pinnacle 30ft/9m is certainly worth a visit – the trick is to stand erect on its tiny sloping summit platform . . . without slipping off!

CASTELL CIDWM   (551554)

This impressive crag sits on the lower slopes of Mynydd Mawr just to the north-west of Llyn Cwellyn. A stream, the Afon Goch, runs down the mountainside to enter the head of the lake and Castell Cidwm overhangs its north bank. The crag lies on private land and should be approached from the south end of the lake along a forestry track (no vehicles permitted) in about thirty minutes. Parking is sometimes possible at the farm at the start of this track (568539) provided the farmer's permission is

Adam Rib, pitch 2

sought; if this is refused, the nearest alternative is Rhyd Ddu village.

   The main facet of the cliff is its gently overhanging south-east face which gives strenuous and deceptively steep routes on smooth compact rock. On the L a large curving band of overhangs leads into the centre of the face, whilst just R is a smoother area of rock which bulges at the top and has a prominent R-leaning V-groove at its foot. On the R, a huge sloping overhang caps the steep diedre rising up from the foot of a grassy rake which slants up R-wards to the cliff top. *This rake is the normal descent path.* A large grassy terrace stretches along the foot of the cliff and is best gained from its L end.

293 **The Curver** VS 180ft/55m **

J. Brown, C. T. Jones, 1960

A fine climb which follows the gangway on the L of the face to break through the roofs at a weakness. The easiest climb on the face. Start in a corner, below the start of the gangway under the roofs on the L side of the face.

1. 60ft/18m. 4c. Climb up to the start of the gangway. Follow this R to a niche and peg belays.
2. 120ft/37m. 4c. Continue traversing with a long step round a bulge to gain a ledge. Follow this on good holds past a PR until a difficult move is made into a small corner. Finish up this – an airy pitch.

294 **Central Wall** E3 180ft/54m ***

A Bell, J. Clements (2 pts), 1964/FFA: W. Wayman,
N. G. Shepherd, 1978

This brilliant climb up the centre of the cliff is very sustained and at the upper limit of its grade. Start from a block belay in the middle of the grass terrace below the clean cut V-groove.

1. 80ft/24m. 6a. Go up broken rock to the foot of the groove and climb it to a difficult L-ward exit at its top. Move awkwardly L to a block and PR. Climb the difficult wall above

Castell Cidwm

to a resting place on the L below overhangs, PR. Step out L and surmount these strenuously, moving L past two old PRs to a ledge. Peg and nut belays.

2. 100ft/30m. 5b. Move L a few feet, then go diagonally back R to pull over a roof on good holds. Follow the ramp/groove to its top. Make a very bold move up the overhanging wall for a hidden hold on the L and continue more easily to the top.

295 **Vertigo**   HVS   130ft/39m ***
J. Brown, B. D. Wright, 1960

An excellent open and exposed route, weaving up the face to the R of Central Wall. Good holds appear when needed. Start at the R end of the terrace, below and to the L of black slabs leading up to a scoop, 20ft/6m R of Central Wall.

1. 60ft/18m. 5a. Traverse diagonally R for 20ft/6m. Where the slab steepens, step L, then R-wards to climb a scoop past the L end of a long overhang. Exit R from this with difficulty, PR, on to a ledge. Traverse 15ft/5m R to a good stance and peg belay.

2. 70ft/21m. 4c. Move R round the arete to reach a steep flaky crack. Take this on good holds to a bulging section above. From the foot of a short chimney, traverse R for 15ft/5m to finish.

296 **Dwm**   HVS/A1   180ft/54m **
J. Brown, H. Smith, 1960

A superb climb taking the diedre and capping roof on the R end of the crag. Some pegs may be needed for the final pitch! Start on the grassy rake below the obvious groove.

1. 60ft/18m. 5a. Climb on to a large block and move L across a steep wall to a niche. Climb steeply up on good holds then move across to a crack on the R. This leads to a good stance and peg belay.

2. 60ft/18m. 5a. Climb the bulging wall on the L end of the ledge to another ledge, PR. Traverse diagonally and delicately R, crux, to a small stance in the corner below the overhang.

3. 60ft/18m. A1. Climb the corner to the overhang and traverse underneath it on pegs (some of which are old or

missing) into a bottomless chimney. Go up this to finish
suddenly on top of the crag. This pitch goes free at 6a!

LLECHOG   (597537)
Llechog lies cupped in the rim of Cwm Clogwyn to the west of
Snowdon. Attaining a maximum height of nearly 500ft/140m,
this large north-east-facing cliff looks quite imposing from a
distance. Yet as one advances up Cwm Clogwyn, it can be seen
that there is a lack of continuity; the cliff consists of a maze of
short slabs and grassy ledges with a considerable amount of
poor and shattered rock. A Central Couloir divides the cliff up
into two sections; the Eastern Cliff on the L has little coherent
rock, but our climb lies on the Western Cliff, to the R, where
three prominent slabs stacked one on top of each other, and
leaning to the L, stand out from the jumbled hillside.

There are two main approaches; the shortest takes about an
hour and follows the Snowdon Path from Rhyd Ddu car-park
(571526). Where the path veers east at 595538 continue around
the flank of the mountain and contour up into the cwm to
beneath the cliff; alternatively, follow the Snowdon Ranger
path from 565551 up into Cwm Clogwyn and so reach the foot
of the cliff – longer but easier.

297 **Resurrection/Erection**   E2   400ft/121m *
J. Perrin, N. J. Estcourt, M. Yates, 1970/H. I. Banner, J. Yates,
M. Yates, 1982/P. Williams, H. Walton, 1988
This excellent hybrid route is well worth the walk in to reach it,
and will appeal to those of a pioneering bent, and lovers of
solitude. The line is fairly devious, taking a fine collection of
pitches which although escapable, give some wonderful
climbing on rough sound rock set mainly at slab angle. Just R of
the lowest of the three slabs is another larger slab with a
straight L edge which rises from a grassy rake. Start by
scrambling up for about 50ft/15m to belay in a bay L of a
prominent pillar, L of the toe of the slab.
1. 60ft/18m. 5a. Climb directly up thin cracks to the grassy

Llechog – Cwm Clogwyn

ledge below the large slab. Scramble up to good nut belays in a crack on the R.

2. 50ft/15m. 5b. Step down and traverse L above a bulge, across the base of the slab on small holds with a couple of delicate moves to gain a ledge on the arete. Layaway up a short subsidiary groove with a step L to a cramped stance and nut belays below a corner and crack.

3. 70ft/21m. 4c. Climb the corner and crack then step R to a ledge. Take the slab above, or step back L, and continue to a grass ledge. Scramble diagonally across and down to the L to belay below the large slab.

4. 100ft/30m. 4c. Follow the edge of the slab up R-wards to a short R-facing corner. Climb this to a ledge on the L. The delicate groove above leads pleasantly to a shallow scoop. From the top of this, drop down the back of the slab for 20ft/6m to

nut belays at the foot of the next slab, below a crack.

5. 120ft/37m. 5c. Climb the crack in the smooth slab to a small niche. Follow the L branch, then traverse boldly to the arete, footholds, and runners, below a thin crack. Enter the crack and follow it on sustained layaways to the top. A superb finale. Good belays 20ft/6m back. Scramble up easily to finish.

Descend 55yd/50m L of the wall (facing out) just beyond the Central Couloir (in fact down a L-hand branch, again facing out) to join it. The top of the descent is steep and needs care; or skirt round the lower end of the cliff.

CRAIG Y BERA (545542)

Perched majestically on the southern slopes of Mynydd Mawr above the Rhyd Ddu to Nantlle road, the tottering ridges and pinnacles of Craig y Bera are a striking sight. The main climbing interest centres on Pinnacle Ridge, a broad-based buttress which meets the drystone wall running up from Drws y Coed.

The shortest approach is directly from below, up alongside the stone wall, but the farmer who lives directly below the crag and owns the land up to it refuses this means of access at present. The alternative approach is to walk in from Planwydd (568539) in the Cwellyn Valley (the start for the Castell Cidwm approach) along the officially marked path up Mynydd Mawr, before breaking off R-wards and contouring along to the foot of the cliff in around an hour.

298 Angel Pavement HS 580ft/176m *

C. P. Brown, A. J. J. Moulam (AL), 1946

A unique expedition taking the triangular slab and long gangway on the L side of Pinnacle Buttress. The climbing is serious with long and poorly protected runouts, and there is some dubious rock, but the hard section is very short and the position is magnificent. Start in the centre of the slab, about 30yd/27m L of the wall.

1. 140ft/43m. Climb directly up the slab to a grassy terrace. Thread belay at its R end.

2. 140ft/43m. Go diagonally L across the steep slab on good holds, then continue directly up it to a stance and belays below the overhang in a crack on the R.

3. 100ft/30m. 4b. Climb the narrow slab L of the overhang with difficulty, crux, and continue up the groove on more vegetated and broken rock to a small grass ledge.

4. 100ft/30m. Climb the rib on the L to a grassy area, then move across L below steep walls to good ledges.

5. 100ft/30m. Scramble up over pinnacles and generally easier ground, still rather loose, to the top. Descend down the scree-filled gully just R of the buttress. The obvious spiky arete on the opposite side of the gully is Sentries Ridge (Diff).

CRAIG YR OGOF (CWM SILYN)   (517502)

This splendid crag lies in the hills to the south of Nantlle, overlooking the twin lakes of Llynnau Cwm Silyn. It is best approached by following the road which passes through Tan-yr-Allt to Llanllyfni until a turn L is made at 481521, signposted to Vronlog Quarry, along a very narrow lane which leads after a mile and a half to Bryn Gwyn Farm. Cars may be left in the field just beyond the farm where the lane turns into a grass track which continues across fields through three gates to the twin lakes. A scree slope leads up to the crag. Approach time forty-five minutes.

Craig yr Ogof has two main faces at R-angles to one another. The north face has a shallow cave, the Ogof, set at half-height. Beneath this a wide ridge of slabby rock which tapers as it rises, The Nose, leads to a verdant pasture below the cave, whilst above and R is an area of steep grooves and overhangs capped by a grassy terrace, Sunset Ledge. The south-west face comprises a single sheet of rock, the 350ft/98m Great Slab. To the R of this across Amphitheatre Gully lies the broken Amphitheatre Buttress.

Descent: The Great Stone Shoot provides a descent to the R of Amphitheatre Buttress.

299 **Crucible** HVS 300ft/91m***

B. Ingle, R. G. Wilson (1 pt), 1963

A classic route trending diagonally L across the wall between the Ogof and the Great Slab, towards a huge roof which is turned on the R by some exposed climbing. Start 40ft/12m L of the Great Slab on the R-hand side of a depression, below the prominent central groove in the upper wall; Codswallop E2 5b.

1. 100ft/30m. 4c. Climb the middle of the three grooves to an overhang, then step up R into another groove. Go up this then move back L to a triangular overhang at 60ft/18m. Move up L into yet another groove. Ascend a few feet then step R above a roof and move diagonally up to a stance.

2. 80ft/24m. 5a. Traverse L and down slightly on to a perched block and go up the corner above to an overhang. Surmount this using a point of aid (5b free) and continue up L to a sloping ledge. Traverse L into a groove then move down to gain a small sloping ramp. Follow this across a very steep wall to a crack in an obvious groove. Ascend a few feet to a small stance and belays.

3. 120ft/37m. 5a. Climb the groove to the top of a large perched block. Take the rib on the L until it is possible to step back R into the main corner. Continue until the angle eases at a resting ledge, runner. Traverse R across the slab then go delicately up to worrying holds under the roof. Make a blind swing down R into a niche from which another step R leads to the foot of an easy-angled groove. Climb this to Sunset Ledge. Descent: a short traverse R leads to Ordinary Route (Diff) on the Great Slab which is easily reversed; this will be preferred to the normal descent by most climbers.

300 **Jabberwocky** E2 210ft/63m**

R. Evans, J. Yates, M. Yates (1 pt), 1970

An excellent route with a sensational second pitch up the grooved arete R of the central groove of Codswallop. Difficulties are short and sharp. Start about 20ft/6m L of the Great Slab, below the arete, at a short grassy groove.

1. 100ft/30m. 5a. Ascend the groove for 20ft/6m to a grass ledge. Move up L on to the arete and follow its R edge by the line of least resistance to a sloping stance below the steep upper wall.

2. 110ft/33m. 5c. Step up the L wall from under the small roof to gain a good spike. Make some awkward moves back R into the main groove. A few fingery moves lead to a small sharp hold, then move boldly L on to an exposed gangway. Follow this easily up L until a difficult move up leads to a small slab. Cross this to the arete on the R, and step R again into a shallow groove leading easily up to Sunset Ledge. Descend as for Crucible.

301 **Outside Edge Route**   V Diff   390ft/118m ***
J. M. Edwards, C. H. S. R. Palmer, 1931

One of the great Welsh classics: steep but with good holds and superb views. Start 20ft/6m R of the L edge of the slab, below a large semi-detached block.

1. 60ft/18m. Climb a groove which slants R to just below the block. Move R and go up to a stance by its R edge.

2. 80ft/24m. Move steeply up on to the next ledge. Make a rising traverse across the wall on the L to the arete. Follow this to a ledge and belays (Ordinary Route comes in from the R here).

3. 50ft/15m. Go 20ft/6m up, then 20ft/6m L along Sunset Ledge to a grassy corner and slab leading up to a rib. High thread runner. Traverse L down and across the rib to a second rib. Climb this to a grassy ledge and high belay on the brow of the buttress.

4. 80ft/24m. Climb up and L to the foot of a grassy crack. Take this and its continuation until the crest of the ridge is reached. Go up a few feet to belay.

5. 120ft/37m. Easy climbing up the ridge leads to the top. Descend down to the R of Amphitheatre Buttress.

Cwm Silyn – Craig yr Ogof

302 **Ordinary Route** Diff 360ft/109m *

D. R. Pye and party, 1926

This, the original way up the slab, takes a L-ward slanting line:
a fine climb with large holds which 'goes' in wet weather.
Belays are numerous, and pitches may be split as desired. Start
40ft/12m L of the R-hand corner of the slab at a grass-topped
pedestal, 20ft/6m above the scree.

1. 90ft/27m. Climb the wall above on the R then trend easily
L-wards up along ledges to good belays below a broken groove.
2. 70ft/21m. Continue diagonally L to the edge of the slab and
ascend this to Sunset Ledge. Move L along this past an obvious
open chimney to a high thread belay on its L rib.
3. 80ft/24m. Move back R and climb the chimney to a short
slab 40ft/12m up. Take the slab and nose above to belay on a
ledge where the angle eases.
4. 120ft/37m. Go round to the L and ascend without difficulty
to a prominent little step in the ridge above. Go over this past
large spikes to scramble up along the summit ridge. Descend as
for Outside Edge Route.

303 **Kirkus's Route** VS 320ft/93m **

C. F. Kirkus, G. G. Macphee, 1931

An exhilarating route up the R-hand side of the Great Slab
giving nicely sustained climbing. Start 40ft/12m L of the
R-hand corner of the slab, as for Ordinary Route.

1. 90ft/27m. 4b. Climb the wet slab to an overhang. Turn this
on the L to gain a traverse line. Follow this L-wards for 20ft/6m
then go up into a diagonal crack which leads to a niche round a
corner on the R. Climb up steeply for 20ft/6m to a block belay.
2. 60ft/18m. 4b. Move delicately L, across a groove to gain
small holds leading up to a staircase. Follow this up L to a good
spike runner. Stride L into a groove and go up this to belay on a
grass break.
3. 70ft/21m. 4c. Climb diagonally R up on a smooth slab

On the Outside Edge Route, Great Slab, Cwm Silyn

Craig Cwm Trwsgl

capped by a small overhang. Take this direct to a grass ledge
on the L.
4. 90ft/27m. 4c. Climb straight up on good holds to an
overhang which is passed on its R-hand side. Continue easily
up cracked grooves to the summit ridge. Descend as for
Outside Edge Route.

CRAIG CWM TRWSGL (CWM PENNANT)   (550494)

This remote and seldom frequented crag lies at the head of Cwm Pennant on the northern slopes of Moel Lefn. Its main cliff faces west, and on closer inspection is quite broken with ribs, buttresses, and overhangs, jumbled up with grass and heather terraces. Peregrines nest here year round, and are under surveillance by the RSPB and NCC. Around to the L of the main cliff, a fine diamond-shaped slab of rough dolerite lies hidden, overlooking Bwlch Cwm Trwsgl where the quarryman's path runs over the col between Y Gyrn and Moel Lefn before dropping down into the Beddgelert Forest.

Turn off the A487 Caernarfon to Portmadog road at Dolbenmaen (507432) and follow the narrow winding road up into the cwm for around four miles, keeping L at two junctions. After passing through a couple of gates at the farm of Braich y Dinas, a parking spot is reached at 540492. Cross the stile and follow the footpath due east up the hillside, eventually bearing round to the R through a ruined building into Cwm Trwsgl, opposite the main crag. Take a path up the hillside to reach some disused quarry workings. The slab gradually comes into view, across the cwm, to the R. Contour round along the track until due north of the slab, then come back south to its foot.

304 **The Exterminating Angel**   E3   180ft/55m ***

J. Perrin, D. C. O'Brien, 1974

This superb esoteric outing is bold and technical on its first pitch, but the rock is immaculate. Start below a fluted tongue of rock, directly beneath a prominent ledge and tree at half-height.

1. 60ft/18m. 5c. Ascend the V-chimney to the R of the fluted tongue to a foot-ledge on the L. Move up to a thin horizontal crack running L-wards. Follow this until a precarious move up can be made to a fragile spike below the overlap, or continue L via thin moves into a corner then climb back up to the same point. Pull round the overlap on to the slab above. Delicate moves, first up, then across R-wards, lead to better holds, runners, and at last, thankfully . . . the ledge.

2. 120ft/37m. 5a. Traverse across to reach the prominent slanting crack splitting the L side of the slab. Climb it to a difficult finish. Take the grassier slab behind to belays; these require some cunning to arrange, and there is the odd peg or two lurking hidden in the grass. Descend well over to the L of the crag.

Tremadog

This popular fair-weather area, the focal point of climbing in south Snowdonia, consists of four main crags spread over three miles along the escarpment running east-west just above the A487/A498, both roads meeting in Tremadog Village.

CRAIG Y GESAIL   (544413)

The most westerly of the Tremadog outcrops is reached along the narrow lane which starts opposite the Post Office in Penmorfa, a small village lying one mile west of Tremadog. Follow the lane for about 400 yd/400m to park near the gate of Tiddyn-Deucwm Isaf, making sure that vehicles are not impeding access to the fields. A track leads up to the farm from which a faint path leads up to the cliff in about fifteen minutes.

   The cliff is fairly broken, steep buttresses being separated by vegetated gullies. The most obvious landmark and reference point is the large area of slabs forming the lower part of Princess Buttress. To the R across a vegetated area lies Midas Buttress with its steep front face split by a horizontal break at half-height on its R side; to the L is Sheerline Buttress split by a central groove, Clutch (VS), whilst a rock tower rising out of vegetation on the extreme L of the cliff gives two good VS climbs: The Castle and The Chateau. The easiest descents lie down the well-worn paths at either end of the crag, i.e. to the R of Midas Buttress, or the L of The Castle.

305 **Bramble Buttress**   V Diff   190ft/57m *
M. J. Harris, J. Neill, 1953
A pleasant outing up the prominent rib on the L-hand side of

*Bramble Buttress:
the final moves*

Sheerline Buttress on large holds. Start at the foot of the rib
where the rock is worn.
1. 70ft/21m. Climb a series of short walls on the L of the rib to
the foot of a small corner at 30ft/9m. Ascend this then move R
to the crest of the rib which leads up to the top of a pinnacle.
Stance and belay behind it.
2. 60ft/18m. Go L and up a groove, then move back R to climb
the arete. Scramble up through trees to the base of the final
wall.
3. 60ft/18m. From the L side of the wall. Climb up trending
R-wards to finish.

306 **Javelin** HVS 210ft/63m
D. P. Davis and party, 1957

An interesting route with a bold first pitch. Low in the grade.
Start at the foot of the slabs on the L side of Princess Buttress by
a small tree.

1. 100ft/30m. 5a. Climb the slabs L of a small overlap, trending
L to a large block under the overhang. From the top of this, pull
on to the wall and go up to the L side of a sharp rib. Make a
bold move up the rib for a small hold then reach the horizontal
arete. Follow this to belay at the foot of a small wall behind.

2. 40ft/12m. 4a. Climb the wall then take a grassy line up
L-wards to a ledge below the final wall.

3. 70ft/21m. 4c. Climb the L-hand groove and continue up a
short wall from the top of which a corner crack gives an
enjoyable finish.

307 **Touch and Go** VS 120ft/36m. *
R. James, P. Benson, 1957

A popular route with an energetic top pitch. Start at the foot of
a V-groove capped by an overhang, in the centre of Midas
Buttress.

1. 70ft/21m. 4c. Climb the groove to the overhang. Step out L
and traverse delicately across a wall to a good ledge. Gain the
ledge 10ft/3m above.

2. 50ft/15m. 5a. Mantelshelf on to a ledge at the foot of a short
groove above and R of the stance. Climb this to the top of a
flake. Step on to the wall and climb it to the top.

CRAIG Y CASTELL (558405)

This crag lies behind the village school at the west end of
Tremadog. A short lane leads up to the L of the school. Go
along this, and its continuation until just past a stone wall with
a wire fence on top of it where a path leads R-wards across a
field to a boulder field. The crag lies just above. Approach time,
ten minutes. Care should be taken to avoid blocking the lane
when parking. The nearest official car-park is in Tremadog
village square.

On the L of the cliff is a large slabby area capped by overhangs. To the R, an area bristling with more overhangs has a fine slab rising up to meet it. A central V-groove runs the full height of the cliff, its L arete comprising a slabby nose of rock cut off at the base by large roofs.

308 **Creagh Dhu Wall**   HS   200ft/60m ***

J. Cunningham, W. Smith, P. Vaughan, 1951

One of the finest Welsh 'Severes'. This superb climb reaches the central V-groove from the L, then moves back L to tackle the crest of the buttress. Start on a well-worn ledge, by a large block to the L of the central groove, and below a large overhang at 40ft/12m.

1. 90ft/27m. Scramble up to a tree at the foot of the corner. Climb this and a tricky slanting crack, runner. Foot traverse R into the corner crack which quickly leads to a large terrace.
2. 80ft/24m. Follow the horizontal crack out L on to the crest of the buttress. Climb straight up in a fine position to belay on a good ledge.
3. 30ft/12m. 4b. Climb up L to enter a sloping and polished groove with difficulty, crux. Finish either L or R of the small overhang. The shallow groove directly behind the stance can also be taken at VS 4c. Descend down the scrambling path on the R-hand side of the cliff.

309 **One Step in the Crowds**   E1   170ft/52m

A. Evans, S. Tansey, S. Beresford, 1979

An enjoyable climb up the buttress just L of Creag Dhu Wall. Start by a large block as for Creag Dhu Wall.

1. 50ft/15m. 5b. Go up past the tree at the foot of the corner, as for Creag Dhu Wall. Step L into a steep groove and climb this taking care with a dubious flake. Step R below the overhang on to a rib, then go up with difficulty to a sloping ledge. Belays on the R in Creag Dhu Wall.
2. 120ft/37m. 5b. A diagonal crack splits the overhang. Use this to gain the sharp rib to the L of the ledge below a second crack. Climb this, moving R to better holds. Step L into a

groove/crackline and take this, then a flake crack on the R to
the large overhang. Pull over this and step round the arete on
the L whence a thin move up a slabby wall gives an exciting
finish.

310 **The Wasp**   E1   170ft/51m **
J. Brown, C. E. Davies (5 pts), 1960
An excellent climb with two contrasting pitches; a strenuous
crack precedes a precarious groove. Start at the bottom L-hand
corner of the slab which lies below and R of the large overhangs,
just R of the centre of the crag.
1. 90ft/27m. 5b. Climb easily up the corner for 30ft/9m. Move
L and up on to a pinnacle below a slanting crack in the
overhanging sidewall. Climb the crack (which is especially
strenuous for the weak or ageing) to a difficult exit.
2. 80ft/24m. 5b. From the L-hand end of the ledge, climb
directly up the prominent V-groove/corner; sustained,
technical and awkward, to a L-ward exit.

Pellagra, E3 6a, 5c, climbs the corner just R of the crack of The
Wasp, exiting L at the roof on to the large ledge. Its second
pitch climbs the slab, 20ft/6m R of The Wasp's V-corner, to a
long overhang, where it traverses L to finish up The Wasp.

311 **Tensor**   E2   220ft/66m **
J. Brown, C. E. Davies (2 pts), 1964/FFA: H. Barber, 1973
A spectacular way through the roofs R of Pellagra. Start R of
The Wasp at the foot of the slab.
1. 90ft/27m. 4b. Take a more or less direct line up the centre of
the slab, finishing up a short groove on to a small ledge.
2. 100ft/30m. 5c. Step down L and move across on to the slab.
Move up and traverse under the large overhang to a groove at
its L side. Climb this to a good foothold. Step R, hard, and go up
to the roof, PR. Make a long reach and pull over the roof into a
groove, crux, which leads to a stance.
3. 30ft/9m. Finish more easily via the groove above.

Craig y Castell

312 **Tantalus** HVS   220ft/66m *

H. I. Banner, J. Neill, 1955/Pitch 2: D. Yates, G. Simpkin (1 pt), 1964

A good route which sneaks around the R end of the Tensor roof with some exposed climbing. Start at the foot of the slab as for Tensor.

1. 90ft/27m. 4b. As for Tensor; or the R edge of the slab can be taken: Tarantula, E1, 5b.

2. 100ft/30m. 5a. Climb up ribs and grooves on the R until it is possible to cross the wall on the L to a PR. Make a difficult and exposed move past this to gain the arete. A thin move across the slab on the L leads to better holds and a stance above the Tensor roof.

3. 30ft/9m. Finish up the groove, as for Tensor.

CRAIG PANT IFAN   (570406)

One mile east of Tremadog village, this excellent crag rises from trees, 300ft/93m above the A498; less than 400 yd/372m further along the road lies the other major outcrop of the area, rising from a sub-tropical forest: Bwlch y Moch.

Handily, for climbers, situated between these two crags is Eric's Café, and a car-park which provides a welcome retreat for those rainy days, or midday brews. The approach to Pant Ifan is via a stile about 150yd/139m along the road towards Tremadog. A path marked by the occasional white arrow leads up across a boulder field to its foot where a well-trampled traversing path gives easy access to all of the routes.

The L end of the main section of cliff is dominated by the wide tower of Peuterey Buttress perched above vegetated slabs. An obvious (from below) overhanging chimney, Strapiombo HVS, splits the centre of the tower, while Poor Man's Peuterey climbs cracks up the slab to its R. Next come three massive overlapping slabs, each sporting a barrier of overhangs and separated by two clean R-angled corners; Barbarian on the L, and Scratch. R of Peuterey Buttress, across a dirty gully, a clean rib, Integral, E2 5b, 5b, rises up to the L end of some enormous

overhangs breached by The Toit, E4 6a, and other harder
problems, best approached by abseil!

Further over, across more vegetation and broken slabs, and
to the R of the approach path, lies the steep wall of Strangeways
Buttress; beyond this is a smooth black wall with a steep square
corner on its R-hand side: Vulcan. After this, the crag
deteriorates, its lower half becoming shaly, although a good
route, Hogmanay Hangover, HS, takes the groove at its
extreme R edge.

The usual descent is down the somewhat eroded steps of
Porker's Gully, just to the L of the main crag; tricky at the best
of times, this path becomes lethal when muddy! Another
descent, also tricky, may be made down a poorly defined path
through the woods to the R of Hogmanay Hangover; this is
difficult to locate, and an abseil escape may be necessary.

The topography of the crag is best established from the road.
Routes are described from R to L.

313 **Vulcan**   E3   190ft/58m ***
B. Wright, C. Goodey (artificial), 1962/FFA: R. Fawcett, 1977
The impressive L-facing corner on the R side of the smooth
black wall R of Strangeways Buttress is steep, technical, and
very sustained. A brilliant pitch in the modern idiom. Start by
following the traversing path R-wards past a rib of rock,
Strangeways Pinnacle, until it is possible to scramble up to the
front of a small slab in the vegetation, well below and just R of
the corner.

1. 70ft/21m. 4a. Climb the slab and continue direct up rock
and vegetation to a tree. Traverse L across a slab to nut belays
on a small stance below a steep crack.
2. 120ft/37m. 6a. Climb the crack round a bulge to a short
smooth groove. Thin bridging up this, PR, leads to a roof
(Falcon moves R here). Step L into the remorseless and
unforgiving corner which yields, sometimes, to fingertip
laybacking and bridging up to an overhang. Pull around this to
a rest. Continue with slightly less difficulty up the corner above
to finish. An immaculate pitch.

314 **Falcon**   E1   120ft/37m **

R. James, M. Petrovsky (artificial), 1962/FFA: J. Clements, 1964

A popular route which breaks out of Vulcan to take the wall to its R. Start from the belay at the top of the first pitch of Vulcan.

1. 5c. Climb the crack around the bulge, PR, to a short smooth groove below the overhang, as for Vulcan. Bridge up then step R to a small ledge immediately below the overhang. Swing round on to the face on the R and follow improving holds to the foot of a steep crack. Climb this past a couple of difficult moves to the top. A fine pitch.

315 **Scratch Arete**   VS   200ft/60m **

B. Ingle, R. F. Jones (1 pt), 1962

A climb of character up the R arete of Peuterey Buttress. Hard for its grade. Start: follow the traversing path L-wards for about 30yd/27m below vegetation to where a rib and shallow groove run up to the foot of a crack, 25ft/8m before the rock step in the path.

1. 100ft/30m. 4c. Climb the rib and shallow groove to a ledge at the foot of the crack. Go up this moving R at the top to an awkward finish round the bulge. Belay slightly L.
2. 100ft/30m. 5a. Climb the slab trending L then R to join the arete just below the overhang. PR around the corner to the R. Step up L and make a long reach round the overhang for a small hold. A committing pull and quick step up gain good holds, a runner and the end of the serious difficulties. Finish directly up the edge of the slab.

316 **Scratch**   VS   170ft/51m *

A. J. J. Moulam, W. R. Craster, 1953

The easiest route up this piece of rock has a fine second pitch up the R-angled corner, R of Barbarian. From the step in the path, traverse up L, then scramble up to the foot of the massive square R-facing corner: Barbarian.

1. 70ft/21m. 4b. Climb the slabby wall for a few feet. A gently

Craig Pant Ifan – Main Cliff

rising R-ward traverse leads past a block to a good ledge and
tree belay at the foot of the corner.

2. 100ft/30m. 4b. Climb up on to the block on the L. Continue
up the polished corner, with good protection, until holds lead
R-wards, across to a small ledge and crack. Finish up this.

317 **Barbarian**   E1   160ft/48m **

C. T. Jones and party (artificial), 1958/FFA: J. Brown, c. 1960
The huge corner in the centre of the overlapping slabs is a
powerful and intimidating line. Yet the difficulties are
relatively modest. Start by traversing up L-wards from the top
of the rock step in the path to belay as for Scratch, at the foot of
the corner.

1. 50ft/15m. 4b. Climb the wall just R of the corner, then move
into the corner and go up to a cramped stance at a ledge on
the L.

2. 110ft/33m. 5b. Surmount the overhang; difficult. Continue
up cracks in the slab above to a niche below the second
overhang. Pull out on to the L wall and get a finger jam with the
R hand, in the crack above. Awkward. A strenuous pull now
enables a layback position to be attained. Move up to a ledge
on the L, PR. Step back R into the groove and finish carefully
past a rattling block in the L wall. Good tree belays, and an
abseil descent point.

318 **Fingerlicker**   E4   170ft/52m ***

R. James, D. H. Jones (artificial, as Victimization), 1964/FFA:
P. Livesey, J. Lawrence, 1975.
A very strenuous testpiece which takes the overhanging
chimney/crack in the L wall of Barbarian, before crossing it
L-wards to join the upper reaches of Silly Arete. Well protected,
this route is often ascended with rests. The grade is given for a
free ascent; non-thugs need not apply. Start at the foot of
Barbarian.

1. 65ft/20m 6a. Climb L-wards across the slab into the
overhanging chimney. Squirm up this and pull out into the
crack. Take this on good finger-locks past a particularly

strenuous section just below a small overhang. Pull over this and climb the short corner to an easy R-ward traverse across into Barbarian at the cramped stance.

2. 105ft/32m. 6a. Climb Barbarian over the overlap then make a difficult traverse L across the overhanging wall to the arete. Move round on to a thin slab and a finish up Silly Arete.

319 **Silly Arete**   E3   150ft/46m ***

J. Pasquill, J. Nuttall, R. Evans, 1971

An immaculate route up the compellingly obvious R arete of the Pincushion slab which lies just L of Barbarian. The best slab climb at Tremadog! Scramble up to the foot of Barbarian.

1. 30ft/9m. 4b. Move L and climb a short groove in the arete. Swing out L to a tree, at the foot of Pincushion chimney, and belay on this; this pitch is usually omitted in favour of an approach along Pincushion, Pitch 1.

2. 120ft/37m. 5c. From the tree, which bends alarmingly (though not quite as much since the end of the branch broke off), step R and climb the arete moving slightly L at 15ft/5m. Step back R and follow the arete to the overhang, large tape runner. Surmount the problematic overhang (some are doomed to spend ages here!) above the Pincushion chimney on tiny crystals then move back R to the arete via a small prominent flake, just above. Continue delicately up the edge to a narrow ledge. A few steep moves up lead to a finger jam, a small ledge, and a sigh of relief. Finish easily up the crack.

320 **Pincushion**   E2 (HVS with 2 pts)   190ft/58m ***

D. P. Davies, M. J. Harris, R. R. E. Chorley (artificial), 1956/FFA: H. Barber, c.1974

A popular route with only a short really hard section to pass the overhang. Well protected. Start: 30ft/9m up the slab, and 20ft/6m L of the tree protruding from the Pincushion chimney, is another tree which has an enormous root dangling down. Begin just R of this.

1. 50ft/15m. 4b. Climb a shallow groove then its R arete. Step L below a tiny overhang with a long reach for a tree root.

The delightful upper reaches of Silly Arete

Traverse R from the prominent broken branch, past a small
tree in a groove to gain the tree at the foot of the chimney.
(Great Western, VS, follows the diagonal crack on the L to
finish up the next slab over.)
2. 140ft/43m. 5c. Climb the chimney to the roof; large spike
runner on the R. Move L with extreme difficulty past a PR, crux,
and pull over on to the slab; 5a with 2 pts. Follow the crack
until it bends sharply R. Climb diagonally R on pockets to

another crack. Continue up to the overlap. Traverse R below
this past two PRs to finish up a short slanting crack.

321 **Poor Man's Peuterey**   S   255ft/77m **

G. J. Sutton, J. Gaukroger, 1953

A very good route which always seems to have someone on it.
Start 20yd/18m L of Pincushion, below a damp fault line which
runs directly up to the obvious deep chimney cleaving the top
of the buttress; Strapiombo, HVS 5a.
1. 50ft/15m. Climb the groove for a few feet then step R on to
the rib which leads to a good tree belay.
2. 40ft/12m. Continue up the damp groove/cracks to another
tree.
3. 45ft/14m. Traverse R to reach an open stance on the edge of
the slab.
4. 100ft/30m. Climb up on the R, then move R on to the
exposed nose and ascend to a small ledge. Follow the cracks in
the slab above in a delightful position to a step R. Continue to a
good stance.
5. 20ft/6m. Finish up a short chimney on the L: loose. Or,
sneak off R-wards.

About 300yd/280m L of the main crag, past a few isolated
buttresses, lies the prominent Two Face Buttress with its
impressive overhangs. On its L is the descent path of Helsinki
Gully. The buttress can be reached by bushwacking across via
an indistinct path, from the foot of Peuterey Buttress, or, more
pleasantly, by wandering across the summit fields from the top
of Porker's Gully. A small outcrop, the Upper Tier, soon comes
into view and Two Face Buttress lies below it, and to our L.

322 **Helsinki Wall**   HVS   140ft/43m *

J. H. Longland, B. E. H. Maden (1 pt), 1955

An excellent climb up the west face of the buttress. Start in
Helsinki Gully at the L end of the obvious traverse leading
across a yellow coloured slab.
1. 60ft/18m. 5a. Traverse R across the slab to a ledge, then

climb up bulges and move back L to a niche. Make a hard move
R into a diagonal crack which leads more easily to a stance on
the arete.

2. 25ft/8m. 4c. Step down and traverse L below overhangs then
climb the obvious break and trend L to a stance below the steep
upper wall.

3. 55ft/17m. 5a. Climb the wall and groove past a PR to the
overhang. Make a hard move L and go up to a steep crack.
Take this via a final layback to a sudden finish.

323 **Stromboli** HVS 210ft/63m ***

H. Smith, C. T. Jones, 1956

This route gives exciting climbing through the overhangs on
the front face of the buttress at a surprisingly amenable
standard. Low in its grade. Start near the bottom L-hand
corner of the buttress, below a curving groove capped by a roof.

1. 90ft/27m. 4c. Climb up to the foot of the groove, or traverse
into it. Ascend the groove until a long stride R gains the arete.
Move R across the shattered wall and climb up to a stance and
belay; Olympic Slab, VS 4c, finishes direct via cracks in the
slab above.

2. 40ft/12m. Descend to the R, then go across to climb a small
corner to a good ledge and belay.

3. 80ft/24m. 5a. Climb up towards a wide capped chimney for
15ft/5m until level with a large overhang on the L. Move L
below this using underclings, and so gain a good hold at its L
end. Pull up on to the slab and climb it to a second overhang.
Turn this by the V-chimney on the R to reach the upper slab
below the final roof, PR. A thin step up R, and a long reach
gains the crucial finishing hold. Hitler's Buttock, E5 6b, takes
the short hanging groove and the three bands of overhangs
between Stromboli and . . .

324 **Sexual Salami** E4 80ft/24m ***

J. Redhead, K. Robertson, C. Shorter, 1980

A brilliant, finger-searing test piece which threads an intricate

Craig Pant Ifan – Two Face Buttress

and devious way up the R side of the front face of the buttress. Start from a ledge just R of the main face, reached by a traverse R from the second stance of Stromboli, or better, by abseil.

1. 6b. Climb the slab just L of the R arete for 15ft/5m. Step L and pull round on to another slab. Go up to a good undercut and resting foothold. Climb diagonally across, PR, to a small ledge on the arete; Cardiac Arete, E4 6b, continues direct past two PRs from here. Step down and move L with difficulty. A long reach and a desperate pull on a rounded arete enable a slab on the L to be gained. There is a hidden wire placement in the top overhang next to the PR. More desperate moves over the roof lead to the easier finishing groove. A pitch which is hard on the nerves!

CRAIG BWLCH Y MOCH   (577407)

This, the most popular of the Tremadog cliffs, lies just above the A498, a hundred yards or so R of Eric's Café and car-park. At the L end of the cliff, nearest the café, is a steep wall cut by two overhanging grooves in its upper half: Grasper Buttress. This lies between an undercut rib, Valerie's Rib, on the L, and the square cut corner of Clapton's Crack, VS, low down on the R. Next comes Neb Buttress with its easily recognized roof crack, Neb Direct, E3 6a, and beyond this is a slabby wall which terminates in the fine arete of The Plum. To the R is a narrow buttress comprising a fine undercut slab sitting above a steep wall. Above this wall hangs a large inverted tooth of rock, known as The Fang. R again, across more vegetation sits the magnificent Vector Buttress with its impressive overhangs, followed by the fine open wall of Shadrach Buttress. Further along, past a vegetated rock-scarred area and close to the old road, is Merlin Buttress with its two steep walls. After this the cliff peters out into the hillside just before Portreuddyn Castle.

There are two established descent paths; the first runs down through the woods to the L of Valerie's Rib, whilst the second, Belshazaar Gully, lies just L of Merlin Buttress. Both paths are well-worn and marked by white arrows. Under no circumstances should a descent be made through the grounds of Portreuddyn Castle.

325 **Valerie's Rib**   HS   230ft/70m *

P. Vaughan, W. Smith, J. Cunningham, 1951

A fine open route up the L edge of Grasper Buttress. Scramble up to the L of broken rocks to belay on the L side of the rib, level with the large overhang.

1. 20ft/6m. Climb up, then go diagonally R to a stance on the front of the rib, just above the overhang.

2. 120ft/37m. Go straight up to a short groove at 20ft/6m. Exit L from the top of this on to a slab. Climb this for 20ft/6m, then step R on to the nose. Continue up the slab and crack above to a large grass ledge.

3. Scramble up R-wards keeping L of the rockfall to a ledge of detached blocks. Take the steep crack above to a tree. Move L to finish up the broken crack.

326 **Grasper**   E2   160ft/48m **

J. Brown, D. Thomas Bach (5 pts), 1961

A fine sustained and exposed route whose second pitch takes the L-hand groove in the overhanging headwall of Grasper Buttress. Start at a clean slabby ledge on the L and at the foot of the steep wall R of Valerie's Rib, reached by a scramble up from the R.

1. 90ft/27m. 5b. Climb a shallow groove to a narrow ledge then move round the rib on the L into an overhanging niche. Step L again on to another rib and go up the groove on the L to a small overhang, PR. Layback boldly up to gain a good foothold on the R. Move L into a good crack. Climb this to a large spike runner. A short traverse R leads to an airy stance and peg and nut belays.

2. 70ft/21m. 5c. Go up the leaning wall to enter the top groove. Continue by wide bridging past several old PRs to the overhang. A hard pull up, and move out L gain a sharp rib leading to the top.

327 **Zukator**   E4   180ft/54m ***

P. Crew, A. Harris (8 pts), 1964/FFA: P. Livesey, J. Sheard, 1976

The wall and overhanging groove R of Grasper give a very bold, strenuous and technical climb; the ascent of the groove is akin to bridging up a groove in the bottom of an egg, with about as many holds! Start below a corner, Clapton's Crack VS, about 20ft/6m R of Grasper's start.

1. 90ft/27m. 5c. Climb up L into a niche. Move L from this, round the arete to a tiny ledge. Ascend more or less directly up to the top of the steep slabby wall above, moving L on to the Grasper stance.

2. 90ft/27m. 6b. Climb the short wall and groove above to the first bulge, as for Grasper, Make a hard traverse R to the base of the overhanging groove; the ascent of this past two PRs provides the meat of the route!

328 **Christmas Curry with the Micah Finish**

S/HS 270ft/78m ***

A. J. J. Moulam, J. M. Barr, 1953

An enjoyable and popular route up the slabby L wall of the arete of The Plum: the wall R of Neb Buttress. Start at the bottom R-hand side of the wall beneath a triangular slab leading up into a deep chimney.

1. 40ft/12m. Go up the slab and chimney to a tree belay.

2. 90ft/27m. Climb diagonally L to some sloping ledges and continue up a short steep wall. Follow good holds on the R then move back L and go up to a ledge and tree belay on the L.

3. 60ft/18m. Climb the slab above and gain the wall to the L above a small roof. Continue up on good holds to another fine stance.

4. 70ft/21m. The normal finish moves across to climb the corner on the L for 10ft/3m, traverses L to a bunch of flakes, then finishes direct via a polished scoop with a problematic entry. However, a better finish is to take the thin crack behind

Craig Bwlch y Moch – Grasper Buttress and The Plum

the stance then traverse R to the arete to join the top part of The Plum. Follow this on good holds to the top.

329 **The Plum**   HVS   140ft/42m ***
R. James, D. Yates (2 pts), 1961

The arete R of Christmas Curry gives one of the finest routes at Tremadog. If the avoidable bottom crack is climbed, and the whole route done in a single runout . . . it is E1. Scramble up to the bottom R-hand side of the arete where a steep corner runs up to a large roof.

1. 60ft/18m. 5b. Climb the corner to a sloping ledge; it is possible to traverse in from the R to this point. Move L on to the rib and make a few feet of steep ascent to a small ledge below a slabby groove. Climb the precarious groove to a sloping stance and large flake belay.

2. 80ft/24m. 5b. Climb the wide flake crack above to a small ledge. Move R up a short groove. Make a hard step L on to the rib which leads without difficulty to the top.

330 **The Fang**   HVS   200ft/61m **
J. Brown, C. E. Davies, 1961

A fine climb with two contrasting pitches on the narrow buttress with the inverted rock spike, to the R of The Plum. Start at the foot of Striptease Gully, just R of the buttress.

1. 80ft/24m. 5a. Step L and climb a thin crack up to the large pinnacle. Move L into a steep short corner which leads to a ledge on the arete. Move back R across the wall and climb a crack to a narrow ledge and belay.

2. 120ft/37m. 5a. Climb the wall on the L and make a couple of thin moves round the arete to a sloping ledge. Continue L for a few feet then climb up to a flake below the upper slab. Possible belay. Climb the slab trending R at first, then continue direct to the L-hand side of a large block at its apex. Finish easily to tree belays.

331 **Extraction** E2 160ft/48m **

C. J. Phillips, M. Crook, 1975

A superb eliminate on The Fang. Start as for that route at the toe of the buttress.

1. 60ft/18m. 5b. Climb the crack to the top of the pinnacle, as for The Fang. Climb the strenuous bulge above then continue up the thin crack to the narrow ledge and belay, on The Fang.

2. 100ft/30m. 5c. An exciting pitch. Climb across the R wall until a bold move gains a small ledge on the arete. Climb the sloping rib to where the wall above overhangs. Step L round the arete to a hidden finger jug, crux, and so reach The Fang slab. Climb the R-hand side of this to the top.

332 **Striptease** VS 160ft/49m

J. Brown, C. E. Davies, 1961

A worthwhile and interesting climb which remains dry in all but the wettest of weathers. Start at the foot of the gully just R of The Fang.

1. 120ft/37m. 5a. Climb the chimney turning the first overhang on its R. Continue over a couple of bulges to an overhanging wall. Step R and move up to a good tree belay.

2. 40ft/12m. 4b. Step L on to the arete. Finish up this.

333 **One Step in the Clouds** VS 230ft/69m ***

C. T. Jones, R. Moseley, 1958

An exposed and delicate route which is very popular. It climbs the slabby L flank of Vector Buttress. Start at the toe of the buttress, L of a short stepped flake, and below a block-filled corner.

1. 90ft/27m. 4b. Climb up over the blocks to a large tree. Continue diagonally L up the wall to the foot of a polished V-groove. Climb this to a stance by a large flake below overhangs.

2. 90ft/27m. 4c. Go round the corner on the L to climb a shallow crack. Possible tree belay on the L. Move diagonally R to the edge of the overhangs and go delicately up the slab above

until a step R leads to a hard move up a short crack. Stance and belays above.

3. 50ft/15m. 4b. Move R and take a short slab to the start of the obvious traverse line. Follow this to finish with a delicate step up on to the stance.

334 **Nimbus**   E2   165ft/47m *
J. Brown, C. Goodey (1 pt), 1961

A fine exposed route taking a diagonal fault from L to R across the front of Vector Buttress. The climbing is mainly VS, with a short sharp crux. Start from the first stance of One Step in the Clouds which can also be reached by scrambling up to The Fang start, where a short R-ward traverse leads easily round to the large flake.

1. 90ft/27m. 5c. From the stunted tree at the R-hand end of the ledge, traverse R on the lip of the overhangs, below a small triangular roof to a sloping ledge at the foot of a groove 10ft/3m further on. Climb the groove with some very hard moves to pass a flat-top spike, crux. Step R on to a black overhung slab. A few thin moves up this lead quickly to the Vector cave. Peg belays.

2. 40ft/12m. 4b. Follow the fault line diagonally R-wards out of the cave to reach a large sloping stance overlooking the gully on the R of the buttress.

3. 25ft/8m. 4b and ivy. Step down and cross the gully to a tree belay. Either abseil off, or finish up one of the routes on Shadrach Buttress.

335 **The Weaver**   E2   200ft/61m ***
C. Shorter, P. Williams (AL), 1980

A classic companion to Vector which weaves an improbable path up through the overhangs to the L of the parent route. The easiest way up the front of the buttress. Start at the toe of the buttress, half-way up the stepped flake: just L of Vector.

Craig Bwlch y Moch – Vector and Shadrach Buttresses

1. 40ft/12m. 5b. Step L and climb up into a faint groove. Pull directly up the wall above on to the first Vector stance.

2. 120ft/37m. 5c. Step up and traverse 10ft/3m L to a small ledge. Climb directly up the bulging wall past a PR to the triangular overhang on Nimbus. Step R one move and climb a short groove, PR, then step L on to good footholds on the lips of an overhang, crux. Take the short crack to a hanging flake, then go diagonally R to a large TR. Step L and go steeply up a groove to the foot of the final Vector layback. Climb the puzzling corner to good holds and a large stance on One Step in the Clouds.

3. 40ft/12m. 4b. Step R and climb the slabby wall direct to finish up a short layback flake.

336 **Vector**   E2   250ft/75m ***

J. Brown, C. E. Davies (2 pts), 1960

This steep and intricate route through the large overhangs is a masterpiece of route finding. It epitomizes the best that Tremadog has to offer and is still *the* route of the crag. Start at the toe of the buttress, from the top of the stepped flake, immediately R of The Weaver.

1. 50ft/15m. 4c. Climb a short groove and step R on to a slab. Move up L to climb a short steep corner. Traverse 6ft/2m L to belay. (Cream E4 5c, 6a, takes the obscene cleft above then follows Nimbus to the Vector cave.)

2. 80ft/24m. 5c. Traverse R via a pinch-grip move to a thin diagonal crack. Follow this to a huge spike on the R. From the top of the spike make a hard step out L and climb the sustained and polished slab to a bridging rest at the foot of the ochre-coloured slab. PR. Climb past the peg to the end of the overhang and continue up the shallow groove above to another overhang. Traverse L to a cave stance in the centre of the face. Peg belays. A tremendous pitch.

3. 70ft/21m. 5b. Move L to a small ledge and stride across to another ledge. Pull over the roof above on a good jug then

Vector: the Ochre Slab

traverse the slab delicately L-wards to an overhanging groove and flake crack. Difficult starting moves up the groove lead to good holds, and runners. Continue more easily to a large stance on One Step in the Clouds.

4. 50ft/15m. Finish diagonally R as for One Step in the Clouds.

337 Void   E3   205ft/62m ***

R. Edwards and party (1 pt), 1975/FFA: R. Fawcett, 1976

An exceptionally fine eliminate with an exciting finish up a pod and crack on the R side of the Vector headwall. Start at the foot of an undercut groove directly below the ochre-coloured slab.

1. 50ft/15m. 5b. Climb the sustained groove to belay under the Ochre Slab.

2. 85ft/26m. 5c. Climb up and L on to the large spike of Vector. Step L and climb the difficult wall to the foot of the Ochre Slab, PR. Continue past the peg and climb the shallow groove in the arete to the overhang (where Vector moves L to the cave). Climb up R round the corner to a ledge below a bulge. From the R end of this, climb a hidden crack to an overhung stance overlooking the gully; shared with Nimbus.

3. 70ft/21m. 6a. Climb the overhanging crack/groove above the stance into a niche. Exit L at the top on a good hold. Take the bulging wall above with a very long reach past a PR for a good jam. Continue via a crack for 10ft/3m then step R to finish up its continuation. A strenuous and intimidating pitch which is 5c if the peg is used for aid.

338 The Atomic Finger Flake   E3   150ft/48m **

J. Redhead, P. Williams (AL), C. Shorter, K. Robertson, 1980

A very strenuous route with some sensational moves up the underside of the Ochre Slab. Start at the top of the stepped flake, immediately R of the Vector start.

1. 60ft/18m. 5b. A problem start up the wall R of the Vector groove leads to good holds. Follow a diagonal line R-wards to the top of the Void groove. Continue to the Void stance.

2. 90ft/27m. 6b. Move R and climb a short technical groove. Move R on to an ivy ledge. Go up the rib behind to a niche level

with a PR in the ludicrously overhanging L wall. Cross the wall using two undercuts just above the PR (to cross the wall at a higher level is cheating; on the first ascent the wall was crossed even lower) to reach an overhanging crack. Layback dynamically (or otherwise) up this to a PR. Pull up into the groove above with an easier finish to the Void stance; all very dramatic! Finish up the top pitch of Void, or take the exposed crack on the L: the 6a top pitch of Cream.

339 Sultans of Swing E4   190ft/58m ***

J. Redhead, P. Williams, 1980/Pitch 1: P. Williams, J. de Montjoye, 1980

A magnificent girdle of Vector Buttress. The second pitch, which requires good rope management, is one of the finest in South Snowdonia. Start on the L side of the buttress, at the first stance of One Step, and Nimbus.

1. 50ft/15m. 6a. Above is a hanging groove. Traverse R and climb a steep wall to the large overhang. Make a couple of desperate moves up L to enter the groove which eases to the overhang above. Step R into a groove (on The Weaver) to belay.

2. 140ft/43m. 6a. A brilliant pitch. A few moves R lead to an overhanging chimney/crack: Croaker, E3 5c. Traverse R with difficulty with bold moves round the arete into an overhanging crack. A couple of thin moves R across a slab lead to good holds and a sharp spike (this section can be taken at a higher level). Climb the crack above (the top pitch of Cream which continues direct at 6a) and swing R on to a flake. Continue up a few moves until a short traverse R gains the good jug on Void. Follow Void past the PR up to its continuation crack. Take this for about 8ft/2m until a long stride R gains a good finger ledge. Pull up to reach another incut hold from which a step up and jam lead to a shallow corner, and the top.

The slabby wall R of Vector Buttress has several quality routes:

340 **Grim Wall** VS   180ft/54m *

H. Smith, C. T. Jones, H. Fox, 1957

This climbs the L side of Shadrach Buttress with a good steep finish. Scramble up R of Vector Buttress to belay at a tree below an overhanging chimney, Shadrach, in the middle of the face.

1. 100ft/30m. 4b. Climb up and L to a ledge. Go up into the scoop above to reach a large flake on the L. Hand traverse along this to gain a corner on the L. Climb the corner then take the rib on the L to a large earthy ledge. Nut and tree belay.

2. 80ft/24m. 4c. Climb diagonally R and pull up L-wards over the overlap on to a narrow ledge. Traverse L on to a rib and finish steeply up this on good holds; easier than it looks.

341 **Meshach** HVS   190ft/57m ***

R. James, A. Earnshaw, M. Petrovsky (1 pt), 1962

A fine varied route up the highest part of the face R of Grim Wall. Start below the Shadrach Chimney, as for Grim Wall.

1. 110ft/33m. 4c. Climb up a slabby rake leading L to a ledge. Go up the scoop above, then take a shallow groove on the R, and step R to a good ledge. Continue up for a few feet to the Shadrach flake. Step down L into a small niche then climb the wall on the L to a good spike. Traverse L to a corner and continue to the Grim Wall stance; this pitch has several slight variations.

2. 80ft/24m. 5a. Climb diagonally R and pull up L-wards over the overlap on to the narrow ledge, as for Grim Wall. From the R end of the ledge. Pull on to a wider smoother ledge. Step up and move R past a PR using a hidden side-pull to another ledge. Continue direct to the L end of a long narrow ledge. Traverse this to a flake on its R. Step up then move R to finish.

342 **Shadrach** VS   150ft/45m **

A. J. J. Moulam, G. W. S. Pigott, D. Thomas, 1951

A classic direct line up the centre of the buttress. Start at a tree belay below the overhanging chimney in the centre of the wall.

Shadrach, top pitch

1. 50ft/15m. 4b. Climb up to the foot of the chimney. Struggle up this on the inside or outside, depending on stature, to a ledge and belays. For those not into struggling, a crack on the R provides a more pleasant alternative.

2. 40ft/12m. 4b. Move L and pull up on to a flake. The steep slab above leads to a belay at the foot of a huge block/pinnacle.

3. 60ft/18m. 4c. From the top of the block stride across to get established in the shallow groove: difficult. After a few feet, step R to finish up the slab.

343 **Leg Slip**   HVS   200ft/61m *

J. Brown, C. E. Davies, 1960

A worthwhile route up the L-hand of the two obvious grooves on the R edge of Shadrach Buttress. Start by scrambling up to a large tree at the foot of a steep groove capped by a huge roof.

1. 50ft/15m. 5a. Climb the goove, hard to start, and so reach a ledge. (First Slip, E1 5c, continues up to the roof, steps R and climbs the thin groove, steeping back L to finish up an arete.) Climb up a couple of moves, then go across L to a tree belay on a sloping ramp.

2. 65ft/20m. 5a. Follow the ramp up R through the overhang to the foot of a V-corner. Move up a little, make a hard step out to the R arete, crux, then move back L and so reach a tree belay.

3. 35ft/11m. 5a. Climb the groove behind the tree to the roof. Make a hard move on to the L arete and go up easily to another tree belay.

4. 50ft/15m. Scramble up to a grass ledge and finish up the slab above.

344 **Daddy Cool**   E2   185ft/56m

P. Williams, D. Roberts (AL), R. Edwards, 1978

An interesting and varied route up the L wall of Merlin Buttress. Start from the large tree growing 15ft/5m up the L arete of the wall, above some blocks.

Craig Bwlch y Moch – Merlin Buttress

1. 60ft/18m. 4c. From the tree, pull up on to the wall and continue easily to an oak sapling in a corner. Move ʀ past this and go up a shallow groove to a ledge on the ʟ. Take the short wall above to a good ledge, then move ʀ with a long stride into the tree on the ʀ. Descend this to belay.

2. 65ft/20m. 5c. From half-way up the tree, cross the wall on the ʀ to the top of a pedestal. Climb up to get runners in the diagonal crack and step ʀ into a groove. Layback boldly up on to a ramp to reach a inverted V-shaped overhang. Pull over this into a ʟ-sloping groove. Climb this to a rounded ledge. Step back ʀ and move up to nut belays at the start of a traverse line.

3. 60ft/18m. 5a. Traverse ʀ past a hard move to good holds below a short crack with a pod at the top; finish up this. Belay well back.

345 **Merlin/Direct Finish** VS 160ft/48m ***
A. J. J. Moulam, B. A. Gillot, 1956

A steep entertaining climb. Start on the ʀ side of the buttress, on the ʟ side of a bay formed by a severely overhanging wall and a short slab, below a short crack – this is at a lower level and about 10yd/9m ʟ of the slab.

1. 80ft/24m. 4c. Climb crack for 15ft/5m on to a slab. Climb this and its continuation to a tiny ledge at foot of a V-chimney; the ramp of Geireagle runs up to the ʀ from here. Climb chimney/groove exiting ʟ at roof on to easy slabs. Move across and go up to a tree belay.

2. 60ft/18m. 4b. Climb the short slab to the layback crack. Exit ʀ from the top of this and go round the corner continuing up to a tree belay; The Direct Finish, VS 4c, goes straight up from the top of the crack, then traverses ʟ to finish via a thin crack in the centre of the wall on the ʟ.

3. 20ft/6m. 4a. Finish up the steep little corner behind the tree.

346 **Geireagle** E2 155ft/47m **
R. Edwards, J. Edwards (2 pts), 1966

A spectacular climb up the ramp in the overhanging wall ʀ of Merlin. Start below the short crack down to the ʟ, as for Merlin.

1. 135ft/41m. 5c. Climb the short crack on to the slab. Move up to a thin diagonal crack below the continuation slab. Traverse this diagonally R-wards, without much for the feet, to pull over the overhang on to the ledge below the Merlin V-chimney. Climb the hanging ramp diagonally up R to a fierce section, where hidden holds above seem just out of reach! Follow the line of ledges back L with increasing difficulty until a bold swing past a PR gains a good hold on the L arete. Climb the slab to the final corner of Merlin.

2. 20ft/6m. 4a. Take the steep little corner to the top.

Further along the old road, just beyond a large block, a rib below easy-angled slab gives the pleasant Yogi, S.

CARREG HYLLDREM   (614432)

This ferocious little crag towers over the A4085 at a sharp bend, about midway between Aberglaslyn and Penrhyndeudraeth. It is possible to park below the crag, about sixty seconds away! There is no easy way up this sensationally overhanging cliff; all the routes tend to be deceptively steep – slabs are vertical, and the vertical . . . overhangs! On the L-hand side, rising from the foot of the crag is a huge overhang. Further R, at its centre, the crag consists of slabs and ribs capped by yet more overhangs, the most prominent overhanging prow giving the path of Raging Bull, E5 6b. R of this, a concave wall sits above an oak tree and is bounded on its R by slabs. 50yd/46m further over, just past a fence, is a fearsome leaning bouldering wall which gives good sport on rainy days as well as some carnivorous micro-routes.

The descent route is way over to the R down a grassy slope, through trees and back round below the bouldering wall.

347 **King Kong**   E2   150ft/45m *
R. Evans, J. Pasquill, 1974
On the L of the cliff, the obvious flake crack splitting the roof gives a superb outing, ideal for gritstone thugs.

1. 90ft/27m. 5c. Layback up the flake, from the top of which a

bold move over the lip of the roof leads to good holds and a sloping ledge. Traverse R for 20ft/6m into a short groove. Climb it and continue up the slab above to nut belays a few feet below the upper wall.

2. 60ft/18m. 5a. Traverse R along the slab for 20ft/6m to the foot of an overhanging chimney. Climb it awkwardly past a dubious flake to the top.

348 **Primus**   E2   180ft/55m

J. Brown, D. T. Roscoe (2 pts), 1960

The first attack on the crag proves to be no walkover. Start R of King Kong, at the end of the overhangs, just L of a large prominent groove.

1. 75ft/23m. 4c. Climb up to the roof then traverse awkwardly R into the groove. Climb this to a stance and peg belays below the upper overhangs.

2. 55ft/17m. 5c. Cross the slab on the L to the rib. From the top of this make a very strenuous pull up round the bulge to enter the overhanging groove, PR. Wedge and jam the stubborn groove to easier ground and a stance on the R.

3. 50ft/15m. 4c. Step back L and continue up the groove, move L and finish up a short steep corner.

349 **Samurai Groove**   E3   180ft/54m ***

B. Wyvill, D. Mossman (2 pts), 1971/FFA: P. Thomas, M. Fowler, 1979

A wild, wild climb up the overhanging rock just R of the prow of Raging Bull. Start 10yd/9m R of Primus below twin grooves.

1. 60ft/18m. 5a. Climb the R-hand groove to an obvious traverse line, and a junction with the Girdle. Move across to a stance and belay on the rib on the L.

2. 80ft/24m. 5c. Climb the awkward bulging groove behind the belay and move R to a saddle beneath the prow, PR. Move R with difficulty and blindly grope round the ridiculously overhanging arete for the 'Father of all Jugs'. Swing across on

Carreg Hylldrem

Hardd

this to reach a steep groove, spectacular! Climb the groove in a spacewalking position to an overhung niche, PR. Exit up the wall on the L and continue up to the Hardd stance.
3. 40ft/12m. Scramble up broken rock to finish.

350 **Hardd**   E2   160ft/48m ***
J. Brown, G. D. Roberts, N. Drasdo (1 pt), 1960

The concave wall R of Samurai Groove provides the classic of the cliff. Scramble up the sloping ramp behind the large oak tree to reach a small stance at 30ft/9m.

1. 80ft/24m. 5c. Step L on to the steep wall and move across to the foot of a short crack. Climb this past an old PR to an undercut below the bulge and make a delicate traverse L to a resting place. Continue up the smooth slab on the L over some bulges to reach a tiny stance in a fine position. Peg belays. Or, from the resting place after the traverse, climb the crack in the short corner above to a rake, step R and layback round the bulge, and so reach a small stance: 20ft, 5a. Traverse low down L into a groove then climb up to the ledge at the end of Pitch 1.

2. 40ft/12m. 5a. Either climb or abseil 15ft/5m down the overhanging groove below the stance until good holds lead L to easier ground. Move up to a stance. Or, from the stance, continue up the corner, move R to the arete then go straight up to a L-stepping exit: The Direct Finish, E3 6a!

3. 40ft/12m. Finish easily up broken rocks above.

351 **The Hyll-Drem Girdle**   HVS   220ft/67m **
J. Brown, G. D. Verity, 1960

An enjoyable and popular wet weather route which sidles along the fault line below the overhangs. Start at the large oak tree on the R-hand side of the cliff.

1. 65ft/20m. 4c. Follow the obvious break L-wards beneath the bulging upper walls to reach a short groove. Climb this, then make a tricky move on to the slabby rib on the L, crux. Peg belays.

2. 35ft/11m. 4b. Awkward moves across a short slab on the L lead to another rib. Descend the groove on the other side for 20ft/6m to a stance.

3. 40ft/12m. 4b. Move L across the slab to the arete, then descend a broken groove to a good ledge at the bottom R side of the final slab.

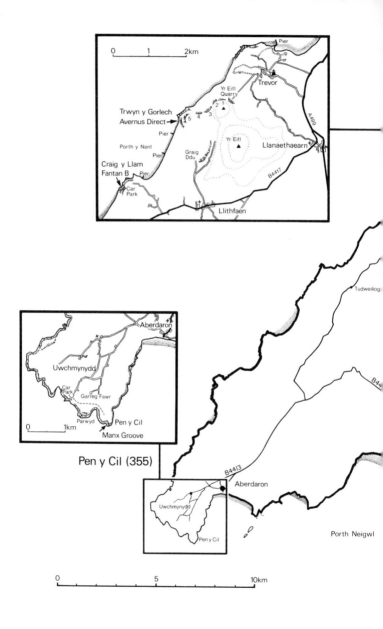

Pen y Cil (355)

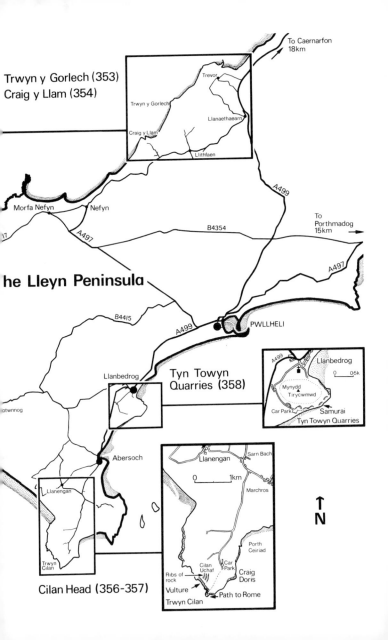

Trwyn y Gorlech (353)
Craig y Llam (354)

To Caernarfon
18km

Trevor

Trwyn y Gorlech

Llanaethaearn

Craig y Llam

Llithfaen

Morfa Nefyn   Nefyn

A499

To
Porthmadog
15km

17

A497

B4354

he Lleyn Peninsula

B4415

A499

PWLLHELI

A497

Llanbedrog

Tyn Towyn
Quarries (358)

A499

Llanbedrog

0   05k

Mynydd
Tirycwmwd

Car Park

Samurai

Tyn Towyn Quarries

otwnnog

Abersoch

Llanengan

Sarn Bach

Llanengan

0   1km

Marchros

Trwyn Cilan

Porth
Ceiriad

Cilan
Uchaf

Car
Park

Craig
Doris

Ribs of
rock

Vulture

Path to Rome

Trwyn Cilan

Cilan Head (356-357)

↑
N

Avernus: the traverse below the rock band

4. 80ft/24m. 4c. Climb a groove on the R for a few feet, traverse L to the edge of the slab and finish direct to a tree belay. Scramble up L, then back R to the top of the crag.

352 **The Weirpig**   E5   80ft/24m ***

S. Haston, solo, 1981

A beast of a route up the centre of the bouldering wall. Start
below a prominent niche in the middle: high up.

1. 6b. To attain the base of the niche is a powerful problem. To
attain a standing position in it is even harder! Exit L with
difficulty then move back R to finish up a broken groove . . . a
pitch which 'takes no prisoners'.

The Lleyn Peninsula

Jutting out into the Irish Sea to the south-west of Snowdon, this
forgotten backwater lies well out of the other mainstream
climbing areas. Yet the Lleyn holds a certain fascination for a
discerning clientele: the climber in search of adventure, the
connoisseur of the esoteric, the seeker after solitude . . . to see
another party is a rarity.

YR EIFL: TRWYN Y GORLECH   (351457)

This large rambling cliff lies on the west side of the pyramidal
seaside mountain of Yr Eifl, about twelve miles south of
Caernarfon. It is seen in profile when driving down the A499
from Caernarfon to Pwllheli as the prominent R skyline of Yr
Eifl, plunging dramatically down into Caernarfon Bay.

The best approach is from Trefor, just to the north. Park at
the far end of the village near the foot of the incline coming
down from Yr Eifl Quarry. Follow a track, then the seashore
path, south, eventually dropping down on to the boulder
beach. The crag is now fully revealed as two huge buttresses,
enclosing three smaller ones above a massive grassy cwm. Our
selected climb lies on the furthest, and largest, buttress, No. 5.

353 **Avernus Direct**   E1   735ft/226m **

G. W. S. Pigott, J. N. Mather, W. R. Craster, 1954/T. Hodgson,
P. Williams, 1988

This unusual, interesting and memorable expedition up the
front of the buttress is a serious undertaking, though mainly at

VS in standard with only one hard pitch, which can be avoided on the L. The rock is compact granodiorite, yet loose in places, with few cracks and generally coated with lichen. The climbing is generally of a low technical difficulty, but with a few sections of steep grass to negotiate, rather unnerving for devotees of the 'clean clip-up' school. Protection is hard to find and crops up occasionally; the exact line is devious, but old pegs are in situ on most of the stances – these are good when backed up with modern hardware.

The route should be avoided if it is wet, as this greatly enhances the difficulties, and a retreat may take on epic proportions if you are caught out above the rock band. From the belay at the top of Pitch 6, an escape up to the L can be made via a two-pitch diversion of 160ft/49m with a wobbly belay, midway.

From the beach, scramble up an earthy gully and traverse steep grass diagonally R-wards, all very gripping, to start about 20ft/6m R, and just up from the toe of the buttress.

1. 40ft/12m. Scramble up to a large flake belay.
2. 140ft/43m. Step up and climb diagonally R for 15ft/5m. Pull up on grass and step L on to a juggy rocky rib. Climb this then trend R over grass to a second rocky outcrop capped by an overhang. From the R end of this, step up L and climb the slab to another grass and rock section to belay on a large block below a lichenous short wall. This point can be reached from below and to the R via grassy ledges.
3. 50ft/15m. 4c. From the flake, climb the wall via a hollow flake, then continue on good holds, trending R to a sound belay below the overhanging rock barrier.
4. 75ft/23m. 5a. Traverse easily L to the very edge of the face. Surmount the steep groove, then climb diagonally R for 30ft/9m to belay in a niche. Friend 2 and wires immediately L.
5. 75ft/23m. 5a. Go straight up just L of the belay for 35ft/11m to a grass terrace. Move R for 10ft/3m. Small grassy ledges lead diagonally R to good belays in a corner, on a narrow ledge, 10ft/3m L of the arete.
6. 75ft/23m. 4c. Move R to the arete and follow footledges

slanting up R-wards to a small V-niche after 35ft/11m. Climb up and surmount the roof. Continue up a rib for a few feet then pull out on to a grass ledge. Move R and go up to a good crack and nut belays below a short rock band.

7. 120ft/37m. 5a. Climb the rock band to a good runner in a crack. Make an exposed R-ward traverse, above a roof, to gain the arete via a tricky swing. Step back L and climb boldly up, holds appearing when needed, to reach some large perched flakes. Clamber over these to more grass and a large flake and peg belay at the foot of a large grassy ramp. A serious pitch which is avoidable on the L via a ramp, honeysuckle slab and incipient groove to easier ground, where a traverse R gains the same spot. This is VS, and the wobbly belay may be taken at the top of the slab.

8. 100ft/30m. 4b. Walk R for 10ft/3m, then move diagonally back L up flakes to a terrace. Move L along this for about 15ft/5m then take the centre of the wall to grass and a shallow groove.

9. 60ft/18m. 4a. Climb easily up behind the belay. Block belays lie 60ft/18m back from the edge. Continue back and contour round the hillside above a small quarry, traversing across heather and grass to emerge at the top of Yr Eifl Quarry. Zigzag down, then descend the incline to collapse in your car!

CRAIG Y LLAM   (333436)
This crag is approached along an old quarry road/track which turns off the B4417 about a mile west of Llithfaen, just south of Yr Eifl. The track winds down and around, heading west, to a quarried amphitheatre (335438) above the point marked 'Caves' on the map, at its end. The cliff, a prominent pillar jutting out into the sea, is invisible from land and is reached via an easy but exciting traverse.

354 **Fantan B**   HVS   600ft/182m ***
P. Crew, I. G. MacNaught-Davies (AL), 1966
A thrilling sea-cliff expedition with impressive situations which has been compared with A Dream of White Horses as an

experience, though Fantan B is much steeper and more
isolated, hence its HVS cachet. The climbing is mainly of a
modest standard though difficulties increase with height to
climax at two small roofs near the top. The rock, granodiorite,
and sometimes suspect, has a ledgy structure. Good belays and
runners are often difficult to locate and a selection of blade pegs
would give both spiritual and temporal comfort; alternatively,
adequate protection may be arranged using wires, micros,
Friends, long slings and a lot of ingenuity.

Descend through a gap on the seaward side of the
amphitheatre via a steel hawser. From the end of this, scramble
carefully down damp grass to rocky ledges about 60ft/18m
above the sea. Traverse L (facing out) for about 200ft/61m
across a greasy guano-covered rock bay to take a stance at the
far side where the crag steepens. Belays are difficult to find.

1. 120ft/37m. Traverse easily R across broken ledges to a
pink-coloured ledge on the arete. Peg, nut, and Friend belay.

2. 100ft/30m. 4a. Make a slightly rising R-ward traverse for
50ft/15m to an exposed position on the skyline. A high step up
the arete, then 40ft/12m of easy climbing gain large ledges over
on the R by a large flat-topped spike.

3. 130ft/40m. 4c. Traverse easily R for 20ft/6m to a point below
overhangs 60ft/18m above. Climb up via the easiest line,
trending diagonally R across the face below the overhangs to a
prominent perched block at their R end. PR. Move round,
avoiding the block which looks ready to topple, then climb the
10ft/3m wall immediatley to its R; this is at the top L edge of a
gigantic broken scoop. Step L and awkwardly pass a PR.
Continue easily along a diagonal rake to a stance on the arete.
Friend belay. Beware of rope drag on this pitch!

4. 60ft/18m. 4b. Ascend for 30ft/9m to a niche at the foot of an
evil-looking groove, much steeper than it looks, PR. A step R
round the corner, a tricky move up, then a short traverse R past
a huge nest (usually in situ) leads to a superbly positioned
skyline stance on a prow. Wire belays.

5. 90ft/27m. 4c. Surmount the roof above the stance on
surprising holds to a ledge. Friend. Climb the short slab to a

bulge. Move R to a PR under the lip. Pull over via the obvious
hold with a long reach for a large flat hold, and so gain another
ledge. Take the slabby wall above to a narrow grass ledge
10ft/3m higher. Traverse 15ft/5m L, then ascend on hidden
jugs, moving L to a large arete stance and Friend belay.
6. 100ft/30m. 4b. Trend up R-wards across the blackish slab
with a tricky step on to a grassy ledge. Move steeply back L to
join the arete. Finish up this to a grassy slope and belays in a
rocky outcrop. Scramble up to the crest of the ridge and
continue to the R over gendarmes etc; or scramble carefully
down over scree and slabs to the terrace above the quarry floor,
before walking off to the R.

PEN Y CIL   (158240)
Pen y Cil is the south-west tip of the Lleyn Peninsula and our
selected climb lies hidden in a small zawn a few hundred yards
to the west. From Aberdaron, take the road up the hill towards
Uwchmynydd and then turn L after abut half a mile, with yet
another L turn after 200 yards. Follow the road for one and a
half miles (ignoring the L turn after one mile) until it becomes a
tarmac track which finishes at a fork. Park a few yards up the L
branch taking care not to block the gates. Continue along this
track through a gate, keeping the wall on the L, to a stile. Cross
this and continue through another gate to a second stile which
leads on to the Pen y Cil Nature Reserve. Descend from the
summit for 300yd/279m to a grassy platform overlooking the
southern tip of Pen y Cil. Turn R (west) and descend to a
sloping grassy area. The zawn lies down to the R (facing out)
with a prominent sea cave at its far side. Approach time,
twenty minutes.

355 **Manx Groove**   E2   230ft/70m **
R. Edwards, P. Sketcher (1 pt), 1967
The fine groove running up to a roof in the centre of the zawn is
steep and technical. It faces Bardsey Island and lies hidden
from the descent. Scramble down the gully bounding the near
side of the zawn which is reached via a Diff traverse into it. The

route is tidal, but can be reached at any state of the tide by a traverse in; from mid to low tide, the groove can be started direct – much better.

1. 100ft/30m. 6a. Climb the black wall on the R for 20ft/6m. Move L to the centre of the groove. Climb the crack with awkward moves past a PR. Step R then back L to reach the top of the groove. A hard move L across a slab gains a large hold. Move up and jam strenuously around the L end of the roof, with a heel hook to gain the slab above. Take a hanging belay here to avoid rope drag.

2. 130ft/40m. 4c. Climb the corner for 20ft/6m then step R and scramble up the tottering hillside, trending first R, then back L to finish. Careful handling of the rock is needed on this pitch!

The next two routes lie within half a mile of each other on the Cilan coastline.

CILAN HEAD   (291235)

From Aberdaron, turn R along the main street and head south for about one mile to Sarn Bach. Follow the road signposted to Cilan. This becomes single track and leads to Cilan Uchaf where there is parking space. The farmer has no objection to car-parking here, but his permission should be sought at the house. Go through a wide gate, R of the house, and follow the walled track to a field. Bear diagonally L up to a gate at its top L corner, then continue across another field to a stile in the fence. Go straight on along a narrow path for about 250yd/232m to a sharp R-hand bend. Keep on in the same line along a faint L-hand branch, gradually descending, until three broken rocky bands dipping down the hillside towards the sea come into view, on the R; a large triangular slab at the foot of the cliff is also obvious. Contour across to the centre of the second band – the convex grassy hillside is *very slippery*. Descend more or less directly to a cracked ledge just below the cliff top and

Manx Groove

356

immediately ʀ (facing out) of the crag. Approach time, fifteen minutes. Abseil down a groove to a sloping rock platform from an old hidden peg and nut belays 25ft/8m ʀ (facing out) of the cracked ledge. The abseil rope should be left in place with prussiks on the end, in case of emergency.

Access to the cliff is difficult, and may be impossible for a couple of hours either side of high tide. At mid to low tide a sandy beach is exposed.

356 **Vulture**   E4   360ft/109m ***

J. Street, C. Jackson (1 pt), 1968

A tremendous climb which requires total commitment. The cliff is capped by a huge barrier of overhangs, and undercut towards its ʀ side. Starting on the ʟ, the climb traverses across just above the lower overhangs before finishing up an overhanging groove on the ʀ; the rock needs careful handling on this, the most famous of all the Lleyn routes. Start from the top ʟ end of a sloping ledge where the overhangs end, at the ʟ side of the crag. Small low nut belays.

1. 90ft/27m. 5b. Climb the wall just ʀ of the white streak to a shale band. Traverse ʟ a few feet until below a short crack. Runners. The crack direct is 6a; so traverse ʀ for 10ft/3m and climb a shallow corner, then trend back ʟ and continue up to a long narrow ledge. (Friends 1 and 1½ slightly up and ʟ protect the second man.) Step back down, traverse ʀ, then move up to a two bolt and nut belay on the first terrace: the aid route Giant crosses here and continues direct over the enormous capping ceiling, on bolts.

2. 50ft/15m. 4a. Womble ʀ-wards along the terrace for 50ft/15m to a high nut and sling belay immediately ʀ of a rocky nose.

3. 130ft/40m. 5b. Traverse ʀ-wards across the wall below overhangs without too much difficulty, and no protection, to a large bong, and a small footledge just before two obvious

The Lleyn Peninsula – Cilan Head

grooves. Cross these and make a sensational swing around the nose on the R. Climb a blocky corner, whitened by guano, to a ledge. Traverse L for 15ft/5m to a larger ledge on a prominent arete. Nut and peg belays.

4. 90ft/27m. 6a. Climb the groove above the belay and traverse L round an arete into a wide bottomless groove. Strenuous bridging and layaways in a fine position lead to an awkward move R to gain the easier finishing groove. Nut and Friend belays just above.

VATICAN ZAWN   (230295)

This is the large zawn immediately east of the very tip of the Cilan, marked 'Trwyn Cilan' on the map. Approach as for Cilan Head to the stile, then angle across slightly L-wards to the cliff top and follow the coastline around L-wards past a small, very steep-sided zawn to a larger R-angled one, whose stratified R wall (facing in) dips down above a cave into the sea.

357 **The Path to Rome**   E3   225ft/69m ***

D. Jones, R. Kay (AL), P. Evans, 1987

A fabulous rising girdle of the R wall of the zawn destined to become a classic. The rock is rough and generally sound Cilan Grit and the position feels surprisingly exposed for such a small crag. Scramble down a grass bank to start at the R side of the zawn on a broad ledge, 30ft/9m below the top of the cliff, reached by a short abseil. Two sets of Friends are useful!

1. 150ft/46m. 5c. Make a descending L-wards traverse down to horizontal tram lines. Continue with feet just above the lip of the overhang to a niche at 60ft/18m. Climb to the top of this, creep L round a large bulge then make a hard step, around to a rest. Move up on good holds and continue easily L along the obvious traverse line, heading towards the open groove below a large roof. Climb down for 15ft/5m about 15ft/5m from the groove and traverse in to an ancient peg belay, backed up with small wires. A brilliant pitch.

Crossing the void on The Path to Rome

2. 75ft/23m. 5c. Climb diagonally L for 15ft/5m passing a PR to enter a groove on the L of the roof. Climb this on widely spaced jugs taking care with the rock, to a cautious final few feet through The Hanging Gardens of Babylon. Belay on a spike well back from the edge.

TYN TOWYN QUARRIES   (335305)

These delightfully situated quarries, five in all, are strung out in a line adjacent to the golden beach on the south side of Mynydd Tirycwmwd, about one mile from Llanbedrog. To reach them, turn L off the A499 at Williams Garage, Llanbedrog, and go through the village to another L turn, immediately before St Pedrog's Chapel. A narrow lane winds steeply up before dropping down the opposite side of Mynydd Tirycwmwd to a track branching off to the L, after three-quarters of a mile. Park at the end, just above the beach in Quarry No. 2. Our route lies in the best of the quarries: No. 4. Walk east (L facing out to sea) along the beach for 400yd/372m past some poles protruding prominently from the beach (the remains of a jetty) – this section may involve an easy rock traverse at high tide. Scramble up a bank into Quarry No. 3, with an obvious rippled wall at its back. Quarry No. 4 comes next, characterized by long shallow stepped overlaps starting at 25ft/8m. Beyond, the grassier Quarry No. 5, behind a group of derelict concrete buildings, has several pleasant routes up the easy-angled slabs on its R side. On sunny days, the heath below the crag is a favourite haunt of adders . . .

358 **Samurai**   E2   220ft/66m **
J. Brown, D. Alcock (2 pts), 1967

A superb and unique route which finds the easiest way up through the steepest section of rock. The first pitch tackles seven overlaps alone, yet the climbing is nearly always in balance! Protection is infrequent but the rock, compact microgranite, gives good friction. Start in the centre of the cliff,

Samurai, pitch 1

about 45ft/14m R of a short hanging chimney low down on the face, and just L of a threaded borehole at 35ft/11m.

1. 80ft/24m. 5c. Climb up to the R-facing corner formed by a small rib at 25ft/8m. Pull out on to this, PR, then step R and make contortionate moves to get established on the slab above. Move R to the situ borehole thread. Undercut up via the borehole above, to good holds. Traverse R for 5ft/1.5m to the arete. Balancy moves up the L side of this gain better holds culminating in an airy swing out R-wards on to a large sloping ledge. Peg and small wire belays in the far corner.

2. 90ft/27m. 5b. Swing R around the arete on to a narrow overhung ledge with a flake crack at its far end. Move carefully up for 10ft/3m to an old PR, just above and L of a detached (but apparently sound) block. Whisper up and move R on to a slab. Climb direct to the capping overhangs before traversing L for 20ft/6m, to pull over just before the arete. Good nut crack and belay in an overhung corner 20ft/6m higher.

3. 50ft/15m. Traverse R for 10ft/3m; 40ft/12m of easy slabs lead to a further 50ft/15m of grassy scrambling L-wards to an iron stanchion belay. Descend across to the L, down the ramp separating Quarries 3 and 4.

Snowdon East

This is another area lying well away from mainstream North Wales climbing – the crags covered by this section provide a refreshing break from the crowds.

The highest concentration of routes is found in the Moelwyns, a delightful low-lying mountain range well to the south-east of Snowdon, around Blaenau Ffestiniog and Tan y Grisiau. Despite being overshadowed by the popularity of the better known outcrops at Tremadog, the cliffs here provide equally good climbing. The selected crags, Craig y Clipiau, Craig yr Wrysgan, Clogwyn yr Oen and Clogwyn y Bustach, all offer a good choice of routes and are typified by their pocketed walls as well as their excellent scope for bouldering.

Further to the north, near Dolwyddelan, is Carreg Alltrem, a small quick-drying crag which boasts a classic route of the area, Lavaredo Wall, with the little riverside craglet of Craig Rhiw Goch tucked away in the Lledr Valley, about four miles from Betws y Coed. North again, and west of Llanrwst, is the secluded and little-frequented Crafnant Valley, whose finest crag is the extremely steep Clogwyn yr Eryr.

Local Amenities

The cliffs in this area are best visited on a daily basis, but if it is required, camping can be found in and around Betws y Coed, Dolwyddelan, and Penrhyndeudraeth, further south. Unofficial camping is possible above Tan y Grisiau in the Moelwyns, near the car-park used to approach these crags. There is a bus service between Llanrwst, Betws y Coed and Ffestiniog which runs throughout the year. Betws y Coed and Ffestiniog are tourists' towns and as such offer the usual range of shops, cafés and pubs. The same applies to Llanrwst, for those visiting Clogwyn yr Eryr.

The Moelwyns
With the exception of Craig y Clipiau, these delightful crags lie immediately above the Llyn Stwlan dam service road,

overlooking the Tan y Grisiau reservoir. A narrow road leading from Tan y Grisiau to Cwm Orthin is followed for a few hundred yards to limited parking at 683455 from which all the cliffs can be reached in under thirty minutes.

CRAIG Y CLIPIAU   (683458)

This impressive crag sits high on the hillside, above slate tips overlooking the village of Tan y Grisiau. Follow the track above the car-park towards Cwm Orthin to where it levels off. A faint path leads back R and upwards towards the R edge of the slate tips, where another path climbs steeply up the crag. Despite its squalid surroundings the cliff offers excellent routes to suit all tastes. It is dominated on its main face by an overhanging grooved prow which rises up from a steep slab, the line of the Crimson Cruiser. To the L is the obvious White Slab with Vestix Buttress further over, beyond a vegetated area. To the R of the steep slab, a rib runs up to twin overhanging cracks. Next, past a holdless overhanging arete, a stepped groove up a steep wall gives the Inverted Staircase. There are two main descents: go easily down a path on the R of the main crag, or take an easy grass funnel to the L of Vestix Buttress.

359 **Vestix**   HVS   140ft/43m
R. Newcombe, G. Ashton, 1965
An interesting crack followed by a poorly protected arete gives a pitch of contrasts. Start below the crack, just R of the prominent arete on the buttress L of the main (south-east) face.
1. 5a. Climb the steep crack to a small niche. Make awkward moves L and round the arete. Move up a little and step back R to the arete. Follow this fairly easily in a fine position to a good stance and belays at the top of the cliff.

360 **Africa Rib**   V Diff   160ft/49m*
R. Buckland, J. Neill, 1953
The L edge of the White Slab gives an enjoyable outing. Start

Craig y Clipiau

by a block pinnacle at the L-hand side of the slab.

1. 60ft/18m. Climb the face of the pinnacle on sharp pockets (or either of the chimneys formed by it) and continue to reach a stance by a prominent rowan tree.

2. 55ft/17m. From the L-hand end of the ledge climb up to a quartz ledge. Continue straight up the rib to belay at a large block.

3. 45ft/14m. Climb the crack above a rib and a large vegetated ledge below a short steep wall. Finish up this.

361 **Asahel** S 170ft/51m*

R. James, R. L. Roberts, 1955

A worthwhile route with some good moves. Start below the R corner of the slab.

1. 110ft/33m. Climb the slab near the corner passing a bulge at 70ft/21m by a traverse R then back L to a small stance.

2. 40ft/12m. Continue delicately up to the overhang. Traverse L to a rib and climb it to a good stance.

3. 20ft/6m. Move round to the R and go up a wall to finish.

362 **Mean Feet** HVS 130ft/39m**

R. James, P. Vaughan, 1957

An entertaining climb which takes the V-groove at the top L corner of the steep slab R of Asahel. Start at the R side of the slab below a vegetated corner.

1. 70ft/21m. 4b. Scramble up into the corner to reach a line of jugs leading L across the top of the slab to a nut belay at the foot of the V-groove chimney.

2. 60ft/18m. 5a. Bridge and jam up strenuously to the top of the chimney, crux. Step back R and climb up to a ledge. Finish up the awkward wall above.

363 **The Crimson Cruiser** E5 130ft/40m***

R. Fawcett, P. Williams, 1980

The overhanging prow just R of the Mean Feet V-groove gives

Asahel: approaching the overhangs

a tremendous route: the best in the Moelwyns. Splitting the pitch reduces the grade to E4. Start in a small grassy corner at the foot of the slab, directly below the prow.

1. 6a. Climb the slab on the R to a bulge. Move up L then back R to reach the top of the slab a few feet R of the prow. Step L into the overhanging groove, go up this and swing R on to a small lichenous slab. Move back L into the groove and continue strenuously up to a tiny ledge on the L. Pull on to this then climb up on hidden holds to a good resting ledge. Make a hard move back up R and continue up the overhanging prow, swinging R in a sensational position to finish via a good hold. A pitch which overhangs by 20ft/6m.

364 **Double Criss** VS 125ft/38m *
C. J. S. Bonington, C. W. Brasher, 1953

The rib R of the steep slab leads to a strenuous finish up the crack in the corner high on the R. Start below the undercut rib which is the L edge of a slabby wall.

1. 100ft/30m. 4c. Climb steeply up the R side of the rib, then go L to its crest. Follow this pleasantly to a move R into a corner. Continue up to a ledge and belay below the final corner.
2. 25ft/8m. 4c. The crack yields to brute force plus a little technique!

365 **Inverted Staircase** VS 110ft/33m **
R. James, A. F. Mason, G. Rees, 1958

A good climb up the stepped groove on the wall of the buttress R of Double Criss. Start below the groove.

1. 4c. Climb the groove or the face direct to a ledge at the foot of the groove. Climb the groove, then move out on to the L wall and go up on good holds to the ledge above. Walk L a few feet to a delightful finish up a short pocketed wall.

CRAIG YR WRYSGAN   (679454)

This is the first crag one reaches along the dam service road, easily recognized by the quarry incline which drops down from a tunnel on its L side. A steep path leads up the incline, then breaks R across to the foot of the cliff which has a simple layout:

on the L is a large quartz slab above which is a steep tower cut
by an overhanging corner. This corner starts from a large grass
ledge known as Y Borfa. In the centre of the cliff are two blunt
ribs, and further over is an easy angled slab beneath a steep
green wall. R again are a few grooves and ribs. The usual
descent runs down the incline from the quarry buildings,
although a longer one can be made down the R side of the crag.

366 White Streak/Honeysuckle Corner

HS 170ft/51m **

G. Dwyer, R. L. Roberts, 1958/J. R. Lees, G. Moffat, 1961

A superb climb, bold for its grade, taking the R side of the
quartz slab on sharp pockets. Start on a grassy ledge by a large
spike, below a square-cut groove at the R side of the slab.

1. 110ft/33m. Traverse up L and move boldly round the bulge
on to the slab above. Climb diagonally R to reach a triangular
corner cutting into the R edge of the slab. Traverse L and make
a hard move up to good holds and incuts, leading to Y Borfa in
a fine position. Nut belays in the wall behind.
2. 60ft/18m. From the L end of Y Borfa, climb the overhanging
corner, which eases after 25ft/8m, in an airy position to the top.
(Daufen, S, climbs the L side of the slab to an easy escape by a
R-ward traverse along Y Borfa.)

367 Y Gelynen V Diff 250ft/75m *

R. Davies, G. Williams, 1953

A classic climb up the blunt rib L of the central V-groove
(Dorcon, VS). Scramble, or climb up to the grass ledge below
the V-groove.

1. 80ft/24m. Move L along the ledge and go up on to the arete.
Continue to a sloping stance and belay.
2. 50ft/15m. Step L and follow the rib up to a stance below a
wall.
3. 50ft/15m. Climb up, first R, then L, and turn a little
overhang to reach a slab. Climb this to Y Borfa.
4. 70ft/21m. Climb directly up the wall, stepping round R to an
easy finish; the corner on the L can be climbed at S standard.

368 **Green Wall**   E3   100ft/30m **
J. Perrin, A. Cornwall (1 pt), 1972
A very strenuous route up the overhanging green wall which
lies R of the centre of the crag. Scramble up to belay below the
corner formed by Green Wall and the almost featureless wall
on the R. The corner is Gethsemane, HVS, whilst a direct line
up the smooth wall 10ft/3m R is Bing the Budgie, E4, 5c.
1. 5c. Traverse L up the slab to a short corner. Climb this then
step R and continue up the bulging wall on good holds to a
traverse line in the middle of the face. Move L a few feet to a
good spike, then climb up and R to a thin crack. Runners. Move
boldly and steeply L to a strenuous, and sometimes dirty, finish.

369 **Space Below My Feet**   HVS   120ft/37m
J. R. Lees, D. W. Walker (some aid), 1961
The arete R of Green Wall gives an enjoyable pitch. Scramble
up to belay below a short vertical crack in the wall R of
Gethsemane.
1. 5a. Climb the short crack, then move diagonally R to the
arete. Continue up this, very steep to start, but gradually
easing towards the top.

CLOGWYN YR OEN   (673449)
This is the second crag reached along the dam service road,
and the nearest to it. There are two faces separated by a blunt
ridge: on the L is the south-west face which is climbed by Pinky,
whilst R of the ridge lies the south-east face with its many easy
climbs on superb rock, the profusion of holds enabling one to
climb almost anywhere at S standard. Descend down the L-side
of the crag.

370 **Pinky**   VS   200ft/61m *
I. G. MacNaught-Davies, C. W. Brasher, 1953
An interesting route with a steep finish. Start on a grass ledge
below a small overlap 8ft/2m up the pinkish wall.

Craig yr Wrysgan

1. 130ft/40m. 4b. Climb up past the overlap, and continue over a bulge at 30ft/9m. Climb directly up the rib for 80ft/24m on incut holds to finish up a short steep wall on to a large sloping terrace. Scramble R across this to belay on a flake just L of an obvious corner.

2. 70ft/21m. 4b. Take the corner past two small trees to a good grassy ledge on the L. Finish up any one of the three cracks above, the R-hand one being the best.

371 **Kirkus's Climb Direct**   S   300ft/90m **

C. F. Kirkus, C. G. Kirkus, 1928

The first recorded climb in the area takes the blunt ridge between the two faces. Start by the drystone wall running up to the toe of the buttress.

1. 70ft/21m. Step R on to the face and climb it, then the slab above to a ledge by a flake. Continue up another slab above the flake, just L of an easy chimney moving R at the top to a stance by some huge jammed blocks.

2. 80ft/24m. Climb the chimney until a long step and swing out R to gain a small ledge. Take the pocketed slab above to a large sloping ledge.

3. 90ft/27m. Move up and L to a shallow groove in the arete. Follow this on good holds to a ledge at 60ft/18m. Step R on to easy slabs leading up to a small stance and nut belays.

4. 60ft/18m. Climb the groove above the belay, then go up easy slabs on the L to belay by a huge block. Scramble to the top.

372 **Slack**   S   300ft/90m **

I. F. Cartledge, J. R. Lees, 1960

A good route up the centre of the south-east face turning the prominent overhang on the L. Start about 80yd/73m R of Kirkus's Climb below slabs leading up to a large flake on a ledge 80ft/24m up.

1. 80ft/24m. Take the slab direct to the R side of the flake.

2. 80ft/24m. Climb the R edge of the flake, step on the wall

Slack: the crux

above and go up on good holds to a possible stance. Continue up a steep crack and so reach a stance below the overhangs.

3. 60ft/18m. Climb up to the overhangs and traverse L to a rib which leads up past them. Climb the rib, crux, then move across R to belay in a corner.

4. 80ft/24m. Take the strenuous corner crack to a ledge and continue up the corner above to a grassy stance. Scramble easily up to the top.

CLOGWYN Y BUSTACH   (672448)

This is the small buttress 100yd/93m L (as one faces the crag) of the descent from Clogwyn yr Oen.

373 **Flake Wall**   HVS   140ft/42m *

D. D. Stewart, T. Kellet, 1955

A splendid little climb. Start on the R of the main face by a large flake.

1. 70ft/21m. 5a. Climb the L side to its top. Step L on to the wall and move across below a shallow V-corner. Climb back up to the foot of the corner, make one move up it, then step L and go up on good holds to a narrow stance. Nut belays.

2. 70ft/21m. 4b. Traverse L to the edge of the buttress on good holds. Continue steeply up to finish.

CARREG ALLTREM   (739507)

This quick-drying crag stands proudly on the east side of Cwm Penamnen, the valley running south from Dolwyddelan. Turn L in the centre of the village to the railway station. Follow the road to a R turn immediately after the railway bridge and continue along it; it becomes a gated forestry track which leads to a parking space, across the valley from the crag, and opposite to it. Follow the track and paddle across the river before going up through the forest to the foot of the crag in about ten minutes.

Carreg Alltrem

The central feature is a prominent corner capped by an overhang, Penamnen Groove, E1 4c, 5b, which is a disappointing climb. Just to the R, an overhanging slanting crack below a steep groove gives the ferocious Civetta, E3 4b, 6a. The routes are described from R to L and the descent lies down Pinnacle Gully, well over to the R.

374 **Lavaredo Wall**   VS   145ft/44m ***
R. James, K. Forder, I. F. Campbell, 1961
The wall on the R of Civetta gives one of the best routes in the area. Start 10yd/9m R of Penamnen Groove, in a groove just R of a detached rock pillar.
1. 75ft/23m. 4a. Climb the groove to a flake on the R at 30ft/9m. A tricky step L on to a ledge leads to easier climbing, and a stance and block belay.
2. 70ft/21m. 4b. From the top of the block, pull up the bulging wall using a good spike on the L, with a long reach for incut holds. Continue direct moving L to finish up an open corner.

375 **Lightning Visit**   VS   130ft/40m *
R. James, C. T. Jones, 1959
A popular climb up the curving groove L of Penamnen Groove. Start at a groove just L of the square cut corner below Penamnen Groove.
1. 55ft/17m. 4a. Take the groove and wall above to a block belay.
2. 75ft/23m. 4b. Ascend to a good ledge. Move R to a pinnacle and gain the V-groove, awkwardly. Finish pleasantly up this.

The L arete of Lightning Visit gives Greenpeace, E1 5b, an airy pitch. Beyond this lies:

376 **Fratricide Wall**   HVS   145ft/44m **
C. T. Jones, A. S. Jones, A. Daffern (1 pt), 1960
A steep and technical climb of great interest. Start below the next groove L of Lightning Visit which leads up to the R end of a grass ledge.

1. 70ft/21m. 5a. Go up the groove to the grassy ledge. Climb the wall directly above and continue up a smooth groove. Go round a bulge to the R, runner, on to a wall. Move steeply up and back L. Continue across L on good holds to reach a stance in a corner below an impending wall.

2. 75ft/23m. 5a. Take the short thin crack behind the belay to gain a sloping ledge. A delicate traverse R along this leads round on to a rock nose. Climb this to another ledge below a steep corner. Go up the corner to where it gets mean; runners. A couple of difficult moves across the wall on the R lead to the arete of Greenpeace. Finish up this in a fine position.

CRAIG RHIW GOCH   (767541)

This steep little south-facing crag is a National Trust property, peacefully situated on the north bank of the Afon Lledr, just below the A470 Bettws y Coed to Dolwyddelan road, about 150yd/138m after it leaves the forest, one mile west of the railway bridge. Parking is a problem, but there is a small rough lay-by on the R, 200yd/186m further on past some bends (two-car capacity). Walk back along the road to a gap in the fence from which a path leads to the cliff top. Descend either side. The iron walkways and ladders set in the riverbank are used for fishing, and are strictly private.

The large diagonal groove of Congl, and the embedded flake, starting point for The Riparian, are obvious features.

377 **Reign**   S   80ft/24m

A. J. J. Moulam, H. Drasdo, 1967

A pleasant climb: the easiest hereabouts. Start from behind a large tree at the L side of the crag.

1. Climb steeply up on good holds, trending L to a ledge on the arete at 40ft/12m. Continue up a rib and a short slab, stepping L at the top to finish. Tree belay well back.

378

379

378 Congl VS 100ft/30m **

R. James, B. James, R. Rowlands, 1965

The obvious groove gives a very fine pitch which is tough for its grade. The groove blanks out above the base of the crag. Start slightly to the R.

1. 4c. Ascend easily to an awkward move L at 15ft/5m to reach a slab at the base of the groove proper. Continue up with increasing difficulty to a steepening, about 15ft/5m below the top. An exposed traverse L on good holds leads to an easy finish; but better, take the obvious direct finish which is short, much harder and superb – HVS 5b. Small wires protect.

379 The Riparian E2 100ft/30m *

J. Perrin, A. Cornwall, 1972

The slabby wall R of Congl gives a route of character: bold and poorly protected near the top.

1. 5c. From the large embedded flake, climb the slabby wall and narrow groove above. Avoiding easier ground on Congl, to the L, step R on to the wall and pull up into a short slim groove. At the top of this make committing moves R, then go up for a prominent pocket. Ignoring the pain, crank up fiercely to gain a distant jug. The groove above is a welcome anti-climax!

CLOGWYN YR ERYR (733604)

This is by far the finest of several small cliffs hidden away in the secluded Crafnant Valley, which runs south-west from Trefriw. Cars may be driven up and parked inside the last gate near the Mynydd Club hut at Blaen y Nant (738602) and *not* at the hut itself. For mountaineers, an approach from Capel Curig is recommended in about an hour. The crag stands out from across the valley, light-coloured and severely undercut at its base, sitting above a scree slope – strictly Tiger Territory. From the parking spot, follow the R fork in the road to Hendre Farm which is passed on its R along a public footpath via two gates

Craig Rhiw Goch

Clogwyn yr Eryr

and two stiles. Turn L along the forestry track and follow it for
400yd/472m or so to a sharp bend. Another stile now leads L to
a laborious scree slog before the crag is reached in about
twenty-five minutes.

The best climbing is on the South Buttress, once the sole preserve of the aid man, but now boasting many fine free routes. The main face is split by three prominent grooves, all undercut. From L to R these are: Clonus, E4 6a, Connie's Crack, E4 6a, and Astoroth. R again, three lesser grooves are the main substance of Beelzebub, E1 5c, Gondor, E2 5c, and Prometheus, E1 5c. The descent for all routes goes down to the R of the crag: scramble R down heather to a marshy grassy area and continue carefully down a steep path which bends back towards the crag over two rock steps, about 100yd/93m to the R.

380 **Phoenix**   E3   150ft/46m ***

J. Ball, M. A. Reeves (AL) (some aid), 1966/FFA: M. Boysen, 1976
An excellent climb, varied and well-protected, up the R-facing corner crack capped by a roof, on the L wall of the buttress. Start below it.

1. 6a. Enter the corner/groove awkwardly and continue up to the roof, crux. Traverse R under the roof then move up on to the arete. Step round the corner and continue up the edge to a small ledge. Possible stance and spike belay 8ft/2m higher. Take the wall above then trend R to join the arete just below the top. Finish easily.

381 **Clonus Left Hand**   E3   150ft/46m **

P. Livesey, P. Gomersall, 1980
A stupendous pitch which starts up the Clonus groove before moving L to finish up Phoenix. Deceptively steep and hard for its grade. Start just L of the huge groove at the L end of the front face.

1. 6a. Pull over the overhang and step R into the main groove. Climb this boldly to a thread in a pocket at 25ft/8m; the first runner. Continue up for another 20ft/6m to an old piece of sling, then make a couple of moves L and ascend on improving holds to join Phoenix. Climb the arete to the ledge and finish up the wall above, as for Phoenix.

382 **Astoroth/Snowdrop Connection**

E3   170ft/51m ***

R. James and party (some aid), 1961/P. Boardman, M. Wragg (1 pt), 1970/FFA: P. Livesey, P. Gomersall, 1978

A brilliant way up the crag. The top pitch is as fine as any in Wales. Start R of the stepped roofs, Connie's Crack, at the base of the R-hand groove.

1.   100ft/30m. 6a. Climb the groove to the overhang. Pass this using holds on the R wall to a second overhang. Step L into a smooth groove which steepens considerably. Chimney up over the funnel of space, then swing on to the R wall and go up to a large pinnacle belay.

2.   70ft/21m. 6a. Traverse L to below a crack splitting the headwall. Climb it; the position is spectacular, there is one desperate move, but the protection is bomb proof! An immaculate pitch. Alternatively:

2a.   70ft/21m. 5a. For Astoroth: climb above the stance to the narrow flake in the groove. Step R, then go up and back L to good holds. Move L from the small tree to finish via a niche.

Central Wales

Lying in the climbing doldrums and overshadowed by the unbeatable variety and quality of the cliffs in Snowdonia, less than an hour's drive to the north, the crags of Central Wales have for too long been dismissed by a majority of climbers as grassy, loose and broken. Indeed, on first appearances their fears would appear to be confirmed; there are copious amounts of vegetation on some of the cliffs and they do lack the size of their northern counterparts. Yet tucked away in the remote cwms and high mountains lies a wealth of good climbing, hidden gems waiting to be discovered by the connoisseur of the esoteric. The pace of life is slow and relaxed here: to see another party is a rarity. The 'Grades and Numbers Game' played by many climbers becomes irrelevant, the accent lying firmly on adventure and enjoyment.

There are five selected cliffs running roughly in a line from north-east to south-west, starting with Gist Ddu, whose rocky ribs stick starkly out from the north end of the Aran Mountains. At the south end, the seemingly endless buttresses of the vast Craig Cywarch complex hide much of their charm under a green mantle, and contain the highest concentration of routes in the area. To the east, perched on the northern slopes of Cader Idris, just above Dolgellau, Cyfrwy, with its distinctive broken rib and slab formation, lies less than a mile from the sombre Craig Cau which rises out of grassy terraces above the dark waters of Llyn Cau, on the opposite side of the Cader Ridge. In marked contrast to the other cliffs, The Diamond, on Bird Rock, is steep and clean, and in the best outcrop traditions lies a mere sixty seconds from the road in the Dysynni Valley near Tywyn.

Local Amenities

The area is poorly served by public transport and a car would seem to be only way to ensure mobility; even the furthest crag can be reached in less than one and a half hours from Llanberis (or forty-five minutes from Tremadog). Camping is no problem. The campsites handiest for Cyfrwy and the north side of Cader lie at the east end of Dolgellau (735176 and 744174) and at 687160 near the youth hostel at Kings. For Craig Cau, the south of Cader, and Bird Rock, the best campsite probably lies at the farm Cwmrhwyddfor (738120). The sites at either end of Dinas Mawddwy (859152 and 860139) will serve those heading for Craig Cywarch whilst the host of campsites surrounding Bala and Llanuwchllyn provide a good base from which to tackle Gist Ddu.

Since the publication of a Central Wales guide in 1973, considerable access difficulties have been experienced on the hills and crags of the Aran range which are privately owned. In 1982 the National Park concluded access agreements with the landowners concerned, for a footpath over the main Aran ridge from Dinas Mawddwy to Llanuwchllyn. This path is the agreed access route for Gist Ddu and is the result of much patient negotiation. Please do nothing to jeopardize this agreement.

The Arans

GIST DDU   (873255)

This remote mountain cliff keeps a lonely vigil on the eastern slopes of Aran Benllyn, overlooking Llyn Lliwbran. It is slow drying as it receives a fair amount of drainage from the copious quantity of vegetation covering the hillside above, but when in condition, its rock is a delight to climb on, being as rough and firm as any in the area.

The main interest focuses on the R-hand side of the Central Buttress where three enormous pillars present an array of powerful lines. The principal corner thus formed is taken by Sloose with the impressive aretes of Aardvark and Scimitar to its R and L respectively. L again, across the lesser corner of The Trench, VS, the third arete of this classic trio is Maoi Man, beyond which easier slanting groove lines are bedecked with grass and heather. Either side of Central Buttress are the Left and Right Wings, climbed by a few poor routes.

The descent is via two 150ft/46m abseils down Sloose: the first from the tree at its top and the second from the prominent jammed boulder at half-height – if an extra rope is taken, it can be fixed in position for the second abseil and recovered at the end of the day, thus saving a lot of valuable climbing time. Alternatively, scramble up to the crest of the ridge and descend well R of the cliff.

Approach along the A494 from Bala branching off along the B4403 in Llanuwchllyn. Park in the car-park opposite the coal yard, a short distance along it. From the sharp bend in the road, just before it crosses the Afon Twrch, follow the gently rising Arans courtesy path southwards for about three miles before dropping down the grassy slopes just north of the crag and contouring round to its foot. Time, one and a half hours. This is the only approach that should be used, so as not to offend the local farmers. Under no circumstances should an approach be made from directly below.

383 **Moai Man** HVS 240ft/72m **

J. A. Sumner, Miss J. P. Hendrickson, D. Brown, 1972

The L arete of The Trench gives a very fine route despite a short scrambling section. Start below the arete.

1. 40ft/12m. 4a. Ascend the arete to a ledge and good nut belays.

2. 100ft/30m. 5a. Take the steep slab above to a ledge on the arete. Step R round the arete and move awkwardly up to a narrow ledge. PR. Climb a crack which leads back L to a ledge on the arete and a good runner. Make a couple of fierce pulls up the short wall above, crux, then continue up the easier-angled arete above. Move L and belay. 40ft/12m of rock and grass scrambling up a large vegetated ledge lead to peg belays below the upper arete . . . these last two pitches can be done in one run-out.

3. 100ft/30m. 4b. Move on to the arete and climb its L edge to a ledge. Finish up the short arete. Scramble across R-wards to the abseil tree.

384 **Scimitar**   E1   240ft/73m **

An extremely good route which unfortunately takes some
seepage on its second pitch. Quite intimidating. It takes a line
up near the edge of the L wall of Sloose, belaying on the arete.
In spite of being a little dirty, low down, the climb is well worth
doing when dry. Start from nut belays below an overhung
groove at the bottom L edge of the wall, above a small tree.
1. 120ft/37m. 5a. Climb the groove to a ledge at 20ft/6m. Take
the steep corner above to the roof via a hard move on to a
jutting ledge. Move R round the roof and climb the crackline on
good holds to a ledge on the L. Optional stance. Continue up
the arete direct, surmounting an awkward bulge to a belay on
the lower of two grass ledges below an overhang.
2. 100ft/30m. 5b. Continue up the arete to the overhang. Move
round the arete on to the wall and follow a line of weakness
trending up R to the base of a curving flake; occasionally wet.
Continue up on good holds just R of the flake to a small ledge.
Make a final difficult move to reach the large ledge at the top of
the wall.
3. 20ft/6m of rock. 5a. Move L and ascend the short and fierce
little wall to heather ledges. Scramble up to belay.

385 **Sloose**   HVS   280ft/85m **

J. Brown, G. D. Verity, 1963

The enormous R-facing corner on the R-hand side of the
buttress gives a thrilling pitch but requires at least a week of
dry weather to come into condition. By delicate climbing on the
outside (as opposed to a forceful thrutching approach) the wet
parts can be avoided. Start directly below it.
1. 60ft/18m. From the foot of the corner surmount the first
bulge, then move R over rock and heather, loose, to large
jammed boulders below an overhang. This wet and unpleasant
pitch can be avoided by scrambling across from the R.
2. 90ft/27m. 4c. Traverse L under the overhang and enter the

The Arans – Gist Ddu

chimney. Climb up strenuously to a huge jammed boulder.
Move up to belays at the ledge on the R.
3. 150ft/46m. 5a. Move back into the corner and ascend the
steepening chimney. Bridge out over some dubious blocks and
round the overhang into the crack above. Continue up on good
holds to where the crack narrows and the holds almost
disappear. Jam up strenuously to good holds on the R wall. The
last short section goes more easily to the abseil tree at the top.

386 **Voie Suisse**   E1   250ft/76m ***
J. A. Sumner, P. Harding, 1984
A tremendous route up the front face of the pillar forming the R
wall of Sloose. The climbing is continuous and the second pitch
is full of surprises! Start about 15ft/5m R of Aardvark below a
groove in the arete.
1. 100ft/30m. 4c. Climb the groove on the R-hand side of the
arete at first, then join and continue up the arete to the large
ledge and Aardvark stance.
2. 150ft/46m. 5b. Take the easy slab to the break in the first
overlap. Pull round this to the L using a large frost pocket. Step
L to a large foothold then move up to a PR, hidden from below.
Make a delicate move up then reach L to good pockets and
continue to jugs under the second overlap. Go L to a break in
the overlap and surmount this R-wards (about 10ft/3m from
the corner of Sloose). Move up to a flake/block. Make another
move up then step L to a thin crackline 6ft/2m from the corner
of Sloose. Finish up this.

387 **Aardvark**   HVS   250ft/75m***
M. Boysen, A. Williams, D. Little, 1966
The huge arete R of Sloose gives an immaculate route at its
standard on perfect rock. The best of the trio here. Start from a
ledge formed by jammed blocks under an overhang, reached by
a scramble from the R: as for Sloose above its rather grotty first
pitch.

Surmounting the overlap on Aardvark, pitch 2

The Craig Cywarch Crags

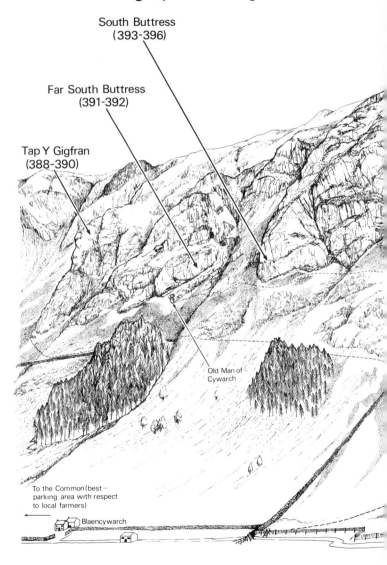

South Buttress
(393-396)

Far South Buttress
(391-392)

Tap Y Gigfran
(388-390)

Old Man of
Cywarch

To the Common (best—
parking area with respect
to local farmers)

Blaencywarch

Central Buttress(397)

North Face
(402-403)

North
East Buttress
(398-399)

North Buttress
(400-401)

Llwybr
Llewellyn

ack to Rhydymain and
nly approach to the
ywarch crags

Afon Cywarch

Philip Gibson

E →

BRYN HAFOD
The Mountain Club Hut

1. 100ft/30m. 5a. Using a jammed block, step up into a niche on the R. Climb the short overhanging crack to gain a sloping ledge. Traverse L to the foot of a groove and climb it to a grass ledge. Move R and take the grassy slab above to the large grass ledge of Sloose, and Aardvark.
2. 100ft/30m. 5a. Climb the slab above trending R to a spike on the arete beneath the large overhang. Move R round the arete then climb a tricky crack moving back to rejoin the arete at a small ledge under a bulge. Surmount this and climb the groove above to a perched block stance.
3. 50ft/15m. 4b. Move L-wards and finish up the arete to the top.

CRAIG CYWARCH

To those used to the large compact cliffs of North Wales, Craig Cywarch, on first acquaintance, seems disappointing. A matrix of buttresses, outcrops and rocky faces seamed by gullies and cloaked in vegetation sprawls lazily and bewilderingly across one and a half miles of hillside at the head of Cwm Cywarch, an almost forgotten valley which cuts up into the south end of the Arans. However, despite its unprepossessing appearance, the crag offers a wide variety of quality routes on compact rock with good wire protection and a surprising degree of exposure.

Leave the Dolgellau–Machynlleth road at Dinas Mawddwy and take the minor road to Aber-Cywarch where a L turn, signposted Cwm Cywarch, leads up along a winding lane, between hedgerows, to The Common. There is unofficial parking at the far side of this at 854185 where two tracks branch off to the L. Continue along the lane past the start of the Hengwm–Aran Fawddwy footpath. A little further on, a wide gate and stony track lead up and across a ford to the R of the house Blaencywarch. Now follow a usually waterlogged track to a stile by another wide farm gate. Cross this (Bryn Hafod, the hut of the Mountain Club of Stafford, sits in front on the opposite bank on the stream) then go over another stile a few yards further up on the L and take the rising grassy footpath to Rhydymain towards the head of the cwm. At the top of a

steepening, a subsidiary path climbs a shoulder in the hillside.
After a short distance, a L fork traverses across down below the
subsidiary buttress of Esgair Felen Isaf (which lies below the
main crag proper), descending slightly to the south end of the
crag and the toe of Tap-y-Gigfran. The R fork continues
zigzagging up, before rising slightly as it crosses the hillside to
reach the foot of the North Face. Approach times vary from
twenty to thirty-five minutes.

From the parking spot on The Common, the general layout
of the crag can be ascertained. The most notable sections from
a climber's point of view lie at the south and north-east ends,
although our selected climbs are spread out along seven
separate buttresses. The two plantations of Nyrs Bont on the L
and Nyrs Blaen are useful landmarks. Above and at the L
(south) end of the main crag lies the amphitheatre of Cwm
Rhychain with outcropping buttresses dotted around its back
walls. On the R side of the cwm sits Tap-y-Gigfran at the start
of the main crag proper. It is one of the largest buttresses at
Cywarch with a long, steep south face which slants up the
hillside to the huge curved capping overhang of Purge. The east
face of the buttress is slabby and vegetated and lies above the
bottom end of the traversing path. Across Cwm Bydyre to the
R, the Far South Buttress sits behind the Nyrs Bont plantation
with the stepped overhangs of The Overlap, low down, an
obvious feature. The path now splits, the lower branch (and the
usual approach from the north) running through the top of the
Nyrs Blaen plantation and under the buttress of Esgair Felen
Isaf, while the upper branch runs above it. Next, across Little
Gully, comes the large triangular shape of South Buttress with
several good slabby routes concentrated on a more compact
triangular area of rock on its lower L side. The narrow confines
of Great Gully, R again, separate the South Buttress from the
poor vegetated Central Buttress with a prominent arch at its
lower L end, sitting directly above Esgair Felen Isaf. Now
comes the deep gash of North Gully and the impressive
overhanging nose of the North East Buttress which forms the R
skyline (when viewed from the parking area). Standing at its

foot, and at the top of the zigzag approach path, the steep little
North North East Tower is a useful marker. Immediately to the
R, the North Buttress is larger and has a clearly defined rib and
groove structure, especially dominant on its L side where the
first and largest rib is taken by Acheron. The R side of the
buttress is delineated by the grassy ramp of Llwybr Llewelyn
running steeply down from L to R, the descent route for this
part of the crag, and one which requires care. Lastly, further
over, lies the intimidating North Face, seamed with quartz and
capped by menacing overhangs.

There have been access problems at Cwm Cywarch for a
number of years and it is in the interest of all climbers to stick
rigidly to the described access route, and also to respect the
Country Code.

Tap-y-Gigfran (845187)

One of the best crags at Cywarch. The south face reaches a
height of 300ft/93m but unfortunately its lower half is very
broken. From the traversing path scramble up to the foot of a
wide vegetated ramp which runs up the hillside parallel with
the crest of the buttress and below the steep south face to finish
at mid-height. The Ramp, as it is known, has several moves of
V Diff standard and is mossy, grassy, and usually greasy!
Above this, a steep wall rising to the top of the crag is split at
half-height by a large ledge; a huge curving overhang rises from
its L end . . . the lip is traversed by Dream Racer while the
corner beneath is taken by Purge.

Descent: at the top of the buttress trend R across a grassy
field to a narrowing at the top of a gully on the R. Scramble over
a blocky col to descend a 15ft/5m hidden gully. Traverse across
a scree shoot and continue contouring across to below the next
crag. Descend a steep grassy couloir to a scree path leading
down to the toe of the buttress.

The next two climbs are reached by scrambling up The
Ramp:

388 **Dream Racer**   E2   175ft/53m ***
J. A. Sumner, R. Thorndyke, N. Caldwell, 1981

A sensational route and one of the finest at Cywarch. It takes a
narrow cleaned wall of pink rock then the edge of the huge
prow above the second pitch of Purge. Start at the top of The
Ramp, up and L of a tree in a small corner formed by cracked
blocks immediately L of the wall. Good nut belays.
1. 75ft/23m. 5a. From the belay, step R and climb directly up
the centre of the wall to its highest point – a surprising pitch!
Sound belays.
2. 100ft/30m. 5c. Move R, then balance up awkwardly on to a
4ft/1.5m flake just R of the corner. Make committing moves
R-wards to a PR at 20ft/6m. A long, long reach gains sharp
holds leading to a ledge and a hidden PR on the 'edge of
eternity'. Move diagonally R-wards for a few feet then enter a
niche round the corner. Udge up to the arete which leads to an
easy finishing slab. Belay at the top of this – a stunning pitch!

389 **The Purge**   E2   (HVS with 3 pts)   220ft/66m *
*J. A. Sumner and party (aid), 1956/N. Robertson, D. McGonigal
(3 pts), 1969/FFA: J. A. Sumner, R. Whitehouse, 1979*

A classic route following the overhanging corner below the
great prow which dominates the south face. Sound rock, good
protection and fine situations make this a trip to savour. Using
the protection pegs for aid turns the route into a superb HVS!
Start from a perched block near the top of The Ramp, a few feet
down from the Dream Racer stance. A rowan 80ft/24m lower
down The Ramp is a useful landmark, and the launching-off
point for The Grafter, E3 6a, which follows the diagonal corner
up under a roof before breaking back L via an open groove to
finish up The Gem (our final selection on this buttress).
1. 80ft/24m. 5c. Stride R off the block to reach a large hold.
Continue steeply to the prominent ledge on the R, below an
overhanging corner. Good nut in a crack on the R. Climb the
corner on layaways past a couple of ancient PRs, making an
awkward, airy and strenuous pull to enter the dirty groove
above. The groove soon relents to a gently sloping grassy

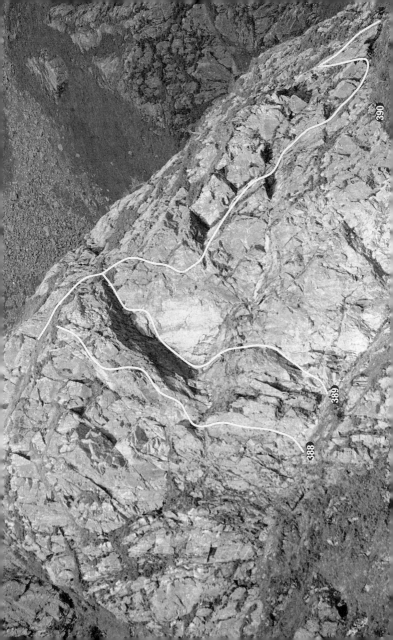

390

389

388

platform. Large iron abseil spike belay in a slab on the R.
2. 70ft/21m. 5c. Follow the crack diagonally R-wards below the
roof to an overlap. Move R to a PR. Make a hard rock-up and
stretch for a crucial quartz hold directly above then step R to a
ledge. Climb back L and take the crack in the corner to a grassy
stance – not as hard as Pitch 1.
3. 70ft/21m. Finish up vegetated rock on the R to a bilberry col.

390 **Incapability/The Gem**   Diff/HS   550ft/190m *

An enjoyable and well-positioned route taking a slabby corner
on the south-east arete of the buttress. Start from just below the
foot of The Ramp.
1. 300ft/93m. Move easily up R-wards to gain the arete. This
gives mainly Moderate standard scrambling with a few steps of
Diff, taking stances as required, to reach a narrow grass ledge
10ft/3m the foot of a large rowan tree where the crag
steepens. Spike belay 20ft/6m to the R.
2. 60ft/18m. Climb a mossy slab to a bulge. Pull over this on
the L and continue up just L of the edge to a peg and nut belay
on another narrow grass and heather ledge.
3. 120ft/37m. 4b. Traverse to the L end of the ledge and ascend
the slab to a holly tree at 20ft/6m. Pass this on the L to a small
block ledge. Move out R on good holds to another slab which
leads to a flat ledge below an overhang. Optional belay.
Surmount the overhang on good holds and take the delicate
mossy slab above to a large square overhang. Traverse L to the
arete and good nut belays at the end of a narrow grass ledge.
4. 60ft/18m. 4b. Go round the corner and make a slightly
rising traverse along ledges for 20ft/6m. Climb steeply up the
exposed wall on good holds, finishing up a short groove to a
rocky ledge. Ancient peg and spike belays.
5. 80ft/24m. Climb R-wards for a few feet then continue
carefully up rock and heather to belay in a grassy hollow.
Belays are awkward to find.

Craig Cywarch – Tap-y-Gigfran, South Face

Craig Cywarch – Far South Buttress

Far South Buttress   (847188)
This is the large triangular buttress situated between Cwm
Bydyre and Little Gully and lying above Nyrs Bont, the L-hand
plantation. A prominent horizontal terrace divides the crag
into an upper and lower tier at about 150ft/46m giving a way
off in either direction to Little Gully or Cwm Bydyre.

As the traversing path emerges from Nyrs Bont, a fence on
the L runs up the hillside through a boulder field towards the
crag. Above and L of its tip, the lower tier of the buttress is
undercut and bristles with overhangs, its L side forming a

stepped overlap. To the L, the steep crack of The Scourge rises up to join the top of the overlaps at about 90ft/27m. Cross the bottom end of the fence and scramble up to the foot of the crag, passing The Old Man of Cywarch, a small rock tower which resembles a human face when viewed from the R, *en route*.

391   **The Scourge**   E1   160ft/48m

G. Kirkham, R. Thorndyke (3 pts), 1969/FFA: D. Beetlestone, P. and G. Gibson, 1980

The prominent bulging crack running up to join the finish of The Overlap will not yield without a fight. Start 40ft/12m L of The Overlap at the foot of the undercut crack.

1. 100ft/30m. 5c. Layaway or jam up around the awkward bulge then continue more easily to the overhanging section. Reachy layaways past a PR gain a ledge just above. Climb up, not as steep as before but with spaced protection, until a line of large holds lead R to a junction with The Overlap. Move across to belay on the R.

2. 60ft/18m. 4b. Go steeply up vegetated slabs breaking out L below a small tree to the grassy terrace. Good cleaned nut slot diagonally up to the L. Escape either by a traverse L into Cwm Bydyre, or R-wards by steep heather scrambling down Little Gully before breaking back below the foot of the crag – or, easiest, by a long abseil (50m ropes needed) from the stance.

392   **The Overlap**   E2   160ft/48m *

J. A. Sumner, R. Thorndyke, R. Cully, 1971

A steep and well-protected line on sound rock up the obvious L-facing stepped corner which usually seeps. Under such conditions it can be very hard indeed. Start below the corner forming the lowest part of the overlap. Belay on good nuts at the base of the wall.

1. 100ft/30m. 5c. Climb the corner to a PR. Make a series of strenuous and delicate moves L, then up and round to the L, crux, and continue to a steepening. Pull out R over the bulge and continue up to the roof. Avoid this on the L then step back R on top of it, continuing across to a stance – a superb pitch!

2. 60ft/18m. 4b. Finish steeply up vegetated slabs just L of a small tree to belay at a nut slot diagonally L, just above the grassy terrace. Descend as for The Overlap.

South Buttress   (848190)

This is the large rambling triangular buttress between Little Gully and Great Gully. When viewed from the path above Nyrs Blaen, the R-hand plantation, the most obvious feature is a shallow gully in the middle of the buttress running diagonally up to the L, and starting from a point about 100ft/30m up the face. The L edge of the gully gives the poor vegetated route, Diagonal Arete, Diff, and also defines the R edge of a more compact and cleaner subsidiary triangle of rock about 200ft/61m high which gives several good medium grade routes.

Descent: go round to the L along a sheep track down into Little Gully and continue easily to the foot of the buttress.

At the foot of Little Gully, a large triangular overhang on the arete of the buttress at 25ft/8m is obvious. The first couple of routes climb either side of this before continuing independently to a common finish.

393 Sweet Baby James   HVS   180ft/55m *

J. A. Sumner, D. G. Armstrong, 1976

A sustained route taking a delicate slab above and L of the triangular overhang. Start a few feet up Little Gully on the side face of the buttress where a narrow slab runs up L-wards to the L end of the overhang. A conspicuous white watermark is a useful marker.

1. 130ft/40m. 5a. Follow the L-ward rising ramp to a steepening which is taken on good holds. Move L and follow the edge to the bottom R corner of the steep slab above. Go up for a good hold then traverse delicately L along a ramp to runners in the corner. Traverse R along small footholds for a few feet then pull up into a groove. Climb this steeply but more easily to a

Craig Cywarch – South Buttress

R-ward exit. Scramble up to the large tree stance on Will-o'-the-Wisp.

2. 50ft/15m. 4b. Move up and L to the large square block. Climb direct to finish by a small tree. Good horizontal nut belays a few feet higher on the R. The two pitches can be run into one 'on the stretch of the rope' if 50m ropes are used. Or better: finish as for Mud Slide Slim.

394 **Mud Slide Slim**   VS   210ft/64m
G. R. Herus, R. Cully (AL), D. Brown, 1972

A pleasant and enjoyable route which traverses R below the roof as a prelude to fine open climbing up the slabby front face of the buttress. Start as for Sweet Baby James below the triangular overhang next to the white watermark.

1. 60ft/18m. 4c. Climb the ramp up L-wards to the steepening (as for Sweet Baby James). Move up and R to reach the roof. Traverse R beneath this to gain the arete and a sloping ledge. Nut belays 6ft/2m to the R.

2. 70ft/21m. 4b. Make a rising L-ward traverse back to the arete and continue up the edge to a diagonal overlap. Pull round this on good holds to land on a slab, continuing towards a shallow niche in an overhanging wall. Good nut belays (as for Will-o'-the-Wisp).

3. 80ft/24m. 4b. Climb straight up out of the niche via a crack: steep. Continue to the large tree. Starting from a point 10ft/3m R of the large square block, climb directly up the final wall moving L at the top to finish.

The next two routes climb the front face of the subsidiary L-hand triangle of the main buttress.

395 **Will-o'-the-Wisp**   HV Diff   310ft/95m ***
J. A. Summer, Miss J. P. Henrickson, 1972

The rising L-ward traverse line across the front face gives a popular outing – the best of its standard on the cliff. Start R of the centre of the front face, 40ft/12m L of the L-hand of two prominent trees. The ground is eroded next to a block, and there is a long narrow overhang directly above, 120ft/37m up the crag.

1. 95ft/29m. Follow the diagonal line of weakness easily L-wards for about 40ft/12m. Move back R along a grassy ramp. Climb a short wall then move L on to a ledge with a thread and nut belays. This pitch can be taken more direct – only slightly harder.

2. 25ft/8m. Step up and take the short steep ramp to ledges. Nut belays.

3. 50ft/15m. Traverse horizontally L along the ledge, then follow good holds for 30ft/9m or so. Move up and go L across a slab pulling over a bulge on to another ledge system. Nut belay.

4. 55ft/17m. Traverse easily L along more ledges and continue in the natural line via a couple of awkward strides before moving up on to a ledge and a niche just before the arete. Nut belays here, below a steep crack.

5. 25ft/8m. Move L and round the arete. Go straight up on good holds, crux, to an easing in angle and a belay on the obvious tree.

6. 60ft/18m. Scramble up to the square block on the L. Surmount this and the corner on the R. Zigzag R, then L along the obvious line to finish by the sapling in the crack. Horizontal nut belays in a large boulder a few feet above on the R.

396 **Bluebell Babylon**   VS   275ft/83m **

A. J. J. Moulam, R. E. Lambe, 1956

An excellent way up the front face from the first stance of Will-o'-the-Wisp. The line is fairly direct via the L end of the long narrow overhang at 120ft/37m, with a finish up the front of a small tower. Start as for Will-o'-the-Wisp 40ft/12m L of the L-hand of two prominent trees.

1. 95ft/29m. Zigzag up, as for Will-o'-the-Wisp, to the first stance.

2. 60ft/18m. 4b. From the L end of the belay block, climb the overhanging wall on good holds to land on a slab. Go directly up this trending L-wards to a belay at the L-hand corner of the long overhang.

3. 60ft/18m. 4b. Move out L and go up on to a ledge. Climb diagonally L for a few feet to a runner then step R and pull steeply up on good holds to easier-angled rock. A vague crack leads straight up to a belay at the foot of the prominent tower.
4. 60ft/18m. 4c. The indefinite crack in the front face of the tower has a tricky move to reach good holds. Move L on to the overlap and climb the narrow rib finishing over perched blocks.

Central Buttress (849193)
Lying between Great Gully and North Gully, this is the most broken and heavily vegetated of all the Cywarch crags. The only rock of any merit centres around an area L of the prominent natural arch at the bottom L-hand corner of the buttress, on the R wall of Great Gully.

From the stile on the L of the track, down below Bryn Hafod, a stone wall runs up the hillside towards the gash of Great Gully, from which a stream issues. Either traverse R from South Buttress, or approach by a scramble up steep grass to the L of the stream to reach the gully mouth.

397 **Shade of Pale** E1 175ft/53m *
J. A. Sumner, I. Warner, 1983
The overhanging light-coloured right wall of Great Gully, around the corner from the arch, gives a quality quick-drying route with a juggy second pitch. Start down and to the R of the light-coloured wall below the L-hand of two grooves.
1. 40ft/12m. 4a. Climb up behind the tree then traverse L along the obvious easy-angled ramp until directly below the overhanging wall. Old peg, nut and Friend 2½ belay.
2. 135ft/41m. 5b. Ascend steeply, just L of the peg, to gain a niche. Climb directly up on good widely spaced holds to a sloping ledge under an overhang, and an old in-situ TR. Pull out L-wards to reach jugs. Step R on to the lip of the overhang and move up to easy ground. Angle up L-wards over easy rock to a belay. Traverse the hillside across a narrow scree-filled gully to a wide shallow gully which gives an easy descent down the R side of the buttress.

North East Buttress   (849195)

North East Buttress forms the R skyline of the main crag when seen from the parking spot on The Common. It lies at the top of the zigzag approach path between the lower R branch of North Gully, and a series of vegetated terraces on its R side which lead down to the path as it crosses beneath. The focal point of the buttress is a very steep nose of rock rising from vegetated slopes for about 250ft/77m. From the large twin-boled rowan at its foot, the face fans out, the inverted V-chimney of Hades, E1 5a, 5b, on the L, and the slanting ramp of Charon, E1 4a, 5b, to the R being notable features.

For climbs on both the North and North East Buttresses, the best way off lies along a faint path running R-wards over the top of the North Buttress before descending Llwbyr Llewellyn, the steep grassy ramp forming its R flank, to the foot of the crag.

To gain the foot of the face, start from a small bay by a tree just above the path: an interesting scramble, first L then R-wards up through 200ft/61m of lush vegetation, lands one at the large rowan. A white ramp runs up to the L: Styx, VS.

398   Stygian Wall   VS   280ft/84m **

J. A. Sumner, D. M. Adcock (1 pt) (AL), 1955

An outstanding route, near the top end of its grade, which zigzags up through some very steep territory. Start from the twin-boled rowan.

1. 100ft/30m. 4c. Climb the white slab on the L (Styx) for 40ft/12m to a tree. Go up behind this for a few feet to good nut and thread runners. Make a slightly rising R-ward traverse across the steep wall to the arete. Pull up around this then move across a narrow mossy slab to a good nut and Friend belay in a corner.

2. 40ft/12m. 4c. Follow the mossy slab up L for 30ft/9m: awkward. Pull up steeply to enter a 6ft/2m high niche. Belays are awkward to arrange.

3. 90ft/27m. 4c. Pull out L-wards and move up to runners. Step back R and traverse R along the quartz slab using hollow blocky handholds. Move up into a block-filled niche. Pull out of this

398

399

into a crack and take the wall above to good belays.
4. 50ft/15m. 4c. Climb the short wall behind trending R to finish.

399 **Strobe**   E3 (E2 with 1 pt)   250ft/75m ***
G. R. Herus, J. A. Sumner (1 pt) (AL), 1973/FFA: A. Grondowski,
C. Little, 1979

A classic route of exceptional quality and character which weaves a line up the nose of the buttress. The outrageously exposed final pitch gives one of the finest pieces of climbing in the area. Start 20ft/6m higher, and 25ft/8m R of the twin-boled rowan, where a short slabby groove runs up to an overhanging corner; thread belay on its R arete (or belay lower at the rowan).

1. 70ft/21m. 5b. Awkwardly climb the R wall of the groove to a ramp leading across to the R arete. Contortions along this lead to a pull around on to a slab, running up in about 30ft/9m to nut belays – some finesse is required on this pitch which may be combined with the next.

2. 40ft/12m. 5b. A stubborn section past a PR gains an easy ramp on the R leading pleasantly to an arete. Descend on the other side to a huge perched block – on which it would seem prudent to sit, but not to belay. Good nuts and a Friend up on the L at the start of the wall on Pitch 3.

3. 70ft/21m. 6a. Move back to the arete and go up to a thread, where the wall overhangs. Either free climb via a single mighty move and a long stretch; or more usually, use the thread to gain a good spike. Climb straight up to a second spike. Traverse across to a weakness in the L arete where a tricky move back R gains a groove. This leads airily to a stance in a corner.

4. 70ft/21m. 4a. Climb easily out R along the edge of the buttress, then traverse 60ft/18m R across steep grass to block belays.

North Buttress   (848196)

Just beyond the large grassy terraces at the R side of the North East Buttress, a great slabby rib thrown down from the top of

Craig Cywarch – North East Buttress

the crag marks the start of the North Buttress. This, along with
the huge curving groove to its ʀ, gives twin middle grade
classics of the area: Acheron and Doom. ʀ again, the buttress is
broken and heavily vegetated in its lower section up to an area
of wet overhangs, corner, and overlapping slabs at mid-height.
Cutting through its ʀ end, just before the ramp of Llwbyr
Llewellyn, a steep V-groove with a sharp overhanging arete to
its ʀ is Jugs Groove, E3 5c.

Descend to the ʀ down Llwbyr Llewellyn (as for North East
Buttress).

400 **Acheron**   VS   480ft/145m***
A. J. J. Moulam, R. E. Lambe, 1956

The massive rib defining the ʟ edge of the buttress gives a
magnificent expedition which is high in its grade. The climbing
is continually interesting and some route-finding nous is
needed. Start a few feet ʟ of the corner of Doom.

1. 120ft/37m. 4b. Take the easiest line to the overhanging lip of
the slab at 60ft/18m. Make a hard pull round the bulge and
follow the crack, then the arete to a small ledge and rowan
sapling below a ʟ-facing groove.

2. 80ft/24m. 4c. Climb the groove to a steepening. Cross the ʀ
wall airily on good holds to land on a nose. Move up the rib on
the ʀ for a few feet to a narrow grass ledge. Either traverse
across this for 25ft/8m to a belay in a quartz corner; or better,
pull on to the slab and trend diagonally ʀ on good holds before
descending ʀ-wards to the same spot.

3. 80ft/24m. 4c. Climb diagonally ʟ across the slab to a small
ledge on the arete below a steep little groove. Ascend this on
commodious holds for 10ft/3m to a ledge. Step down and
traverse ʟ around the corner across a steep wall to good belays
in a corner crack.

4. 60ft/18m. 4c. Ascend the awkward corner crack past a
dubious block or two, to runners. Semi-hand traverse ʀ-wards
below a leaning wall to a ledge on the arete. Move ʀ again to

Craig Cywarch – North Buttress

large block belays below a flaring groove/chimney.

5. 90ft/27m. 5a. Squirm awkwardly upwards to attain a
bridging position at 10ft/3m. Continue up the still interesting
groove, pulling R up a small rib at 60ft/18m. A further 30ft/9m
of heather scrambling gains a block belay just R of a small tree.

6. 50ft/15m. 4b. Scramble across diagonally R-wards to a
runner on a stout tree. Surmount the steep bulge into a scoop
which has a precarious heather exit. Belay well back on the L
amongst large boulders.

401 **Doom**   VS   390ft/119m **

J. A. Sumner, A. Gillis (some aid) (AL), 1968

The huge corner R of Acheron gives a fine route with a strong
mountaineering flavour. Best tackled when the first pitch dries
out.

1. 120ft/37m. 4b. Climb the corner using holds on the R wall as
needed to a steep move R on to a little slab in the corner. Make
an awkward exit R at the top, then climb up grass for 15ft/5m to
a ledge and flake belay – a pitch which is considerably harder if
wet!

2. 100ft/30m. 4c. Traverse R along a ledge for 10ft/3m to a
small arete. Climb up delicately moving first L then back R into
the corner and continue up to an overhang. Surmount this
using an undercut pocket on the R wall and ascend grass for a
few feet to a peg and nut belay in the corner.

3. 120ft/37m. 4c. Climb the corner behind the stance for
10ft/3m then move across into a small niche in the slab. Climb
the crack for a few moves then step L (avoiding a loose flake) on
to a ledge. Follow the edge of the slab to a good spike. From
this, either climb the corner, to a smooth section and make a
L-ward traverse to the arete or, better, continue more easily up
the arete in a fine position to a grassy exit. Nut belays.

4. 50ft/15m. 4b. Scramble across to the large rowan and climb
the steep wall behind it with a tricky exit – as for Acheron.

North Face   (847196)

To the R of the North Buttress, the North Face extends across

Craig Cywarch – North Face

from the grassy ramp of Llwbyr Llewellyn to a large vegetated gully by the rocky tower of Dinas Llewellyn on the R. The L side of the face consists of a huge quartz-seamed wall above a grassy bay, whilst on the R, a reddish wall to the R of an overlapping corner is neatly traversed by Spartan, E2 5c, 4c. Between these two areas, a smooth central wall with a large shield of rock stuck to it rises from a terrace. Below this, a subsidiary buttress with a prominent cave-like opening at its base rises up from a large grass ledge, the starting point for our next two routes. It is reached from the R by a scramble up over grass terraces.

The safest and easiest descent is to continue to the top of the cliff, then walk around the top end of the much smaller Far North Buttress to the R.

402 **Plankwalk** HVS 240ft/73m *
M. Boysen, J. Jordan, 1966
A good climb taking the groove just R of the cave then the easiest line across the smooth central wall to the L. Start a few feet R of the cave at the foot of a ramp formed by a large flake.
1. 110ft/33m. 4c. Go up the ramp and the steep groove above

which slants up R-wards leading to a grassy ledge. Continue up more broken ground to a sloping grassy terrace.

2. 130ft/40m. 5b. Follow a line of weakness on the R then trend diagonally L-wards to a prominent small square block in the centre of the wall. Move delicately L, then step up to a narrow ledge and move L again to reach a small ledge on the L side of the wall. Continue round the arete to finish up an easy gully.

403 Keelhaul   E1   230ft/70m ***

J. A. Sumner, Miss J. P. Henrickson, 1969

A stunning route of 'Shrike-like' quality which forces a direct line up over the shield of rock to the R of Plankwalk. Start by an arete a few feet R of the Plankwalk start, about 15ft/5m R of the cave.

1. 100ft/30m. 5b. Move round the arete and climb a L-ward slanting crack to a ledge on the arete. Make a fierce move up the overhanging arete to reach a shallow groove. Take this to the large grassy terrace shared with Plankwalk.

2. 130ft/40m. 5b. Follow a line of weakness on the R then trend up L-wards to a good spike runner about 15ft/5m R of the prominent small square block on Plankwalk's second pitch. Ascend the R-wards-slanting ramp above to a short corner below a small roof. Move out R under the roof to some old pegs, then make a long stretch up for a good spike above it! Continue for 6ft/2m above the spike then move L to a good nut runner. Climb directly up the wall above to a ledge. Ascend direct to a large block overhang then trend L-wards to the arete.

Cader Idris Area

CYFRWY   (703135)

Sitting high on the northern slopes of Cader Idris, rising up to its summit ridge, Cyfrwy, a massive cliff with a distinctive slab and groove infrastructure, stretches for nearly three-quarters of a mile across the face of the mountain. On the L, the cliff is slightly domed where it attains its maximum height of around

600ft/186m. Its L edge is delineated by the castellated Cyfrwy
Arete with a distinctive stepped profile, the first step marking
the summit of the clean-looking Table Buttress – a celebrated
and obvious feature known naturally enough as The Table.
From a slot behind this, a gully runs down separating Table
Buttress from two huge ribs: Quartz Rib, VS, immediately to
the R, and the much larger 'Rib and Slab', beyond. R again, at
the end of the large terraces crossing this section of cliff, the
deep diagonal Slanting Gully runs up from R to L, with the fine
open overlapping slabs of Slabby Buttress, which give some
outstanding climbs, a little further over, just before the wide
deep gash of One Pitch Gully. Beyond, the long tapering
Western Wing continues for about one-third of a mile before
eventually merging into the hillside.

   The rock is generally compact and offers good friction, but
there are some loose areas, though protection is usually
adequate.

   Follow the Twyn road out of Dolgellau to the Idris Service
Station. Turn L up the hill (signposted Cader Idris) and follow
the road for two and a half miles to the National Trust car-park
at 697153. Take the pony track which starts on the far side of
the bridge (the Fox's Path from the Gwernan Lake Hotel at
704159 is slightly quicker, but parking is a problem) for about
one mile to where it crosses a mountain wall and stream. Break
L along a faint contouring path leading up below the Western
Wing to a point overlooking Llyn y Gadair. A few minutes of
steep scree ascent now lie between the climber and his selected
route. Approach time about sixty minutes.

404 **Cyfrwy by the Table Direct**   V Diff   642ft/194m ***
R. W. Davies, H. E. Chatburn, 1951/O. G. Jones, solo, 1888
This fine mountaineering route is traditionally climbed in
boots, carrying sacks, as a prelude to an Alpine season. It
follows the prominent stepped ridge forming the L edge of the
buttress; the first and largest step is self-evidently known as
The Table. Though the line is well-trodden, there is still some
suspect rock in places. After the first four pitches, the standard

drops to Diff at a junction with Cyfrwy Arete. The largest and most prominent arete of the buttress is split by a groove: Nudging Groove, HVS. A short gully slants up R-wards between the foot of this and some pinnacles on the R. Start near the top of the gully where a dubious pinnacle leans against the wall. Pitches can be 'run together' as desired.

1. 30ft/9m. Go up between the pinnacle and wall to a jammed stone belay.

2. 60ft/18m. Make a rising R-ward traverse for 35ft/10m, then ascend steeply L-wards on good holds to a large ledge.

3. 50ft/15m. Take the crack in the corner on the R to a ledge.

4. 30ft/9m. Move to the R end of the stance, overlooking the gully, then climb L-wards up the wall to the terrace under Cyfrwy Arete.

5. 60ft/18m. Climb an arete, then a corner to join the main ridge.

6. 60ft/18m. Continue along the crest of the ridge to land on The Table.

7. 12ft/4m. Carefully descend into the gap behind The Table.

8. 30ft/9m. Move L to climb a steep little crack and so reach a small pinnacle on the L arete.

9. 50ft/15m. Take the arete above to a large ledge.

10. 60ft/18m. Surmount two walls with a ledge midway.

11. 200ft/61m. Follow the ridge, scrambling over short walls and spikes to the top. Either continue to the summit of Cader Idris; or descend – from a point about 70ft/21m from the top of the ridge, traverse across into a large scree gully on the L which leads down to easy ground running round to the L (facing out) below the base of the buttress.

405 **Rib and Slab**   VS   495ft/152m *

D. Burgess, J. R. Allen, 1960

A varied expedition with an Alpine flavour which just merits its grade – never really hard (unless greasy), but with the odd patch of dubious rock. Protection improves as the height

Cader Idris – Cyfrwy

increases. The substance of the route is the large rib towards the L side of the cliff, just R of the obvious Quartz Rib, with which it shares a common first pitch. Start just R of the foot of the gully which drops down from behind The Table on Cyfrwy Arete, where a prominent narrow rib rises up to finish L of a butterfly-shaped overhang.

1. 130ft/40m. 4b. The crest of the rib is taken in two stages to a grassy R-ward scramble and good nut belay in the wall on the R.

2. 45ft/14m. 4b. Step R and climb the slabby wall moving R to an obvious hold on the arete at 30ft/9m. Step round into a groove and go up to a small stance 10ft/3m higher.

3. 120ft/37m. 4a. Climb the slab on the R for 50ft/15m to steep grass and heather. Scramble up over this keeping just R of the arete to a large sling belay on an outcropping rock about 5ft/2m below the upper slab.

4. 130ft/40m. 4c. Just up on the R and about 12ft/4m R of the arete is a prominent crack; after an awkward start, follow the crack more easily over several small bulges, trending L after 100ft/30m to a good spike belay, but poor stance on the arete – about 20ft/6m below where the angle eases off.

5. 70ft/21m. Climb doubtful rock for 20ft/6m. Scramble easily along the ridge for 50ft/15m to where a wall of flakes necessitates a step round to the R. Either finish up the ridge, or descend. A grassy ramp leads down and across L-wards to rock and heather slopes. A further 150ft/46m of L-ward traversing gains the wide scree gully. Continue down as for Cyfrwy Arete.

Slabby Buttress

This, the cleanest and most compact area of rock, takes the form of an enormous triangle, the base of which runs from Slanting Gully to One Pitch Gully. Its two diagonals meet at the apex of the buttress and are formed, on the L, by a shallow gully running up from a point just above the foot of Slanting Gully, and on the R, by North Arete, Diff, which starts from the bottom of One Pitch Gully. The main attraction centres on the

two clean overlapping slabs, the lower and larger one set to the
R of the upper.

Descent: there are two alternatives, both of which require
care. 1. Traverse into a shallow gully behind the buttress and
climb it for about one ropelength to a col – tenuous if wet!
Avoid the large buttress by a short wall on the R to land on a
grass ledge. Take the grassy weakness in the wall behind to a
sloping ledge after 120ft/37m. Scramble up L-wards to where
the angle eases – 120ft/37m. Walk up L-wards to the top of
Cyfrwy Arete and descend this for 70ft/21m before traversing
across R-wards (facing out) to the scree-filled descent gully, as
for Rib and Slab etc. If it is misty: 2. From the belay spike it is
possible to reach the ground via two long abseils – down to the
runner/belay thread on Route 2/Obsession (155ft/47m) then a
further 125ft/36m to the ground. This will mean leaving two
slings to ensure that the abseil ropes pull!

406 Obsession   VS   350ft/96m **
A. B. Black and party, 1956

A fine interesting route which meanders up the centre of the
buttress crossing the large upper slab from R to L. Start below
overhangs about 22ft/7m L of the slim corner with the faded
white water streak which lies directly below the lower slab.

1. 100ft/30m. 4b. Ascend the cracked slab to the overhangs at
40ft/12m. Move L on to a large perched block forming the lower
L overhang. Climb directly up via the obvious weakness to a
small grass ledge and spike belay.

2. 40ft/12m. 4c. Climb diagonally R for 15ft/5m. Step R to
better holds in a groove then go straight up to a ledge. Low
thread belay on the L.

3. 90ft/27m. 4b. Climb the groove immediately R of the belay
then move L with a long stride above an overhang at 20ft/6m.
Go straight up (a little loose) to a horizontal break with
perched blocks at 50ft/15m. TR on the R. Climb diagonally R
crossing grass at the base of a large slab to a corner on its
R-hand side. Huge spike belay.

4. 120ft/37m. 4c. Step L into the groove forming the R corner of

the slab. Climb it for 20ft/6m then move L and up to gain better holds. Follow these across the slab to a crack on the L edge with flakes jammed in it. Take the crack for 20ft/6m then step R and continue up another crack. Move R again and climb the groove to a good ledge and spike belays.

407 **Gwydrin**   E1   190ft/57m **

J. A. Sumner, I. Warner, 1982

This excellent route gives the best climbing on the crag with a sustained and open pitch up the centre of the large lower slab. Start at a groove 6ft/2m L of the faded white water streak below the lower slab, and about 15ft/5m R of Obsession.

1. 90ft/27m. 4c. Climb the groove to a ledge and TR at 40ft/12m. Above is a steeper reddish groove leaning slightly to the R. Take this awkwardly to a large flat hold then reverse the traverse of Route 2 to a stance on the R of the large lower slab. Nut and thread belays.

2. 100ft/30m. 5b. Step back L on to the slab. Move up then step L again to follow a vague weakness, about 6ft/2m L of the corner. Where it ends, traverse delicately L, PR, to a thin crack. Ascend this moving R to a small ledge. Move up and back L to follow thin cracks to the top of the slab, finishing close to the arete. Nut belay in a corner about 25ft/8m above. Finish as for Route 2 or abseil off.

408 **Route 2**   VS   365ft/112m *

D. Burgess, J. R. Allen, 1959

Another good route in the mould of Obsession, crossing the large lower slab. The somewhat scrappy central section is redeemed by a superbly exposed and bold final pitch. From the groove with the faded white water streak running down its L wall, move round to the R and ascend for 10ft/3m to a 6ft/2m spike belay in another corner, slightly R of centre of the large slab above.

Gwydrin, Cader Idris

1. 75ft/23m. 4b. Bridge up the groove to a grassy ramp beneath the slab. Go easily up R to nut belays.

2. 40ft/12m. 4b. Make a horizontal traverse L across the foot of the slab with a step-down half-way. Stride L round the rib and move up to a stance on blocks at the foot of the groove.

3. 120ft/37m. 4c. Climb the groove to a grassy ledge and TR (or belay) on the L (junction with Obesssion). Move 6 ft/2m R and continue up the nearest (L-hand) of the two corner/grooves with an awkward move to good holds on the R arete at about 10ft/3m. Pass a perched block near the top and step R to the high spike belay of Obsession by the upper large slab.

4. 130ft/40m. 4c. Step R round the rib and climb a crack for 35ft/11m. Good runners. Step R then back L and climb delicately up just R of the arete for 10ft/3m, crux, moving R to improving holds in a short corner. From the top of this move back L to the arete and finish direct via a shallow L-facing corner. Good spike belays.

CRAIG CAU   (712122)

This remote north-east-facing cliff lies below the summit of Mynydd Pencoed, cradled in the arm of the massive spur which curves first south then east from Penygadair, the highest point on the main east–west Cader ridge and the top of the mountain. The crag is large and complex, reaching a height of around 900ft/265m, but it is also heavily vegetated and needs at least a week of good weather to come into condition. Despite this, some superb routes on sound rock await those willing to seek them out; the five selected climbs all have the potential to become classics!

On the L side of the cliff, its predominant feature, the gigantic Pencoed Pillar, tapers up for over 600ft/186m and is bracketed between the deep gloomy gash of Great Gully to the R, and East Gully. Further over, R of the pillar, past an area of vegetation and short walls, the next obvious feature is the Central Rib, VS, which drops down from the summit of Mynydd Pencoed to finish at half-height on a great vegetated terrace. Beyond this, across more vegetated rock, the 200ft/61m chimney/crack of Crack of Cau stands out in a cleaner area of rock, whose R arete is taken by Bird of Time.

The usual approach is from the National Trust car-park (731115) near Minffordd, just north of Idris Gates, on the south side of the mountain where the B4405 Abergynolwyn road branches off the A487. Follow the path up through the wooded hillside, following the stream issuing out of Llyn Cau. From the top of the treeline, the path continues across moorland for around three-quarters of a mile to the head of the Llyn. The cliff sprawls lazily across the back wall of the cwm and is reached along a narrow path either on the L or R side of the Llyn. Approach time, one and a half hours.

The easiest descent lies on the R side of the cliff and takes the scree path which descends to Llyn Cau from the col between Mynydd Pencoed and Penygadair. For Pencoed Pillar, and Darker Angel, an alternative descent is to follow the main ridge path south-east, past the tops of East Gully and Little Gully. The next gully along has a wide bilberry funnel exit; keeping to the heathery slopes on its L (facing out), descend this to a sheep track which slants back down and round to the base of the crag.

The first two routes lie on opposite faces of the Pencoed Pillar:

409 Pencoed Pillar   HV Diff   645ft/197m ***
M. Dalton, H. G. Dalton, 1903

A very fine mountaineering route following the easiest line up the East Face of Pencoed Pillar. After an initial botanical ramble across vegetated foothill slabs, the pillar narrows and steepens in its upper reaches where the exposure becomes breathtaking; thankfully, the holds, stances and belays are all good on this part of the climb. Start low down on the L side of the pillar and scramble R-wards up a large grassy ramp to nut belays just round the toe of a rocky rib. A quartz lump at 5ft/2m is an obvious marker.

1. 120ft/39m. Climb the rib and step R on to a grassy ledge at 12ft/4m. Move R a little then step back L and take the rib to another grassy ledge on the R. Continue up the trodden line

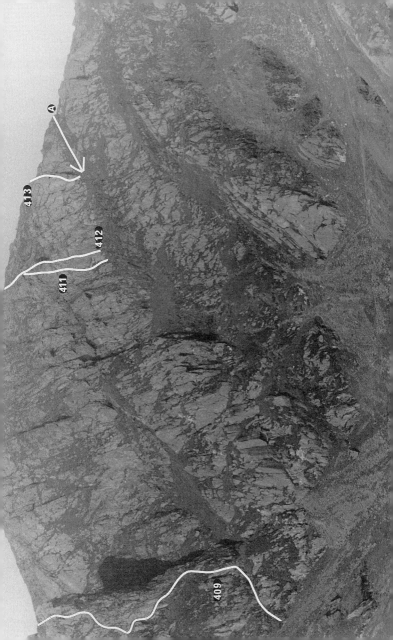

through vegetation, to nut and ancient peg belays in a rocky rib, 5ft/2m above a small rowan tree.

2. 180ft/55m. Scramble diagonally L up vegetation along the foot of the steep grey wall, admiring the flowers, to nut belays at the base of a short chimney/gully – a well-trodden path which requires little or no gear! Intermediate belays on a couple of flakes if needed.

3. 130ft/40m. Climb the gully and short wall above, stepping L on to vegetation at the foot of the pillar itself. Scramble up R-wards to the base of a L-slanting groove with some blocks wedged in it near the top. Climb the groove, using the blocks. Exit L at the top, then pull back R on to more vegetation. Follow the trodden path to a flake thread and belay 25ft/8m higher on the R. This pitch may be split at the foot of the groove after 80ft/24m.

4. 50ft/15m. Make an exposed rising traverse on large holds across the wall on the R, moving up to a large block belay and superbly positioned stance.

5. 90ft/27m. Climb the wall directly above on large holds keeping just L of the arete, to reach a narrow vegetated terrace with good nut belays in a small crack on the L.

6. 65ft/20m. Climb the small corner then go diagonally up a ramp for 10ft/3m to enter a greasy groove. Struggle up this to a flat stony bay.

7. 10ft/3m. Climb up then scramble R-wards up easy ground to a block belay at the pillar summit. Escape along the narrow ridge to the main mass of the mountain.

410 **Darker Angel**   E2   435ft/132m ***

D. W. Shaw, K. Bentham (1pt) (AL), 1974

The sheer west wall of the pillar plunges dramatically for around 300ft/93m into Great Gully and is breached by a superb line of weakness, the substance of a thrilling and atmospheric adventure – probably the best in the area. Start at the bottom L-end of the face below the arete formed at the

Craig Cau

The exposed slab on Darker Angel, pitch 5

junction of the north (front) and west faces. The best approach is along our other selected climb, Pencoed Pillar, breaking out R-wards on its second pitch, before the steep grey wall, via a vegetated groove. Continue trending up R via more jungle-bashing to a stance at the base of an obvious ramp leading up to the R.

1. 150ft/46m. 5a. Climb the ramp then traverse R for 20ft/6m. Move up and continue awkwardly to reach a L-ward traverse line guarded by a flaky block. Follow this across to the base of a short groove and climb this to a spike belay under a small fang of rock.

2. 30ft/9m. Climb R-wards along a grassy ramp to its end. Good belays.

3. 35ft/11m. 5a. Traverse R across a slab to a bulge with a prominent projecting foothold. Move R round the bulge to a small exposed stance.

4. 80ft/24m. 5c. Go up to the R-hand end of the overhang, then follow the tapering narrow slab in a superb position until it disappears and continues as a crack. Climb the crack via some good finger-locks with a hard finish to land on a small stance below a huge roof.

5. 50ft/15. 5c. Ascend to the roof. Traverse delicately L across the slab to reach a rib. Climb up more easily just L of this to gain a stance under another large roof.

6. 90ft/27m. 4c. Go back R for 10ft/3m and break through the roofs to land on a slab. Finish pleasantly and airily up this.

The next three routes lie on the R side of the crag and are reached from the area where the ridge flattens out, just L of the col at the top of the descent path. Scramble down a grassy couloir marked by a prominent quartz streak. Traverse R (facing out) behind two pinnacles then drop down and follow a faint sheep track to a grassy col. Cross another grassy hollow below the arete of Bird of Time, to a second grassy col. Drop down to the track again to a narrowing and rocky step. Descend this and move awkwardly across to a large flake – Touchstone lies at the far end of the mossy quartz terrace – but for Crack of Cau, descend for 20ft/6m and contour across to belay at a flake crack in a cracked wall, just R and about 40ft/12m below the foot of the huge chimney/crack.

411 **Crack of Cau** E1 345ft/104m **

J. A. Sumner, K. Bentham, 1973

The huge chimney/crack high on the R-hand side of the crag
has a committing feel about it, but the climbing is never really
hard – though it may be a little dirty in places. Start from the
flake crack belay described above.

1. 40ft/12m. 4c. From a spike, move across into the corner.
Step up and L on to a ledge on the arete. Spike runner. A few
gripping feet of grass-climbing leads to easier scrambling and a
block belay below the chimney.

2. 40ft/12m. 5a. Climb the steepening chimney, usually dirty,
using holds on the R arete. Move R to a stance a few feet above
the chockstone.

3. 80ft/24m. 5a. Continue up the chimney then bridge the
short steep groove to better holds. Step back into the chimney
and climb easily up to the overhang. Surmount this:
interesting! Spike belays and a small stance in the chimney line
just above.

4. 85ft/26m. 5a. Go directly up the groove above past two
steepenings to a final greasy flaky bulge which is turned on the
R to a good flake belay. Junction with Touchstone.

5. 100ft/30m. Scramble up the grassy gully to an awkward
exit!

412 **Touchstone** VS 380ft/114m *

J. A. Sumner, R. Thorndyke, 1973

A very good route taking a parallel line up the cliff just R of
Crack of Cau. Start at the end of the mossy quartz terrace
below overhanging rock, where a L-ward slanting
V-groove/chimney cuts through the steep wall – 40ft/12m R of
the start of Crack of Cau, and 12ft/4m above it.

1. 40ft/12m. 4c. Climb cracks in the slabby L wall of the
chimney to a thin spike. Step L and continue to a grassy ledge
on the L. Nut and large flake belay at its far end.

2. 70ft/21m. 4c. Move back R for 10ft/3m and climb to a good
nut runner just above a large detached spike. Traverse R,
laybacking around the arete on a good foothold. Step R into a

corner and crack. Climb this, exiting R at the top on to a
narrow grass ledge; large block belay at its L end.
3. 70ft/21m. 4c. From the L end of the ledge, take the scoop to a
steepening at 30ft/9m. Make a long stride R and go steeply up
on large flaky holds trending slightly R to meet the R arete of the
buttress. Nut belays a little higher in a corner.
4. 100ft/30m. 4b. Above is a large overhang. Climb up above
the belay moving out L on to the arete. Follow the narrow slab
above to enter a small cave. Chimney up to a TR. Pull round
and continue up a little gully to a large flake belay. Junction
with Crack of Cau.
5. 100ft/30m. Finish up the grassy gully on the R, as for Crack
of Cau.

413 **Bird of Time**   E1   180ft/54m **

K. Bentham, D. W. Shaw (AL), 1974
The clean-looking rounded arete defining the R edge of the
upper R-hand section of cliff is quite bold, and deceptively
steep, especially on its second pitch. Even better than it looks!
Start at a short chimney below and just L of the arete.
1. 40ft/12m. 4a. Take the chimney then go over ledges above to
a long grassy ledge. Belay in the centre of this.
2. 90ft/27m. 5b. From the centre of the ledge, a crack leads up
to a small ledge. From the R-hand end of this ledge, climb down
to the R, then ascend up R to enter a groove set in the arete.
Climb the groove to a ledge. From its R end, step R, then ascend
the arete to an overhang. Belay over on the R below the roof. A
superb pitch.
3. 50ft/15m. 4b. Move R and enter a chimney. Climb this on
the inside, exiting through a hole at the top.

BIRD ROCK (CRAIG ADERYN)   (643069)
Situated to the south-west of Cader Idris, about seven miles
inland from the coastal resort of Tywyn, the striking dome of
Bird Rock towers over the flat, low-lying Dysynni Valley. The
cliff receives better than average weather and is quick to dry

out, despite facing north and only catching the sun in the late afternoon during the summer months.

From the Cross Foxes Hotel, 766167, on the Dolgellau–Welshpool road, follow the A487 along the south side of Cader Idris to Minffordd, 733115, then the B4405 to Tal-y-llyn. Just over a mile further on, a minor road, signposted Llanegryn, branches off to the R, immediately before a bridge. Continue along this, following the river Dysynni for about three miles to a parking space just below the base of the cliff.

There are three main facets: the Eastern Face, perched up above the quarry, is a large rambling crag of little interest to a majority of climbers; loose rock and vegetation abound, not to mention the liberal sprinkling of guano – cormorants nest here, and there is a climbing ban during the spring and summer months. Similarly, at a slightly lower level and at the R end of the Eastern Face, the scrappy two-tiered Central Buttress also has little to commend it. However, way down to the R, The Bastion stands proudly, almost next to the road, and is by far the most popular of the Bird Rock crags. It presents two faces which meet at a blunt rib, The Buttress. To the R, The Bastion's West Face is rather broken and bitty, whilst to the L, the Diamond Wall, gently overhanging for 150ft/46m, is the jewel in its North Face. Descent: a path runs down L-wards from the apex of the Diamond Wall to a scree slope leading back to its foot.

414   Spike Wall   E1   120ft/37m *

FA: Unknown

A surprisingly steep pitch up the L edge of the Diamond Wall. The holds are large, but the climbing is strenuous and there is some doubtful rock which needs care. Start from a large block which protrudes from the scree a few yards up from the toe of the wall, directly below a pedestal at 33ft/10m.

1. 5b. Ascend steeply to a niche below the pedestal. Move up and R alongside it. Traverse R for about 15ft/5m then pull on to

Bird Rock – the Diamond Wall

a small slab below an overhang. Climb steeply up to the L, via a crack, to a large spike. The bulge above is strenuous and is taken on large dubious holds to gain a R-ward slanting groove above. Follow this airily using holds on the L wall. Move R at the top and finish more easily to block belays at the crest of the wall.

415 **Daisy Belle** E1 130ft/39m **

L. K. Forsey, D. Davies (some aid) (AL), 1964/FFA: J. Codling and party, 1978

A high-quality route which tackles an overhanging groove above the L end of a ledge in the centre of the face. Start from the large boulder as for Spike Wall.

1. 60ft/18m. 5a. Step up from the boulder then traverse R. Move up and go R again to an obvious groove. Make a difficult move up this past a PR, and so gain a ledge on the R. Peg and nut belays.

2. 70ft/21m. 5b. Battle up the overhanging groove above the L end of the ledge past some old PRS to a niche on the L. From the top of this, pull out L on to a slab and continue up, moving L near the top to finish.

416 **Diamond Eliminate** E3 160ft/48m **

K. Bentham, D. W. Shaw (2 pts), 1976/FFA: D. Wiggin, J. Codling (AL), M. Elwell, 1978

A superb route taking a fairly central line up the Diamond Wall. The rock is a little shattered at first but soon improves; protection needs careful attention; the position is sensational, the climbing sustained. Start at the foot of The Diagonal, a prominent slanting rake running up to the R from the toe of The Diamond, defining its lower R edge.

1. 80ft/24m. 5b. Go up bearing slightly L to a large spike at 25ft/8m. Move up R to another spike 6ft/2m above. Follow a thin crack up L-wards to reach a R-ward slanting ramp. Take this for 20ft/6m then make difficult moves directly up over a bulge to reach a line of ledges cutting across the face. Move R to a stance and belays.

2. 80ft/24m. 6a. Step R and climb the smooth shallow groove to
a flat-topped pedestal. Move up and R past an old hammered
nut to reach an obvious hold, crux. Continue to the base of a
slanting slab. Traverse L and move up into the central niche.
Climb this, exiting L to an arete leading up to the top – a
thrilling pitch!

417 **The Bolero**   HVS   150ft/45m **
J. A. Sumner, R. F. Short, 1974

An enjoyable climb which takes rock R of the Diamond Wall
before breaking back L up the prominent groove in its upper R
corner. Start just R of the fence running up to the crag, below a
pedestal at 30ft/9m.
1. 80ft/24m. 5a. Take a narrow R-ward leaning slab to a black
scoop. Runners. Make steep moves L to stand on the pedestal.
Move L and ascend awkwardly, PR. Step L and continue via the
obvious line (The Diagonal) to a ledge and spike belay on the R
of the ivy.
2. 70ft/21m. 5a. Move back down L across the ivy groove to
reach a steep ramp; after a difficult start, climb this to its top.
Climb the steep wall above, crux, and pull up into a V-slot at
the foot of a L-sloping ramp. Take this to a ledge at its tip, then
finish direct up a short steep wall. Belay on large blocks up
and L.

418 **The Buttress**   V Diff   140ft/42m *
FA: Unknown

A fine and popular route which follows the rounded central rib
of The Bastion in three short pitches. Start just above the road
at the lowest point of the cliff.
1. 40ft/12m. Follow the crest of the rib to a large ledge which
slants up to the L. Belays at its top end.
2. 70ft/21m. Move up for 5ft/2m. Pull over the bulge on hidden
pockets and continue on good holds to a grassy ledge at
25ft/8m. Go straight up via a short grassy groove to rejoin the
crest of the buttress. Follow this to a metal spike belay behind a
large block, and below a short overhanging wall.

3. 30ft/9m. Pull up the overhanging wall on large holds.
Scramble up to a grassy ledge and awkward belays. Descend by
taking a grassy ramp up L-wards over the top of The Diamond
Wall.

Anglesey

The sea cliffs of Craig Gogarth, situated two miles west of
Holyhead, offer an almost unique type of climbing which is
only mirrored, but in a scaled-down form, at the fierce 'Little
Big' crag of Rhoscolyn, three miles to the south. Most of the
routes here are only suitable for parties operating competently
at the grade of VS and above, and there is little to entice those
of more moderate ability, save for some attractive coastal
scenery. The situations are usually very dramatic and it is not
unusual for some climbers to succumb to the 'Gogarth Grip
Factor' during their first few visits. Familiarity, however,
breeds a more relaxed understanding (though one will never
become blasé), when both the climbing and the changeable
seas below can be savoured to the full.

Local Amenities
A vast majority of climbers visit the cliffs on a daily basis and
use the conventional mountain areas, especially Llanberis, as a
base. Those wishing to stay over, however, will find adequate
facilities in and around the port of Holyhead. The more
determined and discreet will find unofficial places to camp,
especially at South Stack, where there is also a café – only open
during the summer months. All valuables should be locked
away out of sight; there have been thefts from tents here, even
while the occupants were asleep during the night! Trearddur
Bay, midway between Craig Gogarth and Rhoscolyn, is also a
good place to be based, with good shops, windsurfers for hire at
the Anglesey School of Sea Canoeing and good night life,
especially during the summer, at the Beach Hotel.

Craig Gogarth
The climbing on Gogarth is generally demanding, on rock
which varies from the brittle white quartzite of North Stack to
the solidified talcum-powder-and-mudstone-mix found in and
around South Stack.

    On the harder routes, a cool head allied to temendous fitness

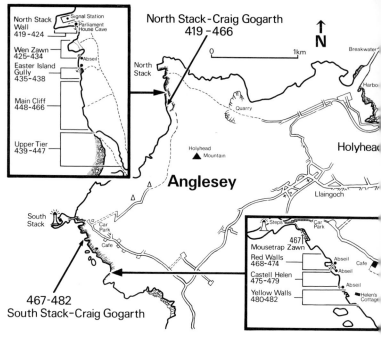

and finger stamina are vital for a successful ascent and parties are advised to tackle something well within their capabilities on their first few visits to the cliff. Most climbs can be adequately protected with nuts, but a large rack of Friends and Micro Mates will be particularly useful for rapid runners and belay back-ups in the flared overhanging cracks of the Main Cliff; these will also require regular checking and lubrication after use to avoid seizure. All in-situ pegs should be treated with caution as they are susceptible to rapid corrision in this damp salty environment. The failure of such rusting items of ironmongery has already caused several spectacular falls, though fortunately none proved fatal.

Access to some areas, especially the Main Cliff and Easter Island, is affected by the tides and visiting climbers are strongly advised to check the times of high and low water. Tide tables may be purchased in Holyhead.

South Stack is the home of several protected species of birds which nest in Mousetrap Zawn and on the adjacent Red Walls. Consequently there is a local ban on climbing on these cliffs during the nesting season, which lasts from 1 February to 31 July.

Approaches

Gogarth comprises ten separate cliffs which form part of the Anglesey coastline between the North Stack (215840) and Penlas Rock (208815) on the west side of Holyhead Mountain, which itself contains many short routes. There are two main approaches to the crag:

Approach for South Stack, Upper Tier and Main Cliff routes
These cliffs are best reached from one of the South Stack car-parks. To get to South Stack, turn L off the A5 at the Valley traffic lights, three miles from Holyhead, and follow the B4545 to Trearddur Bay. Turn L again at 255793 where a twisting coastal road leads past several small coves to another L turn, after three miles; a narrow road runs up to the South Stack café.

The South Stack cliffs – Mousetrap Zawn, the Red Walls, Castell Helen and Yellow Wall – lie just below the café and car-parks. However, for the Upper Tier, the Main Cliff and Holyhead Mountain, a well-defined path runs north-east from the upper car-park past a prominent telecommunications relay station towards the south-facing crags on Holyhead Mountain. The path now splits, the R branch continuing up over the mountain itself to North Stack, while the L branch drops down from a col to a well-worn site at the top of the descent gully, overlooking Gogarth Bay. This is the usual place to gear up. From the foot of the gully, a path, badly eroded in places, contours round the hillside below the Upper Tier: just round the corner beyond the prominent pinnacle, Shag Rock, a little subsidiary branch drops steeply down to the Main Cliff. Approach time, thirty minutes.

Approach for North Stack Wall, Wen Zawn and Easter Island routes
Best reached from the Holyhead Quarries. On entering
Holyhead, follow the A5 (Victoria Road) to the harbour. Turn
L along the Prince of Wales Road, which runs along the
harbour front, and continue along a minor road which forks L
where the main road bears R. This twisting minor road
eventually joins a bumpy earth road leading to parking in the
quarries at 225834.

Follow the path which climbs steeply up the hillside, taking
the L fork when it divides after half a mile. Continue uphill until
the path divides once again. The R fork runs down by some
telegraph poles to the North Stack fog-warning station; the L
fork leads up to a col just above Wen Zawn before dropping
steeply down to the peninsula overlooking the zawn. To reach
Easter Island Gully, a small path leads up the L side of the col
above Wen Zawn, just before some rocks. From a shallow col
immediately after the top of the hill, veer down R-wards
towards the sea. Approach time, fifteen to twenty minutes.

North Stack Wall and Parliament House Cave   (215840)
The fog-warning station perches on a peninsula above a long,
smooth south-facing wall taken by some classic single pitch
climbs. It forms one side of a zawn, at the back of which lies the
huge Parliament House Cave.

The floor of the zawn is reached either by abseil from the
telegraph pole, or from one of the shackles behind the white
wall, or – at low tides – by a tunnel running from the north side
of the peninsula to emerge in the back L-hand corner of the
cave. An extra rope for the abseil ensures an escape in case of
tidal complications or any other emergency that might arise.
The traditional escape route is Green Gilbert, HVS, but a bit of
a 'rock horror' for its grade.

Three hard aid routes accept the challenge of the 100ft/30m
Parliament House Cave roof; on the R, it is breached by
L'Affreuse and The Black Rod, both A3, whilst the L-hand line
is:

Hanging around below The Big Overhang

419 **The Big Overhang** A3 200ft/61m***
D. K. Scott, B. Palmer, 1967

A superb voyage into the world of the horizontal. One of the country's longest roofs provides an interesting excursion into the realm of the aid climber. There is a fair amount of gear in situ, but much of this has perished, or is in a dangerous state. About eighty karabiners seem to be the norm for an ascent, though it has been done with less. A good selection of pegs is needed, not to mention long slings which are essential to prevent rope drag. The initial 30ft/9m of the roof are on poor rock but the remainder is solid. A good way to spend a wet weekend! Start below a sort of pedestal in the centre of the back wall.

1. 40ft/12m. Free climb the crack in the buttress using aid as necessary to an awkward exit and scramble up steeply to a stance hewn out of shattered rock. Ancient bolt belays.

2. 120ft/37m. Above is the massive roof. This is it! Climb up to the roof. Swing out with long reaches for poor pegs in poor rock: strenuous. Continue along two vague parallel cracks; the line is littered with rusting ironmongery. Multi-peg belay on the very lip of the overhang – adds to the experience and can be backed up with a preplaced rope from above.

3. 40ft/12m. Either peg and free climb up the steep wall to finish via a shallow corner, or prussik!

At the R end of the North Stack wall, an arete drops down below the lip of Parliament House Cave. This arete and the groove above it give Wall of Horrors, E2 5c. An obvious corner 30ft/9m L is taken by The Whip, HVS, but loose, whilst 20ft/6m L again lies the thin crack of Green Gilbert.

420 **Blue Peter** E4 130ft/40m **

P. Whillance, D. Armstrong, 1978

The prominent flake crack on the R side of the wall gives a brilliant pitch. Start 5yd/5m L of Green Gilbert below the R-hand side of an overhang.

1. 5c. Climb a short slab then surmount the overhang strenuously to a PR on the wall above. Move up, then L with difficulty to the foot of a thin flake crack. Follow this in a fine position until about 10ft/3m from the top where a step L leads to a short finishing groove.

421 **The Cad** E5 120ft/37m ***

R. Fawcett, C. Gibb, 1978

One of the great Welsh rock climbs. A magnificent route with sustained and poorly protected climbing up the centre of the wall. Still rated as a bold lead. 15yd/14m L of Blue Peter is a flake crack which begins above an overhang; start just to the R at a vague R-ward slanting weakness.

1. 6a. Climb up to a flake at 25ft/8m. Continue boldly up trending slightly R-wards and making for the obvious flaky undercut hold. Friend runner. Difficult moves diagonally R gain a BR and 'resting' foothold. Go straight up the wall for

The Cad, just before the bolt, on the third ascent

25ft/8m by thin and sustained moves. The climbing now eases towards the top – a mind-blowing pitch.

Two other routes utilize the Cad start: The Long Run, E5 6a, moves L after 20ft/6m, then follows a thin crack to the overhanging headwall which is taken on the R before moves back L to finish; The Bells, The Bells, E7 6b, is a virtually unprotectable chop route which leaves The Cad after 30ft/9m to tackle the face on its R . . . seldom repeated!

422 **South Sea Bubble**   E2   110ft/33m **

J. Moran and party, 1978

This good route up the obvious fine flake crack just L of The Cad has a fairly serious start. Start below the flake, under an overhang.

1. 5c. Straightforward climbing leads up to the overhang. Surmount this trending L, crux, and move up to the foot of the flake crack. Climb this on excellent holds to a large ledge below a short wall. Finish up this with surprising difficulty.

423 **Nice n' Sleazy**   E1   110ft/33m *

A. Evans, G. Milburn, J. Moran, 1978

The 'chossy' crackline 20ft/6m L of South Sea Bubble proves better than it looks. Start below the crack.

1. 5a. Go easily up the crack to a steepening at 15ft/5m. After moving L to a good flake the angle starts to relent. Easier climbing now leads to the top.

424 **Talking Heads**   E2   120ft/37m **

J. Moran and party, 1978

An interesting and enjoyable pitch which is isolated at high tides. Start to the L of Nice n' Sleazy – tides permitting.

1. 5b. Traverse L just above the water-line until beneath the obvious overhang. Ascend the wall on good holds to a crack which leads up to the R end of the overhang. Pull over this on large holds, then make a difficult stride L into the final crack. This proves tricky for a few moves, soon easing to the top.

Wen Zawn   (215837)

Wen Slab, a 300ft/93m sheet of white quartzite split by a prominent central crack, Wen, forms the south side of this atmospheric zawn and contains many fine routes. On the north side, a 150ft/46m high peninsula pierced by an enormous arch also provides several good climbs, as well as providing an excellent viewpoint from which to watch the antics of parties on Wen Slab.

Craig Gogarth – North Stack Wall

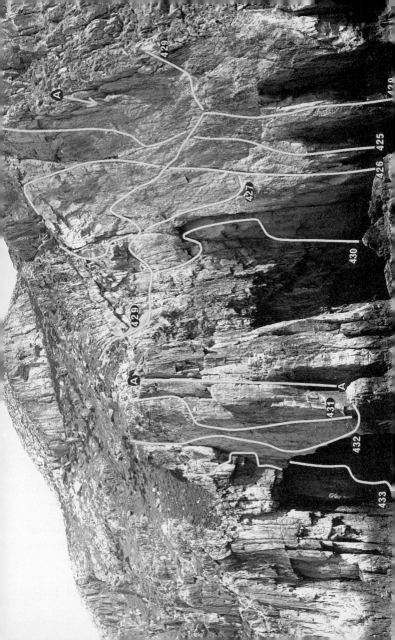

At low tide, gain the bed of the zawn by abseiling down the wall opposite Wen Slab: the line of Uhuru, E1 5b. Leap-frog over the boulders to the base of the wall below the slab. At high tides, the first pitches are inaccessible, and the routes are started from the first stance of Wen. Approach by walking along the top of the slab and scrambling down the seaward side of the arete, which forms its R edge, to a small platform and large blocks. Abseil 120ft/37m diagonally down to the obvious flakes and ledges of the Wen stance.

425 **Zeus**   E2   285ft/87m **

L. R. and L. E. Holliwell, 1970

A bold and absorbing route up the centre of the slab R of the Wen chimney/crack; start from the bed of the zawn, immediately R of the chimney.

1. 85ft/26m. 5a. Step L on to the wall and climb it direct to a steepening. Move L to gain a small niche. Now go up and trend R-wards to a good ledge and spike belays.

2. 150ft/46m. 5b. Behind the stance is a line of cracks. Climb these to a bulge at 30ft/9m. Cross this R-wards with difficulty and go up to a junction with A Dream of White Horses, PR. Continue up bearing slightly L for a further 30ft/9m until it is possible to move R, then move up to a line of overhangs. Step R and surmount the roof at its widest point, then climb straight up with less difficulty. Poor stance and peg belay below the short headwall.

3. 50ft/15m. 4b. Move R to a thin crack and follow it (loose) to the top.

426 **Wen**   HVS   350ft/107m **

J. Brown, M. Boysen, 1966

An excellent route up the chimney/crackline splitting the slab. Very popular. Start in the bed of the zawn at the base of the chimney.

1. 85ft/26m. 5a. Climb the chimney through a natural hole and

Craig Gogarth – Wen Zawn

continue up the shallow groove above to some ledges and peg belays a few feet R of the crackline.

2. 150ft/46m. 4c. Climb the crack pleasantly to a small stance in a shallow chimney.

3. 115ft/35m. 5a. Surmount a bulge on the L and follow the thin slanting crack until an awkward move gains the obvious ledge. Traverse L along this to grass ledges to belays; or finish direct up the main crack – loose!

427 **Concrete Chimney** HVS 230ft/70m ***
P. Crew, J. Brown (AL), 1967

This superb climb takes the arete to the R of the lower section of the prominent rubble-filled chimney splitting the L side of Wen Slab before crossing it to finish up bulges on the L. Start from the first stance of Wen.

1. 130ft/40m. 5a. Follow the obvious line diagonally L-wards to the arete. Climb steeply up the slab above to a thin crack, good runners, and continue up the wall above on good holds. Move L above the overhang to gain the edge of the chimney. Ascend to a small stance and belays.

2. 100ft/30m. 5a. Go directly up the slab and a short crack to a small optional stance below a steepening of the chimney. PRS. Climb up, then move L across overlapping slabs to reach an overhanging groove. Go up this and exit R at the top on to the final bulge of the chimney. Scramble up to the belay.

428 **Quartz Icicle** E2 200ft/61m **
E. Drummond, B. Campbell-Kelly, 1968

Splendid open climbing along the diagonal vein of quartz between Wen and Concrete Chimney. Start from the first stance of Wen.

1. 120ft/37m. 5b. Move diagonally L to the quartz vein and climb it to a poor PR (High Pressure, E4 5c, continues directly up the slab from this point). Make thin moves L, crux, to where the quartz vein opens out into a crack. Follow this past a PR and continue steeply to a PB in a shattered chimney 20ft/6m R of Concrete Chimney.

A Dream of White Horses, pitch 2

2. 80ft/24m. 5b. Climb diagonally R across A Dream of White Horses, then traverse horizontally R to a small curving groove with a crack in it. Climb this, exiting R to follow the thin slanting crack on the R of the smooth slab. Trend L and finish up the crack which leads to the traverse at the top of Wen.

429 **A Dream of White Horses**   HVS   500ft/153m ***
E. Drummond, D. Pearce, 1968
An exhilarating and atmospheric route which girdles Wen Zawn from bottom R to top L by VS climbing in HVS situations. *The* classic of the area. Start from the zawn bed, R of Wen chimney below a steep groove capped by a roof. At high tides, scramble down to a prominent notch in the arete and follow Pitch 2a if the abseil down to the first stance of Wen proves too daunting.

1. 150ft/46m. 4c. Take the L edge of the groove to the Wen ledge . . . optional starting point. Continue directly up the wall to a good spike then trend up R to belay in a small corner.

2. 80ft/24m. 4c. Follow the horizontal traverse line until a few difficult moves lead to better holds and a hanging nut and spike stance in Wen.

2a. 120ft/37m. 4c. From the notch, climb down a groove to the start of the horizontal traverse which leads across to the hanging stance in Wen.

3. 120ft/37m. 4c. Move up then follow a line of flakes diagonally L to a ledge at 50ft/15m. Continue in the same line for another 30ft/9m until it disappears. A L-ward traverse gains good holds leading down and across a short broken chimney (optional stance) to a belay in Concrete Chimney 15ft/5m to the L.

4. 150ft/46m. 4c. Step out L and go up to traverse L under the roof to a PR. Descend a few feet and make an exciting move around a rib for an incut hold. Move up to good spikes then continue across L on massive holds to reach the final slab. Cross this, with a hard move past a rock scar to gain a square-cut groove. Exit L and scramble up L to finish with care. Block belay well back.

430 **T Rex** E3 370ft/114m ***

E. Drummond, L. E. Holliwell, D. Pearce (VL), J. Rogers (2 pts), 1968

This impressive route, one of the best on Gogarth, ascends the back of the zawn through some unlikely-looking territory by strenuous and sometimes technical climbing. Start in the back of the zawn to the L of the rubble-filled chimney below the prominent flake with a small overhang at 20ft/6m.

1. 130ft/40m. 5c. Chimney up behind the flake then layback boldly up to the small roof, good nut. Turn this awkwardly and continue up the groove above to a good runner in a corner on the L. Step back down and follow the line of jugs R-wards across the overhanging wall to a stance and peg belay on the slab – a tremendous pitch!

2. 120ft/37m. 5b. Take the wall above to a slab. Climb this to a
PR under the overhang. Climb down L to another PR and move
L round the corner (care should be taken to avoid rope drag).
Traverse L then go up easier rock to a stance and peg belays.
3. 120ft/37m. 4c. Climb up to the traverse of A Dream of
White Horses and follow this L-wards to finish. Or, for those
who have found the first two pitches easy: The Golden Bough
Finish 75ft/23m, 5c, climbs the golden-coloured groove above
the stance exiting R to finish up a slab!

The next two routes are reached by abseiling down the end of
the peninsula opposite Wen Slab to a large ledge – an extra
abseil rope saves a lot of bother with ropes getting stuck. The
abseil follows the chimney/crackline of The Trap, HVS, a
notorious little problem, whilst round the corner to the L lies a
fine wall.

431 **Britomartis** HVS 190ft/58m ***
D. Alcock, G. Rogan, 1967
An exercise in jug-pulling up the seaward face of the peninsula.
Start from the ledge at the base of The Trap.
1. 120ft/37m. 5a. Climb down a crack and make an awkward
traverse L into a shallow groove, crux. Ascend this and the
steep diagonal crack on superb holds to a small stance and peg
belays.
2. 70ft/21m. 4c. Move R and go up over a bulge on to a larger
ledge. Move R round the corner to finish up a groove without
difficulty.

432 **Spider Wall** E1 200ft/61m ***
L. E. Holliwell, D. S. Potts, L. R. Holliwell, 1969
This superb route climbs the wall L of Britomartis on good,
sometimes hidden holds in an isolated position and just merits
its grade. Start as for Britomartis at the foot of The Trap.
1. 150ft/46m. 5a. Climb down, then traverse across the shallow
groove of Britomartis to within 8ft/2m of the arch. Go directly
up over a quartz-vein bulge to a line of holds leading diagonally

L-wards to the top of the arch. Take the crack for 15ft/5m then
move L to a series of holds leading back R to the foot of a
shallow groove. Climb this to a small stance – on Britomartis.
2. 50ft/15m. 4c. Climb diagonally L across the wall into a
groove (Bluebottle, E2 5b, reaches this point from below) and
follow it to a good ledge and peg belays on the L.

433 **Spider's Web**   E2   (2–5 pts)   220ft/63m ***
J. Brown, P. Crew (5 pts), 1968
A unique and sensational expedition which chimneys out over
the sea, and by some simple but exciting ropework gains the lip
of the arch piercing the peninsula. Well worth doing; one pair
of ascendeurs (or prussiks) is necessary. Start: go across to the
top of the gully about 100ft/30m L (north) of where the descent
path reaches the peninsula. Either abseil or scramble down to
ledges, then traverse R (facing in) across a small channel to a
sloping ledge on the arete, opposite Spider Wall.
1. 30ft/9m. Traverse round at sea level to the large chimney
under the arch.
2. 60ft/18m. 5b. Move R around the bulge and go up to climb a
shallow groove. Move R around the bulge and go up to climb a
shallow groove. Move 6ft/1.5m R and climb the overhanging
wall, crux, trending up R at the top to a small cave and belays
in the bowels of the cliff.
3. 80ft/24m. 5a/A1. Leaving one rope free, bridge up the
chimney above the stance then move out above the sea to a
cluster of ancient corroded ironmongery at the top of the
chimney! Pull the runnered rope through until it comes tight on
the second; tie off this rope and prussik down it clipping into a
PR lower down. From here, continue descending until it is
possible to place and clip a nut just behind the overhang. Pull
across to the lip and clip into an old peg, with good wire
back-ups. From slings on the lip, it is now possible to pass the
prussiks back to the second on the free rope. Using a nut, climb
the wall on the L to a small corner stance and good belays –
rope drag is a problem on this pitch!
    As one rope is attached directly to the cluster of ironmongery

at the top of the chimney, the second can protect himself with the prussiks until he reaches it. He now releases the knot and pulls the rope through until it comes tight on the leader's belay. After prussiking down the rope and establishing himself on the lip, the second, protected by the free rope from above, can untie from the prussik rope and pull it through to be used as normal – an exciting pitch which becomes even more so if the ropework is messed up!

4. 50ft/15m. 4c. Move back down to the R and ascend a short crack to a ledge in the groove. Make an awkward move L to another crack and climb it to finish easily up the rocks above. Or, from the stance, finish direct: The Bluebottle, E2 5b.

434 The Flytrap E1 (1 pt) 265ft/80m ***

J. Brown, P. Jewell, 'Smiler' Cuthbertson, 1978

From the peninsula facing Wen Slab as one looks across to North Stack, two prominent caves can be seen on the intermediate headland 150yd/139m away. This entertaining little route, a good counterpart to Spider's Web, climbs the R wall of the L-hand cave. Start from Wen Zawn and contour across the hillside, then abseil down to sea-level ledges between the two caves (low tide necessary). Move L to the base of a large pinnacle.

1. 40ft/12m. 4a. Climb diagonally L-wards on good holds to a ledge which can also be reached by abseil at high tides.

2. 80ft/24m. 5a. From the L side of the ledge, descend for 15ft/5m and make a slightly descending traverse on small positive holds to the foot of the black groove.

3. 80ft/24m. 5b. Ascend the groove to an obvious R-ward traverse line. Follow this easily to a steepening by a peg. Using this (5c free), reach good holds on the front of the massive chockstone at the head of the cave. Pull out over the chockstone to a good stance and belays.

4. 65ft/20m. 4b. Climb the R wall for 20ft/6m. Traverse R for 20ft/6m to an obvious crack. Finish up this.

Easter Island Gully Area   (215837)

This part of the cliffs lies just around the corner to the south of Wen Zawn where a deep narrow inlet cuts into the coastline. The approach is described in the Gogarth introduction. Scramble down the gully keeping to the R (facing out) of the pinnacle, which from certain viewpoints bears a resemblance to one of the Easter Island statues. The path now steepens, leading down to a sloping rock ledge overlooking the narrow Wonderwall Zawn. Abseil 100ft/30m to the zawn bed – tides permitting. The line of the abseil is taken by:

435   **Supercrack**   E2   90ft/27m*

A. Sharp, C. Rogers, 1974

A fine route, both strenuous and technical. Start at the foot of the abseil below an overhanging crack.

1. 5c. After a brutish first 30ft/9m the crack narrows and becomes very technical, leading to a hard move L just below the top. Finish more easily.

436   **Wonderwall**   E3   150ft/46m***

L. E. Holliwell, D. S. Potts (2 pts), 1969/FFA: A. Sharp, J. Zangwill, 1974

This difficult and exposed route gives magnificent climbing up the centre of the wall opposite the abseil. Start below a crack in the middle of the wall.

1. 6a. Ascend the crack until a move L is made into a parallel crack. Follow this to the overhang, PR. Climb the overhang and step R to the foot of a groove. Go up this for 15ft/5m, crux, then go diagonally L to a narrow ledge. Move back R to the arete. Finish up this.

437   **Phagocyte**   HVS   150ft/46m*

J. Brown, P. Crew (AL), 1967

A fine route up the R arete of the Wonderwall Zawn. Start below the obvious crack just L of the arete.

Craig Gogarth – Easter Island Area

1. 65ft/20m. 5a. Jam strenuously up the crack then move R to a small stance and belay on the arete.

2. 85ft/26m. 5a. Move up R to a flake then go delicately L across the steep wall to finish up the arete, easing towards the top.

438 **Hombre**   E1   210ft/64m **

J. Brown, I. G. MacNaught-Davis (1 pt), 1967

Steep and varied climbing with good protection makes this a popular route. Traverse R from Wonderwall Zawn for about 40yd/37m until the cliff juts out and dives straight into the sea. The obvious groove in the corner so formed is taken by Big Gut, VS; start at the foot of this.

1. 50ft/15m. 5b. Climb a few feet up the corner until a line of quartz holds leads R to the arete. Go steeply up a small groove to a ledge and belays on the R.

2. 120ft/37m. 5b. Climb the groove and then a steep awkward crack to finish – a fine pitch.

3. 40ft/12m. Finish up easy cracks to the top.

The Upper Tier   (216833)

This popular section of cliff consists of a series of walls and bays which vary in height between 150–250ft/46m–77m, stretching from the foot of the descent gully along to the steep grassy area L of Bezel, on the upper R-hand side of the Main Cliff. An important landmark is the Shag Rock pinnacle, which stands in the centre of the Upper Tier, just R of Central Park wall.

All routes are reached along the contouring path at the foot of the descent gully. From the finish of the routes, scramble up rock and grass to join a well-trodden path. Follow this southwards to a rock and heather step. Beyond this a branch sneaks off R, down the hillside to a gully dropping steeply down to the area at the top of the descent gully.

A few yards from the foot of the descent gully, the path passes beneath a huge flake which is taken by Bloody Chimney, VS, on the L, and The Rift, VS, on the R. Twin diagonal cracks slant up the steep front face of the flake to give a desperate but well-protected problem, Strike, E3 6a; the leaning wall just L is taken by:

439 **Barbarossa**   E6   170ft/52m ***
J. Moran, A. Evans (1 pt), 1978/FFA: J. Redhead, 1980

The wall just R of Bloody Chimney overhangs and provides an extended boulder problem, capable of extending most capable climbers. Very technical and tenuous on the crux. One of the finest wall pitches on the crag. Start below a PR protruding from the wall.

1. 120ft/37m. 6b. Make bold moves up to the PR. A finger-ripping few feet to pass the blank section lead to more sustained climbing on tiny sharp holds and a 'rest' at a small overlap. Continue up without much respite to some old PRS. Move R and ascend more easily to a belay – a pitch which is painful on the fingers.
2. 50ft/15m. 4c. Climb the obvious crack to finish: harder than it looks.

Continuing along the path, the next wall is rust-coloured, faces north, and is split by a thin crack which bifurcates in its upper part:

440 **Winking Crack**   E2   220ft/67m *
J. Brown, A. Cowburn (6 pts), 1966

A bold and exciting route which reserves its crux for a wide finishing crack which is still as stubborn as when it was first climbed. Scramble up to a large ledge 30ft/9m above the path and below grooves leading to the foot of the crack (the finger crack with a pod at its top in the smooth wall to the R is The Cruise, E5 6b).

1. 100ft/30m. 5a. Move R to climb a short easy groove. Move L round the arete and climb up L to the obvious groove. Climb the shallow groove until it is possible to move L to a stance and large flake belay.
2. 120ft/37m. 5c. Climb the crack, PR, to a ledge on the L where it divides. Follow the L-hand branch to the small overhang.

Move L then back R and go up twin cracks to the final wide
crack/chimney. Thrutch, battle, and struggle purposefully up
this to finish, crux. The crack can be avoided by a long stride
on to the R arete . . . but then you haven't done Winking Crack!

Next comes Shag Rock with the steep white Central Park wall
around the corner, bounded on its L and at a higher level by a
small amphitheatre.

441 **Central Park**   HVS   180ft/54m *
P. Crew, D. Alcock (VL), 1966
A popular route which takes the deep wide crack starting
half-way up the R side of the wall; the first pitch is rather dirty.
Start in a small niche on the L of the short rock traverse in the
path, below the top crack.
1. 100ft/30m. 4c. Ascend the slabby wall on the L for a few feet
to a shallow groove. Climb this to a ledge on the L, then go up R
to the start of an obvious L-slanting line. Follow this, up a steep
groove and the wall above, then traverse R to good belays at the
foot of the wide crack.
2. 80ft/24m. 5a. Climb the crack, hard near the top, crux, to
belay in the short chimney at the top of the wall.

442 **The Strand**   E2   160ft/49m ***
E. Drummond (1 pt), 1967
A brilliant pitch, pleasantly sustained, following the elegant
crack up the L side of the face. Start just L of the foot of the
crack.
1. 140ft/43m. 5b. Climb diagonally R to gain the crack. Follow
this using holds on the wall past two ancient PRs to a steepening
at the top. A few strenuous moves, crux, lead to a peg belay on
the slab above.
2. 20ft/6m. Go up the broken slab and scramble up grass to
belay well back.

Craig Gogarth – Upper Tier, R-hand section

443 **Park Lane/Doomsville Connection**

E1   200ft/60m **

L. E. and L. R. Holliwell (Pitch 1), 1967/A. G. Cram, M. Yates,
J. Yates (Pitch 2), 1967

A fine hybrid up the L side of the large flake and ramp L of The
Strand.

1. 100ft/30m. 5b. Climb diagonally R to the crack of The
Strand. Take a line of holds L to the bulge. Move L and go up,
then back R into the crack and continue to good peg belays and
a stance on top of the flake.

2. 80ft/24m. 5b. Climb the narrow ramp on the R with
difficulty, PR, then a short crack to a peg belay on the broken
slab at the top of The Strand.

3. 20ft/6m. Finish as for The Strand.

444 **Gauntlet** HVS   210ft/63m **

P. Crew, B. Ingle (AL), 1964

To the L of the small amphitheatre and at R-angles to Central
Park wall is an overhanging wall split by a prominent yellow
scar. This entertaining climb takes the crackline L of the yellow
scar: a good introduction to Gogarth climbing. Start at the foot
of a shallow groove, directly below the crack.

1. 70ft/21m. 5a. Climb the groove and go over the bulge, crux,
to better holds. Continue up until it is possible to move R up the
steep wall to a small stance and peg belay.

2. 70ft/21m. 4b. Climb the groove on the L for 30ft/9m, then
move R into another groove. Take this to a stance and peg belay
on the R.

3. 70ft/21m. 4b. Traverse L to finish up the steep corner crack.
Belay well back.

445 **The Ramp** HVS   180ft/54m **

P. Crew, J. Baldock, 1966

A fine climb taking the steep grey ramp up the wall L of
Gauntlet. Start at the foot of a pinnacle below the ramp.

Craig Gogarth – Upper Tier

1. 100ft/30m. 5a. From the top of the pinnacle, step R to a ledge. Go up the corner past a PR, then climb the slab to some spikes on the L. Pass the bulge in the corner with difficulty, crux, and continue to a large spike at the top of the ramp. Traverse easily L to good belays below a steep corner.
2. 80ft/24m. 5a. Climb to the top of the crack in the corner. Make a blind move R into a bottomless chimney, tricky, then ascend this more easily to finish.

446 **The Eternal Optimist** E2 150ft/46m*

A. Sharp, S. Humphries, 1975

A good route on reasonable holds up the steep corner crack running up to an overhang above the foot of the slab which defines the L end of the Upper Tier. Start beneath the crack.
1. 120ft/37m. 5b. Climb steeply up the lower wall to the base of the crack. Ascend using large holds on the L wall and make a tricky move over the overhang. Continue up with less difficulty to a good ledge and belay on the L.
2. 30ft/9m. 4b. Finish up the crack just L of the belay.

447 **Bezel** VS 160ft/48m*

B. Ingle, P. Crew (AL), 1964

A pleasant introduction to the Upper Tier which takes the curving groove a few feet L of the previous route. Start at the foot of the groove.
1. 50ft/15m. 4b. From the top of the small pinnacle on the L, follow the diagonal crack in the slab up R, then cross the slab on the L and continue up to a small ledge below the groove. Peg belays.
2. 80ft/24m. 5a. Surmount the bulge with difficulty and follow the groove above until it is possible to move R to a stance.
3. 30ft/9m. 4b. Finish up a short crack on the L to the top.

The Main Cliff (215835)

This, the showpiece of Gogarth, is split on its R side by a grassy ramp below which lies a slabby wall broken by two grooves: Simulator and Emulator. Further over (northwards), the next main feature is the 60ft/18m high Gogarth Pinnacle which marks the start of the Main Cliff proper. The central wall of the Main Cliff, continuously overhanging for 300ft/93m, is arguably the most impressive piece of rock in Wales. Two obvious corners climbed by Dinosaur and Mammoth cut this superb part of the crag, which extends along to the prominent R-facing groove of Pentathol. Below this groove, at sea level, sits a huge block which provides a useful reference point. Beyond, the crag gradually dwindles in size, though not in quality, as it merges into Easter Island.

From below the Central Park wall, follow the small path down, as mentioned in the introduction, to land on a ledge below Simulator, VS, the L-hand of the two prominent grooves. Descend a short corner on good holds then make a descending L-ward traverse to the foot of the Gogarth Pinnacle. Pass this on its seaward side to a ledge below the overhanging wall of Rat Race – low tides only. At high tides, climb over the pinnacle, with a short abseil down its lower section. It is possible to traverse fairly easily along the base of the cliff, below overhangs, to the huge square block below the Pentathol groove. From here, the traverse gets harder, VS, leading in 70ft/21m to an overhung corner: Heroin, HVS. After a further 70ft/21m, the traverse line peters out at the large corner of Hustler.

From the finish of all Main Cliff routes (except Imitator, Emulator and Aardvark), scramble up to a well-trodden path contouring along the hillside and follow it south to the descent gully, as for the Upper Tier.

448 **Cordon Bleu** VS 470ft/154m ***

G. Birtles, P. Crew, 1966

An excellent high girdle of the Main Cliff. Mainly S standard climbing, but with a little 10ft/3m wall, 5a, which has slowed many parties. Start at the L-hand end of the Upper Tier below Bezel; scramble down the grassy rake on the L to a large embedded flake, below a shallow groove.

1. 120ft/37m. Move down the rake a few feet. Traverse

horizontally across the slab on the L and go around the arete on good holds to descend a short chimney. Stance and belay on the L below a steep groove, on Gogarth.

2. 120ft/37m. 4a. The L wall of the groove is formed by a large pointed flake. Descend a little then traverse the base of the flake to a corner on its L side. Climb this and traverse L along the top of the massive flake to belay just L of its apex.

3. 150ft/46m. 5a (for the first few moves). Move L and climb the short leaning wall with difficulty into a corner; care needed with runners here to protect the second. Follow the obvious slabby ramp leading across to the L. From its end, possible stance, climb a short chimney, then cross a slab to a large groove. Go up this to a stance on the arete.

4. 80ft/24m. 4b. Move easily round the corner and behind a large flake to finish up a short groove.

449 **Emulator**   HVS   150ft/46m **

P. Crew, B. Ingle, 1964

A clean classic climb up the R-hand groove cutting the slabby wall which forms the lower R-hand section of the Main Cliff. Start below the corner on a sloping ledge 50ft/15m above the sea.

1. 5b. Go easily up to a steepening at 20ft/6m. Pass an awkward bulge and continue on good holds and jams to a bulge near the top. Move R to finish up the arete, or better, continue directly up the corner.

450 **Imitator**   VS   200ft/60m

B. Ingle, G. Rogan (AL), 1966

An enjoyable meandering route on the wall R of Emulator; best combined with Bezel. Start at the foot of Emulator.

1. 100ft/30m. 4c. Pull over a bulge to climb a short shallow groove on the L side of the slabby wall. Make a hard move R to gain the front face. Follow a line of holds leading up R across the face to a short crack. Climb this to a belay.

2. 100ft/30m. 4b. Step L and take a shallow groove to a small bay. Move R and climb the arete to easy ground.

451 **Aardvark**   E2   150ft/46m **

A. Evans and party, 1978

This excellent climb takes a direct line up the Imitator wall
with a hard but well-protected move near the top. Start
15ft/5m R of Imitator below the slabby wall.

1. 100ft/30m. 6a. Move up to reach good holds leading
diagonally L to a thin crack. Climb this, hard, to large holds (on
the Imitator traverse) and continue up to take the L-hand of
two thin cracks over a small overlap to below another overlap.
A difficult move up, then across R on a finger jam leads to
better holds in the R-hand crack. Climb it to a small stance and
belays.

2. 50ft/15m. 4a. Climb easier rocks and grass to the steep path.
Follow this up to belay much higher at the foot of Bezel.

452 **Resolution**   E1   330ft/100m **

P. Crew, G. Rogan (1 pt), 1966

A fine exposed climb taking the arete on the R of Gogarth. Start
to the L of the Simulator groove, in a bay of overhanging friable
rock.

1. 150ft/46m. 5a. Climb the prominent overhanging crack,
Razor Blade Crack, until it opens out into a chimney. Follow
the diagonal break L under overhangs to gain the arete. Climb
directly up into a clean-cut groove leading to the Gogarth belay
at the foot of the groove.

2. 90ft/27m. 5b. Climb the overhanging wall just L of the arete
until a difficult move R after 30ft/9m leads round the arete into
a crack. Go up the crack, easing slightly to a good flake and a
hanging peg belay.

3. 90ft/27m. 5b. A crack on the L now leads to the top of the
block. Step L into a shallow groove leading past a technical
bulge to an easier crack above. Finish up this.

453 **Gogarth**   E1   360ft/109m ***

B. Ingle, M. Boysen (1 pt) 1964

A superb climb. The original way up the cliff provides an
interesting outing. Start at the foot of the prominent pinnacle

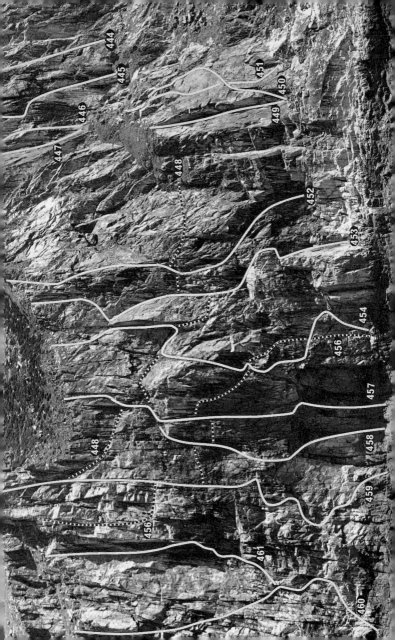

rising from sea level below the R-hand side of the cliff.

1. 60ft/18m. 4b. Climb the wide crack in the R-hand corner of the pinnacle to a stance on its top.

2. 60ft/18m. 5a. Move down and traverse R across the leaning wall and round the arete into a shallow groove. Go up this, passing to the L of the small overhang, then move L to peg belays on the large sloping ledge.

3. 60ft/18m. 4c. From the L side of the ledge, take a short crack and continue up easier ground, trending R to a good stance and belays at the foot of a steep groove, to the R of, and formed by, a large grey flake.

4. 50ft/15m. 4b. Ascend the groove to a small stance on top of the flake.

5. 130ft/40m. 5b. Traverse R for about 15ft/5m across the steep wall to a ledge at the foot of a thin crack. Difficult moves to start the crack, PR, lead to a short sustained section which soon eases. Continue up on good holds over dubious rock to finish.

454 **Rat Race**   E2   380ft/114 **

M. Howells, B. Whybrow (1 pt), 1966/Other teams involved on various occasions

An exciting route with a tremendous pitch across the overhanging wall L of the Gogarth Pinnacle; start on the large ledge to the L of this.

1. 40ft/12m. 5a. Climb steeply up the wall just L of the pinnacle, trending R to the large ledge.

2. 100ft/30m. 5c. Move L and follow the obvious gently rising traverse line past some hard moves at 30ft/9m to reach a chimney/groove. Climb this to the curving overlap, normally wet. Take the crack L-wards round the overlap, crux, then pull back R up a short wall to peg belays and a small stance below the prominent chimney.

3. 80ft/24m. 5a. Boldly climb the overhanging chimney to exit R at its top. Continue up over the slab to belay on Cordon Bleu (to the R of the apex of the massive flake). An escape from here

Craig Gogarth – Main Cliff, R side

can be made up the ramp on the R.

4. 70ft/21m. 4c. Move down R to climb the steep corner/groove which leads to a stance on the top of the flake: junction with Gogarth.

5. 90ft/27m. 5a. Climb back down a little and cross the wall on the L to the foot of a crack. Go up this taking the R-hand branch then move L across the rib to finish up an easier crack.

455 **Positron** E5   200ft/60m ***

A. P. Rouse, P. Minks (5 pts), 1971/FFA: A. Sharp, 1975

A phenomenally steep and intimidating route with outrageous situations. It acquired a legendary reputation in the 1970s . . . the reason becoming apparent a few feet along Pitch 3. Start just L of Rat Race.

1. 60ft/18m. 5c. Ascend R-wards into the scoop then move back L to gain the obvious layback flake. Continue L-wards to a small ramp on the arete then climb a small overlap to nut belays below the chimney/groove of Rat Race.

2. 40ft/12m. 6a. Climb up L to surmount the overhang via a spike. Make a desperate move L round the arete below the next overhang, to get established in a groove. Climb the corner crack to the Rat Race belay below the overhanging chimney.

3. 100ft/30m. 6a. Traverse L to a large spike on the arete; this is it! Follow the diagonal line of weakness (for the strong only) up the wall to a good hold. Traverse L to below the small overhang. Pull round this L-wards and continue direct, easing slightly, until it is possible to step into Dinosaur for the last few feet. Belay on Cordon Bleu.

456 **Ordinary Route** E5   440ft/134m ***

A. Sharp, C. Dale, 1975

A stupendous route with magnificent climbing and unrelenting exposure. The long third pitch across the central wall of the Main Cliff must rank as one of the finest in Britain. Start as for Rat Race.

1. 120ft/37m. 6a. Climb the steep wall L of the pinnacle, as for Rat Race, trending slightly R then back L to enter a groove,

which starts 25ft/8m along the Rat Race traverse. Climb this, exiting L to the top. Surmount the short, ludicrously overhanging wall across L on small positive holds, then make a desperate move up into a groove which leads to the Rat Race stance.

2. 80ft/24m. 6a. Move L to a large spike on the arete and climb the diagonal fault line L-wards to a large side hold; Friend. Traverse L to the small triangular overhang, good wires on its L side, and go over it. Climb diagonally L to step into Dinosaur then descend to a superb hanging stance on a long narrow ledge level with the triangular overhang (a pitch which climbs most of the Positron crux).

3. 130ft/40m. 5c. Move L along the ledge into Mammoth, harder than it looks, and climb up to a small ledge, PR and optional belay. Traverse L across the overhanging wall on the obvious line into Citadel; take this to first small ledges on the L. Traverse L along these to climb a short corner, then move across L to good belays on a large sloping ledge below a small hollow.

4. 100ft/33m. 5b. Step L and climb the steep groove just R of the arete to a shallow cave below twin cracks. Finish up the R-hand crack.

457 **Dinosaur**   E5 (E3 with 3 pts)   350ft/106m**
P. Crew, J. Brown (10 pts), 1966/FFA: R. Fawcett, 1980
An excellent route which now contains very little loose rock. Very strenuous and a very direct way up the cliff with good protection on the overhang. Start below the R-hand of three chimneys in the centre of the cliff.

1. 100ft/30m. 6a. Climb up into the back of the chimney and continue steeply up to the overhang. Make a very strenuous series of moves out L to the arete (or use aid – 5c) to a TR and PR. Continue up to a small stance and belays.

2. 100ft/30m. 5b. Step R and climb the overhanging groove/corner crack on reasonable holds past a small ledge and PR on the L (Ordinary Route stance). Continue more easily to a good stance on the R: on Cordon Bleu.

3. 150ft/46m. 5b. Step L and climb the short wall (Cordon Bleu crux). Move out R to climb the arete on the R of the blank corner to a PR. Ascend the shallow groove on the L past an awkward final bulge. Belay well back.

458 **Mammoth**   E5 (E4 with 2 pts)   200ft/61m *
P. Crew, E. Drummond (6 pts), 1967/FFA: A. Pollitt, 1984
A difficult and impressive route, parallel to, and L of Dinosaur, though rather overshadowed by its two neighbours. Start below the centre chimney, which is in fact a L-facing groove.
1. 120ft/37m. 6a. Climb the back of the groove easily for 30ft/9m to a small ledge. Continue up and L with difficulty under the overhangs to a good TR. Move L round the overhang and climb steeply up to a PR. Bold moves up the friable wall above lead to a second PR (cowboys have been known to lasso the top peg and climb up the rope to clip it). Take the shallow chimney above to a small overhang. Move L and go up to peg belays at the R-end of a long narrow ledge.
2. 80ft/24m. 5c. Climb directly up, PR, to a good small spike. Move diagonally R to a large blunt spike then climb back L to a PR below a bulge. Surmount it, and continue up the groove with less difficulty, exiting R at the top to the flake belay on Cordon Bleu.

459 **Citadel**   E5   (E4 with 1 pt)   320ft/97m ***
J. Street, G. Hibberd (9 pts), 1968/FFA: R. Fawcett, 1977
This magnificent route, very difficult to climb completely free, has a stunning second pitch up an overhanging crack in the central headwall. Start about 50ft/15m L of Mammoth below an obvious line of undercut flakes.
1. 130ft/40m. 6b. Climb up to a PR then move up L with difficulty to the start of the flakes. Traverse R below the flakes to a small niche. Runners. Swing out L and make desperate moves up the overhanging wall to land on a small sloping ledge. Climb up moving R-wards to belay on the long ledge below the impressive crack.
2. 110ft/33m. 6a. Ascend the steep wall then move R to climb

Dinosaur c. 1976

the strenuous and unrelenting crack past an assortment of rotting and rusting in-situ protection to a peg belay on the slab above.
3. 80ft/24m. Climb easily up the groove above to a good ledge. Belay by large blocks on the L.

460 **Pentathol**   HVS   320ft/87m *
P. Crew, B. Ingle (AL), 1964

This good route finds the easiest way up the L-hand side of the central wall of the Main Cliff. An ideal introduction to the crag with only a short difficult section. Start about 20ft/6m R of the large square block on the sea level traverse.

1. 120ft/37m. 5a. Climb up to gain a line of flakes, crux, and follow them R-wards across an overhanging wall to a ledge below a short corner. Climb this for 10ft/3m then move L to a L-facing corner. Climb this to a good ledge on the R.
2. 50ft/15m. 4a. Descend a few feet then step L into a wide crack. Climb it, then move L and follow a line of flakes diagonally up L to a stance below the final groove.
3. 80ft/24m. 4c. Climb directly up the groove, over an awkward bulge, to a good stance on the L.
4. 70ft/21m. 4b. Climb easily up behind the belay to finish.

461 **Big Groove**   E2   370ft/112m ***
P. Crew, D. Alcock (1 pt), 1966

After a scrappy start, the huge L-facing corner high on the cliff provides an excellent finish. High in its grade and quite sustained. Start as for Pentathol.

1. 140ft/43m. 5a. Follow Pentathol Pitch 1, then climb the short corner above to a large sloping ledge and peg belays on the R.
2. 60ft/18m. 5c. From the L-hand end of the ledge, climb over a bulge to a PR in a corner on the R. Make a hard move up the wall on the R to reach a sloping ledge and so reach PRs at the base of the main groove. Climb the groove and continue up a crack formed by a flake in the L wall. Step L to a shallow niche and go precariously up this with a difficult finish on to a sloping ledge. Peg belays.
3. 110ft/33m. 5b. Move L and climb another groove, very sustained, until a hard move near the top gains holds leading L to the arete. Good stance to the L.
4. 60ft/18m. Finish easily up behind the stance.

Craig Gogarth – Main Cliff, L side

462 **The Needle** E3 300ft/91m **

R. Evans, C. Rogers, 1973

A superb steep and strenuous crack up the front of the buttress
to the L of the large square block on the sea-level traverse.
Hypodermic, E2 5a, 5b, take the corner just L of the block,
whilst to the R of it, The Camel, E3 6a, 5b, blasts up a crack
splitting the line of overhangs. Start: The front of the buttress is
split by three cracks.

1. 110ft/33m. 5b. Climb the central crack with difficulty
(normally damp) to a ledge on the arete (Hypodermic comes in
from the R here). Continue up the arete until it is possible to
move L to the foot of the short overhanging groove. Climb this
awkwardly to a sloping ledge, or traverse L then back R up a
deep crack to the same spot. Peg belays.

2. 120ft/37m. 5c. From the R end of the ledge, climb to a PR
(Hypodermic moves R here). Continue directly up the ferocious
crack, the last few moves below a sloping ledge being
particularly trying. Carry on up, easier now, to a large ledge.

3. 70ft/21m. The corner behind the belay gives an easy finish.

463 **Scavenger** HVS 285ft/88m ***

M. Boysen, J. Jordan, 1966

A splendid route on sound rock following a line of shallow
grooves up the buttress to the L of The Needle. Low in its
grade. Start below a huge ledge in the front face of the buttress.

1. 25ft/8m. 4c. Climb the steep wall on good holds to a stance
on the ledge.

2. 140ft/43m. 5a. Climb the groove above for 30ft/9m. Move R
round the arete and traverse R to the foot of a cracked groove.
Ascend this direct to a ledge and belay.

3. 120ft/37m. 4a. Climb more easily up the continuation
groove to broken ground. Traverse off L up grass, or scramble
up R to join the last pitch of Pentathol.

464 **Nightride** E1 235ft/72m **

J. Brown, G. Rogan, 1967

A well-positioned route up the airy arete L of Scavenger. Just L of the arete is a deep bay with an overhanging chimney at its back: Heroin, HVS. Start from the bay, below the chimney.

1. 45ft/14m. 4c. Climb diagonally up R to the large ledge of Scavenger.

2. 70ft/21m. 5b. Go up the corner to the obvious L-ward traverse line at 15ft/5m. Follow this across to the arete and climb a flake on its L side for a few feet. Move R and take the obvious crack to a stance and belay.

3. 120ft/37m. 4b. Move R and go up to enter the wide crack. Climb this to the top and finish up easy ground, or move L into a corner, climb it and finish over broken rock and grass.

465 **Phaedra** HVS   170ft/52m *

M. Howells, B. Whybrow, 1966

An enjoyable climb with a technical start and airy easier climbing above. The arete L of Heroin is split by three short grooves in its lower part. Scramble up L from the foot of Heroin to a spike belay just R of the central groove.

1. 140ft/43m. 5c. Step L into the central groove which is very technical to begin with, and follow it to the overhang. Move L round the arete into the wide chimney crack. Climb this pleasantly on good holds in a fine position to a small stance. Spike and nut belays.

2. 30ft/9m. 4c. Climb easier rock behind the stance and belay well back.

466 **Hustler** VS   130ft/40m ***

M. Howells, B. Whybrow, 1966

A good climb, serious for its grade, taking the large L-facing corner 70ft/21m L of Heroin, at the end of the sea-level traverse. From the bay of Heroin a difficult, VS, traverse L leads to a small stance on the L wall at the foot of the corner.

1. 4c. Ascend the steep crack in the R wall. Climb up another few feet then move L into the chimney above the overhang, Finish airily up this to the top.

SOUTH STACK   (205822)

These fine cliffs, which offer excellent climbing at VS and
above, extend for half a mile south-east from South Stack
lighthouse. Just to the R of the steps running down to the
lighthouse lies Mousetrap Zawn. Next come the two Red Wall
zawns which are best viewed from Helen's cottage, a strange
castle-like structure owned by the RSPB which is perched on
the cliff top below the café and the car-park.

   Immediately below the cottage is Castell Helen, a compact
cliff which contains many easier climbs and is bounded on the R
by enormous overhangs. These peter out into a broken slabby
area leading into a grey and yellow bay capped by barriers of
R-slanting reddish overhangs. Beyond, the cliff rapidly
degenerates into broken hillside.

Mousetrap Zawn

467 **The Mousetrap**   E2   420ft/139m ***
J. Brown, P. Crew (AL), (2 pts), 1966
A magnificent route which weaves a line up the amazingly
contorted rock above the large cave at the back of the zawn.
Low technical difficulty coupled with a big cliff feel have
conspired to make this a popular outing. There are two ways to
the foot of the route. Either descend the lighthouse steps to a
prominent gap between two rocks and scramble down the
grassy L bank of the zawn – tides permitting – or, from either of
the car-parks beyond the café, cross the wall and go carefully
down a grass and heather slope to a large block above the col
between the Mousetrap and Left Hand Red Wall zawns; make
a long abseil down to just above the boulder field in the zawn
bed (the end of a 150ft/45m rope) and scramble down (tricky if
damp). Start on the L of the cave below a huge grey groove.
1. 150ft/46m. 5a. Climb a subsidiary groove on the L to the top
of a pillar. Step R into the main groove, PR. Descend slightly
and traverse R to a foothold in a folded chimney. Pull on to the

The serious traverse on the first pitch of The Mousetrap

rib on the R and climb it. Move up the next chimney for a few feet then move R into another chimney which leads to easier ground. Go across a large sloping ledge to peg belays at its R-hand end.

2. 75ft/23m. 5a. Climb diagonally up the steep wall on the R to a PR in a slanting groove. Pull round the bulge on the R into another groove. Take this more easily to a tiny stance and peg belays.

3. 75ft/23m. 4a. Delightfully easy climbing up the slab leads to a good block and peg stance.

4. 120ft/37m. 5a. Go up into a niche behind the belay. Step R on to the steep red wall and cross this diagonally to the foot of a groove. Climb the groove over a small bulge and continue up to finish.

Left Hand Red Wall

This smooth compact ocean of orangey-red rock contains some of the finest and most serious routes on Anglesey. The three selected routes, not too desperate by modern standards, are all neo-classics.

468   **Pagan**   E4   300ft/91m ***
P. R. Littlejohn, A. Houghton, 1973

A powerful and impressive climb which saunters up the centre of the wall. Though technically reasonable, this is still a bold undertaking. Start as for Mousetrap to the large block above the col. Abseil 70ft/21m to this, then scramble down a grassy ramp to the L (facing out) and past a shallow groove which curves round to the L (the start of Left Hand Red wall, E3 5b, 5c, which moves R at the top to a stance, then continues up a R-ward slanting fault line). Continue down to a block belay at the start of an obvious traverse line, 80ft/24 above the sea. The first pitch is in common with Deygo, E3 5b, 5b, 5c.

1. 70ft/21m. 5b. Traverse R a few feet to a flake, step up and continue R to a tiny ledge below a short grey chimney/groove.

Craig Gogarth – the Red Wall

Pull up L into the chimney and climb it awkwardly to the overhang. Make airy moves across the R wall to a pedestal stance. Ancient bolt and peg belays plus a high sling. Deygo now breaks away along the R-slanting fault line above.

2. 90ft/27m. 5c. Climb up for 10ft/3m then pull across L to a projecting ledge. Move up the wall above trending R to better holds after 15ft/5m, crux. Continue direct for 10ft/3m then bear slightly R to an obvious hold which is used to gain a spike on the L at the foot of the large layback flake. Go up this to a hanging stance at its tip – one of the finest positions on Gogarth.

3. 140ft/43m. 5b. Move R along the flake until it disappears. Go up a faint groove to the start of a traverse line leading back L. Take this, low PR, to a weakness in the wall above. Climb steeply up on small holds (one hard move) using a friable flake to gain the horizontal break. Move up L then back R into a loose groove leading to easier gound. Block belay.

469 **Infidel** E3 260ft/79m **

B. Wintringham, J. Brown, M. Wintringham (2 pts), 1978/FFA: J. Moran, P. Williams, 1978

A superb route which moves L from the col between the Red Walls and climbs the face to finish direct up the Deygo fault line. Start from two large stacked blocks at the top of the cliff (peg back-up advisable) and use a spare rope to make a 140ft/43m abseil to the col between the Red Walls. Scramble down to the L to a point 30ft/9m above where the slab suddenly drops away.

1. 80ft/24m. 5b. Ascend diagonally R on dubious rock to two PRs at 30ft/9m. Climb 10ft/3m L to better holds and follow these to a prominent groove. Take the groove to a good small corner stance with high peg belays.

2. 130ft/40m. 5c. Climb across onto the Deygo fault line and follow this to the large metal spike where Deygo traverses R. Continue up until it is possible to rejoin the line at the level of a PR. Continue up the fault line to belay on the ramp of Red Wall Escape Route, VS.

3. 50ft/15m. Finish up the ramp as for Red Wall Escape Route.

470 **Anarchist**   E1   190ft/58m **

B. Wintringham, J. Moran, 1978

A justifiably popular route on sound rock which takes the wall R of Infidel. Start from the col between the Red Walls (reached by abseil as for the previous route).

1. 120ft/37m. 5b. Traverse L and follow a series of grooves and ledges to a detached flake with a PR at its foot. Climb the diagonal fault line above the flake, PR, to an overlap. Make a hard move R, PR, and traverse to a good crack. Climb this to belay on Red Wall Escape Route.

2. 70ft/21m. Finish up Red Wall Escape Route.

Red Wall

Red Wall is larger than, though not as compact as, its counterpart. Many large crumbly chimney/fault lines seam the crag and most of the routes tend to creep up them. From a large ledge at the base of the wall, 60ft/18m above the sea, a prominent vegetated ramp rises diagonally L-wards to the top of the cliff; this is Red Wall Escape Route, VS, the launching pad for several shorter routes.

Reach the foot of the wall by abseiling from two stacked blocks, 140ft/43m to the col between the Red Walls using a spare rope: as for Infidel. Clip a karabiner to the bottom of the abseil rope and continue abseiling down (on the double climbing ropes) to a small grassy corner about 60ft/18m above the sea: the start of Redshift. A rising R-ward traverse leads to Red Wall Escape Route which is easily traversed to the large ledge. Alternatively, if the tide is out, the bed of the zawn below the wall can be reached via two abseils down the slabby ridge opposite the R side of Red Wall, followed by an easy scramble up to its base . . . much more tedious as the rope invariably sticks on the second abseil resulting in all sorts of epics!

471 **Redshift** E3 280ft/86m ***

P. R. Littlejohn, H. Clarke, 1976

Excellent steep and sustained climbing on good rock makes this one of the best routes on the wall. Start from the grassy corner at the foot of the double abseil, as mentioned.

1. 120ft/37m. 5a. Go up the slabby wall to follow a L-trending crackline. Move R on to Red Wall Escape Route and follow this to a belay by a large block.

2. 120ft/37m. 5c. Climb straight up above the belay for 12ft/3m, poor PR. Move up R then back L below the bulge. Pull steeply over this then step L to gain the groove. Follow the groove, which is very sustained for the grade, in a fine position to a ledge on the L. Move up R to reach a sloping stance and peg belays: junction with Wendigo.

3. 40ft/12m. 5a. Climb L-wards to finish up the continuation groove.

472 **Wendigo** E2 250ft/80m ***

J. Brown, A. J. J. Moulam, 1966

A very fine route, taking a faint curving crackline which becomes a groove system in its upper half. Start from the large ledge and block stance at the foot of the wall. Note that an approach from the col between the walls leads to the stance at the start of Pitch 2: start from here, or continue R to the Red Wall start.

1. 65ft/20m. 4c. Climb a shallow groove on the L to a small ledge below the steep part of the wall. Descend L-wards for 15ft/5m to a stance and belay.

2. 55ft/17m. 5a. Follow the obvious L-wards slanting break above to an overhang at 30ft/9m. Pull steeply R-wards over this and continue up to a small stance in a shallow depression.

3. 105ft/32m. 5a. From the L side of the depression, climb the obvious break to the overhang. Step L across this to the steep wall, then move R and climb up on good holds to a sloping ledge. Move L and follow the corner above to a spike. Move L again and go up to a sloping stance with peg belays.

4. 35ft/11m. 4b. Climb up and R to enter a groove. Finish up this.

473 **Red Wall**   E1   250ft/76m ***

J. Brown, P. Crew, 1966

This classic of the cliff has now shed much of its dubious rock to become quite popular. The climbing is straightforward with only a couple of short hard sections, but the position is very serious and the route is high in its grade because of this. It takes the L-hand side of the two large curving yellow fault lines. Start from the block stance at the base of the wall.

1. 110ft/33m. 4c. Climb a shallow groove on the L to the ledge below the steep part of the wall (as for Wendigo). Take the steep groove on the R, moving R at the top to a small stance and peg belays.

2. 75ft/23m. 5a. Follow the diagonal line up L-wards then move up to a PR. Cross the steep wall on the L to a shallow chimney. Go up a few feet to a small stance. Many belay pegs.

3. 65ft/20m. 4c. Bridge up the overhanging chimney above the stance, PR, and climb the groove above moving R at the top.

474 **Fantasia**   E3   225ft/69m ***

B. and M. Wintringham (1 pt), 1978/FFA: J. Moran, P. Williams, 1979

A superb route with a magnificent second pitch up a steep wall of compact red rock to the R of Red Wall route. Start as for Red Wall, at the block stance below the wall.

1. 75ft/23m. 4c. As for Red Wall.

2. 150ft/46m. 5c. Follow Red Wall until the line goes slightly R. Continue R to cross the floor of a sandy cave. From the R side of this, make an exciting pull round on to the smooth red wall. Climb straight up in a tremendous position, then trend up L to a PR at the top of a small groove. Pass this with difficulty, crux, to better holds and a resting place after 10ft/3m. Continue direct to a good jug, move L and layback up to good holds. Finish up flaky holds.

Castell Helen

This, the most popular South Stack cliff, lies below the RSPB watch-tower, Helen's Cottage. The steep main grey face is

liberally furnished with large holds so that most routes 'go' at a
surprisingly easy standard.

From Helen's Cottage, follow a path diagonally R-wards
(facing out), dropping steeply down then back L to a short rock
wall with two ancient pegs. Make a 120ft/37m abseil to a large
rocky platform in the middle of the wall. Now a 90ft/27m abseil
down a groove below the R end of the ledge (facing in) leads to
a small ledge in the groove 20ft/6m above sea level. Care
should be taken when pulling the ropes through to ensure that
the sea doesn't jam them under the cliff bottom.

475 **Atlantis**   E1   220ft/67m*

J. Brown, D. Alcock (1 pt), 1966

Takes the obvious groove up the line of the second abseil; start
on small ledges below it.

1. 90ft/27m. 5a. Fine sustained climbing up the groove to the
large ledge and peg belays.
2. 130ft/40m. 5c. Climb up behind the belay to a short groove
with a small roof. Go up this with one very hard move then
finish up the long groove on the R.

476 **Rap**   VS   210ft/64m**

D. Alcock, P. Crew, 1966

A good route which climbs directly up the wall L of Atlantis.
From the foot of Atlantis, traverse round the arete to a small
ledge at the foot of the wall.

1. 90ft/27m. 4c. Climb the wall on good holds to finish up a
steep groove leading to the middle of the large rock platform.
2. 120ft/37m. 4b. Climb directly up the wall above the centre
of the platform to a good ledge. Traverse L and continue up a
thin crack which leads to easier ground and a belay at the
abseil point.

Craig Gogarth – Castell Helen

477 **True Moments/Freebird**   E2   300ft/90m ***

A. Hyslop. D. Knighton (AL), 1978/A. Evans and party, 1978

This superb combination gives the best route on Castell Helen. Start on a small ledge just L of the arete as for Rap.

1. 90ft/27m. 4c. Climb the wall and arete R of Rap to belay on the platform.

2. 100ft/30m. 5b. Descend the Atlantis groove for 10ft/3m and make an exposed traverse R along the horizontal fault line to a good rest at 40ft/12m. Either climb the wall above until it is possible to move across to slabs on the R and a peg belay under the obvious overhang, or continue the traverse to its end, then scramble up the slabs to the same point.

3. 110ft/33m. 5b. Move across to the L end of the overhang, PR, and surmount this awkwardly into a small corner on the wall above. Traverse R just above the lip of the overhang for about 10ft/3m. Climb up to better holds and follow the diagonal line R-wards, PR, until excellent holds lead to an easy finishing groove – a serious pitch.

478 **North West Passage**   E1   230ft/70m ***

J. Moran, A. Evans (AL) and party, 1978

A very good route with an exhilarating top pitch. Start on the small ledge at the foot of Rap.

1. 90ft/27m. 5a. Move across on to the wall L of Rap and follow a crack system trending slightly L at first. Go directly up the wall heading for a vague open groove. Climb this to finish near the L end of the large ledge.

2. 140ft/43m. 5b. From the R end of the ledge, climb up to a traverse line at 20ft/6m, as for Atlantis, and follow this R-wards to a PR. Climb up, nut protection on the R, then move L with difficulty into an open groove which is followed to a bulge. Step L, then climb a ledge and crack system up the front of the pillar on good holds. A great pitch.

479 **Lighthouse Arete**   VS   280ft/84m **

A. G. Cram, M. Yates, 1966

This enjoyable route traverses across the base of the cliff to climb its L arete: the easiest route on the wall. Start: traverse L round the arete and continue for 40ft/12m. to a niche at the foot of a thin crack; Pel, VS, goes directly up from here.

1. 80ft/24m. Traverse horizontally L to start, before gently rising to the obvious ledge.

2. 50ft/15m. 4b. Climb the wall on the R into a short crack. Go up this for a few feet then move L round the arete to a small ledge. Go up to belay below a small overhang on the arete.

3. 60ft/18m. 4b. Climb the overhang and continue up the shallow groove above to a good ledge on the L.

4. 90ft/27m. Climb the broken slab diagonally R-wards to the abseil point.

Yellow Wall

Yellow Wall is the massive overhung bay, the L edge of which is defined by an area of red easy-angled slabs; a large triangular-shaped grey wall above a huge cave is the last piece of decent rock on the R.

The sloping floor of the bay lies 100ft/30m above the sea. Either abseil from a block 80ft/24m L (facing out) of Helen's Cottage, down a steep wall to the easy-angled slabs and scramble down and around to the L to the overhung bay; or follow a path which starts 200yd/186m L of Helen's Cottage and drops steeply down L-wards (facing out) to sea level; move back along the base of the cliff through a tunnel capped by a gargoyle-like pinnacle to reach the Yellow Wall zawn – low tide only.

480 The Moon   E3   260ft/78m ***

E. Drummond, A. Barley (4 pts), 1971/FFA: A. Sharp, 1974

A brilliant and impressive route which wends an intricate L to R line through the centre of the overhangs. Situations are, quote, 'Strictly space-walking'. Start at the L-hand side of Yellow Wall; broken rocks lead up to an obvious groove – Savage, E1 5a, 5a, climbs this then moves diagonally L across the wall above. Traverse R from the foot of the rocks across vegetated ledges to belay below a short, steep broken corner.

1. 50ft/15m. 4c. Go up the corner past ledges to a good ledge and peg belay.

2. 110ft/33m. 5c. A diagonal band of slabs leads up R-wards. Move R for 20ft/6m then go up to a PR. Gain the steep wall on the R and climb this to another PR. Move R round the corner on to a slab and traverse this R-wards to a PR in the groove. Reverse the groove and climb across to a ledge on the R. Peg belays.

3. 100ft/30m. 5b. Climb directly up behind the stance, first R then L over the overhanging blocks. Move up R to an unusual rest, PR. Continue up a shallow groove, past a PR after 15ft/5m to the top. Iron spike over on the R.

481 **The Cow**   E4   220ft/67m ***
D. Pearce, P. Trower (2 pts), 1976
A difficult and heart-stopping route which jumps over The Moon, climbing directly to the second stance of that route before finishing up the overhanging prow above. Start as for The Moon.

1. 120ft/37m. 6a. Climb up to the R to the obvious slanting overhanging crack; this is usually wet and greasy, requiring the odd aid point. Pull up into the crack, which puts up a real battle, then follow the easier continuation groove to a traverse line leading into a broad corner. Move round the arete on the R and climb thankfully up to the stance and peg belay – an exhausting pitch.

2. 100ft/30m. 5c. Climb the overhang directly above the stance to a PR. Pull round the next overhang to another PR. Enter the groove above with difficulty; it soon narrows uncomfortably, but the position is fantastic! Pull out L on to a slab and continue to the top of the cliff.

482 **The Creeping Lemma**   E2   350ft/107m ***
A. Sharp, S. Humphries, 1974
A superb route taking a counter diagonal line to The Moon

Craig Gogarth – Yellow Wall

from the bottom L-hand to the top R-hand corner of Yellow
Wall. Fine situations and reasonable climbing, with a couple of
hard well-protected sections, have made it very popular. Start
R of, and level with, the top of the cave, on a grassy ramp
leading up to a col.

1. 160ft/49m. 4c. Traverse the grey wall diagonally L above the
cave along a system of ledges. Where the traverse gets harder,
climb diagonally R up a broken slanting groove to belay on the
col.

2. 60ft/18m. 5b. Climb easily L to the end of the obvious ramp.
Move L on to the slab. PR. A wild move round a bottomless
corner leads up L to a good stance and belay; on The Cow, and
The Moon.

3. 130ft/40m. 5c. Move 15ft/5m L and climb the groove to a PR.
Move L along the slab to where it finishes (The Moon is
reverse), then move up and climb across L-wards under the
overhangs with difficult moves past two PRs (if used for aid the
pitch is 5a/b) to the foot of a groove. Optional stance. Climb
the shallow groove to finish.

Rhoscolyn   (257755)
A holiday atmosphere surrounds these south-facing cliffs,
pleasantly tucked away amongst the zawns, coves and beaches
on the south-west side of Holy Island. Despite several worthy
routes in the lower grades, interesting sea-level traverses, and
endless picnic sites, the crags main attraction (for some) lies in
its wide range of high-quality extreme climbs: single pitch
routes with a big 'Gogarth feel', yet without the attendant 'grip'
factor normally experienced on the Main Cliff or the Red
Walls.

Approach by turning L off the A5 at the Valley traffic lights
and continuing along the road to Four Mile Bridge. Take the
first L turn after the bridge and follow the narrow road for
around two miles to park by Rhoscolyn Church (268757). Care
should be taken not to block or restrict the passage of vehicles.

The tricky move on The Creeping Lemma, pitch 2

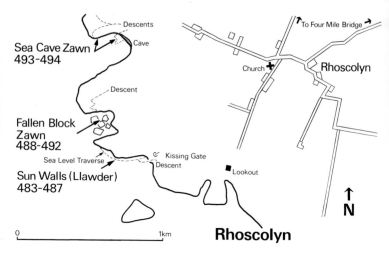

Walk back about 30yd/27m to the start of a track which leads
across a field, and through some farm buildings, before a closed
gate, then a slight rise bring one to a coastguard look-out post.
About half a mile away on the R, the top of the Sun Walls are
clearly visible; around fifteen minutes' walk from the car in
total.

The layout of the crag is straightforward. First come the Sun
Walls overlooking an inlet at its L (facing out) end; next is the
eponymous Fallen Block Zawn, lying at R-angles to the Sun
Walls, with the Sea Cave Zawn and headland just beyond.

The Sun Walls   (a.k.a. Llawder)
A central overhanging wall is bounded on the L by a steep
orange slab, and separated from a slim red buttress on the R by
the huge corner of Icarus. From the prominent perched flake at
the start of that route an overhanging bottomless groove rising
the full height of the crag gives one of its finest routes: The Sun.
Belays on top are hard to find, but with some ingenuity and
careful arrangement, secure anchorages can be made. A saddle
on the R of the crag, half-way down the descent path, is a good
place to dump gear. Routes are described from R to L.

483 **The Savage Sunbird**   E2   120ft/37m **

P. Williams, G. Peters, 1984

A fine varied route taking the front of the slim red buttress R of
the Icarus corner, finishing up the leaning groove. Start below
the pocketed lower wall, on a sloping platform, 6ft/2m L of the
arete.

1. 5c. Climb boldly up the wall to a ledge at 20ft/6m. Gain
good holds on the sloping ledge 10ft/3m higher. Balance across
L-wards and pull up on to another ledge using large friable
holds. Climb directly up the corner into the deceptively steep
groove which gives sustained climbing to an awkward L-ward
exit – an airy pitch.

484 **Icarus**   HVS   130ft/40m *

P. Buxton, D. Durkan, 1969

The huge open corner bounding the R side of the central
overhanging wall is most amenable up to the final corner. Belay
at the top of a low-angle slab at the base of the wall.

1. 90ft/27m. 4c. Move L and climb steeply up the R-hand side
of the large perched flake to a ledge. Optional belay. Move R to
climb the slabby ramp delicately up its centre to gain the R
edge (or take the corner direct). Continue more easily to nut
belays at the base of the leaning corner.

2. 40ft/12m. 5a. The strong will bulldoze up the strenuous
corner crack making light of the difficulties near the top, but
the weak . . . ? Protection is good. Belay well back.

485 **The Sun**   E3   145ft/44m ***

P. Williams, J. Moran, 1984

The large overhanging groove in the centre of the red wall gives
a uniquely exposed pitch with 'bomb-proof' protection. A
classic of the cliff! There is usually a little seepage at the foot of
the crack.

1. 25ft/8m. 4b. Climb the flake crack as for Icarus to a large
tape belay.

2. 120ft/37m. 5c. From the L-hand end of the belay ledge, PR,
traverse L into the bottomless groove on good holds. Make

difficult moves up to a PR in the seepage area. Just above, the crack dries out and succumbs to forceful laybacking and jamming past a wide section, crux, to a tiny resting ledge at 60ft/18m. Continue more easily now, in an exposed position, before moving R about 10ft/3m from the top. Finish direct.

The next couple of routes are reached from the grassy sloping terrace below the steep orange slab 50yd/46m L of The Sun. Traverse L along the large shaly bands before climbing up just to the R of a small pointed block.

486 **Warpath**   E5   125ft/38m***
J. Moran, P. Williams, 1984
The stunning arete L of The Sun will only be trodden by the brave! The situation is sensational with a degree of exposure rarely encountered on small cliffs. Start near the R-hand end of the sloping grassy terrace at a peg and block belay.
1. 6a. Traverse R, then move up and continue R to the foot of the orange hourglass-shaped slab. PR. Climb to the apex of the slab. Jam wildly over the roof to good holds; above they get much smaller. Continue with difficulty up the strenuous and technical wall, past a PR, to reach a resting ledge on the arete. Finish easily but airily L-wards – awesome!

The Mask of the Red Death, E3 5c, 5c, starts up Warpath, then breaks out from half-way up the orange slab to finish up the prominent crack in the headwall just L of the arete.

487 **Little Queenie**   E1   100ft/30m*
P. Williams, J. Moran, 1984
A fine delicate pitch up the centre of the steep orange slab. Start from the protruding block below the centre of the slab.
1. 5b. Climb up to the ledge at 30ft/10m. Continue up just R of the pointed flake with an awkward move to gain a ledge on the R. Move up on to the ledge above. Step back L and finish

Rhoscolyn – the Sun Walls

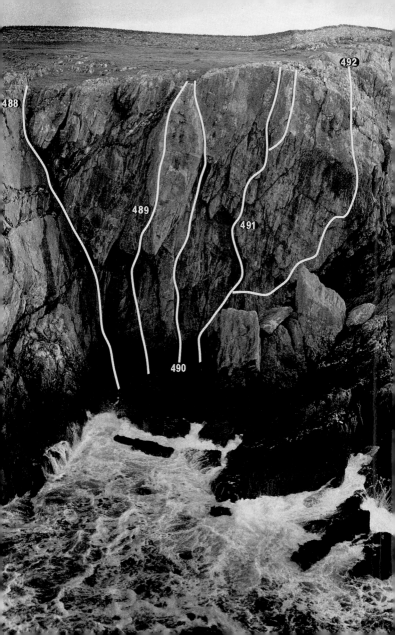

pleasantly up the centre of the slab passing an obvious flake. The corner on the L is Cocaine, E1 5b, best approached up Little Queenie to the first ledge as its lower section is rather scruffy.

Fallen Block Zawn

This atmospheric zawn contains the highest concentration of hard routes at Rhoscolyn and lies just round the far end of The Sun Walls. On the L is the slabby corner of Truant, with The Fin, a prominent hanging blade of rock, jutting out between this and the concave and undercut orange wall to the R. At the top of The Fin, a narrow saddle gives a bird's eye view of the massive blocks lying on the zawn bed. Approach either down a steep gully on the R (facing out), which houses an angry seagull during the nesting season, or by sea level traversing round from The Sun Walls. Access to some of the routes is probably impossible for about two hours either side of high tide; nonetheless, it is worth waiting!

488 Truant VS   110ft/33m *
D. Durkan, D. Birch, 1970
The corner formed where the R edge of the slab abuts the steep back wall is both pleasant and non-tidal.
1. 70ft/21m. 4b. Climb the corner direct to a ledge. Move into the recess and step L on to a good foothold. Continue up the corner to a flake belay.
2. 40ft/12m. 4b. Climb awkwardly round the bulge on to reddish rock and continue more easily up to finish. An arbitrary central line up the slab is Sea Shanty, VS . . . although the slab has been climbed all over.

489 The Trail of Tears E4   120ft/37m ***
J. Healey, P. Williams, 1984
This elegant route climbs tenuously across the L side of The Fin

Rhoscolyn – Fallen Block Zawn

before finishing delicately up its L arete. Start directly below
The Fin.

1. 6a. Follow the obvious slanting line to the sloping ledge, just
L of the chimney/crackline; step R and fight up this to a PR
(E.P. Special, E3 6a, finishes benignly up the dirty groove
above). Make committing moves out R-wards across the
overhanging wall to a PR. An adrenalin surge enables one to
gain a tiny ledge on the arete. The difficulties are now behind
and the exposed arete may be enjoyed up to the 'saddle' at the
top of the crag.

490 Godzilla   E4   140ft/43m***

P. Williams, J. Healey, J. Moran, 1984

This powerful and impressive route tackles the monstrous
corner at the junction of the R wall of The Fin and the back
wall. A brute of a route, with some exciting moments,
especially on the large roof at 90ft/27m, warily negotiated on
Damoclean fangs of rock which have withstood strenuous usage
– so far! A large rack of gear is needed.

1. 5c. Climb the corner and groove to a short L-ward traverse
on undercuts at 30ft/9m. Continue up to a rest, just below The
Fin. (The Jub-Jub Bird, E6 6b, climbs the front face, then
moves out L from this point, before finishing up the R arete of
The Fin; a truly awesome experience!) Follow the large flake
crack diagonally R to a niche below the roof. PR. Chimney up
past two more PRS until just under the roof. Launch boldly out
on the creaking flakes to attain a sensational bridging position
on the lip. A couple of quick steep pulls lead to easier climbing
up the final groove . . . long slings are essential to avoid rope
drag from under the roof.

491 Centrefold   E3   130ft/40m***

J. Moran, P. Williams, 1984

A solid pitch, sustained and varied, which finishes up the
prominent groove in the central headwall. Protection is good.
Start in the centre of the wall below the prominent diagonal
crack.

1. 5c. Surmount the bulge then move 10ft/3m R. (The Viper, E4 5c, continues direct to the L of the hanging fang of rock, then continues up the overhanging crack before pulling out L to finish up a slab.) Climb the slight awkward groove to a ledge, Continue up the steep flaky corner/crack to a bold swing out R on to a short leaning wall. From good holds and runners at the top of this, battle up the crack splitting the overhang above. Undercut R into the interesting finishing groove; either take this direct, or better, climb up a few feet, then traverse out to climb the flake in the R arete: 5b.

492 Magellan's Wall   E4   155ft/47m ***

J. Moran, P. Williams, 1984

A magnificent route which navigates the lip of the concave wall before ascending cracks in the R arete.

1. 35ft/11m. 5b. Follow Centrefold to the top of the slight groove. Move 8ft/2m R to belay by the foot of the impressive twin cracks (Dreams and Screams, E6 6b, takes these cracks direct and is alarmingly strenuous).

2. 120ft/37m. 6a. Traverse R and then climb up using the obvious undercut to gain a tiny ledge. Move R and climb a shallow groove to good holds by a PR. Continue R to the hanging rib. Ascend this boldly, to finish up a slab.

Sea Cave Zawn

Not quite as good as the previous areas, but the next route is certainly worthy of attention.

493 Electric Blue   E3   110ft/33m **

S. Haston, T. Saunders, 1983

A superb trip along the juggy line crossing above the lip of the sea cave, with one or two electrifying moments; shockingly stubborn in places. Scramble down the low-angle slab to the L-hand side of the cave.

1. 5c. Move into the fault line which soon becomes awkward. A long reach to a spike, then a good jug, just above, precede a section of strenuous bridging and laybacking to gain better

holds. Continue into a slight recess above the centre of the arch.
Move R then undercut up on a spike to good holds. TR. Move
diagonally R to finish in a recess just past the central pillar.

494 **Symphony Crack**   Diff   60ft/18m **

D. Durkan, J. Baker, 1970

A classic little climb for its grade. At the end of the headland
beyond the sea cave is a prominent overhang with a bottomless
corner at its L side. Scramble down towards the end of the
headland, bearing L to a stance and good belays L of the corner.
1. Traverse steeply R across a corner (from which the curving
Toccata Crack, V Diff, rises) into the L-facing corner. Climb
this delightfully on small positive holds to a L-ward escape just
below the top.